The Lost Classics of
Jack O'Connor

The Lost Classics of
Jack O'Connor

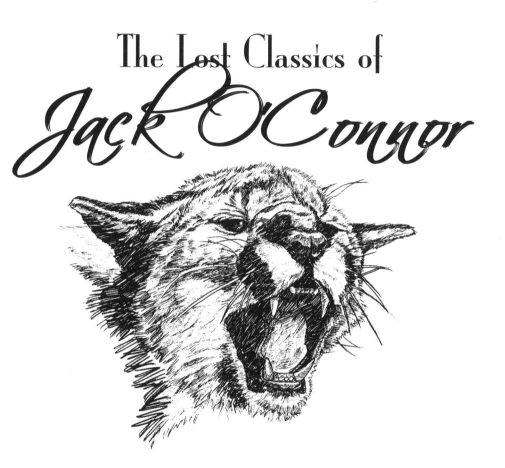

Edited by Jim Casada

Illustrations by Dan Burr

Published by LiveOak Press, Inc., Columbia, SC

The Lost Classics of Jack O'Connor is published by LiveOak Press, Inc. in cooperation with Time4Media. Copyright 2004.

Edited by Jim Casada with assistance from Chuck Wechsler.

Publisher: Chuck Wechsler
Art Director: Ryan Stalvey

Printed in the United States.

Fourth Printing
Library of Congress Catalog Card Number 2004114019
ISBN 0966021231

DEDICATION

To all my treasured gun and hunting writer friends who walk
proudly in Jack O'Connor's footsteps, and for all of the countless
readers, yesterday and today, who admire the work of a true
master of these genres.

Jim Casada –
Opening day of dove season, 2004

V

ACKNOWLEDGEMENTS

Those who have done much "digging" in the field of sporting literature know there are not nearly as many reference tools, indexes, bibliographies, and other research aids as they would like. Tracking down articles by, and information on, an individual author, even one of Jack O'Connor's renown, can be a tedious and time-consuming process.

In the compilation of this work, a number of individuals who also happen to be real O'Connor "buffs" contributed appreciably to my endeavors. Foremost among these is Eldon "Buck" Buckner. Buck knew O'Connor well, offered invaluable insight on Jack's pen names and his articles in *Outdoor Life,* provided photographs from his collection of memorabilia, and was of vital assistance in a variety of other areas.

Dale Arenz, who owns an extensive collection of old sporting magazines and has spent countless hours in compiling lists of articles by individual authors, kindly shared pertinent information with me. Lou Razek of Highwood Books, who specializes in accumulating and selling back issues of old hunting, gun, and fishing magazines, helped me to acquire scores of those containing articles by O'Connor. He also generously sent me a photocopy of his bibliographical work on O'Connor.

Todd Smith, editor-in-chief at *Outdoor Life,* deserves special recognition for garnering Time4Media's support of this book. It would not have been possible without his efforts.

Another *Outdoor Life* staffer, Executive Editor Colin Moore, helped immensely by tracking down and photocopying half a dozen articles I had been unable to locate, and thanks are due to all the folks at *Outdoor Life* for their support of this project.

Chuck Wechsler, the editor of *Sporting Classics* and a man with whom I have worked closely on a variety of undertakings over the years, goaded and guided me with his customary blend of patience, persuasion, and persistence. He also deserves considerable credit for his input in selecting these stories, as do Larry Chesney and the late Art Carter.

Good illustrations are icing on the cake in book publishing, and Dan Burr deserves recognition not only for his forty black-and-white drawings, but his beautiful cover painting of O'Connor for the dust jacket of our Trade Edition. When this project was suddenly resurrected after a five-year hiatus, Dan worked almost round-the-clock over a two-week period to complete all of the illustrations.

And when it comes to support, I owe a great debt of gratitude to my wife, Ann. She maintains at least a modicum of order in my office, answers the constant questions which are the product of my being richly deserving of the description "technologically challenged," and serves as a sounding board. Similarly, I will always be grateful to my parents for offering me a most precious gift – an upbringing where sport loomed large.

Jack O'Connor did the same for his offspring, and his three surviving children have been supportive of this anthology from the on-set. Brad and Caroline contributed touching reflections on the sporting life as they experienced it as youngsters, and all three – Brad, Caroline and Cathy – deserve a special thanks for signing our Deluxe Edition books. I fervently hope that this book is one which pleases each of them and honors their father's literary legacy in a suitable fashion.

CONTENTS

PART THREE – HUNTING IN AFRICA & ASIA

PART FOUR – MISCELLANY

PREFACE

by *Todd Smith*
Editor-in-Chief,
Outdoor Life

I never met Jack O'Connor, yet through his writings I feel I somehow know him. That ability to connect with people through words is truly the sign of greatness in a writer, and O'Connor was a master.

Like many of you, I grew up reading Jack O'Connor in *Outdoor Life.* For a boy of ten, his stories took me to places I could only dream of, like hunting tigers in India and great, black-maned lions in Africa. Seeing this first-ever compilation of the greatest O'Connor stories to ever appear in *Outdoor Life,* I am reminded that I have the unusual distinction of now being the only person who has been editor of both the magazine O'Connor called home for more than thirty years and the magazine where O'Connor finished his career.

Jack O'Connor retired from *Outdoor Life* in 1972. The following year Ken Elliott, then editor of the soon-to-be-launched *Petersen's Hunting*, convinced O'Connor to come out of retirement and become the magazine's shooting editor. I began my career at *Petersen's Hunting* in 1981, just a few years after O'Connor's death, so we just missed each other.

In the years we worked together, Ken told me many Jack O'Connor stories. One of his favorites illustrates O'Connor's ability to recall practically everything he ever wrote in minute detail. For would-be editors, it also underscores what a stickler he was about his copy.

It seems O'Connor would often call to make the tiniest of changes to manuscripts he had already sent in. On this occasion he was having dinner with Ken, when out of the blue he growled, "Have you read my latest story?"

"Of course," Ken replied with confidence.

"What did you think?" O'Connor pried.

"I think it's the best darned story you've ever written," Ken said, hoping the exaggeration in his voice would appease the man.

"Well," groused O'Connor, "do you remember the paragraph where I said 'my wife may smell like new-mown hay to me, but to a deer she smells like trouble?"

"Sure," Ken said, his confidence waning.

"I'd like you to change that to read 'my wife may smell like hot-cross buns to me, but to a deer she smells like trouble.' "

Ken swore he'd make the change, but the ever-skeptical O'Connor quickly penned the correction on the back of a cocktail napkin and handed it to him. Two days later he called to make sure Ken hadn't forgotten. Now that's a stickler! Yet it is that subtle turn of phrase, that deft ability to hear the tone of good writing in your head and tweak a word here and there until it sings, that separates great writers from the wannabes. At this, O'Connor excelled. Interestingly, Jim Carmichel, who succeeded O'Connor as *Outdoor Life's* shooting editor, is likewise afflicted and equally fastidious about his writing.

Perhaps O'Connor's greatest gift as a writer was his ability to weave volumes of information so seamlessly into his stories that his readers never knew just how much he was imparting to them. Rarely do you come away from an O'Connor piece without knowing a little of the history and geography of where he was hunting, the rifle and load he was using, and the taxonomy of the animal he was pursuing – all beautifully illustrated in rich word-pictures that give us, as readers, the sense that we are right beside him as the wounded buffalo charges or a 40-inch ram suddenly appears on a distant mountaintop.

Knowing how difficult this kind of writing is to deliver, the stories of O'Connor's rows with his editors don't surprise me. His standards as a writer were incredibly high – so high, I suspect, that he probably felt no one could say it better than he, no matter what their editing credentials. And, in many ways, no one ever has, which is why this compendium is so important and why it will no doubt be so well received.

True O'Connor fans will find all of their favorite stories gathered here to savor again. And for those young sportsmen who have never read O'Connor, here is chance to discover a wild new world of hunting adventures from "the dean of outdoor writers."

Enjoy!

INTRODUCTION

by Jim Casada

Like countless others of my generation, my fascination with Jack O'Connor dates from boyhood. I was fortunate enough to grow up in a time, the 1940s and 1950s, that was what O'Connor called the "Golden Age" of hunting. Similarly, my home as a youngster, North Carolina's high country, was a place where hunting and fishing were integral parts of everyday life. There were trout and smallmouth bass to be caught, and abundant small game in the form of cottontails, squirrels, quail, and grouse. Pretty simple sporting fare in some senses, but when the hunting season was closed or when the fishing was slow, the pages of outdoor magazines offered plenty of vicarious adventure.

My family's budget didn't allow the luxury of subscriptions to *Field & Stream* or *Outdoor Life*, and some of the stories in *Esquire* and *True* were a bit too risqué to garner my father's approval. However, the shelves of the local library and the tables stacked with magazines in the barber shop solved that problem. Each new issue of the two top outdoor magazines brought heady fare as their pages took me to the streams of my dreams or on exciting big game hunts. Among the regular contributors to *Outdoor Life* and *Field & Stream* were a number of writers who particularly caught my fancy. Corey Ford's rollicking tales of mischief and misadventure connected with the Lower Forty Shooting, Angling and Inside Straight Club always provided pleasure. Archibald Rutledge was a masterful storyteller. Havilah Babcock and Nash Buckingham stood as a pair of literary giants when it came to wordsmithing on dogs and quail hunting, and Charlie Elliott frequently wrote about subjects with which I had some firsthand experience.

Yet for all the appeal of these writers and others, two individuals had a special hold on a starry-eyed youngster's sporting soul. One was Robert Ruark, a fellow Tar Heel who was blessed, as I was, with a grandfather who loved the outdoors and just happened to be a boy trapped in an old man's body. Ruark's monthly column in *Field & Stream*, along with the occasional feature, offered simple lessons in ethics and conservation in addition to scenarios that any teenager who hunted and fished could readily identify.

O'Connor, on the other hand, filled the pages of *Outdoor Life* with a great deal of solid, practical information along with treating his readers to sport all over the globe. Ruark was "home folks," while O'Connor wrote of hunting in places and for species I could only experience in the realms of imagination. His knowledge of guns, particularly rifles, also fascinated me, for all of my hunting and shooting experiences as a boy, except for some plinking and squirrel hunting with a .22, involved shotguns. I often thought of writing him back then but lacked sufficient courage to do so. Had I only known that part of his contract *required* him to answer every letter (sometimes as many as 3,000 a month!), I would now be the proud owner of a missive I unquestionably would have saved.

In a very real sense, this book marks the conclusion of a pilgrimage of close to a half-century, for I've always thought, since my late teens, that more folks, and more recent generations, deserved the pleasure of sharing O'Connor's wonderful world the way he shared it with me.

Without question, Jack O'Connor ranks as the 20th century's foremost gun and big-game hunting writer. Over the course of a long, extraordinarily productive career, he became a household name. Those who are in their 40s or older remember his work with great fondness, but since his death, an entire generation has come of age without the benefit of ready access to O'Connor's polished, persuasive writings. One purpose of this book is to introduce them to this giant of American sporting letters, but it has also been compiled with long-time O'Connor fans in mind.

On the pages that follow, no matter what your background or previous exposure to O'Connor, you should find something new, for every effort has been made to include only material that has never before appeared in book form. Before plunging headlong into that world, however, let's first take a closer look at the man who was Jack O'Connor.

*J*ohn Woolf O'Connor (known as Jack from an early age) was born on January 22, 1902, in Nogales, Arizona Territory. Until age 13 Jack had an idyllic childhood, thanks to his maternal grandfather, James Wiley Woolf, who doted on the youngster and served as his sporting mentor. "Bird hunting was my grandfather's dish," O'Connor would later write, and Woolf did it in style with "an Ithaca, a Parker, and a lovely Purdey with two sets of barrels and an oak and leather case." He bought Jack his first gun, a little single-shot 20 gauge, and taught him the basics of wingshooting. Woolf also took him on his first camping trip and set him firmly along the path toward a fruitful and fulfilling career.

While Woolf was a somewhat taciturn, undemonstrative man,

near the end of his own life O'Connor would write: "I know now that he loved me and took great pains with me." In *The Last Book*, his posthumously published autobiography, Jack says that "with the exception of my mother no other person has had so much influence on me." The loss of his grandfather when Jack was 13 not only meant that he was suddenly without a sporting compass. It also deprived him of ready access to all the grand outdoor magazines and abruptly terminated what had been a wonderful apprenticeship. From that point on, O'Connor would pretty well be self-taught through astute observation, voracious reading, and plenty of rounds in the arena of hard knocks.

It is worth noting that the sporting deprivations of his later adolescent years influenced Jack a great deal, because once he had a family of his own, he consistently made a point of sharing his hunting experiences with them. His boys and girls, along with his wife, Eleanor, figure prominently in many of the stories reprinted here. The loss of his grandfather was one of the great tragedies of his life, although it paled by comparison with the death of his oldest son, Jerry. After returning from the Korean War, Jerry had plunged into the depths of depression and at age 39, died when he choked on his own vomit while in a drunken stupor.

Anyone who reads between the lines of another of his autobiographical works, *Horse and Buggy West: A Childhood on the Last Frontier,* will appreciate the troubles that haunted O'Connor in his teens. He weathered the storm though, and enlisted in the U. S. Army Infantry near the end of World War I, at only 15 years of age! Only a year later, in January, 1918, O'Connor was discharged because of a medical disability (pulmonary tuberculosis). He finished his high school studies and resumed a military career, this time as a hospital corpsman with the U. S. Navy.

Certainly, these two stints in the service "toughened up" young Jack, and in 1921, after leaving the Navy, he began a two-year course of study at Tempe Normal (the equivalent of a modern junior college). He then spent a year at the University of Arizona before receiving his bachelor's degree at the University of Arkansas in 1925. Interestingly, his degree was in banking and finance.

For a brief period he worked as a junior reporter for the *Chicago Tribune* before enrolling in graduate school at the University of Missouri. It was there Jack met Eleanor, at a mixer dance, and a few months after receiving his M. A. in journalism, they eloped. Following their marriage on September 10, 1927, the newlyweds settled in Alpine, Texas. Thus began a lifelong love affair marked by mutually strong devotion, the occasional clash of strong wills, the rearing of four children, dealing with Eleanor's alcoholism, and countless days spent afield together.

For the next three years Jack taught at Sul Ross State College in Alpine and moonlighted as a newspaper stringer, contributing to several Texas dailies. He was also busy at work on his first book, *Conquest*, which he sold to noted New York publishers Harper & Brothers. The book was quite controversial, thanks to some salty language, and Jack later laughingly reminisced about the furor it caused: "I left Texas with my shirt tail on fire because a character in my first novel had called another a son of a bitch. . . . In Texas many thought the word was a pronoun but they didn't print it."

The book was banned in the El Paso library, but Jack managed to land on his feet, even as the winds of the Depression were blowing at gale force, with a position as professor of English and public relations spokesman for Arizona State Teachers College in Flagstaff. There, to his delight, he found that "the hunting was a veritable Shangri-La."

It was at this juncture that O'Connor began contributing to outdoor magazines. He sold his first story, for a whopping $12.50, to *Sports Afield*, and shortly thereafter a $50 piece to *Field & Stream*. His first story for *Outdoor Life* came in 1934, and he also had articles in *Redbook, True, Esquire,* and other national magazines. Any supplement to the family income was welcome, as his salary was reduced twice in the span of two years, thanks to the worsening ravages of the Depression, even as his first two children, Gerald (Jerry) and Bradford (Brad) were born.

In 1936, encouraged by his success in placing articles in outdoor magazines, he and Eleanor took a trip to New York, where Jack met with the editors of *Field & Stream* and *Outdoor Life*. The latter produced a one-year contract to write 18 articles for $2,700, which enabled Jack to take a sabbatical from teaching. Before long he would solidify his foothold with *Outdoor Life*, find plenty of time for hunting, and complete his second novel, *Boom Town*. He also finished the first of his many sporting books, *Game in the Desert*.

Up to 1945, Jack worked like a madman. He continued his teaching duties, saw the birth of two more children (Catherine and Caroline), and in 1941 was named Arms and Ammunition Editor of *Outdoor Life*. Finally, in the early spring of 1945 Jack was convinced he was sufficiently well established to give up his teaching duties, and he became full-time Gun Editor for *Outdoor Life*. A few years later, eager to escape Arizona's booming post-war population, the O'Connors moved to Lewiston, Idaho. Jack was now firmly entrenched with *Outdoor Life*, and his close relationship with the magazine would last for upwards of three decades. All of the stories in this anthology come from that mutually beneficial partnership, for there can be no doubt that he played a significant role in the magazine's steadily rising circulation.

Along with his steady, consistently high-quality output for *Outdoor Life* (he still wrote a bit for other, non-competitive magazines such as *Esquire*), O'Connor continued to produce books at an impressive pace. The sheer magnitude of his productivity over an extended period of time tells us several things about him as a writer: He wrote fast and well, he worked exceptionally hard, and he had an almost compulsive desire to convey the joys of hunting to his readers. His approach was one every outdoor communicator should strive to emulate. He always tried to take his audience along with him – to carry them, if only in their imaginations, to the settings he described. Whether it was hunting quail in the sagebrush of his beloved Southwest, eating venison tamales in Sonora, or tracking lions in the African veldt, he was a master at reliving his adventures in riveting detail. He made the heady aroma of gunpowder, the camaraderie of evening campfires, the thrill of a difficult stalk so tangible as to seem almost real.

Few writers have ever approached his expertise when it came to sporting guns. A great advocate of first-rate marksmanship and avoiding overkill, he eschewed big caliber rifles when he felt smaller ones would do the job. He was adamant in his opposition to "freebies"; when evaluating new guns and ammunition, he wrote precisely what he thought. Interestingly, his steadfast refusal to be an industry whore served him well, because gunmakers knew they could count on him for an honest, forthright opinion.

While O'Connor kept in constant touch with his readers through his monthly magazine columns and frequent features, posterity knows him best for his books. Overall, he would write 16 full-length books during his lifetime, and two would be published posthumously. Add to those several manuals, major contributions to a number of other books, and countless appearances in anthologies, and you have a situation sure to captivate and confound any bibliophile (much fuller details on his writings appear in the Bibliography.

O'Connor's favorite book editor was Angus Cameron, who for many years presided over all outdoor publications at Alfred A. Knopf. Cameron once laughingly but with great fondness described O'Connor as "a reactionary old curmudgeon somewhere to the right of Genghis Khan" in his political outlook, and anyone who reads Jack's thoughts on editors (both book and magazine) in *The Last Book* will realize that genius came with a heavy price. He could be acerbic, was always opinionated, and never tolerated fools or sycophants gladly.

Jack could also be remarkably generous. One of Cameron's favorite anecdotes concerns the time he worked on the manuscript of *The Rifle Book,* which the author had dropped off before departing on an African safari. On the return trip home, O'Connor stopped over in Spain for a few days to visit the premises of AYA, the noted Spanish gunmaker. There, Jack asked AYA's craftsmen to build a custom shotgun, which in due time he presented to Cameron. No bill was attached stating the cost of this exquisite firearm, and several letters to O'Connor on the subject produced nothing but evasive answers and a strange unwillingness to discuss the matter. Finally, Cameron resorted to the telephone and told Jack, in no uncertain terms, that he wanted to pay for the gun. Jack simply responded that the shotgun was a gift "for past kindnesses," and when Cameron protested, he abruptly cut him off: "Angus, you've got to learn to receive as graciously as you give" (referring to Cameron's careful editing of his books over the years).

Jim Rikhoff, another close friend and the publisher of Amwell Press, recalls similar incidents of generosity and harbors fond memories of Jack's powerful, agile mind. He likes to point out all manner of contradictions in the man, such as the Brooks Brothers suits (O'Connor was always a snappy dresser) and the sartorial splendor which seemed so much at odds with his Western roots. As Rikhoff puts it, "He was an extremely talented but equally complex man . . . a mixture of the sensitive and sensible, of the ribald and reflective, of insight and inspiration, of instinct and intellect."

In 1972, frustrated with the editorial direction of *Outdoor Life,* the 70-year-old O'Connor retired from the magazine (although his name continued for a time to appear on the masthead as Hunting Editor). His final column, "Hail and Farewell," should be must reading for any serious fan. Always a workaholic, he soon signed up with a new publication, *Petersen's Hunting,* as executive editor, and up until his death he had a feature (54 in all) in every issue.

*J*ack O'Connor died of a heart attack on January 20, 1978, while on a cruise aboard the *S.S. Mariposa* en route from Hawaii to San Francisco. In my personal collection I have a number of his letters, including some written while on this cruise, and to the end he was as he had always been – inquisitive, irreverent, probing, and passionate about everything that interested him. His funeral was held in Lewiston, the town he called home for so many years, and his son Brad scattered his cremated remains over a mountain range in the Rockies inhabited by his favorite hunting quarry: wild sheep. Eleanor, who had been troubled by emphysema, would follow him in less than a year.

One cannot escape the conclusion that Jack carefully cultivated an image, and some found him aloof. Always, though, you return to the same conclusion: Jack O'Connor was a man of many talents. He understood the importance of friendship; he prized craftsmanship in guns and the finer things in sport and life; and he consistently produced work of superior quality. His life was full of friends and adventures, the kind that most people can only dream about. Jack was, for example, one of only a handful of men who ever scored a double grand slam on the four species of North American sheep. He made eight safaris to Africa, hunted tigers in India, made two trips to Iran, and hunted virtually every kind of game North America had to offer.

He won the Weatherby Award, was recognized as Winchester Sportsman of the Year, and was inducted into the Hunting Hall of Fame. He hobnobbed with princes, but felt equally comfortable with desperately poor gunbearers in Africa or impoverished beaters in Asia. Most of all, O'Connor was a man who possessed a full measure of that elusive quality we call *style*. As an author, he was unquestionably a masterful stylist, but the same held true in the way he dressed, his feel for sportsmanship, his love of the natural world, and so many other aspects of his life. This is a part of his legacy, as is the significant body of outdoor writing he left behind. It places him squarely in the very forefront of America's rich literature of the outdoors, and once you have read the selections that follow, I think you will readily agree.

A NOTE ON SELECTION

*J*ack O'Connor was a prolific writer throughout his adult years. While posterity will remember him, and rightly so, primarily for his books, there is wit, wisdom and no small degree of whimsy in his magazine articles. For the most part the information and expertise they contain has, after the passage of only a generation or so, been forgotten.

He wrote for a number of major magazines, among them *Field & Stream, True, Petersen's Hunting* and *Esquire*, but the heart of his vast literary outpouring graced the pages of *Outdoor Life*. Literally hundreds of those stories and columns, embracing a span of some four decades, can today be found only in remote attic corners or on seldom visited bookshelves.

The purpose of this book is to resurrect some of the finest of these "*Lost Classics*" so that older sportsmen can once again enjoy his worldwide adventures while younger readers discover one of the greatest hunters of yesteryear.

I have made every effort to include *Outdoor Life* articles that have never before appeared in book form. However, as someone who has undertaken a number of previous works of this nature, I am all too aware of the possibilities for overlooking a story or two that might have previously appeared in an anthology or other volume. If you discover such a slipup, I encourage you to contact me about it. Likewise, clues as to the whereabouts of any obscure O'Connor stories would be appreciated.

A number of considerations entered into my choice of selections. Obviously, literary quality was a factor, as was a desire to have a work truly representative of O'Connor's diverse hunting career. Since much of his hunting took place in the desert Southwest, species such as Gambel's quail and Coue's deer figure prominently in this anthology. Yet Jack traveled widely in search of sport, and every effort has been made to provide representative coverage of his hunts in terms of both species and geography. Accordingly, the reader will find stories on most of the big game animals in North America as well as in Africa and Asia.

Jack O'Connor was a gregarious fellow, and he especially enjoyed sharing his hunts with family and friends. The first section acknowledges this, though you will find his wife Eleanor and their children in stories scattered throughout the book. Hopefully, the end result is a reasonably balanced cross-section of material written by O'Connor as a hunter, as a passionate outdoorsman, and as an incredibly knowledgeable student of the natural world.

If this work receives the reception that O'Connor's enduring work richly merits, there likely will be a sequel, focusing in large measure on sporting guns as opposed to this book's concentration on hunting.

Most of these stories originally saw the printed light of day as feature articles, for it was through this medium that O'Connor best exhibited his storytelling abilities. Whether you are a hunter, shooter, serious student of our sporting past, or simply someone who enjoys a good read, these pages afford plenty of opportunity to sip and savor the heady literary wine which was O'Connor at his best.

THE O'CONNOR LEGACY

by Bradford O'Connor

*J*ack O'Connor often wrote that the caribou was the most handsome of all the world's big game animals, even more so than North America's wild sheep and elk and Africa's sable and kudu.

To him, the caribou was beautiful, but dumber than a tuft of tundra. He'd rarely encountered a more dim-witted creature and considered it unethical for a hunter to take unfair advantage of the caribou's stupidity.

That will explain why he commanded me, his then teenage son, to put my rifle back in the scabbard that September afternoon nearly 48 years ago.

We were less than a week into a month-long hunt southeast of Atlin Lakes in northern British Columbia, when two bull caribou approached our string of pack horses. For the next ten minutes or so, Dad and I watched the bulls trot up to investigate the horses, then trot off, nostrils flaring and tails raised after getting a whiff of human scent. The bulls returned moments later having already forgotten what had scared them off in the first place.

This was the beginning of the rut and the bulls had obviously mistaken our horses for cow caribou. We shouted, cursed and tossed clods of dirt at the addled bulls, finally driving them off.

The largest sported a gargantuan rack with the most massive shovel Dad ever had seen. Its antlers were certain to have scored near the top of the record book. This was my first northern hunt, so the urge to shoot had been almost irresistible.

Dad didn't have to lecture me on hunter ethics to explain why he didn't want me to shoot. I knew. To have popped that bull would have been akin to blasting a bunch of mallards rafting in a pond. Besides, the caribou season did not open until the next morning. This seemed to be a moot point to me, because we were days away from the nearest road and law-men, but a quite serious matter to Dad who said that getting a jump on the season simply was not an option.

"You'll get another chance," he assured me.

He was right. On the last hour of the last afternoon of our hunt, after running nearly a mile to keep ahead of the wind, I shot a bull with enormous antlers that earned the top medal for mountain caribou in the 1951 Boone & Crockett competition.

For a caribou hunter, this was about as fair as a fair chase can be, and a far cry from popping that sex-befuddled bull earlier in the hunt.

Dad wrote about the hunt later in *Outdoor Life (see There IS A Santa Claus)*. This soon triggered a stampede of caribou hunters to the Atlin area. By the early '70s my caribou had slipped from No. 7 to 35 in the record book, with several of the best bulls shot in the Atlin country. I often wonder how many record-book caribou were taken in the rut, victims of their own self-destructive stupidity, by hunters who paid no heed to the concept of fair chase.

That hunt in 1951 was one of my first lessons from Dad on hunter ethics. No, he never lectured me about hunting ethics nor did he lecture his many readers in his books and magazine articles.

But the message was there, an embedded part of a much larger picture he painted of the hunting experience.

He wrote in such a vivid, descriptive manner that the readers were transported on the hunt with him. It required little imagination to feel the lingering warmth of a grassy bed vacated moments before by a ram, to see the red autumn rust forming on arctic willows, the woodsy smell of a campfire, or to hear the cackle of a pheasant rooster exploding from the brush.

Dad's passion for sheep and sheep hunting was known throughout the hunting world and his message on ethics was contained in almost everything he wrote on the subject.

Alas, the message must have been too subliminal, for many did not get it.

He fretted over his role in creating a Grand Slam hysteria. He is said to have been the fifth person to bag all four varieties of North American wild sheep, and he blamed a new breed of affluent and highly mobile hunter for turning the Grand Slam into a status symbol. He said too many Grand Slam seekers were so driven by greed and ego that they cared little about the sights, sounds and smells of sheep country. They were out for instant success and prestige, accomplishing in days what required weeks of tough hunting for others before them. Out of the greed grew an industry of unscrupulous outfitters who promoted quickie hunts, often flying their hunters to the base of mountains where rams had been spotted a day or so earlier.

I met one such hunter who had stashed his rifle and duffel in his office while he awaited the go-ahead call from his outfitter. He got the call shortly after arriving at his office, hopped a jetliner to Anchorage, shot his ram the next morning, and was back home the following day. He said that his objective was to score a Grand Slam in a year. I lost track of the guy, but he probably achieved his goal.

In the book *Sheep and Sheep Hunting,* Dad wrote: "I have written a good many stories on sheep hunts. Some of the boom in sheep hunting may well be laid to my doorstep. I hope that when I arrive at the Pearly Gates, Old St. Peter does not hold it against me. He may well do so – and if he does, I shall not argue. I simply will bow my head, turn around and go down below where I belong."

But Dad's message was not totally lost. I like to believe that he had played a role in an awakening of hunter ethics and a growing awareness that to preserve our sporting heritage we must clean up our act. I'm convinced of this, because many leading hunter-conservationists have told me they were great Jack O'Connor fans and were inspired by his writings.

Today, most of the shenanigans that tarnished the image of hunters and hunting in the '60s and '70s are unthinkable. Resource managers – with the enthusiastic support of sportsmen – have gotten tougher on game-law violators, and associations of guides and outfitters have done a commendable job of policing their own members.

Hunters are pumping vast amounts of money into wildlife conservation through organizations such as the Foundation for North American Wild Sheep, Safari Club International, Rocky Mountain Elk Foundation, Game Conservation International, Ducks Unlimited and a host of others. These hunter dollars protect and enhance wildlife habitat and support critical research into disease and nutrition, migration patterns, and relationships between predators and prey.

I like to believe that Dad's writings – and sometimes rantings – contributed to a heightened concern for the environment. In Arizona, he witnessed the devastating impact of overgrazing on a fragile desert and its wildlife, and he saw the same happening after his move to Idaho.

In public meetings, magazine articles and letters to the editor, he warned that the frenetic dam-building activity of the 1960s and 1970s would inundate an important Idaho elk winter range and devastate steelhead and salmon runs on the Snake and Clearwater Rivers. He locked horns with the Corps of Engineers and the many who saw cheap hydroelectric power and river barging as panaceas for all of society's ills.

The dams were built anyway. Since then, the states and federal government have pumped millions if not billions of dollars to stave off extinction of some fish runs. Today, there even is serious talk about removing some of the dams to restore the runs.

Dad was a prolific writer, a workaholic who until his late '60s often boasted that he never had taken a true vacation. He slept in his office so he could get to his Royal typewriter quickly in case he woke up at 2 in the morning with a story idea, which he often did. He'd carry paper and a pen almost everywhere he went, often pausing in mid-conversation to jot down an idea or observation.

Dad's hunts – all of them, even his afternoon sashays from home or office into the Arizona desert for quail or jackrabbits or in later years for upland birds or rockchucks in Idaho – sooner or later showed up in his writings.

That Dad wrote more than 1,200 articles for hunting and fishing magazines, authored two novels, an autobiography and about a dozen books on hunting and firearms was known to most of his fans. Few, however, are aware that he wrote romantic novellas and articles for *Redbook, Mademoiselle, Readers Digest, Cosmopolitan, Esquire,* the literary magazine *Midland*, and other magazines popular in the 1930s and 1940s; or that he once was a cub reporter in Chicago at the time of Al Capone and later was a Hollywood correspondent; or that his western novel *Conquest* was banned from the El Paso library because librarians thought the salty language of the book's characters would shock readers.

Literary critics throughout the U.S. gave the book highly favorable reviews, as they did later with his second novel, *Boom Town,* but that did little to placate the good citizens of West Texas and Arizona where there was talk of publicly flogging him. The book created such a stir among the pious that he was forced to quit his job at Sul Ross College in Alpine where he taught English and journalism.

Few Jack O'Connor fans are aware that he earned a bachelor's degree at the University of Arkansas in banking and finance in 1925. He never told me why he chose to study banking, but I think that it had a lot to do with his admiration for his maternal grandfather Woolf, who was chairman of the board of the Tempe (Arizona) National Bank. His grandfather also loved bird hunting and owned fine shotguns, including an English Purdey with two sets of barrels. This, too, rubbed off on Dad.

Blessedly few knew something else about Dad: He was a

prankster who rarely passed up the chance to pull off a practical joke.

One victim was Lee Sproul who had hunted tigers with Dad in India in the 1950s. Sproul, a kindly, soft-spoken East Coast lace manufacturer, had been invited to visit Father and Mother at their home in Lewiston, Idaho. Before his arrival, Dad found a ramshackle house nearby with a porch stacked high with junk and a yard littered with rusting car bodies and old washing machines.

Dad fetched Sproul from the airport, then drove to the old house, opened the trunk and began to unload Sproul's luggage.

After an awkward silence, Sproul cleared his throat and said: "But, Jack, I am sure I will be very comfortable here."

For the rest of Sproul's stay, he was fair game. Even Mother got into the act, putting rubber novelty-store vomit on the poor man's jacket. Sproul was very forgiving, because he and my parents remained good friends.

Mother – bless her soul – was a willing collaborator in other pranks. The victims usually were sorority friends my sisters Cathy and Caroline had invited home for the weekend. Mother would start serving dinner by announcing that she was developing a toothache. As the dinner progressed, her moans became louder and louder until, finally, Dad would say:

"Eleanor, I have to pull that damned tooth out."

And she'd whimper: "Oh, don't, Jack, please don't."

At that moment, Dad would head into the kitchen and emerge with pliers in one hand and an elk tooth, its roots painted blood red, hidden in the other.

As the horrified girls looked on, Mother would scream in mock agony, while Dad pretended to pull the elk tooth from her jaw.

The joke was great fun until the night a panicked coed fled, ran to a nearby house and phoned the police. Minutes later, a squad car pulled up and two burly cops pounded on the door, demanding to know what was going on.

In the fall of 1953 Dad sent a letter to me in Korea written on stationery filched from a mortuary. I learned later that he had sent other letters with stationery taken from such places as churches, collection agencies and used-car dealerships.

Dad could not pass up a good gag even if he knew it could put his career at great risk. In 1938 Ray Brown, editor of *Outdoor Life*, asked Dad if he wanted to be the magazine's gun columnist to replace Ned Crossman, who had committed suicide. Brown liked the two sample columns Dad wrote, but there was the formality of filling out the necessary employment forms.

Father apparently had neglected to fill in his date of birth. Brown sent the following message in the terse language of the telegram:

HOW OLD JACK?

Dad's reply: JACK FINE... HOW OLD RAY?

Brown, who was well known for his explosive temper, must have been in an exceptionally mellow and forgiving mood because Dad got the job and remained with *Outdoor Life* until he retired in 1972, then went on to write for *Petersen's Hunting*.

I recently attended a party in Reno hosted by Bob Lee, one of Dad's longtime friends and hunting companions.

"One thing I admired most about your father was that he was the only outdoor writer to admit that he'd occasionally miss a shot," said Lee.

Dad did miss, but rarely.

One of my earliest hunting memories was of tagging along with Dad for coyotes and jackrabbits in the desert north of Tucson. I saw him down two coyotes in a row, one at 250 paces and the other at 300. Over the years, I accompanied him on hunts in Mexico, Arizona, Idaho, Wyoming, Montana, British Columbia, The Yukon and Africa, and I can't recall seeing him botch a shot.

On our last upland hunt together a few months before Dad's death in 1978, a big pheasant rooster flushed from a clump of brush about 50 yards away. I didn't shoot, but Dad shouldered his 28-gauge Arizaga, said, "well, hell," and fired, dropping the bird. We stepped off 70 yards. The rooster was hit by a single No. 6 pellet in the head.

Dad was known as the father of the .270, which is not quite accurate. But he was so keen on the caliber in his writings that the .270 became the pet rifle of thousands of Jack O'Connor fans. He'd readily admit to me that the .30-06 was in the same league as the .270, yet somewhat more versatile. It was a .30-06 loaded with 220-grain "solids" that Mother used in Zambia in 1969 to kill her first and only elephant.

His love of the .270 and his affection for such kindred calibers as the .280 Remington, 7x57 and .257 pitted him against writers he dubbed the Big Bore Boys, who preached that these calibers and their wimpy breathen were inadequate for elk and foolish choices for deer. Dad argued that it was not the caliber so much as where the shot was placed that counted. An elk shot in the lungs is just as dead with a .270 as with a .458, he maintained.

His jousts with Elmer Keith, the leader of the Big Bore Boys, provided years of great entertainment for readers of outdoor magazines.

Though Dad has been dead for 26 years, I still receive dozens of letters and calls from his fans. Some are from men in their twilight years who had met or corresponded with Dad. Yet a surprising number are from hunters and gun enthusiasts in their mid or late '30s who were barely old enough to read during the peak of Dad's writing career.

What is most gratifying to me is that my three teenage grandsons – Riley, Michael and Andrew Pleas – are devout fans of their great grandfather, worshipping a man who died four years before Riley, the oldest, was born.

These boys will never hunt Bengal tigers in India or Urial in Iran, and it may be they never will afford a Big Five African safari, but they have inherited a fondness for fine guns, are getting to be good wingshots, and have shown a love and respect for what they hunt.

This is the Jack O'Connor legacy I cherish most.

A Daughter's Rememberances

by Caroline O'Connor McCullam

*M*y father's dearest wish was to make a hunter out of me. He began grooming me when I was barely an adolescent. He invited me to come along on pheasant hunts on those bright fall mornings that stirred him to gather the guns and the dogs, have my mother put together a sack lunch, and head out toward the harvested wheat-fields near Pomeroy or Tammany.

Dad sang all the way, old familiar tunes, driving in his meandering, preoccupied way. We had no radios in our cars at the time, for he believed that the automobile was a means of transportation and nothing more. I would be in jeans, an Eddie Bauer down jacket, and boots from Abercrombie & Fitch. I was a pudgy child and not terribly attractive in such clothing. I longed to be lanky, large-busted and glamorous – an ambition which was never to be entirely realized.

Still, I loved going with my father on these rather eccentric forays. Years after his death, I remember those chilly autumn days, the crunch of frost and plowed earth underfoot, the smell of sagebrush as it warmed in the sun. I remember how he would splay the barbed wire apart so I could climb through unsnagged, sharing sandwiches and carrot sticks and black olives and a thermos of hot V-8 Juice. At these times my loquacious father talked very little, but we were comfortable without conversation.

He had a series of lunatic, ill-bred Brittany spaniels that he would set loose on the countryside wearing cow-bells on their collars. His theory was that the clanging of the bells hypnotized the pheasants, and he wanted to know where the dogs were, as they responded neither to commands, nor to profanity, nor to the police whistle he kept on a string around his neck. When the bells went silent, he'd charge off through the brush and stubble fields in the direction of where he last heard them. Usually, he found the dogs on point, just where the noise had stopped. There would be an explosion of wings and cackling; and *BOOM, BOOM,* the birds would sail down in an arc or plunge to the ground, and then he would dash over to grab them before the dogs could tear them apart. Dad missed few birds, of course. He was an excellent shot.

He loved to watch the dogs work the fields, slipping back and forth through the underbrush and up shadowed draws, noses to the ground, all instinct and energy, the music of their cowbells fainter and then nearer. He saw such beauty in it. "God, isn't this wonderful!" he would say. It was part of his world that I would never again enjoy. Forces more powerful than he determined that.

I was allowed to carry a shotgun – sometimes my mother's Arizaga 28-gauge sidelock, a delicate beauty with lovely checkering and engraving. Often, my father encouraged me to take a shot, but I missed almost every one. My early promise at skeet had vanished. Later, we found that the sight in my right eye had suddenly and mysteriously deteriorated. By then it was too late: I was in the throes of adolescence, and for years my father lost me to all except worry and aggravation. Fortunately, he had my brother Brad, who was his cherished hunting companion, second only to my mother, who would accompany him on expeditions around the world.

My father sang all the way home after each of our pheasant hunts. Slapping his leg in rhythm, he was sometimes an entire orchestra: a muted trumpet, a trombone, a clarinet, the percussion section. *"Deedly dee dee dah dah DAH! slap! slap!"* The dogs were panting in the back seat, their eyes rimmed red with fatigue; there was the smell of sweat and doggy breath and earth caked on the soles of our boots. I rolled my eyes but smiled because he was so happy and so funny. I was too young to be terrified by his driving, which was legendary among those who had been his passengers. I felt loved, and safely encapsulated in the little Jeepster with its Isinglass snap-on window covers and its pathetic little heater rattling away.

The last time I saw my father alive was in late December of 1977. We had all gathered at my sister's house in Seattle to wish my parents bon voyage as they stopped on their way to San Francisco to board an ocean liner for Hawaii.

I was in a miserable state with an injured back, and I was numb with pain medications. I didn't stay long. I hugged him goodbye; his cheek seemed very warm. Did I sense that anything was wrong? I don't know, but during the next few weeks before his death, I was weighed down with a terrible sense of foreboding. If anything, I was worried about my mother's health. Her lungs were ruined from years of smoking and illness, and she was on oxygen several times a day. But it was he who died aboard ship. We escorted his body ashore on a terrible grey day in San Francisco.

It has been over 25 years since he died on that ship, on January 20, 1978. He was two days short of his 75th birthday. My mother died six months later, just kind of dwindled away in their house with its staircase and hallways full of the furry hides and splendid mounts of animals from around the world, the smells of leather and books and gun oil. I can still open the drawers of some of the furniture that was theirs and breathe the odor of their house. I miss them still.

XXX

PART ONE
Family & Friends

hanks in large measure to being outspoken to the point that the word "diplomatic" must have been absent from his vocabulary, Jack O'Connor was viewed by some as a difficult fellow, incapable of getting along with anyone. Once, for example, when a Corps of Engineers spokesman was assuring a group of Idaho sportsmen that there were no plans to build a dam in the area, Jack jumped to his feet and growled: "That is a goddamned lie, soldier boy, and you know it!" He then read a clipping from an Oregon newspaper in which the same official had said the dam would indeed be constructed. Such forthrightness notwithstanding, perceptions of Jack as a cold-hearted curmudgeon could not be further from the truth. He was a generous, gregarious man who reveled in friends and who deeply loved his wife and family.

Jack O'Connor had an obvious talent for making friends, notwithstanding his sometimes acidic comments about those in the hunting industry in his autobiography. He was, in fact, precisely the sort of man any of us would enjoy as company around an evening campfire with a glass of snake-bite medicine in hand or at our side with an enraged Cape buffalo bearing down. He was a staunch friend, generous to a fault, and devoted to those whose acquaintances he cherished. You will see ample evidence of that not only in this section, but throughout this book.

O'Connor's love of his family is even more obvious. Jack shared his passion for hunting with Eleanor and took great pride in her marksmanship, and in each and every one of the many sporting milestones attained by his family. Eleanor and the girls and boys loom especially large in this section, but you will join all of Jack's loved ones at various points throughout the book. In this regard, he was a model for the "pass it on" perspective many of us believe is the surest, most meaningful way to ensure the future of hunting and fishing.

THE KID GETS HIS BUCK

*Jack O'Connor certainly must have
looked back to this story with fond
longing considering the tragic turn in his
oldest son's adult life. Here, after the
sort of misadventures and bad luck that
would have dampened any youngster's
enthusiasm, Jerry kills his first whitetail
buck with one perfectly placed shot.*
May, 1943

*J*erry was just short of 11 when he started deer hunting, and he
didn't want to get a buck *very* badly – no worse, say, than he
wanted to pilot a P-38 or be a Marine. He was a very good shot
with any rifle, and I wouldn't have given much for a buck's chances if
it got up within 200 yards of Jerry in a good open spot. He had been
shooting a .22 since he was six – at first a single-shot and then a sweet
little Winchester Model 75 with a scope – and had developed a pair of
eyes that could detect the flick of a jackrabbit's ear behind a bush a
hundred yards away, and he had long, thin legs that could carry him
mile on mile through desert and canyon.

The first time Jerry tried a high-powered rifle, I was afraid
that the recoil and muzzle blast might make a flincher out of
him. However, he made the transition without the slightest
trouble. Shooting my .270, he kept five shots in the six-inch bull
of a 100-yard small-bore target, at 200 yards.

At that, he had nothing but bad luck the first season. We tried
for mule deer, but on the first trip neither of us got a shot, and he
still calls the section where we hunted, "The Place Where All the
Deer Are Does and Fawns." We saw more than 40 animals, all
told, but not an antler in the bunch. Then Jerry had a cold, the
next trip, and couldn't make it. When I said good-by, a couple of
big tears squeezed out and ran down his cheeks.

So for months, next year, he looked forward to the opening
of the season, the way most kids look forward to Christmas.
Then his principal topic of conversation was, "When the Season
Opens and I Go Out and Get My Buck." In his room he had a
calendar with the opening date circled in red, and as each day
passed he solemnly crossed it off.

3

*T*he day before the season opened, we arrived at the ranch of our friend, Frank Siebold, a few miles north of the Mexican border and in some of the best whitetail country in the Southwest. Frank had the horses in the corral, was waiting for us, and in a few minutes I was off up a rocky country road in the car with an extra saddle, Frank's bed roll, and the camping gear, headed for a well several miles out in the back country. Frank and Jerry followed with the horses, and by the time they showed up, I had the tent pitched, a fire going, and supper cooking.

When the alarm clock jangled the next morning at 5:15, Jerry was already up, dressed, and had a fire going; and long before daylight we finished breakfast, saddled, and were off. Our objective was a long, steep range called Limestone Mountain, which rose about 1,500 feet above our camp. It was cut by canyons and filled with deep basins. Evergreen oak, cliff rose, mountain mahogany, and manzanita dotted its flanks and grew thick in the canyons, and on the high ridges gramma grass reached to the horses' knees.

By the time we had worked through the three miles of rolling hills and canyons that separated us from the main ridge, the sun was up – bright, warm, and welcome after the biting cold of early morning. Frank and Jerry went up a trail that ran along a deep canyon, where Frank had almost always seen deer when he was working cattle, and I took off up a ridge half a mile away. We were to meet on top, and there was always a good chance that we might run bucks across to each other.

Sign was thick and the whole country looked "deery," and as I rode, I half expected to see a buck sneaking out below me. But if there were any in that canyon, they sat tight, and I rode to the top without event.

Presently I heard the brush popping and Jerry and Frank showed up. They, too, had seen deer, but nothing that looked like a buck, so we plotted a new course of action. About a mile away was what was known as the Big Basin, a thickly wooded hole which dropped about 500 feet and was surrounded by steep, rocky hillsides. It had almost always produced shots at bucks, so we decided to take a crack at it.

According to plan, Frank dropped into it and worked along the bottom while Jerry and I traveled the north side on foot. Now and then, far below us, we could hear a rock roll, and we knew that Frank was coming.

We had gone no more than 50 yards when out of the corner of my eye I saw a deer get up at the very bottom of the basin. He flirted a white tail and was gone in one jump, but I had a very strong hunch that he was a buck. Then I heard the heavy, sullen bellow of Frank's scope-sighted .30/06 – *pow, pow, pow!*

Yelling for Jerry to follow me, I started off at a dead run across a point so I could get a shot if Frank had missed. I traveled about 200 yards before I got in the clear; then I sat down, switched off the safety of the .270, and waited. On the far hillside nothing moved but a bluejay. Then Frank's .30/06 boomed again, and far away, at least 500 yards from where I sat, I saw a deer trotting through the brush. He was too far away for me to see antlers, even with 8X glasses, but he was a large deer, dark and deep-chested, and the fact that Frank, who had seen him at close range, was still throwing bullets at him convinced me he was a buck.

I had plenty of time to shoot, so for a moment I sat watching, trying to estimate the range. For the first shot I held about three feet in front of his nose with the horizontal crosshair about level with the top of his back. I could see the dust fly just beneath his belly. On the second shot I gave him the same lead, but held what looked like about two feet over his back. He jumped into the air and then I didn't see him again.

Jerry, who had found the going pretty rough, came puffing up just then, and we sat there watching the place where the buck had disappeared. Nothing moved. Then Frank's voice came up from below: "Hey, what the heck happened to that buck?"

"I think he's hit!" I shouted back. Still no sign of life across the basin.

Frank went back to wrangle the horses, and Jerry and I crossed over to the place where the buck had disappeared. No buck. While I was looking around to be sure of my bearings, Jerry found a stone with a spot of blood on it. We took up the trail – such as it was. There was a fleck of blood about every 15 or 20 feet, blood from a slight muscle wound. After three hours of laborious tracking over rocks, we gave up. Evidently no legs had been broken, or lungs or guts touched; the wound was surely a very slight one. That buck is the only one I have ever hit and lost with a .270. Of course, I cannot be certain, but it is my hunch that I hit him in the neck, and the wound couldn't have done much more than draw blood.

*B*y that time the sun was beginning to slant toward the west and we started back toward camp. When we got to the tent, we found that Frank's sister, Doris, had ridden in to hunt with us the next day. We pitched an extra tent for her and laid out a spare bed roll. Before we turned in, we laid our plans for the morning. East of the trail which Jerry and Frank had followed to the mountain top the day before, there

5

lay a series of deep, rough canyons which looked "bucky." We decided that Frank and I would hunt them near the heads and that Doris and Jerry would ride along the bottom where the going was not so tough.

By 11 o'clock Frank and I had covered six or seven canyons and had put an average of five does and fawns out of each. But no buck. Finally, we came to canyon that we simply could not cross with the horses, so we had to drop a thousand feet to the bottom where Doris and Jerry awaited us. They, too, had seen deer but no bucks, and all of us were puzzled.

As we sat there talking, I could see the canyon that we had found impassable from above. It headed out into a nice basin, with grass deep and rich and cliff rose, or "buck brush," growing thickly. As I looked, the strongest kind of hunch came over me – that a buck was waiting up there.

"Frank," I said, "let's not pass that basin up. If I were a buck, that's exactly where I'd be!"

We started up the side, and when we came to a point where we could overlook the basin, we got off, took the rifles out of the scabbards, and started using the glasses. Suddenly about 300 yards away, and a couple of hundred feet above us, a buck popped up and began running beneath a rimrock. I overled him the first shot, but got him right behind the shoulder the second. He was a nice, fully mature four-pointer with a good, though not exceptional head.

I got my horse to him and brought him down. Jerry inspected him with big, disappointed eyes. "Dog-gone it!" he said. "Why didn't you tell me to come if you knew that buck was there?"

Later we headed back to camp. My buck was across the saddle and I was leading my horse. The others were riding. A couple of miles from camp, Doris said quietly: "There are two bucks up on that hill – a big four-pointer and a pronghorn. Get the big one, Jerry!" she added.

He piled off, as excited as a kid could be, and reached for his rifle, which was in a scabbard forward along the horse's neck, but the beast shied and ran off about 50 yards. The mount was a round-backed rascal, and we had found that Jerry couldn't carry his rifle butt to the rear on the left side, as he should have, because it pulled the saddle over too much.

Seeing how matters stood, I grabbed my .270 from its scabbard and handed it to Jerry. Those dumb bucks still stood there, about 200 yards away, but the kid didn't shoot.

"Knock over the big one – the one to the left, Jerry," I urged.

"I can't see through the scope, Daddy!"

Noticing that Jerry wasn't going to shoot, Frank cut loose then, but missed, his shot kicking up dust just beneath the big buck's belly. Off they went, over the hill and far away. I examined the scope of the .270. The buck I'd slung on my horse had bled on the ocular lens, and one couldn't any more see through it than through the side of a house. Jerry's face was a study in disappointment, but all he said was: "What lousy luck!"

The next day was a perfectly wonderful one for not hunting deer. A storm was brewing. Long, white cloud streamers fled across the sky and the wind howled a gale. Deer, of course, lay tight. Occasionally we kicked a doe out of her bed, but by midafternoon we hadn't got a shot.

About that time I got another hunch. We were not far from a long, sharp hill where we'd often seen deer, usually bucks. The south side was bare and smooth, but the north was cut with beautiful canyons thick with oaks and deep in rich grasses. We plotted a campaign for it. I was to ride along the ridge, while Frank and Jerry would go below. Once before I had acted as jump dog there for a friend, and had got him a fine, big, five-point buck.

So up I went. Now and then, 500 feet below me, I could see Jerry and Frank working slowly along. Every time I came to the head of a canyon, I tied the horse, went carefully to the edge and – keeping out of sight – watched with the glasses. One canyon produced a doe and a fawn, but I knew bucks were close by when I found their big, heart-shaped tracks.

I had covered about three-fourths of the hill and my heart was sinking when – at the bottom of a canyon in some thick brush – I saw a movement, then another. About the same time I heard below a click of iron on rock and knew that Frank and Jerry were riding there.

Then one of the gray shapes in the brush stepped out into the open. It was a big, four-point buck. Two more, bucks, but small ones, probably spikes or two-pointers, came out. All stood watching the place where Frank and Jerry were riding. Then two more showed up, a medium-sized buck with a small, four-pointed head, and another big fellow following close behind.

It was interesting to watch those deer through the glasses. Not having spotted me, they'd snake up the side of the canyon, tails down between their legs, pausing now and then to look back toward the place where Jerry and Frank had disappeared. For a couple of minutes the bucks were pretty jittery, but then they calmed down. A big four-pointer reached out and grabbed a mouthful of browse. Feeding, the herd began to move slowly up toward the head of the canyon. The danger was passing them by and they felt safe.

Keeping behind some brush, I dropped back over the skyline and then crossed the ridge and ran, out of their sight, to where I could see Frank and Jerry. Presently, far below me, they came into sight, and I gestured to attract their attention.

They were two canyons beyond the one containing the bucks, and I knew that with the wind blowing a gale, there wasn't much chance of their being heard. Nevertheless, I was on pins and needles until they had pushed their laboring horses up the hillside to where I stood.

Climb off and grab your rifles," I said quietly. "There are some bucks over in a canyon. Maybe you can each get a shot."

The kid didn't climb off – he fell off with the little .257 in his hand. Frank followed with his .30/06. At the edge of the canyon where I had last seen the bucks, not a thing was in sight. Jerry sat down on a point where he could see anything that moved, and there he waited, but I noticed his lips beginning to tremble with disappointment.

Then I saw, about 70 yards away at the bottom of the canyon, a suspicious movement in an oak thicket. The glasses showed me a gray coat, then an antler, and a moment later the biggest buck of the bunch walked out.

The kid had been pretty shaky, but the sight of those antlers calmed him down. The little .257 cracked and the buck was down and very dead. When we dressed him out, we found that the 100-grain bullet had drilled him exactly through the heart.

"Gee, Daddy!" Jerry shouted. "I had buck fever until I saw that buck; then I didn't have it any more . . . I just shot him."

The proudest kid in Arizona led his horse off the mountain that afternoon. Every few minutes he would stop to see if the buck was riding all right. It was five miles back to camp, but what's five miles if there's a buck riding on our horse's back.

JACKRABBITS FOR THE BOYS

O'Connor wrote a fair amount about varmint hunting and enjoyed it a great deal. He realized that plinking for jackrabbits, coyotes and the like was a good way to improve his shooting skills in the field. February, 1944

We had promised the two boys a jackrabbit hunt if the reports were better, and they were – C's instead of D's and B's instead of C's. Each of the boys had an A in a rather vague subject called "nature study." It is usually the only A either of them drags down, but that shows in what direction their interests run anyway. They barged in on us that afternoon the report cards were distributed, faces beaming, waving the cards and demanding that I keep my promise.

Since Pearl Harbor, there haven't been so many varmint hunts in the family, and we all look back a little wistfully on the days when, at the drop of a hat, we'd get up before dawn and head out after coyotes, or, when the kids came home from school, how we'd dash out for a couple of hours of crow and jackrabbit shooting. But now we were restricting our use of gasoline and tires.

However, now and then we did go out. Carroll, my hunting companion, took his car one time, I the next. The kids always want to go. As a matter of fact, I get more kick out of it when they do. A jackrabbit to me is only a jackrabbit; but to the kids, he is Big Game – a combination of antelope and mountain sheep and whitetail deer. And cottontails? Well, to those two boys, little Molly Cottontail is like a jackrabbit, only more so. They like to

9

hunt them and to eat them, and they're pretty darned good cottontail shots.

So that particular late-winter afternoon, the hunt was on. I consulted the vice president in charge of supplies. She agreed to prepare the lunch and to go along. I called Carroll and pretty soon he showed up. We loaded rifles into the car and away we went. My wife carried her favorite little .257 with a 2^{1}/4X Noske scope, and a supply of handloads using the little .25/20 soft-point bullet weighing 87 grains and traveling along at 2,900 feet a second. Carroll was armed with a 23-D Savage altered to K-Hornet and fitted with a 29-S Weaver. Jerry, the oldest boy, used his Winchester Model 75 sporter with a 29-S scope, and Bradford, who is nine and who won't use his own .22 because it is a single-shot, carried my rather heavy (for him) Model 52 sporter with a 330 Weaver. My own rifle was a heavy-barreled single-shot 2-R Lovell with a .440 Weaver.

The section we chose to hunt was a high, sloping plain covered with yellow gramma grass and spotted with mesquite and paloverde. Terrain was open and level, ideal for fancy running shots on rabbits. To the east a few miles, a great wall of purple, timber-covered mountains, tipped with snow, jutted against the sky. In the lowlands where we hunted, it was pleasantly warm, but when the winds came down from the peaks that reached 8,000 feet into the sky, they were icy cold.

Not far to the south, the Arizona-Mexico border lay, and to the north was a bombing range. All the time we hunted those beautiful grassy plains, great four-motored bombers droned and circled through the winter sky.

Our usual procedure in hunting *liebres,* as jackrabbits are often called along the border, is to park the car along a ranch road and then get out and take a turn on foot, spreading out so that the rabbits are likely to run from one hunter to another. Carroll and Bradford formed one wing, Jerry and I another, and Eleanor was the center. We hadn't gone more than 100 yards from the car on that first jaunt when two enormous antelope jacks broke out of a bush where they had been lying down and angled off to the left. I saw Carroll throw his rifle to his shoulder, and dust popped up just under the leading jack's nose. Confused, the jack turned, ran back a few feet, stopped, and sat up. That was a tactical error, and an instant later I heard the hollow plop of the K-Hornet bullet. Running like thistledown, with the characteristic sitting position of his kind, the second jack went directly past Eleanor about 75 yards away, and she made about as pretty a running shot as I have ever seen. The little 87-grain bullet, traveling more than 1,000 feet a second faster than its designer ever planned, connected squarely amidships, and the jack disintegrated.

I drew the next – two more antelope jacks running directly away from me and about 200 yards away. I registered a miss, just under the tail, and before I could reload my single-shot rifle, both were out of sight. I redeemed myself a moment later, though, with a standing shot at a good 225 paces.

It was still a bit early for the rabbits to be moving and feeding. All we'd seen had been resting under bushes and we jumped them out. I sat down, took my 8X glasses, and looked under every bush within range. Soon I was rewarded with the silhouette of a big antelope, squatting under a bush, thinking no doubt of unlimited fresh, green grass and another and better world where there were no coyotes and no humans armed with varmint rifles. I got those crosshairs on his shoulder, and when the little 47-grain spitzer bullet landed, he never knew what it was that had hit him.

In case you have never seen an antelope jackrabbit, it is the largest of American jacks and about the size of the big varying hare. A good-sized one will weigh ten pounds or so, and the fact that the antelope jack wears an erectile patch of white hair, which it can flash like a real antelope, accounts for its names of "antelope jackrabbit" and "white-sided jackrabbit." That white patch also makes a swell target, as crosshairs look beautifully black against it, even late in the day when it would be hard to hold on a less conspicuous animal.

Our friend, the white-side, is the most common jackrabbit of Mexico and is found in the border states as well. He is a rather dumb creature, in habits much like his namesake, the pronghorn antelope. He is given to running off a little way, and then sitting down, and he likes the plains better than the brush, also like the pronghorn. The familiar black-tail jackrabbit, found all over the West from Montana to Arizona and from California to Kansas, is a far smarter critter.

*J*erry, who so far had not had a shot within range of his .22, was by this time muttering bitterly to himself. "You shoot too soon, Daddy!" he remonstrated. "I don't get a chance!"

I let him go into the lead then, and we circled farther to the left so the others would not frighten the rabbits. The animals had just begun to move, and had hopped out from behind their bushes to feed. In a quarter of a mile, Jerry got three, all shot within 90 yards and all of them taken offhand. For a kid of his age, Jerry is an excellent shot and also a fine stalker. Wise to the ways of the desert, he has hiked ever since he could walk. I spotted one black-tail at about 300 yards. It was busily feeding, and we decided to see how close we could to it by going the long way around and by approaching with the wind in our favor. We got within ten yards of the unsuspecting beast before Jerry took it.

In the distance we could hear the others shooting – the roar of Eleanor's .257, the sharp snap of Carroll's Hornet, and occasionally the feeble pop of Bradford's .22. We were a couple of miles from the car by then, so we turned and headed back. Soon we saw Eleanor in the distance and moved over to meet her. The three of us were together when Jerry, who was ranging in front of us like a bird dog, ran into the convention of cottontails – young, fat, unsophisticated cottontails that fry tender and brown in the pan. Jerry, who is usually a cool shot, then had an unaccountable attack of buck fever. The cottontails were literally all around him, so thick he couldn't make up his mind which one to shoot at. He emptied his rifle and got only one; then reloaded the clip with hands shaking so badly he dropped it twice. However, he finally got hold of himself, and with his second clip he killed two.

Our first circle had produced good, average jackrabbit shooting, with some cottontails thrown in. On the second, we hit the jackpot. We drove a few miles east to a wide, rather bare flat we knew of. On the edge, we parked the car and got out.

"Look at those antelope jacks!" Bradford cried. "There are three of them!"

"No – five of them!" Jerry yelled.

The two boys were looking in opposite directions. The whole plain, a mile square, was literally dotted with jacks.

Grabbing their .22s, Jerry went in one direction and Bradford in another. A moment later, we heard them shooting jacks from ambush and saw the animals go down. Eleanor, Carroll, and I formed a skirmish line and went into action. In the next half-hour, as the sun gradually slid down toward the west, and the chill of the winter afternoon began to settle, we shot jacks running, jacks loping easily along, and jacks sitting. It was the sort of shooting that the varmint hunter and high-velocity, small-bore nut usually encounters only in his dreams.

The most spectacular shooting of the afternoon came when, after having had our share of hits and misses, good shots and bum ones, we jumped a band of seven big antelope jacks, which often run in bunches, and cut them all down – about half of the run – before they could get into a long thicket of mesquite. Then, right after that, Eleanor made the longest shot of the day, with a beauty on a big, lone black-tail that ambled out of the mesquite in spite of all the shooting, and stopped about 300 yards away.

Eleanor sat down and held just so she could see the tips of the jack's ears over the top of the post (or at least that is what she claimed), and when she pressed the trigger we saw the jack flatten, and a moment later the plop of a striking bullet came floating back. A strange huntress, this wife of mine. She is a skillful shot who knows no theory and refuses to learn any. She should have known that it was impossible to hit a jackrabbit at 300 yards when she was sighting with a 2^1/$_4$X scope, that the shot demanded at least a 6X job. But she hit it anyway.

It was just about too dark to shoot by then, and the boys came in grinning happily and babbling of their luck and skill. The rivalry between the two kids is pretty strong, and by the time they got through shooting their rabbits over again, they were killing most of them 200 yards away.

*T*he jackrabbit has his faults. He eats a lot of grass and browse, which ought to go to fatten precious beef cattle. The old ones are not good eating and are usually covered with ticks and warbles. But for the evergrowing tribe of varmint hunters, who dote on precision shooting with anything from a .22 Long Rifle, high-speed to a .220 Swift or even a .30/06, the jackrabbit is in a class by himself. He affords the best training for big game hunting I know of, and the man who can pluck off a jack at 200 yards won't have much trouble hitting a deer or antelope a lot farther off.

Jerry is going to start hunting big game when the next season rolls around, and even now a flossy little .257 is being finished up for him by a gilt-edged riflemaker. jackrabbit trained as he is, I'll be willing to bet that he gets the first real pronghorn antelope he has a fair shot at. I wouldn't want to be in that antelope's place, as Jerry has been trained on its namesake.

13

CHRISTMAS PRESENT DEER HUNT

*Riveting story lead-ins were not
O'Connor's strong point, but here he
sets the tone perfectly. His Christmas gift
to Jerry and Eleanor was a mixed bag
hunt down in Sonora, which back then
abounded with game, including both
whitetails and mule deer. Their guide,
Santiago, figured prominently in several
other O'Connor stories.
December, 1944*

*A*mong other things, there were two slips of paper in the stockings of my wife, Eleanor, and my elder boy, Jerry, that Christmas morning several years ago. Each slip read: "Good for one trip to the Gulf of California, with a swim in the surf, a look at bighorn sheep, shots at mule and white-tail deer, at quail, coyotes, and foxes."

Eleanor has hunted in Mexico many times and so has Jerry, but neither of them had ever been on the wild, beautiful Sonora coast of the Gulf of California, where tall and gray mountains come down to meet the blue seas. It is a rough, primitive country with little water, bad roads, and no service stations. But there is game there – lots of it.

For more than 200 miles from the Mexican border to Tiburon Island – where the Seri Indians, the most primitive and backward race in North America, make their home – great desert bighorn sheep are found on the rugged mountains that jut into the sea. Antelope run on the sandy stretches, while little mule deer slip like ghosts through the thick desert forests of thorny paloverde, mesquite, ironwood, cholla, and saguaro. There are quail there, too, though not so many as one would expect in a wilderness country, and there are swarms of predatory animals – coyotes, foxes, wildcats.

*B*y driving long and hard and leaving our Arizona home early, we had hoped to camp along salt water the first night out. However, we had made our plans without taking into consideration

15

the one Mexican immigration official at Sasabe. Just before we crossed the border, the whim had struck him to close up shop and go quail hunting. We had to wait until midafternoon before he got back. But there is a silver lining to all clouds, and ours was some very fancy coyote shooting on the way south.

Only a few miles from Sasabe we saw two of these little prairie wolves battling over a jackrabbit they had just killed. Jerry, who was 11 then and already one of the most enthusiastic hunters in North America, grabbed his .22 and put a high-speed hollow-point bullet right behind the shoulder of one of them. The coyote ran 150 yards, then fell, and was dead when Jerry got to it. It was his first coyote in several tries and he wouldn't have been any more pleased if he had gotten a moose.

The second coyote came out of a batch of three that were attacking a desert mule deer doe. As we stopped the car, the wolves ran in one direction and the rescued deer in another, but Eleanor stopped one coyote and shot a leg off another with her .257. My own prairie wolf came a few miles farther on. He trotted across the road a couple of hundred yards away, then stopped behind a bush to look us over. With the scope on my .270 I could make out his outline dimly; so, saying a prayer that the bullet would not be deflected enough to miss him, I touched her off and the welcome plop of the striking bullet came floating back.

The next day, twenty-four hours after we had left Sasabe, we stopped the car in a pass in the Picu Mountains for our first glimpse of the sea. Twenty miles to the west it lay before us – blue, calm, and endless. Far out in the placid water we could just make out uninhabited Angel de la Guarda (Guardian Angel) Island, and along the coast, great red and gray mountain ranges, as barren-looking as the face of the moon, shouldered into the surf.

Rancho el Datil, the last place of human habitation on the road, was a score of miles behind us. In front of us, in all the vast area of plain and hill, and mountain and seashore, there was not a living human.

At certain seasons of the year, Mexican fishermen make their headquarters at Port Libertad, catch sea bass for the market, and poach bighorn sheep by shooting them with .30/30s from their boats. In the summer when the fruit of the organ cactus is ripe, Papago and Seri Indians invade the desert, and now and then Americans come to Libertad to fish and hunt. But for the most part, there are no human beings along that beautiful coast.

Our first objective was to find some sheep, so the next morning we drove over the sand dunes to a low red range of hills where sheep sometimes stop on their way to higher mountains and where literally dozens have been killed by Mexican fishermen and by Americans.

Eleanor carried a 16-gauge shotgun and I a miniature camera with a telephoto lens. We saw no sheep and no sign less than six months old. However, we did see quail – lots of them.

A tropical variety of Gambel's, they differ slightly in coloration from the birds of the same species in Arizona and California, with a rich yellow replacing the buff. They were the only educated quail we found on the trip, and they hid and flushed like veterans of a Southern California hunting season. Eleanor was the gunner and I the bird dog, and after an hour or so we had a respectable bag.

I had to deliver on my promise of seeing bighorns, so the next day I herded my flock into the Cirios. We made a dry camp on the sands not more than 50 yards from the sea and just below a great barren mountain that rose a thousand feet straight out of the breakers. The Cirios get their name from a curious tree that grows there and nowhere else in Sonora. At first sight the trees look like nothing on this earth. Mexicans call them *cirios* (wax candles); the first American botanist who found them christened them "boojum trees" and tacked a long Latin name on them. My own first reaction was to call them parsnip trees, as they look like a gigantic parsnip turned upside down.

While the wife and the boy were marveling at these trees, I picked up sheep sign. That very morning a big flock had walked over the spot we chose to camp in. The next day we saw them. Taking the lead along a steep ridge, I spotted a flock of ewes and lambs, but they were out of sight before Eleanor and Jerry could come up. Back at camp, though, the sheep delivered themselves C.O.D. We were cooking lunch when I saw a three-year-old ram on the skyline, watching us.

While Eleanor was getting a good look at him with the glasses, another ewe showed up a bit farther away. Those sheep must have stood there for an hour.

That afternoon it began to cloud up and I didn't want to be caught there in the rain. Besides, I had already delivered the promised swim in the surf, and the sight of bighorns, quail, and coyotes; now it was time to try our hand at deer hunting.

17

*T*he next afternoon we were back 40 miles from the coast at a *tinaja*, or tank, where the cattle of the pioneer Aguirre family watered. We had borrowed a couple of horses from the Aguirres and we had acquired Santiago to take care of the *caballos* and to guide us around. Santiago punches cows for the Aguirres, and when he isn't punching cows, he is a trapper. He is a very nice guy, a crack hunter with eyes like an eagle, as you shall presently see. We were the first *gringos* he had ever known, and he spoke not one word of English.

About the time we had the camp set up, Santiago came up with the horses, and I thought we might take a short turn around camp to look over the country and decide where we would hunt in the morning. I rigged the scabbard up on my saddle, adjusted the stirrups for these long legs of mine, and Santiago and I set forth. My chances of getting a deer that first afternoon were about one in a thousand. The wind was howling and great gray clouds were scudding across the sky. It was bitter cold, particularly for warm Sonora; and if I hadn't presented Santiago with a sweat shirt before we left camp, I believe he would have frozen in his cotton shirt and thin cotton jumper.

In the flats we saw fresh sign of the big desert mule deer, and in the hills, the heart-shaped tracks of the little white-tail. But no deer. Then, as the sun headed down in the west and we turned toward camp, Santiago pulled up his horse and said, in Spanish: "I see the tail of a mule deer."

"Where?" I asked.

"On the second hill."

I got off the horse, took my 8X binoculars, and tried to see that "tail of a mule deer." No could do. The hillside was at least 500 yards away and thick with paloverde trees.

"There!" Santiago said. "There it is again. I believe it is another."

"All right," I said. "Let's go on foot."

*W*e hobbled the horses and – keeping trees and brush between us and the deer – sneaked through a wide arroyo, over a little ridge, and into another arroyo about 200 yards from the paloverdes where Santiago had glimpsed the deer.

I sat down and put the glasses on the spot once more. It wasn't easy to see anything, because the hillside was in deep shadow and the setting sun fuzzed the lenses. But in a moment a doe walked out of the trees and glanced around. Then another doe came out. Then a three-point buck. I let the glasses drop, dug my heels into the ground, and was about to plant a bullet behind the buck's shoulder

18

when Santiago touched my shoulder and whispered, "No, wait! Look to the left. There's a great big buck – oh, very big!"

I saw him then, an enormous buck that looked as big as a horse and carried a head like a rocking-chair. He had evidently caught our movement and was getting out of there, leaving the does in his harem to their fate. I just glimpsed him as he went over a ridge into a side draw. I didn't have time to shoot, but that one look was enough to make my heart jump.

"Come on," said Santiago. "Let's cut him off."

Having trapped and punched cows all over the country, he knew just where to go to intercept that buck. We had to go about 400 yards, and I doubt if it took us much more than a minute. We scrambled up the ridge, winded and puffing. A doe, one of the big buck's harem, was trotting along about 50 yards away. Then his nibs came into view, trotting along with the power and majesty of a fine harness racer, nose in the air, his great antlers laid along his broad back.

I shot offhand, and winded as I was, my first shot was a miss, just in front of his brisket. At the second shot he whirled and headed back for the ridge, but I was sure he had been hit. On the third he went down as if pole-axed, and lay still.

A grand buck he was, with a fine head, the grandfather of all of the bucks in that section and one of the finest Sonora mule deer I have ever seen. By Western classification he was an eight-pointer, since he had eight points on one antler; by Eastern classification he was a fourteen-pointer, since he had that many points altogether. We didn't get to weigh him, but I am convinced he would have dressed out at somewhere between 225 and 250 pounds.

Seeing what a Sonora vaquero can make a horse do is something to astound an American. In the United States, that buck alone would have been considered a big load for a horse, and it was all Santiago and I together could do to get him on. But once the buck was lashed fast, Santiago got aboard with him. Stumbling and with his legs buckling, the stout *caballo* made his way back to camp.

Arriving there, I found that Eleanor had collected a bag of quail while I was gone; also that she had discovered, by taking a shot at a fox on a nearby hillside, that the extractor of her .257 was on the fritz and that she would not be able to shoot it again until we picked up a new part back in the States.

So the next morning, although insisting that the stock was too long for her, she set out with my pet .270. I put the 16-gauge pump in my own scabbard just in case a covey of quail saw fit to attack me, but mostly I went along for the ride.

Again the wind from the south was sweeping over the desert. Big white clouds with gray bellies rode the blue sky above us, and now and then one of them let go a few drops of rain. All in all, it was a wonderful day *not* to hunt deer, and for a long time we saw nothing.

Then, in a particularly fine bit of country where the interior valleys were all tracked up by deer, I told Santiago and Eleanor to ride over to a saddle that commanded two valleys. I planned to circle a hill and see if I couldn't run something over to them.

I hadn't gone 300 yards when I saw a movement on the hill above me and a whitetail doe got up. I stopped and watched. A big buck with a warty, heavy-beamed head and many points popped out of the brush and stood looking at me. Then a three-pointer joined them.

Some instinct must have told those *venados* that, although I had death in my heart, I couldn't do anything about it with a pump gun and No. 7$\frac{1}{2}$ shot. I was only 50 yards away, yet they stood staring at me as if I were the darnedest sight they had ever seen. But this wasn't getting Eleanor a shot, so I put on my fiercest look and said "Boo!"

Instantly their three big white tails, which looked as large as the deer themselves, went up – and away scampered all three animals. A moment later I heard the .270 crack – once, twice, three times.

When I negotiated the ridge, I saw Eleanor and Santiago below me in the valley, bending over a deer. The smaller buck and the doe had come into view below them, bounding swiftly over low brush. Eleanor's first shot had just clipped the buck in the flank. She swung farther ahead the next time and the bullet landed right in his chest, killing him instantly at the top of his bound. Then, frightened by the noise, a gray fox had popped up on an opposite hill almost 300 yards away. Eleanor held just over its back as it stood there, and killed it with a single shot.

"Lady," said I, when I had surveyed the carnage, "I'd hate to see you use that .270 when you had taken time to practice up!"

Santiago, who had never seen such shooting in his life, was absolutely goggle-eyed. Before that time the little woman had fired the .270 exactly once and that was some years ago when I first got it. Then, she had said that the stock was too long for her and that the gun kicked like a mule. All of which goes to show that rifles may kick when fired at targets – but not when fired at game!

Poor Santiago. I am afraid he has some queer ideas about American women. He thinks they are all dead shots. He also thinks they make their husbands cook breakfast for them.

The first morning he looked rather queerly when I built the

fire, cooked breakfast, and brought fried quail, bacon, toast, marmalade, and coffee to my wife on a tray. When I did the same thing the second morning, he called me aside and asked me confidentially if all American women lie abed while their husbands cook breakfast. I said it was an old American custom, and now he looks upon female *gringos* as a deadly but useless race of women who toil not, but can shoot like sixty.

That afternoon when we got back to camp, Santiago's impression was further strengthened. Quail were calling all around, so Eleanor took the 16 gauge and started out to gather some birds for supper. Santiago went along to pick them up. It was the first wingshooting he had ever seen, and when he came back carrying the birds, he had a dazed look in his eyes. Meanwhile, Jerry had been having the time of his life with his .22. While we were out hunting, he had potted a gray fox, some quail, several jackrabbits and cottontails.

Mexican law allowed us each another buck, but instead of going out that afternoon, we skinned and quartered the two we had so we could hang the meat in the cold wind where it would chill and dry. A buck in the cold storage locker, they tell me, is worth two on the far side of the hill.

The long-threatened rain began in earnest that night. Next morning the desert was gray and sodden – and it was still raining. Dry, most Mexican roads are pretty bad; wet, they are enough to make an American howl for the Marines.

A few days before we had swum in the bracing surf of the gulf and basked voluptuously on the warm sands of the beach. But all that day, as our car labored and slithered through the mud, we were climbing. At Santa Ana we ran into snow, and when we crossed the border at Nogales, it lay six inches on the ground. From summer to winter in one trip. Sheep, two kinds of deer, rabbits, quail, and predators – all in a few square miles. Well, that is Sonora!

THE GALS MEET THE CHAMP

The Champ was a savvy old whitetail that seemed more than an equal for any hunter. In this piece though, reminiscent in many ways of Archibald Rutledge's famed tale, "The Lady in Green," two Dianas (his wife, Eleanor, and Doris Siebold, the sister of a good hunting buddy) find the medicine for the Champ and another buck. The men complete the trip empty-handed.
October, 1946

We called him the Champ because – well, he was the Champ: The shrewdest, foxiest, coolest, smartest whitetail buck that ever made a deer hunter wonder why he hadn't stuck to golf. It would be trite to say that the old buck bore a charmed life: It would also be to some extent true. That buck's life was charmed, because he made it that way by being just a little cooler and smarter than the hunters who tried to "reduce him to possession," as the language of the lawyers quaintly puts it.

I have hunted most species of American big game, from the enormous, phlegmatic moose to the little javelina and the swift, slender antelope, and I'm convinced that the smartest animal of them all is the whitetail deer. Of all whitetails, those little fellows called Arizona whitetails – found from west Texas to western Arizona and south through northern Mexico – have, I think the most on the ball. And of all the whitetails I have run into, the Champ was the smartest of the lot.

For years he frisked, dozed, fed and begat his kind in a range of hills which afforded little cover and almost no safe retreats. The Black Hills, as they are called locally, are a few miles north of the Mexican border, and from the highest ridge one can see the village of Patagonia, Arizona, about three miles away; a paved highway; and the ranch house of our friends, the Siebolds.

The range is only about four miles long and a mile wide. Oaks grow in the canyons and along the north and west slopes, but most of the hills are bare except for tall, rich gramma grass which grows high and thick after the summer rains.

The hills are on the Siebold allotment and the Siebold cattle run there, but actually the hills are yours and mine – part of the national forest system. Anyone can hunt there, and for the last 50 years, many have. There is so little cover that all the dumb deer have long since been killed off, and those that remain are the smartest animals that I have ever had the privilege of hunting. The Champ came from a long line of smart ancestors, and he was probably the smartest of the lot.

It seems incredible that he could have survived for years in a small area of relatively open country, yet he did. Frank Siebold hunted him every season for years, got in a few shots, but never hit him. His haunts were well known in the village of Patagonia, and if the Black Hills are well sprinkled with empty, corroding .30/30 cases, it is because they were fired at the Champ by desperate hunters who shot even though he was out of range. I got two cracks at him myself, when he was running swift and free through the oaks of a deep canyon 400 yards away.

Once I saw him get up beneath a point, with a hunter standing just above him, and sneak around underneath and escape *behind* the hunter – who, by the way, never knew he had moved the Champ until I told him about it. That buck was not only smart, he was lucky. Once I posted my wife in a saddle between two ridges and tried to move him past her. I did, but just as he slipped out of the oak thicket, my wife's horse saw him before she did. The horse snorted – and the buck faded back out of sight before my wife could get off a shot.

The Champ was the most tantalizing deer I ever went after. Those who hunted him would hear rocks roll, look up to catch a glimpse of him, but he'd be gone before it was possible to shoot. He never bedded down where one jump wouldn't put him out of sight. Other bucks might stop on a ridge a few feet from safety for one last look. But not the Champ! He simply scrammed, disappearing as if he possessed the magic secret of invisibility.

The more I hunted the Champ, and the more I heard about him from Frank Siebold and other hunters, the more convinced I became that one hunter going out alone would never get him. Unless somebody knocked him over soon, no one would, because the Champ was an old deer. He had first been noticed as an exceptionally big buck, with a head much larger than average, about six years before his death, and when he was finally killed, he was probably 12 years old. In other words, for a whitetail deer he surely was no spring chicken!

In the ten years from the time he become a legal buck until he met his end, he had scored technical K.O.s over a lot of run-of-the-mill, fair, good, and first-rate sportsmen. One of the best hunters I have ever known went out after him, saw him three times in one day without getting a single shot, and was so discouraged that he never again would even go near his haunts.

"That doggone buck's too smart for me," he said. "I don't mind hunting deer and not getting one, but I resent being made a fool of. I've crossed him off the list!"

That got to be the general notion about the old buck. A lot of people knew where he lived, but they also realized that didn't do much good, and for the most part they did their hunting in other spots.

It was the Champ who got Doris Siebold, Frank's sister, interested in deer hunting. She was a magnificent horsewoman, but for some reason had never been interested in hunting. When my wife and I came down to the ranch to hunt, she would usually go along. She knew every trail and every canyon in the country, and she had eyes like an eagle; but for some time she didn't get the yen to shoot at anything.

Then one day Frank came home to find her practicing with his .22. She announced that from that day forth she was a deer hunter.

"I have been going out with you for a long time," she said, "and it doesn't look too tough to me!" So she kept on with the .22 until she got pretty good, and then shortly before deer season began, she tried her hand with a scope-sighted .30/06.

he day before the season opened, my wife and I pulled into the yard of the ranch house around suppertime. We caught up the horses we were to ride the next morning and then, after we had eaten, we held a council of war.

Frank wanted to head right for the Limestones, a rough, heavily timbered ridge, cut with deep canyons and full of deer, but about six or seven miles to the north. Doris held out for the Black Hills.

"I've seen that big buck you call the Champ a dozen times in the last three months. I *know* I can get a shot at him."

"Forget it!" Frank hooted. "Sure you can see that buck out of season. He'll stand across the canyon and look at you, but he knows when the season opens as well as we do, and tomorrow morning he'll be long gone the moment we put a foot on the place."

But Doris was determined, so we laid our plans. The big buck was most often found on the southern end of the mountain closest to the ranch house. If a hunter approached from the north along the ridge, the Champ simply dropped over a bluff at the south, rimmed around under it, and took refuge in deep, wooded canyons to the west. If the hunter came up under the bluff and the buck was bedded there, he would cut over the top.

We decided that if Eleanor (my wife) and Doris went up the canyon to the east of where he so often bedded, they might get a shot at him as he went over the bluff. On the other hand, if he were bedded or feeding on top and came down over the bluff, Frank and I might get a crack at him. Well, anyway, it was possible.

The next morning it was still dark and cold when we finished breakfast and went to the corral to saddle up. A chill wind was blowing from the north and the stars were big and bright. The first morning of a hunt always goes slowly. Stirrups have to be adjusted, lunch and rifle scabbards tied on. By the time we got going, it was becoming rapidly lighter, and when we reached the rocky lower slopes of the Black Hills, the sun was not yet up but visibility was good.

Eleanor and Doris had farther to go than we did, so Frank and I got off our horses and waited 20 minutes before we cut around along a rocky trail under the bluff where the Champ so often bedded. Higher and higher we went. A cruising owl, headed home after his night's hunting, swept by over our heads and in the distance, a coyote howled. But not a sign of a deer, not even a glimpse of the white fans of the few does and fawns sometimes seen on this side.

Then, on the other side of the point, a rifle cracked in the chill dawn air.

"That would be Eleanor!" I said, recognizing the sharp blast of her little .257.

There was another shot, also sharp, followed by the hollow boom of Doris's .30/06.

Frank and I piled off our horses and dragged our rifles out of the scabbards in case something came our way. On the other side of the point, the rifles were still speaking.

Nothing came. We waited a minute . . . five minutes.

"It wasn't the Champ they jumped," Frank said. "If it had been, he'd have headed for this bluff."

Just as he said it, I saw a deer, and I needed no second look to know it was the Champ in person.

*I*t was plain that he hadn't been shot at. Instead, he had everything under control. He knew where Doris and Eleanor were, but they did not know where he was. He was trotting coolly along, right at the edge of the bluff, looking back over his shoulder. The sun had just come over the horizon. Frank and I were still in deep shadow, but up there on top, the clear, direct rays shone on the Champ and picked out his magnificent antlers, which glittered as if he wore an electric light bulb on every point.

I had been carrying the .270 with the chamber empty. Now, as quietly as I could, I eased a cartridge into the chamber and tried to settle down on those sharp-pointed rocks into a good sitting position.

The Champ was about 350 yards away and some 500 feet above now, trotting easily along at the foot of the cliff. Since my rifle was sighted in for 300 yards, I tried to hold a trifle high and what looked like half a length in front.

I shot – and the bullet kicked up dust from a boulder right in front of the Champ's brisket.

The old buck switched on his super-charger then, and Frank and I caught only a glimpse of him as he tore through the oaks at the foot of the cliff.

"Missed him!" I said.

"What did I tell you?" Frank demanded. "No use to shoot at that doggone buck. He just can't be hit!"

27

I walked over to my horse and took hold of his reins to lead him up the steep slope. Then shooting broke out above us once more. Four times Doris's .30/06 spoke.

"That's Doris!" I said. "I bet she got a shot at the Champ!"

"Nuts!" Frank responded gloomily. "If she did, she missed him."

But let us go back to the female end of the expedition. When Eleanor and Doris left us, they rode around the point and headed up the canyon. Halfway up they saw four deer, which had evidently been watering below, start running up the big ravine; but it was so dark there that they couldn't see antlers. They piled off their horses, however, got out their rifles, and waited.

Presently, when the deer were about 300 yards away, Eleanor made out antlers on one and immediately opened up on him.

She shot four times and hit him three, but all shots were low and behind, for she was underestimating the range. Doris also saw antlers on another deer, shot twice, but missed.

After her fifth shot, Eleanor saw her buck falter and go down high on the ridge above her, so she jumped on her horse and rode uphill as fast as she could spur him along.

Doris, however, took her time. She was pretty depressed, because she had thought deer hunting was easy, and now she had missed the first buck she had ever shot at. She put the .30/06 back in the scabbard, but instead of mounting, she slowly and gloomily led her horse up the steep canyon. She was about to pull out of it, when she heard my shot. She stopped, got out her rifle, and waited.

Then, here came the Champ himself, headed right for her, running from Frank and me. She admitted later that she got a terrible attack of buck fever, and that he had traveled 50 yards or more before she could find enough strength in her arms to lift her rifle.

She could hardly breathe, she told me later, and the rifle swung and bobbed all over the place. One moment the post in the scope would be right in the animal and the next it would be six feet off. She had seen the Champ many times before, but never through a hunting scope and with greed in her heart.

Finally, she managed to pull the trigger. The rifle boomed; the Champ went into high. On her fourth shot, the Champ went down, hit. Then he struggled to his feet and stood there groggily. Doris took careful aim, pressed the trigger – and the firing pin clicked on an empty chamber. Her rifle was empty, and for the life of her, she could not remember how to reload the thing.

She jumped on her horse then and galloped over to where she had last seen Eleanor.

"Quick!" she shouted when she found Eleanor bending over her buck. "I've got the Champ wounded and I don't know how to load this doggone rifle!"

Eleanor filled the magazine for her and together they rode to the place where Doris had last seen the great buck. He was gone, but he had left a wide blood trail.

"He's hit solidly," Eleanor told her, "He won't go far."

She was right. About 200 yards from where they took up the trail, they saw the Champ struggle painfully to his feet under an oak below them.

Struck again with buck fever, Doris shot at him and missed and he started to move off. But the count of nine was already hanging over him.

"Take your time, Doris," Eleanor said, "and *squeeze* the trigger. He can't possible get away!"

Doris shot again, and the big buck went down for keeps.

A few minutes later Frank and I rode over the ridge and found Doris camped there with the buck, as if she were afraid it would jump up and elude her again.

"Well, I got him," she shouted. "I got the Champ!"

He was a fine buck, but a very old one, with 18 points altogether – ten on one side and eight on the other. His antlers were irregular and palmated with age. He was almost toothless and noticeably thin.

"Too bad you shot him," Frank said. "If you had waited a few hours longer, he'd have died of old age."

"You shut up. You're just jealous!"

So, Frank and I dressed the two bucks out, loaded them on the gals' horses, and saw them off. They were back at the ranch before the chill was out of the morning air.

It was dusk that night before Frank and I rode in, empty-handed. Eleanor and Doris in the meantime had the two bucks skinned and quartered and wrapped in cheesecloth.

And that is why the Champ no longer runs on his rocky ridges and makes fools of well-meaning hunters. It is also the reason why friends of ours kid Frank and me. "Better take the gals along to shoot your deer for you!" they say.

THERE IS A SANTA CLAUS

Brad joins his Dad for a hunt for "Santa Claus' reindeer," hence the title. What an adventure it turns out to be. After countless miles of walking and plenty of practice in the school of futility, the teenager finally gets his chance. The result is a bull carrying what Jack describes as "the darnedest set of caribou antlers I've ever seen."
February, 1952

I'll never forget the day my son Bradford saw his first set of caribou antlers. He had been out playing when the express truck came, and returned just in time to see all the mounted trophies of a Canadian hunt being uncrated in the patio.

He was about ten then, a blond, knobby-kneed kid whose blue eyes looked very pale and very big against skin burned brown by the sun. He admired the sheep horns, the goat and grizzly hides. But what bowled him over was the caribou. He fingered the great curving anglers with their many points, wanted to know what the characteristic shovel was for, stroked the snow-white mane.

"Gee, this is pretty!" he said. "He's even prettier than the sheep." Then he turned to two pals of his, who were examining the trophies. "One of these days when I get big," he told them, "I'm going to hunt in Canada and when I do, I'll get a caribou bigger than Dad's."

"Yeah," they jeered. "That'll be a long, long time."

To him it *was* a long time – eight years – but to me it seemed like a weekend, as anyone who has watched a son grow from his 10th to 18th year can testify. One day he was a grubby urchin who loathed combing his hair and whose chief interests were marbles and back-lot softball; the next he was a sharp-looking young man in a brown tweed jacket and gray flannels who had an eye for the girls.

When he was ten, the boy was already a jackrabbit-and-

31

cottontail hunter of several years' experience. He shot his first round of skeet when he was 14 and quickly became good enough to win some Class B medals. I was with him on the great day when, at 13, he shot his first whitetail buck, and I remember that when the buck was down, he got a belated attack of buck fever so virulent he couldn't stand up and I virtually had to carry him down the mountain to look at his trophy. We hunted other whitetails on the Sonora Desert of Mexico, javelinas in southern Arizona. I still remember that bitterly cold October night on Idaho's Salmon River when he came into camp in triumph with a horse he had led 4,000 feet off a mountaintop to the river. On its back was his first mule deer.

But during all those years, we dreamed of the time when we'd hunt together in the wild Canadian north, to get a ram and a goat, and particularly a caribou. Then, in the late summer of 1951, our dream came true. Both of us decided it was then or never, because in another year he'd be out of high school, and Uncle Sam has plans for husky lads of that age.

*F*or hunting companions we had Dr. E.G. Braddock, retired surgeon, and Vernon Speer, bullet manufacturer. We traveled a couple of thousand miles by plane, steamship, automobile, and packtrain to the Atlin country in the extreme northwest of British Columbia. This is the fabled Cassiar district, bounded on the north by the Yukon and on the west by Alaska, a country little hunted and little known, a land of goats and grizzly bears and Fannin sheep – and of the great Osborn caribou, an animal almost as large as the largest elk and with the finest antlers of all mountain-ranging caribou. Watson Smarch, a Yukon Indian pal of mine, was keen to see this area, so I'd asked him to join us as horse wrangler. Our guide, Harry, was also an Indian.

We did not get a good look at a caribou until we had been out a couple of weeks and were moving our camp from Porter Lake to Surprise Lake over the shoulder of a big mountain. We were far above timberline in a rolling country of scrubby arctic willow, meadows of grass and moss, and barren, snow-splotched basins where tiny frigid streams trickled through beds of gray slide rock.

The first Osborn caribou we saw was a cow. She appeared out of the head of a draw half a mile away, jittering nervously around and gaping at us with nearsighted eyes. We had the wind on her, but she'd heard us cursing our stubborn and contrary packhorses.

When Watson and I shouted "Caribou!" in one breath, Doc

Braddock and Bradford piled off their horses and broke out binoculars, the better to gaze upon this simple and befuddled cow.

"A caribou!" said Brad.

"Well, I'll be – doggoned!" said Doc.

"You'd have thought that they were looking at nothing less than a dinosaur. A calf joined the cow, then another cow. Presently, seven caribou were clustered there, gaping at us. Gradually we edged nearer until finally they hoisted their little white tails and took off with their long-paced, springy trot.

"Caribou," said Bradford. "Santa Claus's reindeer! Just imagine my seeing them!"

"Maybe we'll see a bull," Doc suggested hopefully.

And we did. Not many minutes passed before Watson held up his hand to get my attention, then pointed. About a mile away, sharply silhouetted against a ridge, was a big, white-necked bull, head down, lost in thought about whatever bull caribou think about. Again Doc and Bradford piled off their horses and brought the binoculars into use. Here at last was shootable game.

"Boy! Get a load of that," Bradford breathed. "He's as big as a bull elk."

We were about a quarter-mile from the bull on the ridge when a packhorse snorted and we turned to see two other bulls trot out of a shallow ravine to look us over.

*D*uring the rut the caribou bull is the most stupidly reckless of animals. We had the wind on these big fellows, and to their feeble eyes our heavily laden packhorses apparently looked like voluptuous caribou cows. They rushed up to within 50 yards, stopped, ran back, approached again.

One was a good trophy, but the other was out of this world. His antlers were long, massive, and many-pointed, and his shovel formation was terrific. I'd seen some fine bull caribou in my day, but this was probably the best of all. I ran off 30 or 40 feet of color film with the movie camera and then, as the bulls came closer, I trained my still camera on them.

"I'll match you for the big one," I heard Bradford say to Doc, as he jerked his rifle from his saddle scabbard.

"O.K.," said Doc, likewise going for his musket.

"The season isn't open yet," Watson reminded them. "This is the twenty-ninth. You can't shoot caribou until the first of September."

"Better let them alone," I cautioned. "They tell me these B.C. jails get pretty cold in the winter."

So the two caribou hunters, sighing like wounded walruses and with their faces studies in despair, put their rifles in the scabbards and climbed slowly back onto their weary horses.

"Heck," said Bradford bitterly. "That big bull makes the one in our trophy room look like peanuts. Of all the doggoned luck – to see him when I can't shoot him."

"Oh, well," I said cheerfully, "keep your shirt on. We have two weeks left and maybe you'll see one just as good. Maybe even better."

The kid looked at me sourly. "I'll bet!" he snorted.

As we rode off, the two amorous bulls stood on a ridge and watched us, gloriously beautiful, astoundingly dumb. But what trophies!

Brad got his next chance a few days later, after the season opened. He, Watson, Harry, and I were scouting a new piece of country in the hope of locating some sheep, and at noon we stopped in the high point of a pass far above timberline. Watson was eating a sandwich when he noticed the sudden flash of something white a mile away and far below us in the scrubby timber. He picked up the glass and made out a bull caribou traveling toward us. What he'd seen was its white neck.

"Well, Brad," he said, "here's your bull caribou. You don't need to go after it. He'll come to us."

Presently the bull emerged from the timber and we got a good look at him. About all that could be said for his rack was that it was fair. Brad sat down and slipped off the safety of his .270. When the bull drew broadside, he followed it for a moment in the scope. Then he took the cartridge out of the chamber and put his rifle down.

"I don't want him," he said.

"Not big enough?" I asked.

"No. I'm not going to shoot a bull until I see one as big as the baby we passed up."

During the next ten days Brad got a ram and a fine billy goat, and Doc shot the largest grizzly I've seen. But neither forgot the big bull they had passed up. He was legal game now and they felt that all they needed to do was go back to the same ridge and they'd find him still jittering around.

But he wasn't there. We made our last camp on the road that led to Atlin, but still within striking distance of the caribou mountain. Those strange and restless animals had gone, however, and during a long day of hunting, not one did we see.

That night the gloom was so thick in the cooktent you could almost see it. Finally the boy spoke up.

"Next time I see a bull like that big one, I'm going to take a chance on going to jail."

No one spoke. We all knew he didn't mean it. We let him go on.

"Well, maybe not," he said, "but now I'll never get any kind of caribou."

"Brad," said Harry Johnson, "don't give up hope. We've got one more chance."

"Where?" Brad asked, brightening slightly.

"I know a mountain where I always used to see caribou at this time of year. Bulls too."

"Lead me to it!"

"Well, we can't take horses. We'll have to go in the truck, climb about 2,000 feet, and walk at least 15 miles. Are you game?"

"I'd do it barefoot for a bull as good as the one I couldn't shoot," Brad said.

So at dawn the next morning the two wilderness-hardened youngsters took off on a desperate last chance. First they drove the truck 20 miles to the very end of a rough and miserable wagon road that led to a long-abandoned placer mine at the head of a lonely valley. Then they piled out and struck off above timberline to the series of peaks and basins which ten years before, Harry said, had held a herd of caribou.

Harry thinks that, all told, they walked, climbed, and ran about 25 miles that day. The traveled light, with one pair of binoculars, one rifle, and sandwiches tucked into their shirts. They'd toil up a ridge, stop, glass the basins below. Then they'd climb to another vantage point and glass some more basins.

By noon they'd seen a couple of Fannin sheep miles away on a distant peak, but no caribou and only a little old sign. Both were young, tough, and in good condition, but as time went on and they saw nothing to cheer them, they grew tired and thirsty. They were in an area of little water and hadn't had a drink since leaving camp hours before.

They stopped for a rest on a rock-slide where the whole side of a great cliff had broken off and tumbled into a valley. They could hear water, tantalizingly unavailable, trickling below them.

Tired and discouraged, Brad gloomily contemplated the long miles back to the truck.

"Too bad," Harry said. "Places change in ten years."

"Yeah," said Brad. "But we couldn't have got a caribou sitting in camp either."

"That's right," said Harry. Then he added without conviction, "Maybe we'll see something yet."

He picked up the binoculars again and idly put them on the skyline a couple of miles away. Then he almost fell backward.

"Caribou!" he said. "Great big bull. Damnedest bull I've ever seen. Three cows with him."

"Bigger than the one I couldn't shoot?"

"Way bigger!" said Harry.

"I can't believe it!"

Brad reached for the glasses and focused on the caribou – four of them. Two cows were lying down, but another cow and a bull were feeding. As Brad watched, the bull took a few steps toward the ridge, silhouetting his antlers against the sky. It took no caribou expert to see that this was a bull of bulls.

Brad whistled. "Harry," he said, "you're right and I love you like a brother. Let's got get him."

"We got to hurry," Harry said. "They might move. Caribou are crazy that way."

So, hardened and trained down fine by 30 days of hard going in the mountains, the two took off at a dead run, their thirst, their weariness forgotten. They descended the ridge they were on, to get out of sight, then ran for more than a mile. Next they climbed a peak and cut across to come on the caribou from above and behind.

It took them over an hour to make it, but they finally emerged near the rocky knob where they had marked the bull. He was still with his three cows, and at close range he looked even better than he had through the binoculars. He stood there with his white neck, flaring nostrils, and great, heavily palmated antlers sweeping back and forth, and Brad knew that here was one bull in thousands.

The boy sat down, fed a cartridge quietly into the chamber of his .270, put the crosshairs of the Weaver K-2.5 behind the bull's foreleg, and squeezed the trigger. The bull pitched forward, twitched a few times, and lay still.

Brad and Harry both let out wild yells of triumph. Then they ran over to the great bull and measured the main beam of each massive antler. Brad knew my own best caribou, which he had long admired, had one main beam of 51$\frac{1}{2}$ inches. He could not believe his eyes when he now read 57$\frac{1}{2}$ inches on the steel tape, so he measured the beams again. Once more the tape read

57^1/$_2$ inches for the longest one. This time he believed it, and he and Harry let out another whoop.

But they didn't have time to tarry. They gulped down dry sandwiches, skinned out the head, and cut off a hindquarter and the backstraps. Then, carrying about 100 pounds apiece, they took off across ten miles of rough country toward the car.

Doc and I were in the cooktent devouring moose filet mignon when we heard a couple of triumphant yells above the rumble of the truck. We ran out to see Brad and Harry pile out, grinning like horse players who've hit a daily double. Sticking up out of the truck bed was the darnedest set of caribou antlers I've every seen, the longest and the most massive. The shovel was not very well developed, but the antlers had 34 points, a tremendously heavy top portion, and beams of 55^1/$_2$ and 57^1/$_2$ inches. The rack is one of the great caribou trophies of all time, and should rank high in the world records. A tentative check indicates it's the fourth largest ever taken.

"Maybe you'll win the Boone and Crockett Club's annual award with that head," Watson told Brad.

"Nothing to it," Brad said. "All you've got to do is to pass up the fair ones and the pretty good ones till the big ones come along. Now that first one we saw was pretty good, but nothing really special!"

A Family Affair

*Most fans of the man overlook
O'Connor's love of fine bird dogs and
wingshooting. Here, Caroline joins her
father for a late-season hunt with Jack's
dog of a lifetime, a Brittany named Mike.
The trio enjoys a banner day on quail
and finishes up with Caroline's sweet
redemption on a big old pheasant rooster
she had missed earlier in the day.*
August, 1962

The little valley had been swarming with quail when the season opened, and it had contained a surprising number of pheasants, too. But that had been almost a month before. I didn't expect shooting as fabulous as I had run into the first day when I had nailed three big, fat cock pheasants in addition to a limit of quail – or even hunting as good as on the second day when all the pheasants seemed to have left the country, but when I had taken my ten quail in no more than 30 minutes.

I hadn't been back since then, as the valley was a long way from any wheatfields and by no means top pheasant country. The visiting firemen who had been shooting with me had all been doing our gunning in areas more productive of the gaudy cocks. But now the season was drawing to a close, the visitors were all gone, and my daughter Caroline and I were bound for nothing more ambitious than a modest quail shoot. The members of my family would rather eat the tender, delicately flavored little California valley quail than pheasants.

It's a lovely little valley, this. It lies between high grassy hills, and a sparkling stream runs through little sagebrush flats and patches of willows. Once a ranch house had stood beside the little stream, but it had long since been abandoned to decay and vandals. Now, all that was left of it was a stone foundation and a few gnarled trees hung with small, bright apples.

Many a fine day of shooting have I had in the valley. Mostly I have been after quail, but one of the good things about the place is that I never quite know what will turn up. Now and then a cock pheasant adds spice to the quail shoot. In years when Hungarian partridge are plentiful, the valley always holds two or three coveys of these fast-flying, wild-flushing birds. The biggest surprise I ever had there came a couple of years ago when my Brittany spaniel Mike came to a point about 20 yards on one side of the stream in high grass at the foot of the hill. Afterward, I remembered he had the same sort of sneaky expression on his face that he wears when he points a deer. At the time, though, I assumed he was on quail. I walked in. A covey of chukar partridges took off all around me with a sound like tearing silk. They are big, rather slow-flying birds that are all white meat. I gave such a start that if they had been quail, I probably wouldn't have got a feather, but I recovered and nailed two with the fast-handling little 28 gauge double I was carrying that day – and with No. 8 shot.

*B*ut I digress. On the particular day I am writing about, my daughter Caroline and I parked the station wagon beside the creek, put our two Model 21 Winchesters together, and let out my dog Mike. This Brittany is my most cherished possession – the darndest bird-finder I have ever seen, a tough and wiry little dog with a choke-bored nose and the ability to read bird's minds.

I say he is my most cherished possession, but whether I own him or he owns me I cannot say. For $9^1/2$ months a year I serve him faithfully. I clean his runway, feed him, take him for walks, give him dry runs on birds out of season. For $2^1/2$ months a year he presumably works for me, and together we scour the beautiful uplands for birds. Without Mike I'd be a poor bird hunter indeed, and without me and my shotgun, Mike would get few birds himself. For the long closed season, I call the turns; but when the birds are legal, Mike is the boss. When his nose tells him nothing is around, he humors me by answering my hand signals in the best field-trial manner. But when he is on scent, he takes over, regards me with a gentle and pitying eye, tells me in his dog language that I don't know what I am talking about, but that if I'll only pay attention, we'll have some fun.

In his years afield, he has learned that the way you pin a running cock pheasant is to circle it and come in on it from in front, and that to hold one tight for two or three minutes while I come wheezing and scrambling up a steep hill is to get right on top of it and petrify it with fear. But he has also learned that getting right on top of a covey of Huns won't work. When Hun smell hits his nostrils he points at 25 or 30 yards.

So this day I motioned for Mike to take off downstream. Caroline and I followed, one on one side of the creek, the other on the opposite side. Mike quartered back and forth into the gentle breeze that blew into our faces. Now and then he paused and looked at me to tell me he hadn't located a single smell. Once I sent him into a nice-looking patch of scarlet sumac glowing against a hillside, a spot where I had often found coveys, and where now and then Mike would stand a ringneck. A little later, he went into the foot of a long brushy draw which came down from the hills above and emerged at the head of it. He watched Caroline and me for a moment, then trotted down the hill to rejoin us. I could almost see him shrug his shoulders.

Puzzled and discouraged, Caroline and I turned to head back toward the car. Mike continued to work along ahead of us, glancing back now and then to see if I had any ideas or any directions. We walked right through a sunflower patch that a few weeks before had exploded with quail. We found fairly fresh dusting places, a few feathers, but no birds. Mike combed a patch of high grass we had missed on the first turn. Again no results.

"What's the matter with Mike?" Caroline demanded a little pettishly, shifting her shotgun from one arm to another. When she doesn't get action, her gun gets heavy and her feet hurt. "Why doesn't he find birds?"

"Undoubtedly because there aren't any birds around here," I said.

"Did they kill them all off? Look! Here are some empty shells."

"I doubt it," I said. "Let's watch Mike. If he doesn't find something pretty soon, we'll go up this side creek."

*M*ike was taking his time and enjoying the outing. He stopped and smelled at a rabbit hole, investigated the dry and disintegrated carcass of a winter-killed domestic sheep, looked at me, shrugged his shoulders.

Then a little eddy of wind came down from the hills. I saw him stiffen, wave his nose gently in the air. Then he turned around, looked at me with narrowed yellow eyes, and started up the hillside. He disappeared in a brushy draw. Then we saw him come out, high on a grassy slope. I knew he was on scent, not strong scent, but he did have something.

"Watch Mike," I said.

By this time he was 300-400 feet above us and a quarter of a mile away. Something attracted my attention then and I looked away. When I glanced back, he was on point, a little dog as stiff as a statue, a tiny white spot against the yellow, frost-cured grass up there on the hillside.

"Well," I said, "there are our birds. Old Mike's done it again."

Maybe swimming and dancing gave Caroline the muscles in those legs, or maybe she inherited them from the same bog-trotting Irish ancestor from whom she got her dark brown hair, her blue eyes, and fair northern skin. Anyway, she can really cover country. While I labored up the hill, pausing now and then to get my breath, she took it on the run. I was still only halfway up when I saw her coming in behind Mike, her gun at ready. Mike hadn't even twitched an ear all this time, and I knew he had a covey under his nose.

I saw her walk in front of him and kick at a clump of grass. But instead of a covey of quail, a big cock pheasant with a tail that looked six feet long came thrashing out, cackling derisively. She hesitated, then finally shot – once, twice. I saw one lone feather float down. The rooster volplaned by me at about 70 yards, swerved to the left, and finally lit in a brush patch along the stream not too far from the car.

When I joined Caroline she was almost at the point of tears.

"That darned old pheasant," she said. "I hate him. I was expecting quail, and when he came out, it scared me to death."

"You hit him, I think," I told her. "When we get down there, we'll find him."

"We never will," she moaned. "I feel so silly."

When I looked up, Mike was no longer in sight. We hiked to the top of the ridge and there he was, just on the other side, again on point. This time I knew it was quail. Like any artist, Mike has his little mannerisms, and through them I can generally tell what kind of game he is on. He was trained on pheasants and would rather hunt the big birds than anything else. When he is on one, he has the same gone, trancelike look in his eyes that a cool cat gets when he listens to a fancy bit of trumpet work. If he points a bobcat or a hiding whitetail deer, as he does now and then, he looks pretty sneaky about it, as if he knows he shouldn't do it but just can't help it. When he's on quail he plainly thinks he's slumming. He enjoys hunting the little birds, but just can't take them very seriously and has a sort of a what-the-hell attitude toward them that reflects in his stance and his expression. If I miss a pheasant, something that doesn't happen very often, Mike never fails to look around at me as if I had broken his heart. But if I miss a quail, which I do with great regularity, he doesn't even care enough to chide me. So now it was quail.

I motioned for Caroline to go in and make the flush and followed behind her to one side. About 25 of the little black bombshells boiled out – most of them right in front of and directly away from Caroline. But one curved low and wild past me. I didn't swing fast enough with the first barrel, but I caught up with the second and it bounced. I heard Caroline shoot, turned to see Mike darting around in the low sage after a wounded and running bird with Caroline right behind him. Then Mike made a lunge and a grab and had it. Caroline took it away from him.

"See," she whooped, holding it up. "I got one!"

"That's good, honey. Let's follow Mike."

Most of the birds had flown across the little basin up there in the hills and had landed on the opposite side. They were pretty well scattered. Since the grass that grew between patches of sagebrush was fairly high and thick, I expected them to lie well. Mike shot across the basin after the birds and almost turned a somersault when he hit scent and slammed into a point. Five birds that had landed in a cluster took off, and between us Caroline and I managed to get two.

Caroline was having the time of her life. She had the youth and the stamina to stay close to the cruising Brittany, and every now and then I'd hear her shrill "He's on point!" Once she and the dog disappeared on the other side of the ridge for half an hour or so. I heard some miscellaneous shooting. Presently, the tinkle of his bell announced that Mike was returning to see what had happened to me. Caroline was not far behind, grinning happily.

"See, daddy," she said. "I got three more and you weren't there to help me."

There were quail all over the hilltops and through the little basins filled with grass and sagebrush. Offhand, I'd estimate that we must have had contact with at least 15 coveys that afternoon, and I'd likewise guess that the average number of birds to a covey was around 15. Often we blundered into birds when we were cutting across the basins to spots where Mike was on point.

*W*e didn't get our birds without considerable expenditure of ammunition. The California valley quail comes off the ground like a rocket, and he can fly as fast after he has traveled two feet as he can ever. For his size, he is a noisy little devil when he gets up, and he startles the socks off the innocent hunter. He is dark and hard to see as he blends with most backgrounds. Because of his noise and his inconspicuous coloring, he appears to be going twice as fast as he really is. Even on level ground, the quail hunter tends to think the birds will be in the next county unless he shoots quickly. He tends to hurry his shot and misses.

But just put the little rascals in the hills where flights are generally up and down at sharp angles as well as curving, and then the shooting really gets grim. I remember one Waterloo the girl and I had. Mike stood four successive singles on a steep hillside, and in each case the birds flew sharply down as each of us fired both barrels. We didn't even nick one.

I partly redeemed myself a little later when Mike and Caroline were off on an expedition. I was walking right along the edge of a bluff that was probably about 75 feet high when a bird took off at my feet. I nailed it, saw it plummet down in a shower of feathers. Then another took off – and another. When I had shot the third, I began to feel a bit foolish. Could I find them?

I cut around and got down below the bluff to look for the birds. The grass was thick and high, and I was afraid that without Mike's help it would be like looking for needles in the haystack. But presently I saw a feather fluttering on a blade of grass, then another, and another. The three birds were in a small triangle, stone dead.

By this time my jacket seemed fairly heavy, and I decided it was time to count the birds. I had exactly ten – the limit. When I got on top again, Caroline and Mike were working over a gently rolling hilltop for singles. Every now and then Mike would go on point and Caroline would boot out a bird. I followed, taking a picture occasionally. Suddenly, after she had nailed a little cock that had exploded into a pile of feathers just as he was about to clear a bush, she turned to me in disbelief.

"Daddy," she said, "I've only got two shells left. I won't tell you how many I brought with me, but I brought a lot."

"Better save those," I suggested. "You have plenty of quail now and you might run into that pheasant you missed."

As we headed down the draw toward the car, Mike found and pointed two singles and one small covey. When we kicked them out and didn't shoot, he looked at us as if we'd lost our minds.

When we got down in the valley, the sun was behind the hills, and after the bright, dry upland basins, it was damp and pungent with willows and water, chill with evening. Mike cruised around ahead of us in his businesslike manner. Occasionally I'd see him stop and his nose work as if he had caught scent so faint that even he couldn't quite identify it. His bell tinkled gently as he hunted in and out of the cover on both sides of the creek. We were almost through the cover where I thought the pheasant might still be if it had really been hit. Then I became aware that his bell's tinkle had stopped.

I held my fingers to my lips for silence, then motioned for Caroline to follow me. Mike was on point on the other side of the creek in some good cover beside a fence. I didn't have to look at him twice to know that this time it wasn't on quail. He had that gone and goofy look in his eyes.

I motioned Caroline to go in, but she began to jitter.

"It's that pheasant again," she whispered. "You shoot him. I'm afraid I'll miss."

"No you won't," I hissed. "Go on in."

"Will you shoot if I miss?"

"O.K., then, I'll shoot if you miss. Now get ready. Go up behind Mike. The bird's right on the other side of the fence. I'm going to throw a rock and he'll come out.

She walked in, and when the stone hit the fence, the rooster boiled out. Her first shot missed, and I was bringing my gun up in case her second didn't connect. But when she fired again the bird went down. I could see his long tail sticking up out of the grass.

"Where is he? Where is he?" Caroline cried excitedly.

"Dead as Nero," I told her. "Didn't you see where it fell?"

"I didn't even see it fall," she told me. "I didn't want to see myself miss that pheasant the second time, so I closed my eyes!"

PART TWO
Hunting in North America

*J*ack O'Connor is most closely associated with hunting
Coues' deer and wild sheep, yet he spent plenty of time afield
dealing with many other kinds of big game including elk,
antelope, mule deer, caribou, brown and grizzly bears, and moose.
Whatever the species, Jack always managed to find delight in the
many and varied aspects of the quest. This might involve hunting a
record-book trophy, "guiding" his boys to their first deer, or
savoring venison tamales around a mesquite campfire in the
Sonoran desert. It didn't really matter. For him it was the
experience, the thrill of it all, that mattered, and he reveled in
sharing it with others.

O'Connor could be egotistical and arrogant, but he could also be a
genuinely warm human being. He derived great pleasure from
seeing – and writing about – the hunting successes of family and
friends. He was, to be sure, a highly competitive hunter, and record-
book listings meant a great deal to him. But his competition focused
on the animal, not outdoing other hunters. At times, his excitement
at the triumphant moments of others fairly jumps from the page.

Over his career, in one form or another Jack wrote several
hundred pieces describing big game hunts in North America. Unlike
contemporaries such as Archibald Rutledge, who pursued the same
buck in print time and again, virtually all of his material was
original. It was always fresh, always filled with a breathless sense of
reality, and never pedestrian in the sense of reeking of just another
story to meet yet another deadline.

The stories included in this section range widely in subject matter
and geography, from Mexico to Alaska and the Yukon. Jack
O'Connor exhibited a consistently high level of craftsmanship
throughout his writing career, but to me, he is at the peak of his game
when writing about the desert Southwest and the Canadian North
Country, two regions that he loved passionately and knew intimately.

SCAREBEAR

Grizzlies, the Yukon equivalent of voodoo, and juking around an O'Connor jinx combine for a first-rate story. You'll enjoy some of Jack's dry humor and how he could turn camp talk into literary magic. September, 1951.

The little Indian village by the lonely Yukon lake was abandoned, a scene of desolation and broken hopes. As we came upon the scene, doors of the log cabins swung in the wind on creaky hinges. Windows were broken and some of the sod-covered roofs had fallen in. The meat-drying racks were rotten and rickety, and the ground was strewn with litter, as always happens where people move away.

Bleached by the sun, spongy from rain and chewed by porcupines lay the skull and antlers of a fine bull caribou, also one horn of a bull moose, with part of the skull attached, and the horns of a Dall ewe, still with the snow-white hairs around the base. Inside the cabin we found a broken-down sewing machine and a vintage-model phonograph with a morning-glory horn. In another were two Winchesters, a Model 93 pump gun and an old Model 79 single-shot rifle for some big black-powder cartridge. Both actions were frozen solid with the rust of many snows and many rains.

Red Earley, Herb Klein, and I poked about in the ruins, waiting for the pack-train to catch up.

"What happened to the people who used to live here? Where did they go?" Herb asked Charlie, our Indian guide.

"Long time ago bad sickness come," Charlie told us. "Many people die. Others get frightened and move away."

I was puttering around, wondering if the action of the Winchester single-shot was salvageable, when I was startled by what I thought was a ragged child standing alone in the yard. It was a little effigy of a man, and was built around a pole driven into the earth. It wore a battered cap, a decaying shirt and trousers, and it carried a stick that was plainly supposed to be a gun.

"Hey," I shouted, "I've found a scarecrow!"

"No," said Charlie as he came around to look. "Not scarecrow – scare<u>bear</u>. Indian people make little man out of old clothes. They put

49

gun in hand and stand him up. Then beer come to rob cache and break in house. He look and see man standing there with gun. He get scared and run."

"That's a new one on me," Herb said. "A scarebear. Might call it a bearcrow."

"No, scare the beer," Charlie insisted, afraid we hadn't got it right.

"The idea may be new to you, Herb," Red said, "but not to me. I'm very well acquainted with a genuine scarebear – namely me. I'm the original scarebear. I've got something that jinxes me on grizzlies. I've spent hundreds of bucks on grizzly trips. I've worn my feet off up to the knees stalking them. I've hunted them in Wyoming, in Alberta, and in British Columbia, and this is my second time after grizzlies in the Yukon. You know what?"

"What," I responded dutifully.

"I've never even got a shot at a grizzly!"

"That's tough," I said sympathetically.

"Tough? It's fantastic. On anything else I have luck – sheep, caribou, goats, antelope, deer, anything. But grizzlies, no. If I'm in black bear country I can't push a rock off a cliff without conking a black bear, but when they were handing out grizzly luck, they forgot me. I've seen about 35 grizzlies, but I haven't got a shot at a doggoned one!

"Every time I've glassed a grizzly and tried to stalk him, something's happened. Once in Alberta we located a fine big grizzly. We made a good stalk and were within 200 yards of him when some screwball in the party happened to see the bear from a half-mile away and threw a shot at it for luck. My guide and I were just about to come out of the timber and gather in that bear. We heard the shot and, sure enough, the bear was gone."

"You've played it tough," I commiserated.

"You haven't heard the worst," Red said bitterly. "Now I'll break your heart! Once we sneaked up to within 150 yards of a big grizzly and waited for him to show. Then I saw a bear walk out into a little open place. I thought it was the grizzly, so I shot, and down it went. But what do you think? It wasn't the grizzly at all. It was a lousy black bear that came bumbling along at the last minute. That's what I'd shot. The grizzly heard the shot, of course, and scrammed."

*R*ed's outburst explained a lot to me. He and I had just finished a week's hunting near Pilot Mountain. We had each shot a beautiful Dall ram, which to me is the cream of North American trophies. Red had taken his sheep in his stride. But he was really interested in grizzlies, and every time we found a track or a place where the great bears had dug for ground squirrels, he stiffened like a bird dog at the scent of quail. Actually, Pilot Mountain wasn't very good grizzly country, but that hadn't discouraged Red. He hunted from dawn until dark.

"I'll tell you what, Red," I said now. "I'm usually very lucky when it comes to grizzlies, and I'm pretty well caught up on my grizzly hunting. Suppose I go right with you the next time you hunt bears, and maybe my good luck will offset your back luck."

"Brother," said Red, "if you can, you will really be making medicine."

While we stood there examining the scarebear, we heard the packtrain coming, so with Charlie in the lead, we hit the trail.

The Indians had used it for years, but I believe ours was the first big packstring ever to go into this rugged country. The pack boxes took a beating on the thick jackpine, and the horses kept getting hung up between the trees. Part of the time the trail skirted the edge of the placid, lovely lake, but it also crept through muskeg, across streams, and over ridges. Soon, a few miles distant, rose the long, L-shaped mountain range where Red was to hunt grizzlies.

"Good beer country. Lots of beer, old man who live here long time ago tell me," Charlie said. "Lots of beers reason for little man to scare them. Beers steal meat, kill Indian hunters. You get beer all right."

"Let's hope so," said Red. "This is my last shot. If I don't catch a grizzly this time, I'm going to stick to golf."

We hit our campsite at the far end of the lake. Generations of Indians had used this same spot, and in every direction there were stumps of trees that had been cut down with stone axes. Not far from where we pitched our tents we noticed dried grizzly dung on the ground and claw marks on a tree.

"Cheer up, Red," Herb said. "Sign all over the place."

"Doesn't mean anything to me."

*E*arly the next morning, while Herb went after sheep, Red and I rode out toward another mountain with Charlie and Moose Johnson as guides. We pushed through willows, skirted muskeg, and every time we topped a rise, we could see ahead of us the rolling, open sides of the mountain above timberline.

"Red," I said, "you're going to shoot a grizzly this morning. I feel my luck working."

51

"Maybe my jinx is working too," he said gloomily.

About two miles from the mountain we stopped in a little wet meadow, tied our horses and used our binoculars on the long ridge ahead of us. We hadn't been there a minute when Charlie said, "I see a beer."

He sure did! A brown grizzly was eating berries and moving along slowly about a quarter of the way up the mountain.

"Well, Red," I said. "What did I tell you?"

"I'll be damned!" he said. Then his face clouded. "You don't know my luck. A bear a couple of miles away isn't *my* bear. It'll go into a draw and then we'll never see it again. You watch."

"Well," I said, "let's make time so we can get up to him before he decides to lie up for the day."

We booted our reluctant horses through spruce thickets, willow bottoms, and musket. Now and then, when we hit a high spot, we'd grab our glasses and take a look at the bear. He was still here, still feeding, still moving slowly along the side of the mountain, a bright brown spot against the drab green of the brush.

We tied our horses a quarter of a mile from where we expected the grizzly to be. Red took his .300 Magnum out of the scabbard, and slipped a cartridge into the chamber. All the Yukon natives have profound respect for bears, and Charlie is no exception. He unlimbered his .30/30 and Moose Johnson took my .30/06. I was along just for luck, so I took my 16mm. movie camera. If there was going to be a battle, I'd record it for posterity.

Cautiously we stuck our heads over the ridge. The bear was waddling along from bush to bush about 400 yards away.

"Let's wait and see what he does," Moose suggested.

"No," I protested. "Let's get as close as we can and shoot it."

Grizzlies have poor eyes, and in wilderness country, they aren't very wary since they have no enemies. On the other hand, nothing can disappear as quickly as a grizzly. One can walk into the thin brush of a little draw and vanish. My own theory of hunting grizzlies is to have the wind right, then travel toward the bear as fast as possible. Speed is far more important than trying to keep out of sight. I wanted to close the range on the bear fast, because even if he saw us and ran, I felt that Red could cut him down on that open hillside.

*W*e had a council of war, and decided to sneak to a patch of trees about 50 yards closer to the grizzly. All went well. From our hide-out, we feasted our eyes on our prospective victim.

"Great big fellow," said Charlie

"Big as a horse," Moose agreed.

"He's got a skull two feet wide," O'Connor observed.

"Golly, I hope he doesn't get away," said Red nervously.

Crouching, we trotted over the soft lichens another 50 yards to a patch of stunted spruce. The bear was across a wide ravine, innocently chomping berries.

"We can get a hundred yards closer," I said. "Come on, let's go."

"No," Red whispered. "I've played with my luck long enough. At last I'm going to get a shot at a sure-enough grizzly. How far is he away?"

"About 300 yards."

"Where should I hold?"

"Just under his spine."

"Watch my smoke! If he charges, throw that movie camera at him."

Red's first shot was just over the bear's back. The bear paid no attention. Red worked the bolt of his .300, got the bear in the scope, and shot again. The bear dropped and began rolling slowly downhill as limp as a bag of meal. No flouncing around. No bawling. Just a dead bear.

"You kill him," Charlie said quite unnecessarily.

Red jumped to his feet, let out a Texas yell, then shouted, "Look at me, by golly. My jinx is over! I'm a grizzly hunter!"

Come to find out, the bear wasn't 300 yards away, probably nearer 250, since Red and I got 275 paces over rough ground to the place where it had stopped rolling. And "he" became a she, a medium-sized lady bear, which is not unusual since almost all grizzlies are "he" until they are killed and they are always "big." Red had hit her in the right ear.

For minutes Red sat by his trophy, staring at it, fondling its long, golden-brown fur. He was one of the most delighted people I have ever seen.

*M*oose and I left Red and Charlie to skin the bear and went to see if we could find one for ourselves. After a bit Red happened to look up in the direction where we had gone. He told me later that he thought he saw a black horse.

"What's Jack coming back for?" he asked Charlie.

"Maybe forget something," said Charlie, glancing up.

After a few minutes Red looked up again. The horse had no rider, and Red wondered if I'd got thrown.

He picked up his binoculars. What he saw through them was an enormous grizzly, a beautiful silvertip. He was on the move and, since the wind was right, he walked past Red and Charlie and the dead bear without paying any attention. Moose and I, apparently, had ridden on one side of the ridge as the big bear walked along the other. The sight of that beautiful bear made Red's trigger finger itch. But, fine sportsman that he is, he didn't shoot.

Moose and I didn't see another grizzly on the trip, but one night as we were coming back to camp after a long, fruitless day, we heard a terrific fusillade on a hill about half a mile away. Red and Herb had run into a big male grizzly, and the shooting was to scare him out of some willows where he had taken refuge. They came in just about dark, hungry and happy and carrying a beautiful silver-tipped hide.

It looks as if I'd done a pretty good job of transferring my luck to Red. Maybe I'm the scarebear now!

DWARF DEER IN SONORA

In one of his many Mexican trips, Jack gets a first-hand opportunity to check out stories he had often heard about tiny deer, sometimes called fantails or by Mexicans, cabritos *(literally, goats). Accompanied by Eleanor, he kills both the tiny deer and larger whitetails. As a bonus they also bag some Benson quail, a species that had never been recorded that far north. March, 1963.*

The dark, aristocratic-looking little Mexican was gossiping with the clerk in the game department office in Nogales, Sonora, when I went in there some years ago to buy licenses for my wife and myself. Neither of them noticed me, and I stood there, impatient to buy the licenses and get it over with. The Mexicans, I am convinced, are the people who invented red tape, and all that day I had been going from office to office and building up a sheaf of papers. I'm sure conditions have improved in Mexico now, but at that time I had to buy a membership in a hunting club, which presumably would be responsible if I stole any cattle, shot any *vaqueros,* had an automobile accident, violated the game laws, or tried to bilk any citizens out of their *dinero.* It was either that or put up a $100 bond.

Then I had obtained a tourist card, an automobile permit, and I had gotten an arms permit from the general in charge of the department. I had produced a certificate from the chief of police in Tucson, Arizona, saying that I had not been in jail recently and was not at the time under indictment for murder, treason, or grand larceny. All that may sound simple, but it wasn't. It had taken me all day and no small amount of *mordida,* which in Mexico means "the bite." Now my final hurdle was the game license. Then, presumably, my wife and I would go flying through the border with no more trouble than a little more palm greasing.

The little dark man and the game warden were still talking, and I half listened as I admired a calendar advertising some brand of Mexican beer and showing an Aztec priest in a Sioux war bonnet about to plunge a knife into the voluptuous breast of a scantily clad maiden.

"Have luck on the last trip, Pedro?" the warden asked.

"Much," said the aristocratic-looking little character. "Many *venados* and two *cabritos.*"

I pricked up my ears. *Venado* is the word for the Arizona whitetail deer, but *cabrito* means small goat. There are no native wild goats in Mexico.

"What is this *cabrito*?" I asked, breaking into the conversation.

"A very small deer," Pedro told me, "a deer about half the size of the *venado.*"

"Are you sure they aren't young *venados*?" I asked.

"They are all different," he assured me. "All the people know the difference. They are so small that the countrymen always call them little goats."

I was familiar with the old story that in southern Arizona and Sonora, there was a diminutive deer smaller that the regular Arizona whitetail. I had heard it from many ranchers and prospectors, even from my own pioneering grandfather. I had talked the rumor over with game officials and biologists, and they had hooted at the notion. Nevertheless, it was one of the most enduring myths of the Southwest. Sometimes these little deer were called fantails, a name often applied to the regular Arizona whitetail. They were also called dwarf deer and Sonora deer. The trouble was that many talked about them, but no one ever produced one.

After I got my licenses, Pedro and I wound up in a restaurant where we devoured enchiladas, frijoles, and tamales, washed down by some excellent Hermosillo beer. When we parted, I had a map showing me how to get to *cabrito* country. Pedro struck me as being not only a nice guy, but an honest and intelligent one. There might not be such a thing as a dwarf Sonora deer, but I was convinced that he thought there was.

A couple of days later, my wife and I arrived at the place indicated by Pedro's map. It was at the point where the chain of high hills runs east of the Nogales-Hermosillo highway all the way from the border to about 125 miles south. There, this continuous sierra begins breaking up into scattered low hills. In places, the sierra thrusts peaks up to 9,000 feet or thereabouts, but most of it, I'd imagine, averages around 6,000. We camped at a point where a clear, cold stream breaks out of the hills by way of a beautiful canyon about a quarter of a mile wide. The road we had taken ended by a cluster of adobe houses, a couple occupied, the others vacant and in various states of repair.

Ramon, a slight, discouraged-looking Mexican whose old mother and father had a couple of rocky fields and an adobe hut up the canyon, was apparently the No. 1 boy around, so we got permission to camp in one of the least dilapidated huts. His wife swept the earth floor with a willow broom, and Ramon agreed that if we'd cross his palm with a bit of silver, he'd be on hand very early with some horses.

"Are there many *cabritos*?" I asked.

"No many but enough."

"Many *venados*?"

His face lit up. "In some places there are many," he told me.

I broached a jug of *tenampa*, a Mexican liquor made of rum flavored with port wine, and when I gave him a belt of it, he volunteered the information that there were also some *burros* (mule deer) down on the flats, some javelinas, a few lions, and occasionally a *tigre* (jaguar). I gave him another slug of *tenampa* and he told me that he had once killed a *tigre* with a rock after it had been cornered by his dogs.

Ramon, it appeared, made a precarious living by occasionally punching cows for a rancher who lived about ten miles away, doing a little placer mining, killing javelinas for their hides, raising some corn and chile in the *milpas* (fields) up the canyon, doing a bit of trapping for coyotes, bobcats, and foxes, and shooting a deer now and then when he had cartridges for a battered old .30/.30 which he proudly showed me. He owned about a dozen wiry little horses and a mule and a couple dozen half-witted chickens. Ramon could neither read nor write, and his kids had never seen a doctor, or the inside of a school, nor had any of them ever worn underwear, gone to a barber, or had a pair of shoes. But they had fun.

Doves that had been feeding all day up on the sierra were now shooting down from the high country to roost in the big cottonwoods along the stream. They started at about 7,000 feet and plunged downhill all the way to about 4,000. They were coming over the little cluster of huts so fast they sounded like jet planes. I found that by swinging fast and leading them about 20 feet, I hit one occasionally. I had better luck when I went down by the cottonwoods and potted them after they had put down wing flaps and were coming in for a landing. Before long I had enough for supper, and presently good smells came out of the hut where Eleanor was making them into a stew.

*R*amon didn't surprise me by showing up at the crack of dawn, as he had promised, but he did make his appearance about 8:30, and before long we had our saddle scabbards tied on, our stirrups adjusted, the canteens filled and our lunch in the saddle bags.

He led us on a trail that climbed gradually along the side of a canyon toward the high country. Our camp was in the region of desert growth like paloverdes, cholla, saguaro and cat-claw, but as we climbed, we soon began to see the little evergreen oaks which the Mexicans call *encinos*. There were not many cattle in the country at the time, and the grass grew high and thick. We hadn't ridden over a mile from the ranch when two does and three fawns, flaunting white tails that looked half as large as they were, ran out of a little clump of oaks.

Three or four miles from camp, we were rimming around an enormous basin when a fine whitetail buck with a handsome head jumped out of some brush below us and about 300 yards away. I thought I had seen antlers when he jumped, and the 8X binoculars showed them plainly.

"Nice buck!" I yelled to my wife as she scrambled off her horse.

She opened fire with her scope-sighted .257 as the buck dodged in and out of the oaks. Untouched, he crossed the little creek in the bottom of the basin, and started up the other side. *Bang, bang, bang!* The rifle went dry. Eleanor reloaded and opened up again as the buck climbed up the far side of the basin, getting farther and farther away. I could no longer see antlers; all I could make out was a little toy deer with a gray body and a shiny white tail.

The buck was now clear across the basin, just under the rimrock on the far side. He must have been pretty winded by that time. Either that or he felt safe, because he wasn't going very fast as he moved uphill and diagonally to our right. He was now so far away that all the glass showed me was that conspicuous white tail and a suggestion of a gray body moving through tall yellow grass.

Again Eleanor was reloading, still full of fight.

"He's so far away that all I can see is his tail," she told me. "Where will I hold now?"

More as a gag than anything else, I told her to hold 50 feet over him and about 20 feet in front. She shot – and the little white tail disappeared.

"Where did he go?" she demanded, panting.

"I can't see him any more," I told her. "I'll be damned if I don't believe you hit him."

"I held just where you told me," she said smugly.

I turned to Ramon, who had been watching this appalling waste of expensive ammunition with a cynical smile. "The buck is wounded," I told him.

He looked at me as if he felt I had lost my mind.

"I believe not! That is impossible."

I marked well the spot where the buck had disappeared and kept my eye on it during the half hour it took to ride over there. When we were about 100 yards from the spot, Ramon's pack of dogs suddenly started barking and rushed into a clump of manzanita.

Out came the buck, jumping along like a kangaroo and making surprisingly good time on two broken front legs. I could not shoot without hitting a dog, and the whole mob finally wound up in the bottom of the basin, 1,500 feet below, where the dogs cornered the buck in front of a big boulder. The hillside was too rough for horses, so there was nothing for Ramon and me to do but go down there and finish the buck. With him holding one antler and me holding the other, we then dragged him up to the horses, over rocks, over cliffs, through brush.

One of the buck's legs was broken above the knee, the other just below. How far he was away when he was hit I would be afraid to guess, but it was by far the longest shot I have ever seen made on a deer.

Getting the buck out of the basin and back to camp used up a good part of the day and most of my energy. We took some of the meat, but gave most of it to our hosts. While I nursed my Charley horses and did the camp chores late that afternoon, my wife took one of the children as a guide and retriever and went up to see if she could find some quail.

As I labored, I heard her shooting, and presently she returned with half a dozen birds.

"These are funny looking quail," she said. "What kind are they?"

I did a double-take when I saw that they were the Benson or "elegant" quail, the most beautiful of all North American quail. The cocks have gray breasts and gray heads, but the rest of the bird is bright orange, and their long topknots are a lighter yellowish orange. At the time we discovered the Benson quail in the little valley, it was the farthest northerly record for the species, and as far as I know, it still is. The northern limit of their range was supposed to be in the Yaqui Valley some hundreds of miles south.

There were four or five large coveys of the birds around the little *milpas*, but we found them nowhere else. Later we were to see the Mearns quail up in the tall grass of the hills and Gambel's quail down in desert flats, but not a sign of Bensons except in the *milpas*. Ramon told me they had always been there, even when his old father was a youth, and that he had never seen them anywhere else. But we still hadn't found a *cabrito*.

*N*ext morning, not far from camp, I nailed a small buck, and since we had the meat situation in hand, we spent the day hunting the mythical *cabrito*. We saw plenty of deer in the brush of the high country, but when I asked hopefully if they were *cabritos,* Ramon always shook his head.

The following day our break came. We were at least ten miles from camp and nooning by a little tinkling rill high in the mountains. It had been quite cold the night before, and heavy frost still lay in the shade. But out in the sun, in the fragrant grass, it was warm and pleasant. Eleanor and I were munching our sandwiches, the horses were dozing in the sun, and Ramon had a little fire built for his tin can full of coffee.

Suddenly he hissed, *"Cabrito!"* and pointed up the hill. A deer was standing there. Apparently it had been bedded down in the grass and had intended to stay hidden, but the sound of our voices had made it curious so it had stood up to look us over.

I was afraid to take time out to look it over with binoculars for fear it would take off. My .30/06 was leaning against a tree behind me. Without making any sudden movement, I fed a cartridge into the chamber, got into a tight sling, and lined up on the deer. My rifle was sighted in for 200 yards, and since the deer appeared to be somewhere between 250 and 300 yards away, I held right at the top of the shoulder and squeezed off the shot. The deer disappeared into the grass.

"You got him," Eleanor said.

"You missed," said Ramon, shaking his head. "The *cabrito* ran into the oaks."

"He's full of prunes," Eleanor said to me. "I saw it fall."

"Let's go look," I suggested to Ramon.

I didn't know what to think. I had called a perfect shot, and Eleanor swore the deer had fallen. That was likewise my impression. I decided to climb up for a look-see.

About 50 yards from the spot where I had seen the deer fall, I paused for a moment to get my breath. Suddenly, right at the top of the ridge, I saw a big whitetail buck jump. I threw a hasty shot at him, missed, then ran over the ridge in the direction he had taken.

The moment I got to the other side I saw him running to my left about 200 yards away across a draw. I sat down, swung just ahead of his nose and saw my shot throw up dust just behind him. I led him farther the next time, and he slid on his nose like a runner diving into home plate.

I assumed that this was the deer I had shot at when we were eating lunch and that I had wounded him. But when I got up to the buck, I found only one bullet hole, and I thought that strange. Furthermore, he was a regular Arizona whitetail (Coues' deer) and by no stretch of the imagination could he be called anything else.

I had taken his insides out and had started to walk back to the ridge where I had jumped him in order to signal Eleanor and Ramon when I heard brush popping and the hooves of their horses rattling on stones. Both were grinning as they rode up.

"We have your *cabrito*," Eleanor shouted. "I just knew I saw it fall, so when we came up to bring your horse and see what you had shot at, I went over and looked in the grass. There it was, dead as a mackerel."

It was tied behind Ramon's saddle, so I went over to take a look. It was a forkhorn buck, but the smallest whitetail buck I had ever laid eyes on. My guess was that it wouldn't weigh more than 40 or 45 pounds field dressed, maybe not that much. The top of his disproportionately large tail was a flaming orange, and his gray body had a pinkish cast. But it was his head that interested me. It was long, narrow, and mouselike without the pronounced orbital region of the regular Arizona whitetail. There was no doubt that he was related to *Odocoileus couesi,* but he was a different-looking creature. We rode over to where my big buck lay and put the two down together for a photograph.

And our luck was not yet over. As we rode home late that afternoon in the deep chill shadow of the canyon walls, we saw a small doe trot out from behind an oak and stand watching us almost concealed by the tall grass.

"*Cabrita . . . embra! Tira la!*" Ramon hissed. And that meant that it was a *cabrito* doe and that we must shoot it.

Eleanor piled off her horse and put a 100-grain .257 bullet right where it would do the most good. The doe's teeth showed her to be a fully mature four-year-old, but I doubt if she weighed a great deal more than 30 pounds.

*R*ain fell during the night, and the next day we spent resting, eating delicious venison, and going out briefly in the afternoon to get a few quail for breakfast. The next day was cold and overcast, but it did not rain, so we rode up into the sierra again and knocked over a buck apiece, both ordinary Coues' deer.

A few days later in Tucson, I turned our specimens over to Professor S. A. Nichol of the University of Arizona, who had been as interested in the dwarf-deer legends as I had been. After much measuring of skull and comparing of data in reference books, he pronounced the two little deer to be the Sinaloa whitetail, a diminutive, sub-tropical relative of the larger Arizona whitetail.

At the time, our two little deer got considerable publicity, and now that hunters knew what to look for, other specimens began to show up. It turned out that there were pockets of the little Sinaloa deer not only in Sonora, but in brush areas of southern Arizona. Here was a myth that had some basis in reality.

Much rather windy stuff has been written about the small size of the regular Arizona whitetail by those who have only a superficial acquaintance with it. It is a small deer, but not as small as some would have us believe. The average, full-grown, four-point buck will field dress from 80 to 95 pounds. Any buck weighing over 100 pounds is large, but every year many are killed in southern Arizona that weigh around 110. The largest I have ever killed weighed 117$^{1}/_{2}$ pounds, if I remember correctly, and the largest I have authentic dope on weighed 128. In many areas (in parts of Texas, for example), the Virginia whitetails are no heavier, and the Key deer of Florida are smaller.

But the little Mexican brush deer, fantail, *cabrito*, or whatever you want to call him, is only about half the size of the Coues' deer. When we first looked over those we had shot, we found that the large areas of red on them gave their blue-gray coats a pinkish cast. The regular Arizona whitetail often has, for his size, rather imposing antlers, but the little *cabritos* have antlers in keeping with their size. Often in full-grown bucks the points are no more than nubbins, but occasionally one will turn up with a small but beautiful and perfectly formed four- or five-point head. As it turned out, I have never shot another.

How the tiny deer have invaded the north and have kept their identity interests me, as one would think they would breed with their larger relatives and disappear. The answer is that they probably do, and that they survive only in areas of very heavy brush and high, thick grass.

Possibly the same unknown factor which has led to the invasion of the Southwest by other tropical species has forced the *cabritos* north. Fifty years ago the coati-mundi (which the Mexicans call *chulu*) was unknown in Arizona, but now it is quite common. Now and then a *tigre* comes wandering over the border and is taken in Arizona. Occasionally, a rare lobo wolf crosses the line into Arizona from Sonora, and the border mountain ranges fill up with Mexican mountain lions about as fast as the native lions are run down and taken.

The skulls and hides of the little *cabritos* my wife and I took on that trip are still, so far as I know, among the specimens of the department of zoology at the University of Arizona. Likewise, so far as I know, there are still little red-tailed dwarfs in the brush and high grass of the Sonora hills. Some day I'd like to go back and take another crack at them.

THE BIG RAM OF PILOT MOUNTAIN

Hunting with Texas friend Red Earley, Jack explores an unlikely spot in the Yukon Territory and gets a splendid ram – his biggest ever. As a footnote to this story, another friend, Herb Klein, was delayed in taking part in the trip because of illness. When he did show up, he topped Jack's ram with a record-book sheep, a story that also appears in this anthology. January, 1951

The first time I ever hunted Dall sheep – those beautiful snow-white rams with golden eyes and yellow horns – I was up in the glaciers around the head of the White River, near where the southwest corner of the Yukon Territory is jammed right up against Alaska. The area is beautiful and wild, and for 30 years the late Jean Jacquot outfitted parties there. The creeks were named for outside sportsmen and their wives – Count Creek for a member of the European nobility, Edith Creek for the wife of a hunter.

For one month I did nothing but look for a great Dall head, heavy, massive, long of curl, and large of base. I picked up some other game as I went along, but what I was looking for was this super ram. I worked hard for him, but he never came within range of my binoculars.

I remember one day when Field Johnson, my Indian guide, and I made a long climb to the top of a range, then a three-mile stalk through the darnedest canyons ever dreamed up, to look over a bunch of 14 rams. I didn't fire a shot.

Toward the end of the trip, while we were working out of a jack camp, cooking over smoky willow fires, getting wet, freezing, I took my two rams the law then allowed. I am sure I got the two best heads I saw. Each was in the record class, but *not* that dream ram.

Perhaps, I thought, my big fellow awaited me in the Petty Mountains, northeast of Whitehorse, where the white Dalls and dark Stones come together to form the hybrid, so-called Fannin sheep with gray saddles but white heads and necks. No luck! I hunted there, but during as tough a two weeks as I have ever put in, I didn't fire a shot at a sheep.

All this time my big dream ram was waiting for me in a dinky little range I could see from the Alaska Highway. A couple of times I had noticed it and said to myself, "Looks as if there might be a few sheep there!" Then I had forgotten it as hardly worth the gamble.

But fate works in curious ways, and last August Red Earley of Texas and I found ourselves tying saddlebags and scabbards onto our saddles as our outfit prepared to leave old Whitehorse-Dawson road. We were out to try our luck in this range I had seen so many times with its blue peaks tipped with snow thrusting up from the dreary, dark-green spruce forest.

At first, fate seemed more or less against us and had been from the start. Herb Klein, the companion who was to hunt with us, had developed strep throat at the last moment and wouldn't be able to join us for a week. The little range into which we were packing hardly seemed rough enough or extensive enough to hold many sheep, and it seemed too accessible. To top it off, the rain caught us a few miles from where we had left the road, and when I say rain I mean *rain*.

Water poured down on us in sheets. It got so bad that for a while we abandoned our saddle horses and took chilly refuge under some spruce trees. Anyone who has ever pitched camp in a blinding rainstorm knows how much fun it was. Finally, though, we had the packs off, a fire built, the tents up, and gradually we got dry and comfortable.

It seemed to Red and me that we were hunting Pilot Mountain on pretty scant evidence. Ours was the first party of trophy hunters ever to go into it. Actually, the country hadn't been hunted by anyone in years. We saw an old Indian meat cache one place, but what trails we encountered were not pack trails, but old dog trails that were long unused. Neither Moose nor Charley, our two guides, had ever been in the range before, and what dope we were operating on came from an ancient Indian meat hunter we had encountered in a camp on the road.

There were, he told us, some sheep on Pilot Mountain – not many but some. We would find them, he said, if we went up the main valley through the pass. Just on the other side we would come upon two small lakes. Beyond them we could look to the right and see a big basin rimmed with shale slides and rocky peaks. In this basin we would find this beautiful, snow-white Dall sheep of the arctic and subarctic ranges in the Yukon and Alaska. The old man had not been in the range for ten years, he told us; but the last time he was there, he had shot a young ram for meat and had seen several.

To Red and me this seemed like a long gamble. Many things can happen in ten years. The sheep could have moved to another range. Wolves could have killed them off or driven them out.We were all the more skeptical when, as the rain continued, we glassed the surrounding peaks and shale slides and found not so much as a sheep trail.

But Red and I *talked* a good sheep hunt, to bolster our lagging spirits during the time the rain continued to pelt down. We related our respective feats on previous trips into the head of the White River, in the Stone sheep country in northern British Columbia, and in the bighorn ranges in Alberta and Wyoming. Every time the rain freshened and the clouds clung lower on the peaks, we'd draw closer to the stove in the cooktent and shoot a couple of more rams.

Moose Johnson, my Indian guide, was not the least pessimistic. "Don't worry." he told us. "We get rams. If we don't get um here we get um somewhere else. Plenty big rams in all these little ranges. Moose and I, we discovered, were practically twins. Both of us were born on the same day of the same month of the same year – he in the Yukon, I on the Mexican border. But while I was wasting my time behind a desk, Moose had spent most of his years hunting. He and his distant relative, Field Johnson, with whom I had previously hunted, are the most famous of all Yukon sheep guides.

But rain cannot last forever and there came a day when we began to notice that the dirty gray clouds were lifting from the sodden peaks. Then we began to see holes in the overcast that showed blue sky. The rain slackened and then ceased, and on the morning of our third day in camp, we awoke to find the weather good enough to go out, and we were in the sheep-hunting business.

ur first camp had been one of desperation, so the plan was for Moose, Red, and me to go up the canyon, find the mysterious basin, and hunt, while Charley, Harold the horse wrangler, and Odin the cook moved camp in a new location. Then, that night when we came in, we would cut the trail of the outfit and find camp all set up again.

Following the directions of our ancient Indian, the three of us rode up the canyon four miles. We came to the pass about which he had told us. Beyond it, sure enough, were two little lakes. We climbed up above timberline on the bench to the right, and there we saw a great basin hemmed by mighty peaks. To its left was another, smoother basin that rose gradually to a ridge about three miles away.

We got off our horses. Moose took my 9 x 35 binoculars and almost instantly said, "I see three sheep!"

There they were, clear at the head of the second basin, feeding on the rich alpine grass. Moose declared that they were rams, but under those light conditions and at that distance, neither Red nor I could swear to it.

From where we first glassed the sheep, we followed a draw and kept out of sight until we were a bit more than a mile from them. Then I set up the spotting scope and found the sheep in it. They were rams all right, three of them. They were not, however, anything to make a trophy hunter's heart beat particularly fast. The best one had a full curl and was around seven years old. The others were younger and smaller.

We took turns staring at them, trying to decide whether to make the stalk or not. Suddenly Moose said, "I see another ram. I can just see his nose."

"Let me take a look," I said.

Exactly where Moose said it would be – in a hollow about twenty feet to the right of one ram was the tiny white triangle of a Dall ram's nose. As I watched he shifted his position, and I could see the golden base of his right horn.

"Moose, I can see the base of his horn now," I said, "and it looks big."

Moose and Red took turns at the scope and on the strength of that glimpse of horn, we decided to make the stalk.

Red and I had already agreed that I was to have the first crack at rams and he was to have the first crack at grizzlies, if we were together when we encountered game. I had always been lucky on grizzlies, whereas Red had been lucky on everything but; in many years of hunting grizzly country, years in which he had seen many, he had never got a good shot at one.

So off we started. If we could climb out of the canyon and over the ridge, we could ride above the sheep. But while we were climbing out we'd be in plain sight of the rams and about a mile and a half away. I was afraid of spooking them and voted to tie our horses and begin the stalk on foot so we'd be less conspicuous during that initial climb. Red, who'd rather ride than walk, and Moose outvoted me.

"Don't worry," Moose said. "Sheep won't get scared. Nobody hunts them. They won't know people."

So we led our scrambling, puffing horses up that almost straight-up-and-down slope until finally we got them over the ridge and out of sight. Our last look with the glasses showed that the rams were still there, lying down and chewing their cuds. With their telescopic, wide-angle eyes they had no doubt seen us, but since we were not traveling toward them, they paid no particular attention.

Now began the easiest stalk I have ever made on sheep. We simply rode through a series of little upland basins above timberline for about three miles, as we had to travel a roundabout way to stay out of sight.

Finally, Moose held up his hand. We stopped and dismounted. The sheep, we figured, should be about 200 yards away down the slope, within easy shooting distance. I took my .30/06 out of the scabbard, a camera out of the saddlebags. Red unlimbered his .300 Magnum.

Moose borrowed my binoculars and walked a few feet to where he could peek over the ridge. Then he almost fell over backward. From his frantic signals we could tell that the rams had moved and were right beneath us.

Red and I joined him.

There the rams were, so close we could see one of them blink his eyes, 65 paces from us! Three were just as we had sized them up with the spotting scope, but the ram we had almost missed was magnificent, with great incurved and outswept horns. He and two other rams were lying with their rumps to us. The fourth – the one I had seen blink his eye – was lying broadside.

As I sat there with my rifle across my knees a flock of thoughts raced through my mind. I ought to take movies instead of shooting. It was immoral to take a magnificent ram like that after such an easy stalk on the first day of the hunt. This baby would go better than 40 inches, and the only other 40-incher I had ever shot was a Stone that had fallen to my rifle only after a tough month of climbing, stalking, sweating, and looking over more than 100 heads. I thought of going back to the horse for the movie camera. I wished I had my 35mm. still camera and its telephoto lens. I thought that in spite of our agreement, I ought to give Red the shot.

"You take him, Red," I whispered.

"No, go ahead."

"No, he's all yours."

"Shut up and shoot."

"Don't shot him in the het," Moose whispered to me. "Don't ruin scalp."

I didn't have much choice. The ram was facing directly away from me. I had either to break his neck and ruin the scalp or try to drive a bullet through his vitals with a rump shot. I hated to shoot him either place. Then the ram that was facing sidewise decided the matter for me. He either heard us whispering or caught a glimpse of us out of the corner of his eye. Up he jumped and away he went. Instantly, the other rams followed. The fat was now in the fire.

I threw up my rifle and pressed the trigger with the crosshairs sharp and black against the broad white fanny of the great ram. Nothing apparently happened. I worked the bolt, shot again. The ram ran perhaps ten feet more and went down.

The three survivors dashed around a point with Red right after them, and I ran to the top of the ridge where I could see the shooting.

"Take ram in the lead," Moose shouted.

Red sat down and his big .300 cracked. His shot was just to the right. By the time he got lined up for his second shot, the rams had strung out single file and the lead ram was about 300 yards away. At the rifle crack, the ram went down.

With the shooting over, I went over to look at my ram and almost fainted. It was the most beautiful ram head I had ever laid my eyes on, long, massive, symmetrical, the sort of trophy the sheep hunter dreams about but seldom sees. I had known it was good, but not *that* good. Here was the ram I'd dreamed about all those years!

"Good heavens," said Red when he joined me, "that will go 15 inches!"

"Forty-one," I said, not daring to voice my hopes.

"Forty-three," Moose said.

I really had ram fever now. I sat down to ease my shaky legs.

"I've got a steel tape in the saddlebags," I told Moose. "If you'll get it we'll measure this baby!"

*C*ircumference at base of each horn was 15¹/₂ inches, terrific for a so-called thin-horn sheep. Longest curl showed 45 inches. However, the first measurement later proved optimistic and the longest curl was less than 44, still one of the greatest heads ever to come out of the north country, and surely one of the most beautiful. The only thing I regretted was that he came so easy, but I suppose I earned him knocking myself out at the head of the White River and in the Petty Mountains.

He not only had the largest head I'd ever got a look at on a live sheep, but he was the largest and heaviest Dall I'd seen. From the top of his shoulder to the bottom of his chest he measured 22 inches, and he was 44 inches long from chest to rump. A month after he was shot, his dry horns and skull weighed 50 pounds! Since he was built with the round barrel and broad fat back of a beef steer, he couldn't have weighed less than 250 pounds on the hoof, maybe more.

When we went down off the mountain that day, we took the heads. The next day we went up and brought down all the meat with a couple of packhorses and the whole outfit lived on those rams until we got a moose. It was darn great living, too!

Alex Davis, our outfitter, was sure this magnificent ram of mine would win first prize for the year in the Boone and Crockett Club competiton for big game heads. Then our delayed companion, Herb Klein, showed up, rushed out, and got a Yukon ram to make mine look puny. But that's another story!

HOW TO CATCH A RECORD RAM

After O'Connor took his Pilot Mountain ram, long-time Texas friend Herb Klein belatedly joined the party. He killed a huge Dall and Jack makes a convincing case that it should turn out to be a world record. February, 1951.

*I*f you're interested in collecting a world-record sheep head, I can tell you how to go about it. First, get a strep sore throat, so you have to stay home for a week instead of departing with your hunting companions. Then, miss the plane connection at Seattle, Washington, and lose a couple more days. The next step is to arrive in Whitehorse, Yukon Territory, and stay up late cementing the bonds of friendship between the United States and Canada. Once you reach that point, the rest should come relatively easy.

Simply hire a plane to overtake your companions, who have been creeping along through muskeg and forest by packtrain. Land on a lake where camp is set up. After a leisurely breakfast, set out with your guide and find a ram. Then make your climb and kill the ram. It will be a new world record.

*A*ll this sounds cock-eyed, but it's exactly the way Herb Klein of Dallas, Texas, managed to take a new world-record Dall sheep when he, Red Earley, and I were hunting in the Yukon last August.

The curl of one of his great horns measured 47⁷/16 inches after drying for ten days. Further, it is the only top-flight sheep head that has been killed cleanly by a sportsman. One record ram was wounded by a hunter, then tracked down and dispatched by the guide. Another was murdered in the winter in the deep snow of a park, smuggled out, and sold to a head collector. And the head currently listed in the record book, *North American Big Game,* as the No. 1 white or Dall sheep, is strictly a phony. According to the data, it was shot in Alaska in 1927 by Patsey Henderson. Except that it was not shot in Alaska, not shot by Patsey Henderson, and was not a Dall sheep, this listing is accurate.

Actually, the so-called world-record Dall was a very black Stone sheep killed southeast of Carcross, Y.T., just north of the British Columbia border by Billy Smith. Patsey Henderson's brother, Billy, gave it to Patsey, who conducts a sort of museum at Carcross for the Whitehorse & Yukon Railway and who gives a spiel for the tourists. Patsey eventually sold it to the late Dr. Henry M. Beck, the head collector, for $170. Dr. Beck then put a Dall scalp on this Stone sheep head and claimed the world record. The curls were 47$\frac{1}{2}$ and 47 inches long.

Following a tip from Johnnie Johns, Yukon outfitter, Them Kjar, director of the Yukon Game and Publicity Department, did the detective work on this. Patsey Henderson and Billy Smith are still alive, and Kjar has their sworn statements as to the origin of the "record" ram.

So Herb Klein's big Dall appears to be tops. The measurement of 47$\frac{7}{16}$ inches was made with a steel tape in Whitehorse by Them Kjar. With two or three months' more drying, it cannot shrink to less than 47.

*B*ut to get to the hunt. Hard luck seemed to haunt Herb from the start. I was supposed to meet him and Red Earley in Seattle the night before we were to fly to Whitehorse, but the moment I registered at the hotel which was to be our rendezvous, the clerk told me to call Operator 16 at Dallas. I did so with a sinking heart, and in a moment I heard Herb's voice on the phone, saying his doctor had chained him to his bed for a week. As soon as he got over his trick throat, he would start catching up with us.

In Whitehorse Red and I worked out a plan with Alex Davis, our outfitter. We would hunt sheep on Pilot Mountain, then pack back to the old Whitehorse-Dawson City road, cut across it to a lake not far from a sheep range, and hunt bears there while waiting for Herb to join us. At the appointed time a plane showed up all right, but it did not contain Herb. Instead, there was a telegram that he had missed the flight to Whitehorse because the Seattle airport was fogged in and the plane he was on could not land. He'd be in three days later.

The day before, Red had killed a grizzly on the big round mountain adjacent to the rugged sheep country. At our suggestion, Paddy Jim, Herb's guide, had taken a horse and binoculars and had gone out to scout for sheep. The first mountain he glassed – a big, rugged, sharp-crested job right at the edge of sheep country – yielded sight of two rams.

Both, said Paddy Jim, were large, and one was a lulu. Paddy estimated that it had 45-inch curls, but I was skeptical. A man can hunt sheep for a couple of lifetimes and never lay eyes on a 45-inch head. If he gets a shot at one head in the 40s, he's much luckier than most. Paddy also claimed that the second ram would go more than 40. I lifted my eyebrows and winked at Red. After all, Paddy had got a look at the rams from about a mile and he only had a 9X glass, not a spotting scope.

At the scheduled time, we heard the buzz of an airplane motor. That was nothing unusual, since the country where we were hunting lay on a beam and planes were constantly passing, bound for Alaska. But this motor sounded like a small one. Then one of our sharp-eyed guides caught sight of the plane. It wore floats and presumably contained our long-lost pal. Finally, it circled, landed, and taxied to shore, and Herb stepped out

We gabbed for a minute, and Herb regarded with envy a fine head I had taken a week before.

As I said in my write-up of that hunt (see "The Big Ram of Pilot Mountain" in last month's *Outdoor Life*), it was the best sheep I have ever killed. Each horn had a circumference at base of more than 15 inches and a curl almost 44 inches long. Supposedly, that made it the Yukon record for the year and, by the same token, winner of the annual competition for Dall sheep. Red, who also had his ram and had killed a grizzly the day before, was planning to fish, but I was going back to the bear mountain to see if I could locate a big, dark grizzly that Red had glassed the day before. Wishing Herb good luck with his sheep hunting and Red the same with his fishing, Charles, who was my guide that day, and I mounted our nags and took off.

*N*oon found us high on the side of the bear mountain. We were eating lunch and so far we had seen nothing larger than a ptarmigan. The reindeer moss was soft, the sun was warm, and I was about to fall asleep when Charley said, "I see Paddy and new hunter."

I sat up and got them in my binoculars. They were on horseback, toiling up a long smooth hogback to the right of the mountain where Paddy told me he had seen the rams on the previous day. We watched them for 15 or 20 minutes for want of anything better to do. Then I saw them stop and pile off their horses. They were looking at something on the sheep mountain. I trained my glasses in that direction and saw two tiny white specks slowly moving up the mountainside. On both specks I could see little golden blobs that could be nothing but massive horns, but how good the rams were I could not tell without more magnification.

Then I saw our hunters set up a spotting scope and flop down behind it. First one would look, then the other. The sheep they were watching climbed higher and higher.

Finally, Charley, after a long look through my binoculars, said, "One ram great big fellow, great big head."

"Bigger than the ram I got?" I asked.

"Yes. I think so."

As it turned out, Charley was right, just as Paddy had been right. A Yukon Indian with a 9X glass is equal to a white man with a spotting scope!

When Charley and I pulled out for some more bear hunting, the rams Herb and Paddy were watching were still climbing slowly, still on their side of the ridge. I knew that their plan was to lie low until the rams had bedded and then make their stalk. From the lay of the land, it looked as if the stalk would be a very long one, and I thought that if they made it, they would have to lie out all night. Either that or they would postpone the stalk, go back to camp, and get an earlier start the next day.

Charley and I had no luck on the bear hunt. The weather had turned quite warm for the Yukon, and undoubtedly the bears were all down off the mountain and in the thick timber away from the bright sunshine. We got back to camp about 7 o'clock and ate dinner.

It was still light when we heard a horse whinny and Herb and Paddy rode in, both grinning like the cat that had eaten the rat. Behind Herb's saddle was the darnedest sheep head I have ever seen – and one of the darnedest heads anyone has ever seen! I took one look at it and yelled 47 inches! The steel tape showed it closer to 48. For a man who has just chalked up a new world record, Herb was singularly quiet. Actually, he was exhausted after the long stalk and tough climb, since he had just gotten out of sick bed.

When we were measuring the head, I happened to get a good look at Moose Johnson. The big head I had shot a week before was the best, in Moose's opinion, that any of his sportsmen had taken in his 27 years of guiding. Now it was beaten cold, and Moose's face wore the same expression that is on Junior's face when little baby sister comes home with mamma from the hospital.

Herb and Paddy had seen the two rams, they told us, when they were riding up that big hogback. They glassed them, found them good. Then they set up the spotting scope for a better look – and almost dropped their teeth at what they saw. The smaller ram had an enormously wide spread and heavy horns, but the other was out of this world. His head was of the incurved and outflared type and enormously long. In years of sheep hunting, Herb had never seen anything in the same league.

When they first saw them, the two rams had been down to a creek at the foot of the mountain for a midday drink and were climbing slowly toward the crest, feeding a bit on the way. There was no cover between the men and the rams, so it was impossible to begin the stalk.

At long last the rams disappeared over the crest. The time for action had come. Herb and Paddy led their horses down off the hogback, tied them in some willows by the creek where the rams had drunk, and then begun their long, roundabout stalk. They had to go clear around the point of that sharp-combed mountain, then follow a deep canyon up toward the top and to the rams. The climb was somewhere between 1,500 and 2,000 feet and terribly steep. Much of it was over rockslides where boulders were precariously poised and looking for an excuse to roll. Herb was just out of sick bed, and to him the side of that mountain looked as high as the walls of the Grand Canyon.

"Hurry," Paddy kept telling him. "We haven't much time!" Or: "Don't step on loose rocks. Those sheep will hear us!"

About midway in their climb, they took a quick peek at the big one, and Herb realized that this was a ram of rams.

"Look, Paddy," he said. "If we get that big boy, there's $50 in it for you."

"O.K.," said Paddy. "But hurry – and don't step on loose rocks."

Finally, they struggled to the spot from which Herb planned to shoot. The ram was above them, and Herb could see only about six inches of his back. The shooting would be uphill and from a very insecure position on a rockslide.

As Herb poked his rifle to the fore, the old ram saw him, but he did not spook, as he was apparently unacquainted with men and he was in his chosen country where he could run if they came closer.

Sweating with anxiety, Herb rested his .300 Weatherby Magnum over a rock, found the ram behind the crosshairs of his scope, and commenced his trigger squeeze. He was afraid of over-shooting, so he tried to hold right where he could see the ram's body over the rocks. The 180-grain bullet left the muzzle at 3,300 feet a second and smacked into the rocks an inch or so below the great ram's body. The ram bounced to his feet and took off to get over the crest and to safety.

Then Herb got a break. His next shot was a quick one. It went through the ram's right ear and hit the base of one horn. It knocked the ram down and rolled him 30 yards or so down the slope. If this shot had missed or had been taken with a less potent rifle, the old ram would still be wearing his record horns. Before Herb could work the bolt, the ram was on his feet and tearing toward the crest again. Herb's third shot was a miss. He worked the bolt again.

It was now or never. This was the last cartridge in his rifle and the ram had just about reached safety. He got this last shot off with the crosshairs right behind the ram's shoulder, and as he squeezed the trigger and felt the sharp recoil of the rifle, he saw the ram wilt, lose hold, and come rolling down the rocks.

For a moment Herb lay there, weak from the climb and the excitement. Then he turned to Paddy. "Did you see where the third shot went?"

"No," Paddy told him. "I closed my eyes after the second. I couldn't stand seeing my fifty bucks running away!"

The ram was really an ancient. He was scrawny, thin, and rather small of body. He could not possibly have survived another winter, since he had only four outside nipping teeth in his front lower jaw. He had lost many of his other teeth and those that remained were just about to fall out – so loose, in fact, that as an experiment I pulled one out with my fingers after Herb and Paddy brought the head in.

The ram's annual rings showed him to be 15 years old, the oldest I have ever seen. His horns were so brittle that a bump on a rock had caused him to lose several inches on one side, and they looked as if they were from a head that had lain rotting on the ground for years.

The other ram hung around while Herb and Paddy were freeing the head and meat. Both reported that its horns had an enormous spread and at least 40-inch curls. They last saw him standing on the comb of the ridge, his great golden horns and snow-white body brilliant against the blue sky. He was still trying to figure out what happened to his old pal and what were these strange creatures who carried thunder and lightning with them.

The sheep in this particular range have not been hunted for years. Never before had an outside trophy hunter fired a shot there. Once the Indians had lived in a little village on a lake about a day's pack away and they had hunted the Dall sheep, as I found the skull of a young ram by one of their abandoned cabins and I also picked up the horns of a ewe. But the Indians have died off and moved away, and the only enemies of the sheep are wolves and eagles.

The sheep range there is about 12 miles long. Herb touched only the edge of it. There are other rams in that range, and maybe larger ones. This particular area of the Yukon has many such sharp mountain ranges, rising out of the stunted spruce forest like the sheep ranges 3,000 miles to the south in the Mexican state of Sonora – ranges where even now no trophy hunter has popped a primer.

When we got back to Whitehorse, the news of Herb's great ram had somehow traveled ahead of us and we were greeted like channel swimmers. Alex Davis, our outfitter, was of course delighted, because such a head does business no harm. Them Kjar, the game department director, measured the head and was happy because he wanted to see the locale for the record Dall sheep firmly fixed in the Yukon.

After the tumult and the shouting of our arrival in Whitehorse had died down and we were packing to leave, Herb gazed pensively at his great head.

"You know," he said, "maybe I was a little quick on the trigger. That range is 12 miles long and I looked over only a mile of it. I saw only two rams. Now maybe if I hadn't been so hasty . . . "

Bull Elk in the Brush

After his move to Idaho, O'Connor adopted the Selway Wilderness Area as an equivalent of the desert Southwest from his earlier days. In this story he hunts out of Dave Christensen's Moose Creek Ranch, which was considerably less rigorous than his tent camps in the northern wilderness. The hunt produced his best Idaho elk. October, 1965

About the most pleasant elk hunt I know of for the lazy man, the lover of comfort, and the chap who isn't quite as frisky as he used to be, is one I make now and then out of the Moose Creek Ranch in Idaho's Selway Wilderness Area. When the hunter is back in the hills out of Moose Creek after the big bulls, the hills are just as steep, the brush just as wet, the wind just as penetrating as it is anywhere. But when he gets back to the ranch in the evening, he can take a hot shower, brag about his heroic feats before a big fireplace in the living room of the lodge, and eat a good meal. He can dream the hours away on an innerspring mattress, and in the morning he can put on his long-handled underwear and his wool socks in a room heated by electricity.

There are some other deluxe wilderness ranches in Idaho, but the one on Moose Creek is the only one I have hunted from. It is less than an hour's flying time from my Idaho home, and when the mood strikes me to throw some bullets after an Idaho bull elk, that's generally the place I go.

Moose Creek itself is one of the streams that form the headwaters of Idaho's Clearwater River system. This drains what is probably the most productive elk country in North America. Estimates of the herd run from 25,000 to 40,000. Every year about 4,500 elk are killed on the various branches of the Clearwater – the North Fork, the Middle Fork formed by the Lochsa and the Selway, and the South Fork. Moose Creek is a tributary of the Selway.

There were always a few elk back in the mountains drained

81

by the tributaries of the Clearwater, but virgin stands of evergreen contain little elk food. Around the time of World War I, a series of great fires swept over the country and destroyed untold millions of dollars worth of timber. Brush began to grow in the burns, and with the brush came the elk.

There is an Idaho saying that if the state were ironed out flat, it would be larger than Texas, and that may well be true. Idaho's mountains are high and steep. Once I shot an elk that rolled a few yards and hung up in heavy brush. To dress the elk, I had to go up that hillside from the creek bottom hand over hand like Tarzan. When I reached the elk, I chopped it loose and it fell about 300 feet almost straight down into the creek bottom.

In some places, the fire that destroyed the forests was so hot that all of the soil was burned out to bare bedrock, and nothing grows there now. Most of the vast area is brush, but there are patches of green timber, and some selections were hardly burned at all.

As the brush began to grow, the deer and the elk increased, but good elk country is seldom good deer country. The elk is bigger and stronger than the deer. He eats more and can browse higher. In rough winters, he starves the deer out. Now the Clearwater country supports few deer as compared with elk. I cannot remember seeing a mule deer along Moose Creek, but I have seen several whitetails low along the streams. The Moose Creek area has some Rocky Mountain white goats and is fine black bear country. I am told that in the 1964 season, nearly half of the elk hunters who went out from the ranch shot at black bears and that about a quarter of them brought in trophies.

Because the brush is thick, the hills steep, and the basins wide, shots at elk are usually at quite short or very long range. If a hunter sees an elk on the same side of a basin or canyon, he'll get a close shot, generally through brush. If the animal is on the other side, the hunter will need a good scope, a hard-hitting, flat-shooting rifle, and luck.

Probably the lush days of Clearwater elk hunting are drawing to a close. In many areas, the brush is growing out of reach of the elk. The winter range in creek and river bottoms is badly overbrowsed, and in years of great cold and deep snow, many hundreds of elk perish. A recently completed highway across the mountains along the Lochsa to Missoula, Montana, will greatly interfere with wintering elk. A dam to be built near the mouth of the North Fork will destroy most of the winter range of the North

Fork herd. The dam is a pet project of that most powerful of all lobbies, the U.S. Army Corps of Engineers. To get it authorized by Congress, the Corps enlisted chambers of commerce and powerful lumber interests. Sportsman and conservationists fought it, but as generally happens, they eventually ran out of wind and money. What will finish the great Clearwater elk herd is another dam the Army Engineers are planning on the Middle Fork at a spot known as Penny Cliffs. This will flood out most of the winter range along the Lochsa and the Selway, but by that time, those hills will be too steep for me.

For the next few years, however, this great elk country will remain productive. Many Idaho and nonresident hunters drive in on logging roads, make camp, and hunt on foot. Hundreds of others get packers to take them in and come back at a specific time to pack out their gear and their meat. More deluxe camps are set up by outfitters. In these camps, hunters have but to roll out their beds and unlimber their rifles. They are fed, mounted on horses, and guided.

Early in the season when the elk are very high and the bulls are bugling, clients of the Moose Creek Lodge are packed back into the elk range, where they hunt out of tent camps. As the snow and the cold come on, the elk move down and the hunting is done right from the ranch. Because of the great numbers of elk and the deteriorating winter range, the Idaho Department of Fish and Game allows a 2^1/$_2$-month season back in the wilderness area – from September 15 to November 30. I have never been at Moose Creek right at the end of the season after a hard snow, but I am told that elk are then all over the place. Once when I was helping a pilot load elk quarters into a charter plane before we took off, I could see a dozen elk on a hillside within rifle range.

Generally, the elk are fairly low at Moose Creek by the end of the first week of November, but the fall of 1964 was generally warm and dry in the Northwest. Even back in the mountains it was not very cold and there had been little snow. Ray Speer, of Speer Bullets, my wife Eleanor, and I flew into Moose Creek prepared to hunt for a week if necessary. When the little four-place plane settled down on the long airstrip and taxied up to the lodge, we found Dave Christensen, the manager, waiting for us.

"Anyone want to shoot an elk this evening?" he asked. "A bunch was on the hill this morning, and they're bound to be back before dark."

"I'd consider it," Ray said.

"I might look them over," I told him.

"You can count me out," Eleanor snorted. "As long as I came out here to hunt, I am going to hunt. That would be like shooting a zebra out of a tent on safari."

We moved our rifles and duffel to the cabins we were to occupy. Eleanor had brought the battered old 7 x 57 Mauser she has used from Mozambique to the Yukon, and I had a very handsome custom-made 7mm. Remington Magnum on a Model 70 Winchester action. By the time we had got our things laid out, the sun had gone down over in the west and dusk was falling.

Then Dave Christensen knocked at the door. "Come on," he said, "the elk are back."

The hill to which Dave referred is a large open spot about 600 yards from the lodge. Elk have crossed there for untold centuries. Not a few have been shot there.

While Ray climbed the hill to execute a flank movement, I watched from beside the creek. Apparently the herd was aware that Ray was trying to stalk them, as one by one they moved slowly across the open spot about 300 yards away – cows, calves, and one spike bull. It was almost dark, but through the 4x Leupold scope on the 7mm. Magnum I could just make out the intersection of the crosswires against the spike's shoulder. I am certain I could have knocked him off, but I hadn't flown in to ambush a spike bull and shoot him from a rest on a rail fence.

*N*ext morning, we got our scabbards and saddlebags tied on, lunches stowed away, and our slickers secured behind the cantles. Dave was to guide Eleanor and me, and Vance Baker was to guide Ray Speer. The plan was to hunt in a direction that was roughly upstream north of the main branch of Moose Creek toward a high peak known as Bailey Mountain. We might see elk going in, Dave told us, but he was pinning his hopes on a cooperative maneuver. His plan was for me to watch one area in a big basin at the foot of Bailey, Eleanor another. Ray and Vance would go over the saddle to the north, ride into the basin and through the bottom. Meantime, after putting Eleanor and me on our stands, Dave would go around and drop into the canyon lower down and walk up it. If any elk were moved, he told us, they would probably go up a draw and then over a pass within range of Eleanor or me.

After we bade Ray and Vance goodbye, we continued several hundred yards up the trail toward the pass. Then we tied our

BULL ELK IN THE BRUSH

horses and continued on foot. Dave put Eleanor to the left of the saddle on a rocky outcrop from which she could see most of the basin. Then he led me down to a spot on a hillside.

"If any elk move," he told me, "they'll probably work up that draw below you. Either you or Eleanor will be bound to see them." He then cut around behind me and disappeared into the timber, his little Winchester .30/30 carbine in his hand.

I found a nice dry patch of spruce needles and sat down. About 500 yards away to my left across the basin, I could see Eleanor perched on her rocky point. Below me was a veritable jungle of a round-leaved shrub locally called snow brush. It was thick and from six to ten feet high. At the far edge of this tangle and just this side of the ravine in which the elk were supposed to travel was a tall spruce. The hillside on the far side of the ravine was relatively open, and I uttered a hunter's prayer that if a good bull came along he would travel along, that hill in the open.

Now and then I'd turn my binoculars on Eleanor. I saw her eat her sandwich, and I decided it would pass the time if I ate mine.

Then I heard three shots from the direction where Ray and Vance should be. Three shots and no more. I saw Eleanor lift her rifle and apparently watch something through the scope. I heard a stone roll below me, but I could see nothing. I heard another stone roll farther up. Finally, I saw Dave come out of the brush and climb up to sit on the rocky point with Eleanor.

Half an hour passed. The whole basin was quiet, and except for Dave and Eleanor, the only living thing I could see was a patrolling eagle against gray, sullen clouds. Then I heard a shot from the rocky point. It didn't sound like the sharp crack of Eleanor's 7mm. I put the glass on the point and saw that Eleanor was shooting Dave's .30/30. Why this should be baffled me. She shot four times. I could see that she and Dave were watching something in the bottom of the basin. Apparently she had not scored a hit.

A spruce squirrel chattered back in the timber, and I thought I heard a movement well below me. Then I heard a grouse flush about 150 yards away, below me and to my right. I strained my ears, but I could not hear another sound. However, I had a strong hunch that something was moving below me. I slipped a cartridge into the chamber of my 7mm. Magnum and put on the safety.

Then I looked over toward the point with my binoculars. I

85

could see that Dave was watching me with his. The moment he saw that I had my glass trained on him, he and Eleanor both thrust their arms out and pointed down. Apparently, something was below me and I was supposed to go down.

As quietly as I could, I started downhill toward the tangle of snow brush. Then I became aware of a fine set of elk antlers showing just above the brush. I could see antlers but not the elk. Then the antlers began to move slowly through the brush to the left of the big spruce and toward the open hillside. I would guess they were about 125 yards away. When that fine bull came out in the open, I told myself he would be a dead duck – or at least a dead elk.

The antlers moved slowly around the spruce and then disappeared behind it. I think that at this time the bull caught sight of Dave and Eleanor. Elk, I believe, have the best eyes of all the deer family.

The next time I saw the antlers, the appeared from behind the tree. They traveled to the right for a few feet and then turned and started to come back in my direction.

Would the bull walk uphill through the brush toward me? If he did, I'd have a close and easy shot. Or would he turn to his left (my right) and stroll through the heavy brush around the hill? If he did, I'd never see him again. I made up my mind to shoot if I had even a fair opportunity.

The bull passed through a spot where the brush was a bit less thick than it was elsewhere in the patch. For the first time I could see his head and neck through the brush, but by the time I got my rifle to my shoulder and the intersection of the crosswires on the elk, the tips of his antlers were still visible but his head and neck were concealed. I could see the bull's shoulders and body dimly through the brush. Deciding it was now or never, I squeezed off the shot. I was shooting offhand and just about standing on tiptoe to see better. Nevertheless, the crosswires had looked just right when the rifle went off.

But not one sound did I hear – no labored breathing, no threshing about of a wounded animal, no noise of a frightened elk crashing through the brush to get away.

My hunch was that I had dropped the bull in his tracks. I felt that if he had been missed or lightly wounded, I would have heard him or would have seen him as he ran off. I decided the best thing for me to do was to stay right there for the time being.

If he was wounded and ran off while I went toward him in the brush, I'd never see him. If I stayed put and he went out downhill, I'd probably get another crack at him.

Then I could see that Dave had jumped off the point and was picking his way downhill toward the spot where the elk had been. When he was about 150 yards away he called, "Think you hit him?"

"I think so," I answered, "but I wouldn't swear to it. I had to shoot through a lot of brush."

"Where do you think he is?" he asked.

"He ought to be about ten yards to the right and this side of that big spruce in front of you," I said.

"By golly, he is," he shouted a moment later. "He's down and dead. No, he isn't either! He just batted an eye. I'll give him one in the neck." I was working my way down through the brush when I heard his .30/30 crack.

When I joined him he was pulling the bull into the open so it could be photographed – a fine, big, trophy bull with heavy dark brown antlers with ivory tips – seven points on one side and six on the other. I have shot elk with longer antlers, but never one with a much wider spread or with seven points.

"Hell of an elk," Dave said, "best head anyone has shot out of Moose Creek this fall."

"It's the best bull I have ever shot in Idaho," I said. Then I remembered that I had seen Eleanor shooting Dave's .30/30. "Why was Eleanor shooting your rifle?" I asked.

"Something wrong with hers."

"Such as what?"

"She's got a cartridge jammed in the chamber and can't close the bolt. She says it's one of your handloads and it's no good."

"She ought to know better, but I'll bet she tried to put a cartridge in the chamber and close the bolt on it. You can't do that with a Mauser. The extractor won't jump over the rim."

"I wouldn't know about that," Dave said, "but here was this big bull walking along a hillside about 400 yards away and she couldn't close that bolt. She didn't swear, but she can say 'Oh dear!' in a way that would make a first sergeant blush. Boy, was she burned."

A moment later, the storm and strife came scrambling out of the brush wearing a glare you could light a cigarette on.

"How do you like the bull?" I asked her.

87

"He's a beauty, but he should have been mine. You and your silly hand-loaded ammunition!"

"Let me see your rifle," I said. "Just as I thought. You have only been using rifles with Mauser actions about 25 years, and you choose this time to try to ram one up the spout and close the bolt instead of feeding it from the magazine. Do you remember my telling you that couldn't be done?"

"Yes," she said, "but I'll bet the cartridge that got stuck is no good anyway. Here that beautiful bull was mincing along that hillside like a chorus boy with corns, and I had to shoot at it with Dave's miserable little .30/30 and iron sights. That front bead was bigger than the elk. I might as well have been throwing rocks. I didn't get close enough to scare it."

We took some pictures, dressed and quartered the bull, and laid the quarters on a log to get them off the ground and to let them cool.

I had used the Remington factory load with a 150-grain bullet, and my hold had been all right. The bullet had gone to the left of the spine, through the rear portion of one lung, and through the liver. We did not have time to hunt for the bullet. Apparently that old bull had never read those who have written that the 150-grain 7mm. Magnum bullet is inadequate for elk, and that nothing less than the 175-grain should be used. The bull had dropped in his tracks, as I would have expected since I have used the 7mm. Remington Magnum successfully on elk-sized kudu and sable antelope in Mozambique and Angola. If the big 7mm. isn't an elk cartridge, I have never seen one.

Eleanor told me that when I had seen her looking at something through her scope, she had been watching a cow elk. Afterward, I found out that the first shots I had heard had been Vance shooting to try to turn the cow up toward Ray.

*I*t was dusk by the time we had climbed back up the ridge and down to the horses. As we started down the trail, we could see the lights of the lodge twinkling merrily below us and far away. We were chilled when we got back to our cabin, and never did a hot shower feel better.

A score of years ago I injured the cartilage in my right knee during a little romp with a grizzly bear. Several times since I have hurt it again. A few days before we left on the elk hunt, I hurt it once more while hunting pheasants in a stubble field. When I awakened the morning after I had shot the elk, it had turned up again and I decided to rest it.

After breakfast, Dave left with a couple of pack mules to bring in my elk head and the quarters. Eleanor, Ray, and Vance rode off to the wars. Well after dark, they came jingling back. Eleanor and Ray had cooperated in knocking off a nice five-point bull. They had seen it across a canyon during a little local snowfall. Eleanor downed it with her first shot. It got up and started off, and this time she missed. Ray put it down for keeps.

The next afternoon the weather began to clear. We hopped into Ray's little flying machine and presently we were home. Incidentally, that old bull didn't have an ounce of fat on him, but you could stick a fork in the gravy – if you had a sharp fork.

Record Moose as an Afterthought

Myles Brown figured in a number of O'Connor stories. This one comes from their fall, 1945, hunt in the Yukon. Wild sheep were their primary focus, but Myles ends up killing the biggest moose ever taken in the region. February, 1946

According to all the lore on the subject, the man who gets a record head should hunt long and painfully for it, passing up scores of lesser trophies. For a man to go out and knock off one of the great heads of the species without half trying, seems almost immoral. Yet I suspect that this is what happens more often than most of us realize. A truly great head, one much larger than the average of the exceptionally large males of his species, happens along very, very seldom – so seldom that running into one is largely luck, no matter who gets it.

The largest mule deer head I have ever seen was shot by a meat hunter, a nonresident of the state where the buck was killed. He was hunting out of season and without a license. At least two of the first six record Dall sheep heads were killed for mutton, not for their magnificent horns.

Similarly, J.E. Wilson wrote, in *Outdoor Life* for October 1935, how he annexed the third largest Alaska moose head on record – though he was seeking meat for his larder rather than a trophy. Two men could not shake hands across the antlers, so mighty was their spread. And a couple of years ago an *Outdoor Life* article told how one of the largest mule deer heads ever taken in Colorado was left in the hills by the man who shot it, and how it was only by chance that he went back and got it.

So with all this build-up, here is the story of how the largest moose head ever taken by a hunter in the Yukon happened to be garnered in. It is a very strange tale indeed, because this magnificent moose was shot by a man who didn't particularly

91

want to shoot a moose, and who, even after he started shooting, had no real notion of what an enormous head his bull carried. It is also the story of how your gun editor, who had done a bit of hunting in his spare time, and a veteran Yukon Indian guide, who has taken out head-hunters for the last 20 years, also failed to recognize how exceptional this tremendous head was.

But we'll start at the beginning.

It was toward the last week in August when N. Myles Brown, of Cleveland, Ohio, my hunting companion in the Yukon in the fall of 1945, and I set out from the main camp on the Generk River near the Alaska border to do some hunting for Dall sheep. Our destination was Moose Horn Creek near a spur of the St. Elias range called the Solomon Mountains. We were hunting sheep, not moose, and actually moose were farthest from our minds, because the horns of the bulls were not yet free from velvet.

It would have taken a man with a gift for prophecy to determine that we were setting out on a lucky day. Actually, it looked just the opposite. We were crossing the mile-wide bar of the Generk River that morning when I saw my first big northern timber wolf.

I piled off, lay down, and took a shot at him as he stood there looking at us, wondering no doubt if our horses weren't caribou. Seeing that the Lee dot in the scope of my .270 just covered him from shoulder to brisket, I held him dead on – and shot feet below him. Instantly the explanation came to me. I had held as if he were a coyote at about 250 yards, whereas he was a *timber wolf* at 450. I had blown up on what was probably the easiest shot I'd ever get at a wolf.

Anyway, the wolf took out of there. I held well ahead and over for the second shot and knocked him down with the bullet too far back. He got up, though, and hobbled off, leaving only some blood and hair behind him. I could not hit him again.

I sat there, feeling like 17 chumps rolled into one, when Field Johnson, my guide, suddenly yelled, "Look at that grizzly!"

Myles and I snapped our heads around just in time to see a big grizzly disappear into the timber. He had been strolling up the bar and if I hadn't thrown those futile shots at the wolf, he would have been our meat. I rolled in the sand and beat my head on the boulders.

"Oh why, oh why didn't they drown me at birth?" I moaned.

Like most hunters I'm a somewhat superstitious character, and as we rode along through scrubby black spruce, past muskeg moose meadows and little silver lakes, I reproached myself for the beautiful way I had mismanaged the whole deal. I was sure my stupidity had cast a hex on what had otherwise promised to be the trip of my lifetime – one I had wanted to take since I could toddle – into the great white sheep, moose, and grizzly country along the Alaska border.

*W*e had been traveling three or four hours when we got above the timber at last and were riding over the tops of a series of round hills clad only in scrubby arctic willow and a shrub the natives call bug brush. We weren't far from Moose Horn Creek, and we could see the rugged, ice-clad Solomon Mountains not many miles ahead. My thoughts were on big white rams with golden eyes and yellow horns when suddenly, about 300 yards ahead, I saw two brown shapes moving just over the tops of the scrub willows.

"Grizzlies!" I whispered to Myles. "Two big grizzlies just ahead with their backs just showing over the willows. Let's go get 'em!"

I piled off my horse and put the binoculars on the "grizzlies," but instantly I could see the points on the antlers of two really big bull moose in velvet.

"Two big bull moose," I told Myles. "Let's look them over!"

Field rode up just then and I handed him the glasses. "You bet they're big!" he said as he watched them. "Great big fella. Come along. We shootum those moose, maybe!"

"Oh, rats!" Myles demurred. "I'm a sheep hunter. I don't want to shoot a moose just now."

"Well, come along anyway," I coaxed. "We won't crack 'em unless they're big babies!"

So Myles took his Springfield out of the scabbard and he, Field, and I went sneaking through the bug brush and willows until we came to a little knoll about 150 yards from the moose. Evidently they had not heard us, or, if they had, they thought they were hidden and did not realize that their big antlers betrayed them. The situation was so perfect as to be easy. There those big bulls were above timberline, in very easy range, and there wasn't any way they could get out of sight within half a mile.

We sat down on the knoll and I put my left arm through the loop of the sling on my .270. Then I threw a cartridge

93

into the chamber.

"Look, Myles," I said, "the one on the right is yours and the one on the left is mine. I'll yell to make them get up." Then I raised my voice and shouted: *"Quidado!"*

Those two big bulls lurched to their feet. Brown and black, perfectly enormous, standing well over seven feet at the withers, they went trotting off on legs that looked as long as vaulting poles.

"What do you think of that?" I shouted. "A couple of Spanish-speaking moose!"

I could see that my moose on the left had a very good head with extraordinarily wide palms. A hasty glance at the bull on the right told me he had a wider spread, but I had no real notion, until later, of how much wider. I was too busy knocking my moose over.

As he ran along there broadside, taller than a tent and heavier than a horse, it never dawned on me that this, my first Alaska moose and the largest moose I had ever shot at, was anything but a dead duck. The dot in the scope started behind him, overtook him swiftly, and the shot rang out as the dot swung past his brisket.

I heard the sharp snap of the bullet as it struck; I worked the bolt and fired again. Again I heard the bullet strike. I shot again. This time I was irritated that the moose wasn't down, but on the fourth shot he collapsed and never moved. I had fired all four shots very rapidly, while he was traveling about 50 yards.

Myles's Springfield was still going off in my ear. His moose, although hurt, was still on his feet, very much alive, and working his long legs for all he was worth. Now he looked larger than he had when he first jumped up, but I still had no idea as to the real size of the head that animal sported.

The bull disappeared over a rise, and Myles began to groan. "I didn't particularly want a moose – but now I've gone and wounded one! That means I'll have to track the darned thing down and put it out of its misery." Then he turned to me. "You got me into this, O'Connor. I wanted to hunt sheep – not moose!"

Field and I had been watching for the moose to reappear, because up there above the timberline, there was practically no way he could stay out of sight. Sure enough, we picked him up a moment later, going slowly now and evidently headed for a lake about a mile and a half away. Through the glasses we saw him go there, drink, and then lie down out of sight in the willows at the edge. So, protesting his dire luck, Myles mounted his horse and he and Johnny, the other guide, headed out for the lake to garner in the wounded bull.

Field and I, with the cook and the horse wrangler who had ridden up with the pack outfit in the meantime, went over to look at my bull. He was a fine one, the best moose I have ever shot, with a very large palm and a spread which I guessed to be about 57 inches and which later turned out to be 55. A pretty close guess!

My shots were all in a ten-inch group right behind the shoulder and through the lungs, and we found every one of the .270 bullets just under the hide on the far side. Considering the ease of the shots, that wasn't too good a group, but yet not too bad. I doubt if he would have run more than 150 yards after being hit with any one of them, but bull moose are tough, and it is always smart to keep shooting as long as they are still on their feet.

We photographed the bull, skinned out the head, and cut up the carcass to take back to the main camp. Now and then we took time out to watch the other moose hunters through the glasses as they slowly approached the lake. I was watching when I heard a flurry of shots and saw the wounded bull try to run up the bank, only to be cut down and roll into the lake. I could see the water splash as he kicked for a moment.

We went on with our work then and were finishing up when Myles came riding up with Johnny.

"How's the head?" I asked.

"Look!" he said. "I still don't believe it, but this shows how much spread he's got."

He handed me a leather string with a knot tied in it. I measured my own moose head with it and it lapped over more than a foot.

"Great scott!" I said. "That bull of yours has a spread of around 70 inches, maybe more!" I stepped on the end of the string below the knot and held it up. "Look!" I said. "I am more than six feet tall and this string comes from my toes almost to the top of my head!"

"What do you think of that!" Myles said. "It must be around 70 inches. I knew it, yet I hardly dared hope. Here I would have crawled from Cleveland to Akron on my hands and knees for a 60-inch moose and yet I almost didn't shoot at a 70-incher!" He

95

shook his head in mock dismay.

Skinning out that great head was a wet, cold job there in the frigid water of that timberline lake, but at last it was done – and those great antlers looked bigger *off* the enormous animal that had worn them than they did on. Brown's head made my massive 55-inch seem almost small.

Our 70-inch guess wasn't bad, it turned out. The head measured just a hair short of 70 inches with a steel tape at camp. Jean Jacquot, our outfitter, said it was the largest moose head he had ever seen – and he had been in the Yukon ever since the gold rush. Back in Whitehorse a month later, with the head dry, the velvet skinned off, and the skull sawed in two for easier packing, the spread was 69 3/4 inches, as measured by Canadian government officials.

Since the moose was shot close to the Alaska border, it is evidently of the Alaska species and is therefore the largest Alaska moose ever shot in the Yukon. One larger head of the Canada moose is recorded from the lower Yukon, but it has a spread of only three-fourths-inch more.

Anyway, it is quite a moose, particularly since three moose hunters had it in view for half a mile and didn't have the slightest idea of its size! Probably the reason was that the animal itself was so enormous. It stood more than seven feet high at the shoulder, and on an animated ten-ton truck like that, even a 70-inch head doesn't look too large!

RAM ON A SILVER PLATTER

As O'Connor writes here, "sheep do the darnedest things." He loved to hunt them, wrote a book devoted exclusively to them, and knew a great deal about them. Taking a wild ram is seldom easy, but on this hunt, everything seems to falls into place. June, 1945

There are a good many reasons why hunting the bighorn sheep is one of the most fascinating games an American sportsman can play. Surely one of the major reasons is that the bighorn is the most unpredictable animal in the world. He can be found in more unexpected places, and react in more unexpected ways to different sets of circumstances, than any other big-game animal.

Once upon a time a certain Eastern sportsman had his heart set on getting a really good Mexican ram. He knew that climbing over the rugged Sonora mountains was going to be tough, so for six months before he started on his hunt, he trained earnestly in a New York gymnasium, walked to work, limited his smoking, even bade good-by to beer, and in general built himself up into the professional strong man's double.

He and his outfitter were late getting across the Sonora border the first day of the trip, so they didn't have time to camp in good sheep country. While camp was being made and supper cooking, our sheep hunter heard some quail calling and took a shotgun along to see if he could get a few for breakfast. Less than a quarter of a mile from camp, he walked around a patch of cholla cactus and came face to face with the ram of his dreams, which stood there miles from a mountain, peacefully eating cholla fruit.

He killed it with 1^1/$_8$ ounces of No. 7^1/$_2$ shot, and spent the rest of his trip hunting mule and whitetail deer. Since he had his trophy, he did none of the heroic climbing he had prepared himself for.

No mountain sheep had any business down there on the flat, he thought. Actually, sheep are often found a long way from mountains, and in country you wouldn't suppose they'd like. One of the largest rams ever shot in Sonora was killed while eating peaches from a tree in a little orchard not far from a fair-size town. Once, while hunting antelope in the Sonora dune country not far from the Gulf of California coast, I spotted the white rump patches of what I took to be a herd of antelope a couple of miles away. Somehow, even at that distance, there was something phony about those "antelope." Upon stalking closer, I found they were a herd of bighorn ewes and lambs eating weeds in broad daylight far out on absolutely open plains!

As a matter of fact, bighorns are really not mountain animals in the sense that mountain goats are. They like good feed, soft beds, and easy living; they avoid the roughest country unless their enemies force them there. They use cliffs and crags only as place of refuge to retire to when they are bothered.

Far out in the plains of Montana and Wyoming, there are dozens of little buttes and hills that are called "Sheep Butte" or "Sheep Hill." In the United States today, the bighorns have been driven to the very roughest country and we are used to thinking of them as having been there all the time. Actually, they are now living in country where formerly they used only to flee to. That's one reason why the bighorns of the United States are not doing too well.

Sheep do the darndest things. They are generally conceded to be the wariest of all American game animals – the quickest to get out of sight, the keenest of eye. Good, careful, painstaking hunters have climbed their hearts out for days and weeks trying to get a shot at a ram, and failed. Once in Sonora, I spent two weeks in excellent sheep range, walked and climbed from 8 to 15 miles a day, saw rams every day – *and was out-witted by every ram I saw!*

The last time I hunted sheep in Mexico, my wife and I walked and climbed a good ten miles the first day, saw not a sheep. When we got back to our camp near the seashore, we found that the sheep had been there in our absence. They had tracked up the place and butted some of our equipment over. On that same trip, a ram with a fair but not a shootable head came down to the point overlooking our camp and watched us for more than an hour.

When I say that in Sonora, more sheep probably are killed from seagoing boats than by any other method, it will sound like a tall tale. It's the McCoy. Many of the sheep ranges come right down to the sea. Native fishermen carry .30/30s in their boats, pick the sheep off the points, and let them roll down into the sea. And they are practically the same sort of sheep as those hunted at 9,000 or 10,000 feet *above* sea level in Wyoming!

Once I had hunted hard all day on a high, tough, heartbreaking mountain in the Cobabai Range of Sonora. It was about time for me to quit, when through the glasses I picked up two rams about 300 yards away and partly screened by brush. I worked closer to get a look at their heads. One was a three-year-old, the other about a five-year-old with a complete but very small and tight curl, one that would not measure more than 25 inches along the curve. That type of head, by the way, is often seen in Sonora. Anyway, I decided I didn't want either ram, so making no further pretense at concealment, I started to climb down to camp, 3,000 feet or more below and about five or six miles away.

When those two rams spotted me, they did not flee. Instead, they advanced upon me, stamping their feet, shaking their heads, and acting as if they planned to knock me off the mountain. Keeping about 100 yards behind me, they followed me most of the way to camp and did not leave until they had decided they had chased away a dangerous intruder.

Ever hear of a charging sheep? I have! A Mexican rancher I know once decided he was going to climb a mountain near his ranch and knock over a bighorn – a *cimarron*, he called it. He hadn't seen a sheep and had been hunting for some hours when a sudden summer thundershower came up. He headed for a nearby cave to take shelter, and just as he reached it, two big rams come tearing out of it. One knocked him down – right into a prickly cholla – and ran over him; the other just ran over him. He was skinned and bruised, his hide was full of thorns, and his .30/30 was knocked 50 yards down the mountainside.

In ranges where there are caves, by the way, sheep seek them to get out of winter cold and out of summer heat, or to stay dry. In Sonora, almost every good sheep range is honeycombed with caves and every one is full of droppings. Cave-dwelling herbivores? Sounds cockeyed, but it's true!

I could go on telling tales of the cockeyed things bighorns do – of

99

the great ram I saw crossing a paved highway; of another big ram that came down off his mountain, licked the socks off three domestic rams, took over the ewes, and fathered a whole flock of woolly hybrids; of the ram that jumped onto a prospector's roof and peered down the chimney at the man's astounded wife.

But I'll end this with the odd story of the accommodating ram who delivered himself to me on a silver platter.

*F*irst, let me say that as a rule no sheep hunter has to exert himself harder than I do. Usually I climb, sweat, groan, and in general work my head off for a shot at a good ram. For my Alberta ram, I climbed about 2,500 feet, went down another 2,500 feet, hiked a mile up the rocky bed of a canyon, climbed another 500 feet, shot the ram, climbed down, walked another mile, then rode 14 miles to camp.

But this British Columbia ram was another story – and how!

We were changing camp one day and had just crossed with the pack train into British Columbia when my companion, Jack Holliday, spotted a lone ram bedded down right on top of a grassy ridge about a mile and a half away. We pulled up and looked him over carefully with binoculars. He was a big ram, well worth taking, and from where we were, we thought it would be easy, though slow, to go through the timber, emerge above the ram on the other side of the ridge, and polish him off. It was Jack's turn at rams, so away he went, accompanied by Isaac the guide.

Envying him that exciting stalk and wishing I were in his boots, I rode gloomily along with the packtrain. The more I thought about that big ram on the ridge, the finer he seemed as a trophy.

*P*resently, about half a mile away, I spotted a big lone billy goat running his tongue over the mud at a salt lick. I had the wind on him, and decided to sneak up within range. I cut off from the pack train, tied my horse. The campsite for which we were headed was three or four miles away, so I planned to get the billy, skin out the head and hide, remount my horse, and follow the creek down to camp.

Keeping some little arctic willows between me and the goat, I crawled along on my belly, gradually diminishing the space that separated us. Part of the way led through a muskeg, and the icy water soaked through my clothes. At last I reached my objective. I had my binoculars and my .270 on a grassy hummock in front of me, and as I lay there, I could see my goat still licking away, completely unaware of my presence. As I watched, I could see the wind stir his long white hair. Whenever I wanted him, he was my meat.

By rolling quietly over on my back and resting my head on the hummock, I could see the big ram Jack was stalking, still bedded down against the yellow of the cured grass. The day was young, the sun was warm and pleasant. I made up my mind to wait until I heard Jack shoot: then I'd give that billy the works. I was afraid that if I shot before he got to his ram, I'd spoil his stalk.

I was watching Jack's ram through the glasses and trying to see if I could pick up Jack or Isaac anywhere, when I heard the rattle of slide rock. Several hundred feet above me and more that 300 yards away, something was moving. Slowly I turned over. Outlined against the sky on that rocky ridge was a big ram. I didn't move a muscle as his great brown eyes swept the basin where I lay. Then another ram joined him – and another. In a moment five mature rams stood beside him.

What a quandary! I had six rams and a fine goat within range at one time, and if I took a shot at any of them I might spoil my friend's chance for another ram a couple of miles away. I decided to sit tight and wait.

The leading ram inched his way down the steep slide rock directly toward me, followed by the others. When the flock was a little more than 200 yards away, they came to a stop and turned their attention to the goat at the salt lick. For the first time now I felt I could move. I put the glasses to my eyes so I could take a better look at their heads. All were mature rams at least five years old. One had a wide spread, a second had a medium spread but a complete curl. Neither was in the record class, but each was far better than the average "trophy" ram. Actually, I could have taken both of them, since the British Columbia limit north of the Canadian National Railways route is two; but I'm not a bloodthirsty guy, and one would do very nicely. I decided on the one with the complete curl.

Waiting until all the rams were again watching the goat, I turned over on my back once more and put my glasses on the big ram Jack was stalking. As I did so, he jumped to his feet, looked wildly around, and ran up the point and out of this narrative. A treacherous eddy of mountain wind must have carried Jack's scent to him and he let no grass grow under his feet.

So that was that. Lady Luck had smiled on me that day and not

101

on my companion. I rolled over, took one last look through the glasses at my six rams. The keen eyes that had missed me lying there motionless in the muskeg had instantly detected the movement of the running ram two miles away. He had been frightened, they knew, so they were nervous.

I put down the glasses, picked up the .270 and cuddled the butt against my shoulder. The crosshairs came to rest low behind the big ram's foreleg, and the rifle was as steady as if I were shooting from a benchrest. I must admit I had misgivings. In view of all the sweating and climbing after rams I had done, and all the times they had made a chump out of me, it seemed immoral to get a ram so easily.

For a moment I considered standing up and yelling, and taking the ram on the run. I soothed my conscience, however. "Well, O'Connor," I told myself, "You may hunt sheep another 20 years and never get another on a silver platter."

The crosshairs were still low and just behind the foreleg when I finished the squeeze and the rifle recoiled. I heard the bullet smack into the ram, but neither the ram I shot at nor any of the others moved from their tracks. I could hardly believe my eyes.

Then my ram slowly and gently went over on his back and lay there with all four legs thrust stiffly into the air. The five other rams made no attempt to run off. Instead, they gathered around the dead ram, smelled it, pushed at it. I watched them with amazement. Here, evidently, was a herd of rams that had never seen a man nor heard a gun.

I got to my feet then and walked toward the ram. Until I was less than 100 yards from his fellows, they stood there staring at me. Even when I stood over the dead ram, they still jittered around on the slide rock while I took some photographs of them.

Five mature bighorn rams, the wildest and wariest of all American game animals, acting like dairy cattle! Jack's ram across the basin made off at one breath of man-scent, yet on my side of the basin, five big rams stood around and watched me for half an hour.

Though one horn was broomed, my ram had a good head, but not exceptional for a fully mature ram from that country. He was very old, since his unbroomed horn showed 13 annual rings. Although he was very fat and the steaks we had off him were an epicure's delight, his teeth were almost gone. He had but two teeth on one side and four on the other. All were so loose in the jaw that back at camp, I pulled a couple of them out with my fingers.

Later that afternoon, Jack and Isaac came in after a fruitless day of sheep hunting.

"We heard you shoot once," Jack called as he rode up. "What were you shooting at?"

"A ram!" I told him, holding up the head.

"Well, I'll be –!" he grunted. He was even more amazed when I told him how those six rams had stood around above me for half an hour.

Isaac whistled when he saw how bad the ram's teeth were. "Tell me," he said, "did you shoot him, or *find* him?"

"I practically found him," I answered. "On a silver platter."

SLATE MOUNTAIN PATRIARCH

Jack kills a wonderful Arizona whitetail, but the experience is bittersweet. It was a huge buck, called the "Patriarch" by local hunters, that he was really after. Then, on the way home from Slate Mountain, he encounters a truck carrying the big deer. It is an encounter of the sort that haunts many a sportsman's dreams.
July, 1939

This story really starts a good many years ago. I was living in northern Arizona then, in the midst of as good mule deer country as can be found in the United States. It was a case of being embarrassed by riches, since there were so many hunting spots that I could never get around to all of them. Some were famous all over Arizona. Others, just as good, were celebrated only locally.

One of these is the Slate Mountain section – an area of high volcanic peaks, cinder cones, wide parks knee-high with rich yellow gramma grass. Turkeys range on the mountain slopes, antelope wheel and maneuver, flash their white rump patches in the parks. But primarily it is mule deer country. The animals feed clear up into thick fir and spruce of the high peaks in the summer, then drift down before the chill of approaching autumn. Their winter range around Slate Mountain is thinly timbered, but it abounds in canyons where they can get out of the wind, and it has plenty of winter feed in the shape of dwarf juniper and cliff rose – or buck brush, as the natives call it.

Almost from the first, I was aware of Slate Mountain's local fame as buck country, but I always got a buck somewhere else before I got around to hunting there. It took some plain and fancy stories to draw me in there – and I got them. A cowboy told me how he had ridden into a little canyon one windy day and jumped out a bunch of 15 or 20 big bucks. A woodcutter told me how he saw deer there every time he went in. The supervisor of the

105

national forest told me a dozen tales calculated to make any hunter's mouth water. And through all these stories, an account of one particular big buck ran like a theme song. One hunter who had seen him in gray dawn thought for a moment that he was an elk and did not shoot until too late. Others had grown so excited at a glimpse of him that buck fever made their bullets go wild.

The upshot was that I decided to investigate the section where this big buck ran. It was the first day of the 1933 season, and as I drove out there I felt a bit foolish. In the first place, the stories of the Slate Mountain area sounded too good to be true. In the second, hunting for one particular buck is usually about like searching for the traditional needle in the traditional haystack.

*W*ell, my first Slate Mountain hunt was pretty uneventful – except that I got lost and that I'm convinced I saw the patriarch himself. Alone, I pulled up into a little canyon, changed to hobnails, took a quart canteen, a candy bar, and my Springfield, and set out. I circled the mountain high up where most of the canyons headed, edging along on slippery pine needles. I saw lots of deer sign that day and also some deer, mostly does and fawns and a few small bucks. To the north, over tawny grasslands spotted with purple patches of juniper, I could see the scarlet gash of the Grand Canyon overlined with the blue of the famous Kaibab. To the northeast lay the pink and mauve and yellow emptiness of the Painted Desert.

Dusk was gathering when I started down the mountain. I had been in sunshine, 1,500 feet above the plain, but as I went down it grew swiftly dark, and when I came out of the canyon, I found it wasn't the one in which I had parked the car. I could see my hand before my face, but that is about all. Further, I was in country strewn with volcanic boulders and cut with draws that dropped straight for 15 or 20 feet.

Afterwards, when my friends twitted me about the experience, I maintained that I was not lost. It was the car that was lost. Dimly in the starlight I could see familiar mountain peaks bulking black against the horizon. I knew within a quarter of a mile where I was, but I could have passed within ten feet of my car without seeing it. So I built a fire on the lee side of a dead pine, made myself a bed of pine needles, and caught some sleep.

When the first gray of dawn came, I picked up my rifle and went back to the car, which I located without trouble. I was hungry and I was thirsty, so I opened an iron ration and took a drink from the canteen.

Then I looked up – and there was the biggest buck I'd ever seen. Actually, he looked as big as a horse, and his antlers were so enormous that they showed plainly in spite of the fact that he was more than 200 yards away and in the gloom of timber. I dived for my rifle, but the buck disappeared just as I threw off the safety. I spent an hour that morning trying to find him, but his big tracks showed that he was long gone. So I went back to town, and to coffee and scrambled eggs and the reproaches of a frightened wife who didn't like her husband to stay out all night without telling her about it in advance.

The memory of that enormous buck haunted me, and two days later my wife and I were back there with food and bedrolls and hope in our hearts. As we drove through a big open park east of Slate Mountain, we saw a herd of 40 or 50 antelope, so when my wife said calmly, "A big buck just ran into that draw!" I thought she meant a buck antelope and paid no attention. Afterwards, she said she thought it strange that I showed so little interest, but being a well-trained wife, she did not comment at the time. We drove on up to the slope of a cinder cone, stopped, and got out our rifles. Then I happened to look up, and there, about 400 yards away, were three deer trotting through the junipers, gray against the red cinders.

Eleanor, who is an optimist as well as a good shot, went into action. They were bucks, I saw as soon as I put the glasses on them, but they disappeared into thick juniper unhit as far as I could tell. Then something drew my attention to the saddle between two cones, and I saw a sight I had never seen before and have never seen since – a herd of at least 20 big bucks, all on a dead run. They were in sight but an instant, and with all those antlers against the horizon, they looked like motion pictures I have seen of a herd of migrating caribou.

Figuring that they would skirt the cinder cone to our left, I decided to run over the top and catch them as they crossed an open park to the west. The cone was about 500 feet high, and when I topped out I was winded. Eleanor had fallen somewhere by the wayside.

Cautiously, I circled and when I had gone about 50 yards, three huge bucks came bouncing out, great brown antlers laid back against gray hides. The biggest was truly a monster, and I cut loose at him. The three disappeared into a clump of mixed oak, pine, cliff rose, and juniper at the foot of the hill, just as I got off what I thought was my best shot. Only two came out, and when I got down there I found my huge buck, hit three times from my six-shot fusillade – once in the left ham, once in the abdomen, and once, alas, right through the ear.

107

For a moment I thought I'd got the patriarch himself. When I looked across the open park to the next hill slope, however, I began to moan. The whole hill was alive with deer, but I had eyes only for one – an enormous buck that looked as big as a medium-sized elk as he stood there. I knew then that I might have got one of the patriarch's sons, but I surely hadn't got the patriarch.

I wished my wife were there to take a shot at him, but she wasn't, and by the time she found me, the whole herd had melted into the timber. Leaving her to see if she couldn't hunt one of them up, I cut across the cone to bring the car around from where we'd left it half an hour before. A few yards from where the deer she had shot at had disappeared, I heard the brush crack. When I investigated, I found a buck with both hind legs broken. I would have sworn Eleanor hadn't touched one, but there he was. So we had our bucks, both of us, after as short, as dramatic, and astonishingly lucky a hunt as I have ever been on.

As often happens, the head of the buck I got looked better when it was on the move than it did in the hand. But for Arizona mule deer, the animal was a whopper. He weighed 176 pounds with his head and neck off, his hide off, and half of the left ham cut away. I didn't weigh him field-dressed, but he was probably the heaviest buck I have ever shot.

Fate moved me 300 miles away into southern Arizona the next year, but I still remembered that great patriarch I'd left behind. So the end of the season found me once more in the Slate Mountain country. With me were two University of Arizona professors, Waldo Waltz, and Neil Houghton. Both were authorities on political science, but their education had been neglected, as neither had shot a buck. Our guide and horse wrangler was Slim, a local *vaquero* and an old friend of mine.

We pulled into our rendezvous with Slim late one night after the long drive from Tucson. Neil and Waldo were both pop-eyed with anticipation, as I had been feeding them my best Slate Mountain stories; but when we met Slim by the glow of his campfire, he tossed a little cold water on our enthusiasm.

"It ain't snowed a mite yet," he told us, "and them dad-blamed deer is scattered from hell to breakfast. Most of the big bucks is still high up." Then he added piously, "I sure been a-hopin' for snow since I heard you boys was a-comin'." He glanced up at the sky then, but it was blue-black, perfectly clear, blazing with thousands of stars.

"Has anyone potted that big old buck since I was up here?" I asked.

"Not that I've heard of," he reassured me, "but that ain't no sign somebody ain't knocked him over for meat." Slim, as I may have hinted before, is not exactly an optimist.

However, the Slate Mountain patriarch, through he was destined to remain only a name during the trip, did lead us to good hunting, for we saw our first deer within a quarter of a mile of camp the next morning. We were riding along the edge of a wide, fairly shallow canyon when we saw a movement in some cedars. Deer, all right; but at first we thought they were does and fawns. Neil dismounted and pulled his borrowed .30/30 out of the scabbard just in case. When they ran, we saw one was a buck, a small one; and on Neil's third shot it went down – a two-year old, three-pointer that had still been hanging around the does. The professor had done his stuff.

We split then, Waldo and Slim headed one way while Neil and I rode for the high country, where the bigger bucks ought to be hanging out. We hadn't gone more than a mile when we heard the heavy report of a .30/06. Five shots more or less regularly spaced, then a sixth shot.

"Sounds as though Waldo has connected," I told Neil. "Let's ride back and see what luck he had."

A few minutes later, on the opposite side of a hill, we found Waldo and Slim bending over a buck, another three-pointer that would dress at about 130 pounds. Waldo had hit it with his third and fifth shots. It went down, and a bullet in the neck had finished it when they came up. We ate an early lunch then and planned the balance of the day's campaign. Slim and Waldo would pack the two bucks back to camp, while Neil and I pursued the chance of getting a shot at the patriarch himself.

It was so dark when we returned that night that we had to give the horses their heads to make it possible for us to find camp. We had covered at least 20 miles and had hunted in rough country more than 8,000 feet in elevation. We had seen bucks, too, but nothing to make a head-hunter's mouth water, so we passed them up.

The second day was much like the first. We spared neither ourselves nor the horses, and saw our usual quota of does, fawns, and young bucks, but I did not fire a shot.

The last day of the hunt started out even worse. During the morning it clouded up and rained a little. We saw not a single deer, nor even a single track made since the rain. If deer were there, they were bedded and not moving. By noon the gloom was thick enough to cut with a knife. Slim and I swapped half-hearted stories about the old patriarch – his enormous head, his great weight. By three o'clock we had all become reconciled to our fate. The next morning we'd have to leave with only two bucks, neither of which had a good head. We were 12 or 15 miles from camp, and it was time to turn back. For several minutes we sat on the edge of a canyon, smoked cigarettes, and cursed the weather, the deer, and our luck.

I stood up, ground my cigarette under my heel, and prepared to mount. Then, almost 300 yards away, down toward the bottom of the canyon, I saw something move – something that became a great buck going out from behind a cedar in long downhill bounds. He had evidently been lying there, conscious of our presence, hoping we would pass him by, but getting more and more nervous. When I got up, he couldn't stand it any longer and ran.

I got off my first shot before the others saw him. It was a miss, behind and below. My second kicked up dust just over his back, and my third rolled him in foot-high sage.

Now that I had him down, I began to shake. He was an enormous buck, no doubt of it. He might even be the patriarch himself, and the thought was too much for my none-too-stable nerves. When I had reloaded, I started down the hill toward the spot where he had fallen. At a little over 100 yards he came out, one front leg dangling but behind the cedars. So I took a deep breath, sat down, and held on his brisket. He came down at the shot – down like a ton of bricks – and I knew he was mine.

A minute later I stood over him.

"He's the big 'un, the big 'un himself," Slim was shouting. Surely he was a magnificent creature: fat, heavy, lithe, with a wide, symmetrical head the collector dreams about. An Easterner would call him a 13-point, but in the West he would be a 7-pointer, as he had 6 points on one side and 7 on the other.

"You shore got him!" Slim kept saying. "That's the dad-blamedest biggest old buck I've ever seen."

But the longer I looked at that buck, the surer I was that he was not the patriarch. His teeth showed him fully mature but not old, in spite of the record-class head he carried. "It's one of his kids, Slim," I said finally. "It isn't the old one."

"Well, if I got a buck like that," Neil interrupted, "I'd be darned if I'd kick about him."

I still am proud of that head, as it is one of the three or four largest that I have ever taken, but I am now certain that on that red-letter day back in 1934, I didn't get the patriarch. For I saw him again last year, and that is when this story properly ends.

*M*y wife and I were returning from the Kaibab with two bucks, when we saw a truck turning onto the highway from the direction of Slate Mountain. In it were two bucks, and one of them was the biggest I have ever seen dead. I signaled for the driver to stop.

"You surely have a big buck there! Where did you get him?" I asked, knowing the answer before I heard it.

"Slate Mountain country."

I examined the great buck's teeth. He was very old.

"I'm sort of a semi-pro biologist, particularly interested in game," I told the hunters, "and I'd surely appreciate it if you'd meet me in Flagstaff so I can weigh and measure that buck. He's the largest I have ever seen, and he has one of the best heads."

They promised, but they didn't show up. Why, I do not know. Possibly they were hunting illegally. Surely they must have had guilty consciences of some sort.

And that, I am convinced, was the end of the Slate Mountain patriarch. When he was killed he must have been 10 or 12 years old, as when I first saw him he was fully mature and already had a reputation. I still regret that I didn't measure that head on the spot, as I had a tape with me. My guess is that it would have shown a spread of close to 45 inches and a main beam of 32 or 33.

His weight? Well, I'm a conservative and fairly accurate weight guesser. I'll admit that the biggest Southwestern mule deer I ever saw on the scales went 240 pounds and the largest I have any authentic record of went 261. Admitting all this, I am nevertheless going to stick my neck out and guess the Slate Mountain patriarch at close to 400, dressed.

It is too bad that the old fellow couldn't have fallen to a head-hunter, so those magnificent antlers of his could have been mounted. Yet at that, he has achieved immortality of a sort, as he'll long live in the hunters' tales of northern Arizona. Furthermore, he helped populate the Slate Mountain country with a magnificent breed of bucks, and his descendants will range there, I hope, forever. I'll always be grateful to him, as he lured me into country which yielded me one of my most prized trophies.

MYLES GETS HIS CIRCLE

The material for this story came from O'Connor's second Outdoor Life-*sponsored trip to the Far North. Myles Brown, a friend from Cleveland, Ohio, scores in splendid fashion.*
September, 1946

*U*nless a great deal of good luck enters into it, any sheep hunt includes among its necessary ingredients a lot of looking, a lot of climbing, and a lot of aching muscles and creaking joints. This one I want to tell you about now, is no exception – in that respect, at least.

When N. Myles Brown of Cleveland, Ohio, and I were hunting in the Yukon, Myles seemed to be jinxed. He was an old sheep hunter, too, with trips into the Northwest Territory for Dall sheep and into northern British Columbia for Stone bighorns both behind him. But our first stand for sheep was a complete flop.

Field Johnson, one of our guides, and I put in a long, hard day of climbing, looking with the binoculars, and scouting. We found no fresh sheep sign, our glasses showed no trails in the new-fallen snow up on the peaks, and there were no fresh tracks around a famous sheep lick where, in gold-rush days, prospectors used to lie in wait for their supply of mountain mutton.

Field and I did see worlds of wolf tracks, however, and we finally decided that the predators must have run out the sheep. Then, just as the sun was setting, we put the glasses on three sheep high under the cliffs and across a mighty canyon. There were undoubtedly some sheep in the country, we figured then, but probably not enough to hunt.

In the meantime Myles and Johnny, the other guide, had been hunting in another section. They had even less luck than we did. Except for some ptarmigan and a wolverine, they saw not a living thing. When we finally compared notes and discussed our findings in detail back at camp that night, both Myles and I were pretty discouraged and determined to move. I

113

had at least spotted three sheep, sex undetermined, but Myles hadn't even seen a track.

On our next stand a few days later, a jack camp along Moose Horn Creek at the edge of the Solomon Mountains, my luck improved. I saw only about 15 sheep, but I got one of them, a big ram with a 38 1/2-inch curl. When Field and I finally returned to our little camp above timberline in the willows about 10:30 that night, Myles had still to see a sheep of any sex, size, or description. His face was about as long as the face of any man who weighs more than 200 pounds can get.

"You have proof that there really are sheep here," he said wistfully, looking at the head and cape of the ram I had brought in, "but I'd sure like to lay an eye on one myself." Too bad he couldn't see what was ahead!

In many parts of the north country, it isn't possible to camp with a big outfit wherever the notion strikes you; there simply isn't feed for horses. In the section we were hunting, we were tied pretty closely to the bar of the Generk River where pea vines, the best horse feed in the subarctic, grew plentifully. We went back from the Moose Horn, changed our hungry horses for fresh ones, picked up some grub, and headed straight up the Generk to the Klutlan Glacier.

That night, just as darkness was falling, we blew up our mattresses and unrolled our eiderdown sleeping bags on a moss-and-lichen-clad shelf just above a sinkhole full of water and lined with grizzly tracks. Below us was the great white glacier, with hills and valleys of solid ice and huge crevices hundreds of feet deep. Above us was a series of roundtops that merged into the ice-capped peaks of the Solomons. The next morning when I went down to the sinkhole to get some water for my coffee and to wash the sleep out of my eyes, a skim of ice had formed at the edge of the hole, and there were fresh grizzly tracks that had been made during the night.

Later we found sheep clear up toward the head of the glacier in high, rough mountains and deep canyons, all of which were of volcanic origin, barren and fantastically colored – red, blue, ocher, and the deep black of lava that only yesterday, geologically speaking, had been hot and flowing. Some slopes looked as bare as the face of the moon, but others were tinged green with moss and lichens.

If I didn't look to my left to see that great river of ice, I could imagine myself back in Sonora, Mexico – in the fantastic Pinacates, also volcanic and also great sheep country. And there were sheep here, too; not the brown bighorns of the Mexican desert, but the beautiful pure-white Dall sheep of the Arctic. Against the bright-colored lava were little groups of white spots and far above us on the green slope of a mountain pasture, just below a dazzling-red cliff, about 30 sheep shone and glittered like diamonds in the slanting rays of the early morning sun.

But all those sheep were ewes and lambs; what had happened to the rams? Perhaps they were higher up and farther back in the canyons, though we knew that the wolves had been thinning them out. That very morning, there at the edge of the glacier, we counted the skeletons of 14 mature rams that had evidently been killed the previous winter when deep snows forced them low. We found some ewe and lamb kills, too, but ram kills outnumbered them three to one. Some of the sheep we got the binoculars on that morning were probably immature males, but we knew that we had sighted not a single trophy ram.

The following day we were back again on the Generk bar to get fresh horses and more grub. Myles was going to lick that ram business if it took him all fall.

We made our next camp in pursuit of the elusive Dall sheep high in a big interior canyon of the range. After we pitched our little tent, we got out the glasses and found sheep on both sides of the canyon – a little herd here, another there, but all so far away we could not tell whether they were rams or ewes.

The next morning Myles and Johnny pulled out and went clear to the head of the little unnamed creek that flowed down the canyon bottom. Field and I went upstream a couple of miles. Then we turned off and climbed into a side canyon that opened up on more of that fantastic country of lava and volcanic ash. Some of the ridges were green from grass and lichens, and above them the peaks were capped with solid ice.

Even a novice could have told that we were in great sheep country. Trails were everywhere, cut straight and sharp against the volcanic hillsides. High above us were a few scattered white dots that we knew were sheep. We had to have altitude, so up that canyon we went. A two-hour climb put us on a saddle right at the top of the range.

We could see new canyons, new glaciers, new peaks. While the frigid wind right off the glaciers tore at our clothes, we lay there using the glasses. About 30 sheep were in sight, high above the canyon we had just climbed, but so far as we could tell, there wasn't a ram among them. Far across a glacier below us, lying snow-white on great

115

black points, were other sheep which we decided were probably rams, but going after them and getting back that day was out of the question.

Field turned the glasses higher on the ridge where we were lying. Suddenly he stiffened and said, "I see rams!"

More than a mile away a herd of sheep we had not seen before was moving off a peak down a ridge right against the skyline. We could tell that all were rams, but as we were without a spotting scope, we were uncertain about their heads. It did seem logical, though, that in a bunch of 14 or 15 rams there would be some good trophy possibilities, so off we went.

*I*n order to stay above the sheep we had to cut across the heads of half a dozen canyons. I used to say that the sheep mountains of Sonora were the toughest in North America, but when I did, I took in too much territory. The Yukon mountains where we hunted that day are so steep that every rock in them is looking for an excuse to roll. Several times we had to dodge big boulders that simply got tired of sitting where they were, hurtled down toward us and disappeared far below, crashing, leaping and roaring in the depths like cannon fire.

To go directly toward the sheep, we scrambled down into the head of each canyon, then climbed almost straight up toward the next ridge. With nothing horizontal in sight, I found it difficult to tell the difference between what was straight up and down and what was *almost* straight up and down. Once I got stuck on the face of a cliff with a drop of a couple of hundred feet below me. I couldn't go up, down, right, or left for a few minutes, but with Field's coaching I found a handhold, pulled myself over a ledge, and placed my feet on something solid enough to feel safe again.

Finally we toiled up the last slope. Far below us, on a point projecting way out in the middle of a tremendous canyon, were 14 rams – but not one had a trophy head. They were not more than 250 yards away and the 8X binoculars brought them close. Some were feeding, some were resting. For an hour I lay there, just watching those beautiful sheep, so white against the green lichens. They scratched out their beds with their forefeet. They chewed their cuds. A couple of them had a sparring match that wasn't very serious.

Reluctantly we left them, still undisturbed, and worked down the ridge on which we had been glassing. It was relatively easy going, as we had a sheep trail almost a foot wide and six inches deep to follow. At last we were off the mountain and in the bottom of the next canyon. We had nothing to do then except climb to the top of the range again to the saddle where we had first seen the rams, then make our way down the canyon into the one where we were camped. It was pitch dark when we got in.

Myles was back, dog tired and creaking in every joint. It was the old story – ewes, lambs, young rams, but no trophy ram. However, just before sundown he had seen some big rams right under the glaciers, and despite his weariness, he was determined this time to make a jack camp and get his ram.

The next morning he and Field set out with a bedroll behind the saddle of one horse and some food in the saddlebags. If they got a ram that day, all was well. If they didn't, they could share the bedroll for a night.

I had sworn that I wouldn't hunt that day, but after Myles and Field pulled out, I began to use the glasses and almost immediately discovered eight sheep a mile or so away from camp, feeding in a grassy saddle right at the top of the range.

If I had only taken a spotting scope, I would have saved a lot of wear and tear on my legs, but I didn't have one. A pair of binoculars lets a man do too much wishful thinking in sheep hunting. As I watched those eight animals, I decided that the law of averages was bound to make them big rams, and also that the climb looked easy. I was wrong on both counts.

While Johnny stayed in camp with the horses, I took off. About three hours later, my creaking legs had carried me above the sheep. All were young rams, none more than six or seven years old.

On the way back to camp, I shot a couple of ptarmigan in the head with the.270. Johnny and I broiled and devoured them along with a caribou steak the size of a platter. You can't beat a feast like that!

That night when I turned in beneath the northern lights, I was expecting to hear Myles and Field come in, but when I awoke the next morning they were still missing. With nothing better to do, I climbed to the ridge in the opposite direction from where I had hunted before. I saw two beaten-up old rams with badly broomed horns, more than a hundred ptarmigan, and some caribou. Every now and then I'd turn my glasses down toward the creek bed at the bottom of the canyon to see if I could pick up Myles and Field.

At last I was rewarded. I saw them coming around a point far upstream. They were traveling slowly, one walking, one riding. As they came closer, I could see that they had been lucky at last. Behind one of the saddles were white spots that could only be ram heads.

Back at the camp, they told their story. They had glassed three

117

rams, two big ones and one smaller one, about 3 o'clock the previous afternoon. The animals were lying right on top of a ridge absolutely impossible to approach. Field knew they would move eventually, and if they came toward Myles and him, all would be well. The men waited and waited. They grew cold, hungry, and cramped.

Then, just about sundown, the three rams got up, stretched, looked around, and disappeared over the ridge at a leisurely walk.

Field grabbed Myles's rifle and set out on a dead run up the mountain. Myles followed close behind. When they reached the place where the rams had been bedded, they saw the three below them and about 100 yards away. Myles was winded, but he sat down and went to work. In a moment his Yukon sheep hunting was over, for two rams were down.

One of them had a complete curl, a full circle, in other words. The other had the most massive head with the largest base I have ever seen on a thin-horned sheep. The horns had been badly broomed; in every way the head resembled that of an old Mexican ram, whose brittle horns often lose eight or ten inches by brooming.

In spite of the fact that it was almost dark, we laid the two heads out on a log and I took the first of a series of pictures of the trophies, making a few more the next day. That done, Myles heaved a big sigh.

"Gosh but I'm glad those rams are behind me," he said. "Now I can take it easy, hunt caribou, and enjoy life!"

WHAT, NO WHITETAILS?

Whether in Asia, Africa, or Arizona, O'Connor liked nothing better than to make his way to a special and unlikely place and come away with a great story. This is such a piece, from early in his writing career, in which he ventures into a region where the authorities insisted that no deer could survive. January, 1939

*I*f I had to pick the American big game animal that has given me more real pleasure than any other, I think I'd choose the Arizona whitetail. I like the big mule deer, the majestic elk, the great, brown mountain sheep, the gaudy antelope; but for real, deep-seated thrills, little *Odocoileus couesi* is my favorite. The flash of his big, white "fan," the sight of his small, compact antlers, his sleek, gray body scurrying through the brush – well, they give me, more than any other animal, those moments of high ecstasy which make a man a sportsman.

Then, too, the whitetail, as I know him, is a mysterious little devil. His race has never been accurately classified, his habits have never been thoroughly studied, and even his habitat has never been correctly mapped.

This is the account of a hunt for whitetails in a region where, according to the authorities, no whitetails live. Maps of their distribution show the whole coastal desert of the Mexican state of Sonora is devoid of them. Actually, I have seen them there by the hundreds. I told a scientist that once, but he raised his eyebrows, and pulled out a distribution map to show me. I was wrong, he was right – the book said so. Further, he told me, the whitetail could not exist without open water. So again I was wrong.

119

Hence the trip about which I am writing.

When I went into Sonora in the fall of 1937, I wanted to bring back a whole family of desert whitetails for the Arizona State Museum, so my skeptical scientist friend could see them.

So one November night I pulled up at the ranch of Epifanio and Alfonso Aguierre. Rancho El Datil, or "the date" as Americans would say, is the last permanent habitation between the Altar Valley of Sonora and the Gulf of California. Beyond it is a wilderness, without roads, without permanent water except for a few scattered holes, without domestic animals, and with no inhabitants except less than 100 Seri Indians, living on, and near, Tiburon Island. These Indians will eat anything that walks, flies, or crawls, and for many years were reputed to have been cannibals.

Epifanio and I planned the hunt. We decided to pack in 30 miles to Las Mochis, near which the Aguierres were invading the wilderness by sinking a well. There we could water our horses, which would give us a wider range of operations.

But we planned without the weather. We awoke to find my usual Mexican luck – it was raining. My visit at the ranch lasted a week instead of the few hours I had planned. I hunted in the rain almost daily, more for something to do than anything else.

At last it cleared, and we packed into the Las Mochis country and camped. To the west was desert, ending in the rocky, desolate beaches of the gulf. To the north, clear to the American border 200 miles away, was virgin wilderness. To the south, clear to the port of Guaymas, was likewise nothing, except for a fisherman's camp at Kino Bay.

The sun was going down that evening when, leaving a couple of Eppie's *vaqueros* to make camp, Eppie and I rode out through the fantastic jungle of pitahaya, saguaro, and ironwood to see what we could see. Delighted, we found tracks of desert whitetails. We also saw mule deer tracks, and cholla patches, where bighorn sheep had been eating the fruit.

On the eastern side of a tall, black volcanic cone, I shot a buck mule deer. We saw him through an opening in the ironwoods about 50 yards away, and I piled off and let him have it. He was young and dumb. Instead of running, he stood there looking at us, but when my rifle cracked, he went away in high bounds, clearing low brush like a hurdler. He came down at my second shot – a fluke snap that knocked one of his antlers off. The first shot, I discovered, had drilled a neat little hole through his heart and had gone out with no expansion.

As we rode back to camp with the buck behind Eppie's saddle, I felt misgivings. The gun I had taken in was a .257 Remington belonging to my wife, a beautiful little weapon with a 2^{1}/$_{4}$X Noske scope. In her hands, it had shot two-inch groups at 200 yards, but it had never been thoroughly tried out on game, as the two bucks she had killed with it had been hit in the neck and in the spine. If the bullet action on this buck was indicative, I knew I was in for trouble. I longed, then, for the old Springfield I had carried on so many Mexican trips, or for the vicious little 7mm. with which I had killed seven head of big game with seven shots. But there I was with the .257, and it was up to me to make the best of it.

The next morning, Eppie and I rode for the highest peak in the Las Mochis range ten miles away. It was an exploratory trip, but it produced plenty of game, as everything was moving and feeding after the rain. We counted 12 desert mule deer, all the same smaller variety as the buck I had killed the previous evening. We also saw a whitetail doe and fawn.

By noon we'd seen 23 head, and the end was not yet, for we were to find the happy hunting ground for whitetails – a chain of low, gray hills between Las Mochis and camp.

We were jogging along a canyon when a good doe ran out a couple of hundred yards away and above us. She flinched at my first shot, went down at the second, then got up again, and stopped behind a little ironwood tree.

Through the scope, I could see her dimly behind the branches and I shot again. As the rifle cracked, she rolled down the hill. One of the first two shots was in the lungs, another pretty far back. The third, the one that killed her, had passed through the branch of the tree first and hence had opened up. Those first two shots had drilled neat little holes and delivered no shock, exactly like the one on the buck. Moral: When you hunt deer with the present version of the .257 Remington bullet, carry around a tree to shoot through!

We started for camp with the doe, and those magic hills started producing whitetails. Five ran out of one basin, three out of another. For a mile, we saw the distant flashes of white fans through the brush almost constantly. I have hunted little old *Odocoileus couesi* in Arizona, Texas, Sonora, Sinaloa and Chihuahua, from the Mogollon rim to the Yaqui River. Never

121

have I seen them so plentiful as in that little range of hills in a desert where they are not supposed to exist. I went to bed that night full of the tenderest, most delicately flavored venison I have even eaten. In the morning – well, Eppie and I were going to do big things.

But the rain and Hugo came together. With Hugo in camp, I did not mind the rain, as Hugo belongs to an almost extinct species – the wilderness prospector, the sort of eccentric dreamer who opened up the great bonanzas of the West in the last century. He is a Swede, almost 75, and for 40 years he has tramped that last wilderness, carrying his bed, his pick, and his pan on his back, living on quail, rabbits, lizards, land turtles, the eggs of the great sea turtle, mesquite beans, pitahaya fruit, wild honey. He carries a few pounds of *frijole* beans with him as an emergency ration. Flour is a luxury to him, and the bacon I fed him was the first he had eaten in a decade. But he was a mine of information on the plants and animals of that last wilderness.

Hugo shared our shelter, helped eat our beans and venison, as long as the rain lasted. Then, on the third day, in spite of an overcast sky, he announced the storm was over, shouldered his bed roll, called Seri, his dog, and headed our for the Sierra Azul de los Indios, 50 miles away. The rain would fill some potholes he knew of, he said, and, in that great, barren range where few white men have penetrated, he practically had a gold mine in the bag.

Clouds were still heavy the next day, but acting on Hugo's advance information, I took one of the *vaqueros*, a nine-year-old Papago boy named Juanito, and hit out for the little granite hills. Eppie departed on some project of his own. We found deer, but as the Mexicans say, they were *muy broncho* (very wild), and those brushy hills are no place to shoot running deer 200 to 300 yards away, as practically all shots must be taken offhand. A couple of times, I saw bucks with good heads. I would have risked trying to cut them down with my old Springfield or even with a 7mm., but with the .257 I didn't shoot.

Late afternoon found Juanito and me still deerless, and the little imp was calling me *"el muy malo cazador,"* the very bad hunter. The sun was headed down when I decided to hunt back along a high ridge which overlooked brushy basins. The heart-shaped tracks of the little whitetails were everywhere.

Then, as I was riding along, a patch of gray in the brush below me caught my eye. I pulled up my horse to look – and two bucks exploded out of the brush. They had heard us, seen us, smelled us; but they were trying to bluff it out. The small one, a spike, tore up the relatively open side of a hill. I shot, heard the bullet strike, and saw him stagger. Then I whirled to take the big one and shot as he dashed through an opening. Again I heard the bullet strike, and I also saw he had the biggest head I had ever seen on a whitetail – long of beam, wide of spread, and incredibly massive.

Again he hove into view for an instant, and I saw I had broken his left front leg at the shoulder. I was convinced I had a new record in my grasp. But it was not to be. I never got another open shot, and the best I could do was to keep pouring bullets at his ghostly shape hobbling through the brush. But no soap. He slipped out of the basin in brush so thick I did not know he had left until I tracked him out. Frothy blood told me his lungs were hit. A high-speed .30/06 or .270 bullet would have anchored him on the spot, but not those trick .257s.

With Juanito following, riding and leading my horse with the spike buck on the saddle, I stayed on the track until dark. Blood all the way, but no buck; and, when we rode home that night, I was one of the sickest hunters in all North America. I still had faint hopes of returning in the morning and taking up the trail, but even that faded when a slow drizzle set in. The memory of that beautiful, massive head still haunts me.

Luck, which denied me the great buck, did produce me a record head, but alas, it was killed by a lion. The whole skeleton lay under a tree, complete, where the big cat had eaten his fill. The antlers measured slightly less than 20 inches both in spread and beam. It was very massive and the brow tines were huge. It is the best Arizona whitetail head I have ever measured, and, as far as I know, is the record.

Eppie and I landed in camp from opposite directions that night, soaked to the skin by a shower that caught us several miles from camp. Eppie, who wanted some venison to dry, had shot another mule deer and reported seeing a bunch of sheep, one a big old ram, feeding miles from a mountain right out on the cholla flats.

*N*ext morning I set out with Eppie toward the west. About 10 o'clock we were cutting through a basin formed by fairly low hills when two bucks got up and started tearing along the hill slope. My ineffectual little .257 started spitting and Eppie was busy lobbing .30/30 bullets. Down came one buck in plain sight. Then the other rolled head over heels.

123

As he fell, I heard hooves thundering and Eppie yelling: *"Hai Chihuahua* there go our horses!" Nervous from the shooting, one had flinched against a cholla and stampeded. The other followed suit. Two hours later we were back after chasing two *caballos* gone wild all over the desert. We found Eppie's buck but not mine. We hunted, swore, held consultations, read each other's palms. Still no buck. Curious as it may seem, other deer had obliterated its tracks while we were chasing the horses.

We were about to call it a day when a buzzard dropped out of the blue and lit on a saguaro some 200 yards away. Then a crow joined him, then another buzzard. And below them, lodged behind thick brush in a crevice between two rocks was my buck. The .257 bullet had broken a rib going in, but had slipped between coming out. His whole chest cavity was full of blood, but he hadn't shed a drop on the outside. When we turned to chase down the horses, he had got up and run, falling in the one spot where he would be almost impossible to find. I'm sure I never would have found him if that buzzard hadn't shown the way. Anyway, the episode taught me a lesson – it will be a long while before I take anything for granted, and that includes the reports of naturalists and the killing power of a rifle I haven't tested.

My whitetail hunting was over then. As Arizona whitetail heads go, mine was a good one; as Las Mochis heads go, it wasn't even a fair average. For almost every mature buck I saw had a head that would make the eyes of the hardened head-hunter stick out a foot.

One of these days, I'm going to make another trip to those magic granite hills in that beautiful wilderness where no whitetails are supposed to be. I'll take my .30/06 to anchor the game and a rabbit's foot to bring me luck. Those super bucks are there, I know, and I've got my sights set for one.

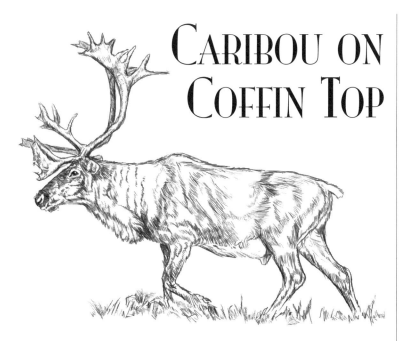

CARIBOU ON COFFIN TOP

*This story was one of several
that came out of Jack's first trip
to the Canadian Rockies (in the
summer of 1943). He gets a fine
caribou with a mule deer thrown
in for good measure.
August, 1944*

We stood high on a knife-edge ridge, far above
timberline and almost astride the British Columbia-
Alberta border. The icy wind of the north country tore at our
faces and sought the crevices in our stout woolen clothes. Just
below us a marmot that had survived the excavating activities of
the grizzly bear who had torn his whole village up whistled at us
indignantly, and a flock of ptarmigan – conspicuously patterned
with white and brown against the green of the lichens –
squawked and cackled as only ptarmigan can. Far across the
basin over which we had just come, land as weird and empty as
the face of the moon, a lone Rocky Mountain goat was slowly
going from some place to some place else, in the calm,
deliberate, and thoughtful manner of billy goats.

Below us the ridge fell away sharply – bare slide rock, then
patches of moss and lichens, and finally great timbered shoulders
that swept down into the purple fir forests where a little stream

meandered like a silver thread. Beyond, the country rose again into more high country like that on which we stood – big, rough ranges, spotted with the white irregular masses of glaciers and topped with jagged peaks.

"See that mountain over there with that big, flat-topped affair that looks like a coffin?" Roy Hargreaves, my outfitter, asked. "Well, we call that Coffin Top, and it is the doggondest game country you ever saw!"

"Better than this?" I asked incredulously, thinking of the astonishing numbers and variety of game we had seen out of camp – bighorns, goats, caribou, deer, moose, and grizzlies.

"Well," Roy considered, "maybe not *better,* but as good. You'll see everything except sheep. And caribou? You think you've already seen some caribou. You haven't – not compared with what's in the Coffin Top country, anyway . . . . Look! I see some caribou now."

He was right. Far away, tiny specks against the white expanse of a glacier, was a herd of 50 or more caribou.

The next afternoon, after a long day with the packtrain, we pitched camp by Forgetmenot Creek, a little willow-choked stream that wandered through a wide valley that lay at the foot of Coffin Top. As soon as the tents were up, Jack Holliday, my companion, and I began looking the mountain over with glasses. The lower slopes were thickly timbered with big fir and spruce trees, but higher up, the big trees gave way to the dwarfed alpine fir the mountain men call shin-tangle, because right at timberline it grows in a dense mass. Anyone who has ever walked through it can understand the suitability of the name. Still higher were nothing but moss and lichens on gray slide rock, and on the very top of the mountain was the big gray "coffin," with its flat top and perpendicular sides – a mesa, in the language of the Southwest.

As we watched, two big buck mule deer, one still in his yellowish summer coat but the other in the gray of fall, walked out of a patch of shin-tangle and began to feed in the clearing. Below them was a big bull caribou with a dark body and snow-white neck.

"Wow!" Jack shouted. "Get a load of that big buck. I want him!"

"We'll go up there in the morning," Roy said as he joined us, "and maybe we'll kick that boy out. He's got a nice head, hasn't he?"

So it came to pass that early the next morning, when the upper slopes of Coffin Top were first bathed in the clear direct rays of the rising sun, Roy, Jack, Isaac the guide and I were pushing our puffing horses through the last patches of shin-tangle toward the mountain top. I happened to be looking at the right time, and I was the only one who saw the buck. He jumped out of his bed and dived into the trees. Jack piled off, hoping to see him as he came out below, but it was not to be. So we put the buck in our list of things to be attended to later.

On two sides, Coffin Top dropped 2,000 feet or more in sheer cliffs of solid rock. On the side toward camp, it sloped down at an angle of about 45 degrees, and to the south, it was connected to another mountain by a long narrow saddle. By the time we got up the slope to the comparatively level top, the sun was well up, the sky was bright blue, and the day was warm – or rather, it was warm enough so that, with a suit of long-handled underwear, a pair of wool pants, a wool shirt, a sweater, and a leather wind-breaker, I wasn't a bit chilly. Jack seemed to be doing right well in a few layers of wool topped by an eiderdown jacket.

We worked around the north side of the mountain, topped a little rise, and saw seven bull caribou bedded down on a small glacier. We had the wind on them, and even though they were only about 600 yards away, they paid no attention to us. Jack decided to take the largest one, so, leaving my rifle behind and taking on a load of cameras, I set out behind him for the stalk. We dropped into a ravine to stay out of sight and emerged less than 200 yards from the herd.

The actual execution was done with a .22 Varminter equipped with a 440 Weaver scope – the same rifle with which Jack had killed a grizzly a few days before. His one shot hit the caribou in the neck and severed a large artery. The bull ran about 200 yards and fell, leaving a wide trail of blood behind him. Roy came up then, and while he was skinning out the head and taking a load of meat, I went over to see where the mountain dropped off to the west to see what I could see.

Across the saddle on the next mountain, another herd of caribou was taking its noonday siesta on a glacier, and in the big basin to the north, I made out single animals here and there. In the valley half a mile below, a grizzly stalked across an opening and disappeared. As I walked back to report, I saw a billy goat walking majestically right at the edge of the cliff about a quarter-mile away. The one shot had disturbed him and he was changing

127

bedrooms. We were right on the continental divide, and on every side giant, snow-covered peaks rose straight into the sky.

After we had eaten our sandwiches, we hunted along the cliffs and saw in all about a dozen goats. Some of them were on the British Columbia side of the mountain, and I wanted a good hide for a rug, but any one of them, if shot, would have fallen half a mile. We contented ourselves by climbing partway down the face of that incredible cliff and taking pictures of them.

Half an hour later we were on the saddle between the two mountains, sizing up the caribou with our glasses. The herd I had previously seen bedded on the big glacier was still there, and so were the bulls in the basin. One very good bull was trotting along below us, and the glasses showed he had a double shovel and heavy palmated antlers. About a dozen bulls were in sight at from 600 to 1,500 yards.

Then a bull walked out of some shin-tangle and lay down on a patch of snow about 600 yards away. He was some bull, noticeably larger of body and longer of antler than any we had seen.

I handed the glasses to Isaac. "What do you think of that head?" I asked.

"Best we've seen on the trip," was his quick verdict. "It'll go 50 inches easy."

"I'll take him, then!" I said.

We held a council of war. Jack wanted to go over and photograph the caribou on the glacier, and I promised not to shoot until I saw him there. He and Roy set out.

When Roy and Jack had disappeared from sight over the ridge, we worked quietly downhill to a bench somewhere between 400 and 500 yards from the bull – as close as we could safely go. I put a cartridge in the chamber of my .270 in case I'd have to shoot quickly, and waited. We were in no hurry, since the wind was blowing our scent well past the bull, and we were above him and out of range of his indifferent vision.

After what seemed like an age, we saw Jack and Roy on the glacier sneaking up out of sight of the herd. They would soon be in photographic range, so things were going nicely.

Then some cows which had trotted out of a timber-filled creek bottom spotted our bull and went over to pay a call on him. The mating season was about to begin, and from the looks of things, the cows were more enthusiastic about the prospect than the bull, who was an old fellow and doubtless had been a few places. He got to his feet politely when they approached, but as they frisked around him, he regarded them with a cold and fishy eye. I could practically read his thoughts: "I've chased prettier dames away with rocks!"

Rebuffed by the cynical bull, one of the cows began to gaze around her. She spotted Isaac and me above on the mountainside and stiffened. Then the two other cows saw us. Tails up, heads back, they began to circle to catch our wind.

"Oh, oh!" I said. "Here we go!"

The big bull's head went up. He regarded us long and intently. Then he began trotting smoothly along, directly across our line of vision.

I had decided that the bull was somewhere between 400 and 500 yards away, and I had already planned to hold just over his back, since the .270 was sighted for 300 yards. I settled down into a good prone position, and let the bull move along with his back just under the horizontal crosshairs. Swinging with him, I got the shot off with the vertical hair about a length in front of his nose.

"Right over his back!" said Isaac, who had the glasses on him.

I used the same lead on the next shot, but held right on top of the bull's back. He went down as if the earth had been jerked from under him, and I don't believe he even twitched. It was one of the quickest kills I have ever seen and surely the quickest on an animal the size of a big bull mountain caribou.

Later, when we skinned him, we found the 130-grain Silvertip bullet, perfectly mushroomed, under the hide on the far side of the chest cavity. That bullet, I found, gives deeper penetration on heavy game than does Winchester's regular pointed expanding bullet of the same weight and kills the big stuff more quickly.

While Isaac and I were taking the whole hide off the bull for a leather jacket, Jack and Roy came riding up. They'd got those caribou pictures they were after.

The sun was sliding down behind Coffin Top when we headed for camp with the two caribou heads, the scalps, and the hide on the packhorse. We thought the day's hunt was over. It wasn't. We were down in the timber once more when, across a ravine somewhere around 250 yards away, we saw a four-point buck mule deer and a two-pointer.

"Want him, Jack?" I asked.

129

"No; I want the big guy on the mountain!"

It was the first chance I'd had to bag a far-north mule deer without disturbing game higher up on the "must" list, so I got quietly off the horse, pulled the .270 out of the scabbard, and sat down. The two bucks continued to stare at us. The crosshairs came to rest low behind the buck's foreleg, and when I finished the squeeze, he leaped into the air, then dropped from sight. We found him where he had fallen. The Silvertip had taken him about an inch behind the heart.

He was a welcome addition to the larder, since we had finished devouring our mountain mutton and we couldn't get too enthusiastic about moose and caribou. While the others rode on, I dressed him, propped open the belly cavity with a stick, and marked the spot with a handkerchief so I could bring him to camp in the morning.

That night the creeks froze solid, but it warmed up when the sun was well in the sky. Isaac and I rode over to skin and quarter my buck. We could see Jack's big buck – still feeding quietly above timberline on Coffin Top, about where I had jumped him the previous day.

When Isaac and I got into camp with the buck, Jack and Roy had cooked up a plot. They would go up the mountain to the big buck's range, while Isaac and I stayed in camp to act as a signal corps. We would be able to see the buck whenever he was in one of the little open glades between patches of shin-tangle, whereas he would be out of their sight. Whenever we saw the men looking down, we'd signal the buck's whereabouts with a towel.

About 4 o'clock they pulled out, and shortly afterward we saw the big buck come out in the open to feed. Presently, we saw the hunters moving half a mile below and signaled that the buck was above them. I believe that hunt was the most exciting I have ever been on, even though I hunted by proxy and was more than a mile from the game. Guided by our signals, the hunters gradually moved closer to the feeding buck, until finally they were separated only by 100 yards of those thick timberline trees.

Then the buck must have heard them, for he ran up toward the coffin on the very top of the mountain. Unaware that their game had scrammed, Jack and Roy still sneaked through the timber. Finally, we saw Jack look down toward camp with the glasses and we signaled frantically. The hunters ran out, and through the glasses we saw Jack flop to a prone position. The buck was now at least 600, probably 700, yards away – a shot so long as to be almost hopeless.

Then we saw the buck stagger. Presently, we heard the boom of the .270 and the plop of the striking bullet. Three more shots were misses, then the fifth knocked the buck flat. But he was up again and moving off. I knew that Jack had gone up with the magazine and chamber of his rifle full, but with no other cartridges. That meant he had only one left, and the suspense almost killed me. I could see the tiny gray figures of the two hunters. Closer and closer they came. Finally the buck sank down and lay still – and the roar of the .270, when it reached us, came almost as an anticlimax.

An hour later, just as dusk gave way to darkness, Roy and Jack came riding in with a very fine mule deer head, a hind quarter, and two backstraps. They both wore grins at least six inches wide.

The next day when we rode off with the packtrain, Jack looked back at the mountain, practically with tears in his eyes.

"Well," he said, "it's good-by to Coffin Top. But believe me, that mountain doesn't owe us anything!"

THE MYSTERIOUS FANNIN

This story once more finds O'Connor and his son, Brad, in the Far North, where they pursue a cross between the Dall and Stone sheep, known as the Fannin. Jack loved hunting new species or tracking down rumored ones in remote, exotic terrain.
January, 1952

My old pal Watson Smarch, crack Yukon Indian bushman and sheep hunter, appeared quietly at the door of the tent. In his eye was a strangely restless and triumphant gleam.

"Got your spotting scope handy?" he asked quietly. "I think I have found some sheep."

The effect was much as if he'd walked into a fraternity-house living room to announce that Liz Taylor in the role of Lady Godiva was just going by outside on a white horse.

My three neophyte sheep-hunting companions almost threw bones out of joint in their haste to rubberneck. Because he was the youngest, the most agile, and the nearest to the flap, my 18-year-old son Bradford disappeared, like the magician's white rabbit, in a puff of dust. Vernon Speer was right behind him. Even Doc Braddock, who had wasted 40 years doing overhaul jobs on the human anatomy and was taking his first sheep hunt at 70, whipped out of the tent like a man of 21 and almost took half of it with him.

"Where?" all three chorused like a singing-sister act in a nightclub.

"You needn't knock me down and run over me," Watson said plaintively. "If those are sheep instead of white rocks, they are six or seven miles away and they won't run off for a few minutes. All I can see are some white dots over on Sawtooth Mountain. They look like sheep to me."

I dug into a pack pannier and got out the 20X spotting scope and stand. When Watson and I went out to set it up, Vernon, Doc, and Bradford were lined up like kids at a knothole when a baseball game was going on. While they breathed down his neck, Watson trained the scope carefully, focused it, then took a long, long look.

"Yeah," he said. "Sheep, all right. They look like ewes."

"I'll be damned," Doc said after he'd taken a look through the scope. "I've seen them now, those wonderful white sheep. I hope I'm lucky enough to get one."

"You'll get one all right," Watson said as calmly as if Doc's ram was already hung up. "Our motto is: 'we see 'em, we get 'em.'" Then he winked at me.

Until the sun went down in crimson glory behind the great Coast Range to the west and the light on Sawtooth grew so dim we could no longer see, Watson and I moved the spotting scope around to find sheep. We saw about 30, tiny miniatures that through the gray haze of evening looked as if they were pasted on the side of the blue mountain. Some were plainly ewes because they were accompanied by even smaller sheep. Some, we thought hopefully, might be rams. Seeing any sheep at all was good for our spirits.

*N*ext morning the first person to get to the spotting scope was Doc. He was always finding sheep – some feeding, some lying down. Every time he spotted a new bunch he'd say, "You can see these very plainly. By George, if I don't see another thing on this whole trip, this is worth the price of admission!"

It took no very astute observer to realize that Doc would practically give his right arm for a ram – and his left arm for a grizzly. He'd lived half of his 70 years in Idaho's big game country. He had knocked over many whitetail and mule deer, elk, black bear, and goats. He had even shot moose in southern British Columbia. But all this was new to him.

Exactly what kind of sheep we'd find, we did not know, because we were pioneering an area new to this generation of trophy hunters. During the winter of 1950-51, the four of us – Dr. E.G. Braddock, retired surgeon; Vernon Speer, bullet manufacturer; my son Bradford; and I – had decided to hunt the section east of the old gold-mining town of Atlin, British Columbia, which is just south of the Yukon border and east of the

Alaska Panhandle. After a lot of correspondence, we had engaged a Yukon outfit with two British Columbia guides. We arranged a tentative route by drawing lines on a map, but the route proved unfeasible because, as we discovered on the trip, the map did not show such things as muskegs, neglected to put in such minor barriers as lakes that barred our way, and even had some of the marked trails cockeyed.

We jumped off by the way of Vancouver, on a luxurious Canadian National steamship for Skagway, Alaska, where we took the narrow-gauge White Pass & Yukon Railway to Whitehorse. There we met our outfitter and went by truck to the spot where we met the packtrain and took off into the pathless mountains. This is the first report of what we found and where we went in this new country.

Many years ago Bryan Williams, who had been head of the British Columbia Game Department, outfitted from Atlin, but he had hunted much farther south and east. Another outfitter named John Nolan took a few parties out in the 1920s but had then switched to mining. So far as I know, for over a quarter of a century no American dude hunters had been in this neck of the woods.

And even our guides knew little about it. George, the head guide, had never hunted in it. Neither had Watson Smarch, who had gone along as a friend, adviser, and horse wrangler because he was a pal of mine of years' standing. Only Harry Johnson, the other British Columbia guide, knew something about it – and he hadn't been in it since he became enamored of an American uniform and joined the United States Army at Skagway in 1940. Once, years before, he had climbed Sawtooth from the other side with a couple of pack dogs. He had shot two sheep and had taken the meat to Atlin with the innocent purpose of selling it for an honest dollar. The mounties grabbed him, confiscated the meat, and fined him ten dollars, so his memories of the country were on the sour side.

*P*resumably the sheep were the mysterious Fannins, that strange cross between the snow-white Dall and the black Stone. These crossbreeds are found in a long belt of wild, rugged country – beginning at the edge of the Coast Range and running along the British Columbia-Yukon border south of the great Yukon River – that is seldom disturbed except by an occasional trapper or prospector. Over much of it, willows and buckbrush grow higher than your head and when you climb the lower slopes of a mountain, you sink in moss to your knees. No one outfits in the great Pelly Range, in the Yukon, where Watson and I first bumped into each other. Few Fannin sheep have ever seen a hunter or heard a rifle shot – all of which may explain why trophy rooms are not exactly crowded with Fannin rams.

Once, when Atlin was a roaring, booming gold camp that flowered in the wake of the 1897 rush to the Klondike, the game of the section took a beating. But that was long ago. Atlin is now almost a ghost town. Its principal hotel is a bat roost, grass grows in the streets, and the big lake steamers that once carried goods in and gold out, are tied up and decaying along the shore.

It was several days after locating the sheep on Sawtooth before we got around to taking a crack at them. We exhausted the possibilities of closer mountains first, without seeing track nor hair, then moved camp to a big open meadow about three miles from the base of Sawtooth.

Hardly had we set up camp before we had the spotting scope out. Our sheep did not fail us. At one time we had an even dozen in the field of view, but even though they were now about three miles away instead of seven or eight, it was difficult to tell much about them. However, on some we could see the dark, saddle-shape markings that explain the Fannin's nickname – saddleback – and could almost kid ourselves that we saw horns as well.

The mountain looked rough and rocky, so steep that an agile man would do well to climb it afoot. One end, though, looked better – so much better that getting horses up it seemed feasible. If Doc was to get a crack at a ram, a husky horse would have to do most of the leg work.

So the next morning we all took off for the mountain. We floundered through the three miles of muskeg meadow that separated our camp from the base, then began the climb. We went over downed timber, over rocks, through willows and buckbrush, working our way higher and higher until at last we emerged right at timberline on Sawtooth's lofty shoulder. Ptarmigan squawked and clattered as we blundered into a flock. Hoary marmots whistled at us from a rockslide across the canyon. We could look down now, see our yellow muskeg meadow spotted with little blue lakes, our tents white dots against purple-black timber. All around us the grass was rich and green and alpine flowers bloomed white and yellow and purple in sleek green upland meadows in those last fair and lovely days of the dying summer.

As I dismounted to tie my horse to a stunted fir, I found myself beside Doc. His eyes were shining and his nostrils were dilated like those of a race horse at the starting post.

"I know why you're nuts about sheep hunting now," he told me. "It's the country. I've never seen anything so beautiful in my life. If I get a ram, I'll be willing to forget the grizzly."

He had hardly spoken when George climbed up the slope a few feet to poke his head over a rise. He fell back as if shot.

"Sheep!" he hissed.

Sheep indeed! We were in a sheep heaven. Directly above us, seven ewes and five lambs grazed unconcernedly. To the right were three young rams. Up toward the peaks we could see other sheep. All around us were tracks and droppings, and a few yards away a narrow sheep trail had, through centuries of use, been beaten deep into the ground.

We all got out binoculars and feasted our eyes on the mysterious Fannins in their native range. Some seemed snow-white except for black tails, others had not only black tails but distinct gray saddles, and some of the lightest ewes had the darkest lambs.

Doc, Brad, and I were watching sheep when George and Watson, who had gone to do some scouting, came quietly back.

"Doc," George said, "we've found you a fairly good ram. Take a look at him, and if you want him, he's your meat!"

Doc jumped up with speed that belied his 70 years. "Where is he?"

We all got down on hands and knees and inched along out of sight for perhaps a quarter of a mile. Then we peeked over a little rise to see the ram.

He was lying on a rocky knob, bright, alert, as beautiful as an idealized ram in a painting. On each side was a smaller ram to give balance to the composition. I can still see the picture – that beautiful ram with his golden horns, his snowy head and neck, and his brown saddle, gleaming in silhouette against the fantastically blue sky. On each side were the smaller rams, like retainers around a king.

"Want him, Doc?" George asked.

"Sure!" said Doc.

"Well," said George, "we'll have to go the long way around, but we can get to within shooting distance without much climbing."

137

So Doc, George, and Vernon took off. Brad, Watson, Harry, and I lay there just under the ridge half a mile from the rams. We had ringside seats.

*B*elow us was a little basin filled with arctic willow, and from it came the gentle, mysterious trickle of tiny snow-fed streams. In protest against our presence, the flock of ptarmigan that lived there cackled and muttered and once one of them flew so close to Bradford's head that he could have caught it if he had only seen it coming.

The young rams over to our right got filled up and minced up the slope to a rocky spot where they felt it was safe to lie down. There, they made themselves comfortable, chewed their cuds, and looked over the vast and lovely country below. The ewes and lambs we had first seen paraded past us about 400 yards away and disappeared over a saddle.

One of the larger rams we were watching got bored, climbed down from the rock, and fed a little. Watson went to sleep and began to snore.

I wondered if our companions had seen another and fancier bunch of rams and had given up their stalk on these. Time passed. I closed my eyes as I lay there on the ridge, voluptuously warm in the sun, and probably I dozed off. When I opened my eyes and looked again, the ram Doc was after had left his perch on the rock.

I punched Watson, who jumped as if a yellowjacket had stung him. "You've been asleep," I said.

"No," he said. "Just resting."

"Doc's ram has left the rock."

I think he's still around. Probably feeding on the other side."

Another half-hour passed. Brad began to grumble. He hadn't waited 70 years to do his first sheep hunting, but he had waited 18 and that was a long time to him. He wanted to get going.

Then, as I watched, the ram came into sight again, back to his original rock. Then one of his pals showed up beside him.

*S*uddenly a rifle cracked there in the thin air of the lonely mountain. We saw the ram lurch to his feet and stand weaving for a moment. The rifle cracked again and he went down. Then we saw Doc, Vernon, and George – little black specks on an outcrop beyond. The two other rams trotted off to the right. One had a flesh wound on his left shoulder. Evidently one of Doc's bullets had passed through the larger ram, then ricocheted on a rock and nicked this second sheep. We watched him carefully. No bone was broken, and he seemed destined to recover.

When we got over to congratulate Doc, George had already skinned the head out. The ram was about six years old, sleek, fat, and handsome. His saddle was a dark gray-brown; his head and neck were white except around his eyes and (faintly) on the bridge of his nose.

"Well," said Doc, "what do you think of him?"

"Pretty ram," I answered, "but of course I have seen bigger."

"I'll bet you've never seen a bigger ram killed by a man 70 years old!"

And he was dead right, because I hadn't – and never expected to.

SALMON RIVER WHITETAIL

In today's world, in which whitetails have become commonplace over much of the country, it seems remarkable that Jack did not take a northern deer until quite late in his career. In this lengthy account, he expands his list of trophy species during a hunt with Brad and Eleanor on the Salmon River in Idaho. February, 1972

The northern variety of the whitetail deer in its various forms is the most widely distributed big game animal in the United States. Found from Maine to Oregon, it furnishes more sport to hunters than any other big game animal and is responsible for the sale of more rifles and ammunition for the manufacturers and more telescopic sights for the scopemakers. And, because sportsmen buy licenses to hunt it, the money it brings in keeps most game departments functioning.

But unil recently the northern whitetail was to me as strange a trophy as the greater kudu, the desert bighorn, and the ibex are to most hunters. I have hunted all of these fine animals and others just as exotic, but the northern whitetail had always eluded me.

Of all the varieties of northern whitetails, the one least known is the one found in the Northwest. The more plentiful mule deer and the elk sell the out-of-state licenses and get the publicity. In fact, many hunters do not even realize that some of the largest whitetail deer in North America and some of the best trophies come from Idaho, Washington, Montana, and Oregon, and from the Canadian province of British Columbia.

These northwestern whitetails are probably just about as heavy as the famous whitetails of Maine, and their heads compare favorably with those of whitetails shot anywhere. The No. 4 listing in the 1964 edition of *Records of North American Big Game* is a whitetail shot in Flathead County, Montana, in 1963, and I have seen handsome and very large antlers nailed to barns and garages and poorly mounted on walls of backwoods bars and country stores. Mostly, these big whitetails are taken not by trophy hunters, but by backswoodsmen and farmers who are after meat. These whitetails of the Northwest are classified *Odocoileus virginianus ochrourus*.

I grew up in the Southwest, where I hunted Coues' whitetail. I have hunted these fine deer in Arizona, in Sonora, and in the Big Bend of Texas, and I have taken many handsome bucks of this diminutive species. Such small skill as I have at hitting running game I owe to the Arizona jackrabbit and the Arizona whitetail. I have also shot the small but quite different Texas whitetail found around San Antonio. But a good northern whitetail was one of the few major North American trophies I did not have.

I had never laid eyes on a northern whitetail until I moved from Arizona to Idaho more than 20 years ago, and then it took me about three years to see one. I'll never forget the first one I saw. I was hunting pheasants with a wonderful Brittany spaniel named Mike. He had been cruising through a field of rich golden wheat stubble when he went on point at the edge of a grassy swale. I thought he had pinned a cock pheasant, but when I got up to him, he looked at me out of the corner of his eye and wore the sneaky expression he assumed when he was doing something he knew he should not do.

I picked up a stone to flush whatever it was, and threw it at the spot in the grass where Mike's nose was pointed. Out burst a little whitetail doe. Most dogs are convinced that they have been born to be deer and rabbit hounds, but Mike almost fell backward in surprise.

Another time Mike hauled up on the edge of a brushy draw on solid point. I walked in, kicked the brush. A pair of cackling roosters came barreling out. I shot, dropped one of them, was about to take the other when a big whitetail buck sailed out of the brush and headed across the stubble toward a patch of woods. For the rest of the bird season, which mostly at the time ran concurrently with the deer season, I carried a couple of rifled slugs in my pants pocket so that if I jumped another whitetail, I could jerk out a shotshell and slam one loaded with a slug into the chamber. But the news must have got around. I never saw a buck.

A farmer I knew told me he just about had a big whitetail buck tied up for me. He said that the old boy lived in a canyon that bounded one of his wheatfields. That buck fed on wheat all summer and in the fall feasted on the sweet, stunted little apples that fell in an abandoned orchard in one corner of his place.

So I spent about ten days hunting him off and on during the season. His tracks were everywhere – in the orchard, in the wheat stubble, along the deer and cattle trails among the brush and trees, and on the bank of the little little trout stream that ran through the bottom of the canyon.

Keeping the wind in my favor, I still-hunted cautiously and quietly along the trails, taking a few steps, stopping, listening, watching. Once I heard something moving quietly off through thick brush, and I found his bed below a ledge in a warm spot where the sun had melted the frost off the grass. Another time I heard a crash below me and caught a glimpse of his white flag flying. I sat for hours with my back to a tree, waiting for him to show up. He didn't.

"I can't understand why you can't see that buck," my farmer friend said. "I seen him yesterday when I was looking for a stray cow, and Bill Jones seen him from his pickup when he was coming back from getting the mail four or five days ago. Said he wasn't a danged bit wild; stood there lookin' at him. He could have hit him with a slingshot."

*I*n the Northwest, at least in areas with which I am familiar, whitetails are found lower than the mule deer, on the brushy hillsides near wheatfields, and in the wooded riverbottoms back in the elk mountains. They are bold but furtive, and they'll live all summer in a farmer's woodlot.

Some of them grow to be very large. I once knew a man who ran a meat locker in Lewiston, Idaho, my home town. He told me that the heaviest buck ever weighed at his plant was a whitetail. As I now remember, he said its field-dressed weight was around 335 pounds. I have heard of whitetails in Washington as well as Idaho that were about as heavy. I have never seen a deer of any sort that I thought would dress out at anything like 300 pounds, but now and then, one undoubtedly turns out to be that heavy.

I started closing in on my first Northwestern whitetail in the fall of 1969 when my wife and I drove to the ranch of our friend Dave Chrisensen on the Salmon River downstream from Riggins, Idaho. Dave operates an elk-hunting camp on Moose Creek in the Selway Wilderness Area and lives most of the year on the beautiful Salmon River ranch. When I first knew the elk-hunting camp, it was Moose Creek Lodge, a luxurious bit of civilization out in the wilderness. A hunter could go out after elk all day and return at night to a drink around a fireplace, a good meal served with silver and linen, a hot shower, and a sound sleep on an inner-spring mattress. But the area was declared a wilderness. The federal government bought the lodge and burned it down. Now in the fall, Dave's clients fly in to a U.S. Forest Service landing strip a few miles away and hunt elk from a comfortable tent camp near the spot where the lodge used to be. I have shot five-, six-, and seven-point elk out of Moose Creek. Dave and his father Ken took the money they got from the sale of the lodge and their land, and put it into the Salmon River ranch.

As my wife and I drove in that November day in '69, we saw a whitetail buck in a field a mile or so from the ranchhouse. Not long afterward we saw some whitetail does and fawns.

"You must have a lot of whitetails around here," I said when Dave came out to meet us.

"Plenty," he told me. "The whitetails are mostly low down along the creek and in the brushy draws that run into it. The mule deer are higher."

The season around Dave's place was closed then, so my wife and I had to forgo the whitetails. We hunted mule deer in another management area about 20 miles away. But we made a promise to take a run at the whitetails.

Along in August, 1971, Dave called me.

"You haven't forgotten our date to hunt whitetails?" he asked. "No? Well, the season opens October second. Drive down the afternoon of the first and we'll have at them."

My son Bradford, who is outdoor editor of the *Seattle Times* and who is a long-time pal of Dave Christensen and his wife Ann, flew from Seattle and joined us on the drive to the ranch.

One of Dave's successful elk hunters from Moose Creek had come down to the Salmon to try for a deer, and three other hunters who were on their way into Moose Creek for elk were camped down the creek a mile or so from the ranchhouse.

The strategy was simple. Eleanor, Bradford, and I, accompanied by a guide named Stan Rock, would climb about 1,000 feet above the ranch near the head of a canyon that carried a little stream that ran into Dave's creek. After giving us time to get into position, Dave would walk up the canyon on a deer-and-cattle trail that ran along the bottom. There were whitetails and mule deer in those canyons, and with luck we should get some shooting.

It was dark and chilly when we started out, and the sun was not up when we arrived near the head of the canyon. We were high on a grassy ridge. The canyon dropped sharply below us, and the bottom was a tangle of trees and brush. The far side of the canyon was steep, mostly rocks with a few low bushes and sparse grass.

Eleanor had gone on the brink of the canyon. Bradford was 20 feet or so to her left. I was in the process of filling up the magazine of an old pet .270 I had used from northern British Columbia to Botswana and Iran. It was a pre-1964 Winchester Model 70 Feather-weight stocked in plain but hard Franch walnut by Al Biesen of Spokane and fitted with a Leupold 4X scope on the now-obsolete Tilden mount. It has the original Winchester barrel with the original Featherweight contour. The only thing Biesen did to the metal was to put the release lever for the hinged floorplate in the forward portion of the trigger guard and checker the bolt knob.

This is a terrific rifle. I bought it from the Erb Hardware Company of Lewiston, Idaho. Year after year it holds its point of impact. Carry it in a saddle scabbard. Bounce it around in a hunting car on safari, ship it a few thousand miles by air, let it get rained on for hours in a Scotch deer forest, shoot it at sea-level or at 10,000 feet, in the crackling heat of the Kalahari Desert or under the glaciers in the sub-arctic, Stone sheep country of British Columbia, and it always lays them in the same place. It is also one of those rare light sporters that will group into a minute of angle – if I am using good bullets and do my part.

I had just finished slipping the last cartridge into the chamber and putting on the safety when Eleanor, who has eyes like an eagle, said, "Deer . . . two deer. The lower one's a buck."

Two deer were scooting up the far side of the canyon about 225 to 250 yards away. Both were waving big white tails. I could dimly make out antlers on the lower one.

The sight of those flaunting flags across the canyon made me shed 25 years. Once again I was back in my favorite Calelo Hills along the Mexican border of southern Arizona, where I had some small reputation among the local yeomanry of being a fair hand on running whitetails. I sat down quickly, put the intersection of the crosswires just to the left of the buck's head for lead, and squeezed the trigger. So far as results went, it was almost as spectacular as a brain shot on an elephant. The buck fell, started rolling, and tumbled clear out of sight into the brush and timber at the bottom of the canyon.

"Some shot!" said Bradford.

145

The buck was a big one. It had long brow points and four points on each beam – a four-pointer Western count, a 10-point Eastern count. He had been hit rather far back through the lungs. Down there in that narrow canyon, it was so dark that the exposure meter said half-a-second at F.2 would be about right. Since we had no flash, good pictures under those conditions were impossible. Later, someone would come out from the ranch with a packhorse and get him.

By now the sun was up and bright, and while the others went along around the head of the canyon where I had shot the buck and to the head of the next, I stayed behind admiring the scenery. Far below, the little creek glistened through the timber along its banks and as it twisted through the meadows. The meadows were still green, the pines dark and somber, but along the creek, cottonwoods and willows were shimmering gold, and patches of crimson sumac blazed on the hillsides.

Up in the high country at the head of the creek, ridges where the Salmon River elk ran, an early storm had frosted the dark timber with snow. Far below against the green of a pasture I saw some moving black dots. The glasses showed me I was looking at a feeding flock of wild turkeys.

Clear down in the bottom of the main canyon I heard a fusillade of shots. I made a mental note that they were probably fired by the Californians who were going to try for deer before they went in to Moose Creek for elk. I hurried to catch up with the other O'Connors, who were out of sight over a ridge.

I heard two quick shots. Then I saw Eleanor and Bradford, rifles in hand, sitting on the hillside looking down.

"Get anything?" I asked.

"Buck mule deer, sort of a collaboration," Bradford said.

"The heck it was," Eleanor said. "I shot behind it and then Bradford dumped it. See? It's lying down there on the road."

The glasses showed me a young buck mule deer close to 300 yards away.

When we returned to the ranchhouse, we found that the Californians had taken three whitetail bucks out of a herd of eight. The largest had heavy antlers with three points and a brow tine on each side. Though their measurements were the same as those of my deer, this buck appeared to be heavier. The next buck was somewhat smaller than mine and the third was a youngster.

Soon a packhorse came in with my buck. He and the largest buck shot by the Californians measured 18 inches in a straight line from the top of the shoulder to the bottom of the brisket. Both were fat and in fine condition. We had no means of weighing them, but I have weighed many mule deer with the same measurements and they have weighed between 185 and 195 pounds. These two whitetail bucks were every bit as large as four-point mule deer bucks.

I was interested in comparing them to the Arizona whitetails I had hunted so long. They were just about twice as large, since an average large, mature Arizona whitetail will weigh from 90 to 110 pounds. As is true among Arizona whitetails, the top of the tails of the old bucks is a grizzled brown, whereas the upper portion of the tails of the young bucks is bright orange. Oddly, the tails of these big bucks looked to be the same size as those of their southern cousins.

The beams of my buck's antlers were a bit over 23 inches long, and the inside spread was 18 inches. I have never shot an Arizona whitetail with beams anything like that long, but I did take one that had a 20-inch spread. Though the Northwestern whitetail is twice as heavy as his Southwestern cousin, his antlers aren't twice as large.

Sad to say, my underprivileged wife didn't get another shot. We drove up a precarious ranch road late that afternoon and early next morning when the deer should have been moving. We hunted the heads of several canyons and glassed the points and ridges, but all we saw were does and fawns. The bucks had gotten the message.

ANTELOPE APLENTY

Hunting Anderson Mesa in his familiar Arizona stomping grounds, O'Connor and some friends make a hunt during the war years that brings striking success. This piece was written shortly before he resigned his position at the University of Arizona and took a full-time position with Outdoor Life. *It was one of his first articles to appear after leaving academia. May, 1945.*

Although we traveled 30 miles across some of the best antelope country in North America, we saw not an antelope. In past years that drive across central Arizona's beautiful Anderson Mesa would have shown a thousand, spotting the rolling grasslands with white rumps and bellies. Now not one – not a fawn.

My wife and I were in the lead car, as I knew the country well. Now and then, as we stopped to open a gate, we were joined by the rest of my party, and I could see that they were profoundly skeptical of the tales I had told them of the great pronghorn bucks of Anderson Mesa. Their lower lips were hanging down so far they could step on them without half trying. Things lightened a bit when we stopped and talked to a couple of other hunters who were making camp. They actually had seen a couple of antelope from the road. Well, prospects didn't look hopeless after all.

Shortly after noon we checked into the fly camp, where about 30 other hunters had pitched tents; and not long after that Carroll, Al, and I started out for a scout, leaving Al's wife and mine to do the mysterious little things which women always like to do around camp and which come under the head of "creating a homelike atmosphere."

The antelope, the dope had it, were in the timber, such as it was – scattered evergreens that spotted rolling yellow grasslands. A mile from camp we turned off the road and edged the station wagon over volcanic boulders toward a tank where we planned to park before scouting the ridges.

Suddenly a buck antelope walked out of the cedars at the head of

149

the wide draw and stood staring at us 300 yards away. A doe joined him, then another and smaller buck, a second doe, and two fawns. It was evidently a reception committee. Out came three pairs of glasses, and we looked them over. The first buck had a very fair head, and none of the pronghorns seemed alarmed. But antelope season wouldn't open until next morning.

When we got out of the car, the herd suddenly took fright and ran. Anyone who hasn't seen an antelope go into high gear has missed one of the most beautiful sights in the world. They stretch out in a series of long, low, elastic bounds. And in less than 100 yards they can hit their top speed of close to 60 miles-per-hour.

In the next few minutes we saw a dozen other antelope. One herd of five big bucks walked single file behind an intermittent screen of junipers, never seeing us, and less than 100 yards away. Two more bucks watched us from the top of a ridge, then wheeled and ran along the skyline when they didn't like our looks. In the middle of a big flat we spotted a lone buck with an enormous head. Other hunters were scouting that stretch of country; so, antelope-like, he had put all the space he could between himself and danger, trusting to his marvelous speed in an emergency.

After our five-mile circuit was complete, Al and Carroll thought they knew where they wanted to hunt antelope come dawn – right where we had scouted. But knowing the mesa of old, I wanted first to look over the section around Hay Lake, where I had always seen lots of bucks, big ones.

On our way there we saw not an antelope from the road, and Al and Carroll were more than ever convinced that they knew where they wanted to hunt. Seven miles from camp we turned the car off the road, walked about half a mile over a ridge – and stopped short. Below us lay a great valley, rimmed with fairly thick timber, and literally spotted with antelope. About 300 hundred yards away a big buck stood guard over half a dozen does and fawns. Farther on, two big bucks lay at the edge of the timber. About 40 in all were in sight when we topped the ridge, and even as we watched through the glasses, others came leisurely out of the timber, picked us up with their telescopic eyes, and watched us calmly.

And those Hay Lake bucks were for the most part big ones, with heads that would go in the record book!

We made a long circle around the west side of the valley, constantly picking up more antelope with the glasses. Then, about a mile from the car, three does suddenly popped their heads over a ridge, watched us for a moment, and disappeared. Thinking there might be bucks with them, we followed to where we could see two herds of does and fawns, each guarded by a big buck. They stopped a couple of hundred yards away, watched us for a moment, and then put on steam and circled around us. Before we got back to the car we had seen 50 more. We had also evolved a plan. The next morning, Carroll was to go up the east side of the big valley along the edge of the timber. Al and Marion, his wife, would take the west side. My wife and I would then go up about a mile and hunt back toward our friends.

At 4:15 we were up, and with the first gray of dawn we were out in the Hay Lake country, moving toward our objectives. The sky was beginning to silver, but it was still too dark to see well, and even though it was September, it was cold there at 7,000 feet. My wife and I were moving toward the ridge from which we had seen the antelope in the valley below when I spied a group of white forms slipping silently along just below the skyline.

"Antelope," I told Eleanor. "If it's one of the bunches we saw last night, there's a good buck in it."

I grabbed the glasses hanging around my neck, hoping their extra light-gathering power would enable me to make out horns. But I hadn't seen anything except those ghostly white rump patches moving like spooks in the gray dawn when Eleanor's .257 went off beside me and I heard the plop of a high-speed bullet hitting flesh.

"What's the idea?" quoth I. "I'll bet you've hit a doe. You couldn't see anything."

"I have not!" she said positively. "I got a big buck!"

"How could you see horns?"

"I just lay down so I could see his head against the skyline."

It was as simple as that. She could see that big buck's head silhouetted against the silvering sky from the prone position, so she lowered her rifle until the post in the scope disappeared and then she touched it off. The buck was a beauty, with a massive base, long perfect prongs, a well-curved beam of 15$^{1}/_{2}$ inches, and tips white and clear as glass. He had been struck in the spine and was, of course, helpless. Another shot finished him.

Half a mile down the valley I heard a rattle of musketry and knew that Al and Marion were getting shooting. I hadn't fired a shot, so you can imagine the speed with which I dressed that buck.

I hung the antelope in a tree and, leaving my wife to her own devices, hotfooted it up to the ridge where I could see down into the wide valley. Not a pronghorn was in sight. The sun came up as I sat there on the ridge using the glasses in hope of picking up some antelope. Below me the grasslands were rich yellow and the cedars on the ridges were almost black. To the south I could see the pale blue line that was the great Mogollon Plateau, a land of elk, mule deer, and wild turkey, and the summer range of many bands of antelope. Now and then, as I sat there, I heard a shot, mostly very far away. One, just one, came from the direction where Carroll was to hunt, and I suspected that he had his buck.

Then, across the valley, two buck antelope and three does walked out of the cedars into the open. They were in no particular hurry; but their air showed that they were jittery and felt that all this rifle fire boded them no good. They stood there, heads up, all-seeing eyes scanning the country, a beautiful sight through the crystal-clear lenses of my fine 8X glasses. One of the bucks was a good one with a 15- or 16-inch head.

They were around 500 yards away, but I squirmed down among the volcanic rocks into what was a passable prone position, eased off the safety of my .270, got into the sling, and held well above the back of the larger buck. I was satisfied with the way I had touched off – but nothing happened. I heard no bullet hit, saw not dust, no flinching. However, every antelope's eye was upon me. Then the big buck turned and trotted back into the cedars.

The smaller buck stood there facing me for a moment, then turned broadside and lowered his head to grab a mouthful of weed. I didn't particularly want that buck, but I was irked that I had taken a shot with a good long-range rifle and couldn't even see any evidence of where my bullet had landed. Using exactly the same hold, I put the top of the post well above the second buck's back and squeezed. Again nothing happened – no sound of a striking bullet, no dust, nothing. The buck stood there looking at me, and that was that.

"Oh, to heck with it!" I said to myself. "I don't want that buck anyway, and I'm glad I missed him."

Just then the buck fell over. The does immediately turned tail and fled into the timber. I paced off the distance to the place where the buck lay. It was 535 paces, about one-third of which took me downhill and two-thirds on the level over volcanic boulders – probably something short of 500 yards. The bullet, a Winchester 130-grain Silvertip, had struck the buck low and just behind the shoulder. Then it had taken off one of the big veins about an inch from the heart, and finally expanded to about .40 caliber on the far side. At that distance the velocity had fallen off greatly, and the buck had bled to death as he stood there looking at me.

As I was dressing him I heard a whoop and Al hove into view. Marion had her buck, he told me, but as yet he had not connected. Together we carried my buck up to the ridge to the tree where Marion sat gloating. That buck was her first head of big game and she was a very happy woman. The first shot from her 7mm. had broken a hind leg and the second had hit the animal in the chest, killing instantly.

Far across the valley then, at the edge of the cedars, I saw a figure emerge. The glasses told me it was Carroll, lugging the head of a buck antelope. Presently he joined us. My hunch had been correct. That one shot I had heard had been his – and it had done the business. Shortly after sunup he had seen three bucks feeding along through the cedars and had stalked to within 200 yards of them; and at that distance, with Carroll behind the rifle, one shot is plenty. The head was a massive 16-incher, with an exceptionally large base, so pretty that he had to annex it right away.

I went back with him to where the carcass lay and we carried it to the rendezvous under the tree. Not bad. It was still well before noon, and five of us had four bucks. We held a council of war then. The rest of us were to return to camp and get things shipshape while Al stayed on to get his buck. I agreed to drive back to the place where the road crossed the valley and meet him at 5 o'clock.

When the appointed time came, I had skinned and quartered three bucks, eaten a large and satisfying lunch, and polished off a couple of bottles of beer. Eleanor and Marion were both fast asleep in the tent and I felt a bit drowsy myself. At the rendezvous, Al was not in sight. Far up the valley a doe and two fawn antelope were feeding nervously, while a couple of crows with the wind behind their tails blew swiftly across the blue and polished sky. The wind was chilly, but inside the station wagon it was warm and snug . . .

I must have pounded my ear for an hour when some sixth sense awakened me and I looked up the valley to see a lone figure gesticulating. It was Al, and when I had approached to within a couple of hundred yards I could see that he had a buck beside him, a fine one with a big 16-inch head.

He had seen worlds of antelope, he told me, mostly bucks, but the shooting had made them very jittery and he couldn't get within a quarter mile of any of them. Finally, he decided that instead of

153

hunting them he would let the antelope hunt him. So he hid in a little clump of cedars, and three bucks fed within range. He picked out the biggest, but as he swung his rifle around, they all started to run. His first shot with the 7mm. hit the antelope he wanted in the flank, quartered its body, and came through to rest in the neck.

Back at camp, we found that our luck had been typical rather than exceptional, for every one of the 30 hunters in that area had connected!

The next day we checked out. Literally dozens of heads worthy of inclusion in the record books had been taken, but nothing very close to the long-standing world record ($20^5/16$ inches in outside curve) was listed.

With gas and tires short, there won't be much hunting on the magic mesa for a while, and when peace comes, some of those plentiful 15-inchers may have added enough horn material to become the new No. 1 trophy. Anyway, I know of some hunters who are going back to find out!

STONE RAMS DON'T COME EASY

*O'Connor enjoyed some great
experiences in the Far North in the
years immediately after World War
II. This piece relives a demanding
but ultimately rewarding Stone
sheep hunt in British Columbia.
January, 1947*

A little after noon, two and a half days from the Alaska
Highway, the pack outfit scrambled a few hundred feet
almost straight down into Nevis Creek. Those two and a half days in
northern British Columbia had been tough going – brush, thick
jackpine, muskegs where the pack horses plunged and wallowed,
hillsides two feet deep in moss where every step was an effort, and
swarms of mosquitoes as large as robins and as ferocious as wolves.

After a cold summer, that wilderness area had turned
unseasonably warm. All day, as I led my horse through muskegs and
windfalls, I was miserably hot, and those first nights I roasted in my
down sleeping bag.

When I got a look at the steep cliffs and shale slides of Nevis
Creek, my bedraggled spirits began to lift. The canyon looked *sheepy*.
I have seen mountain rams in canyons just like it from Mexico to the
Yukon, and I hoped that I was to see my first Stone sheep –
something I had wanted to do all my life.

Frank Golata, the famous Dawson Creek, B.C. outfitter and Stone sheep guide, was leading the outfit and I was right behind him. Strung out behind were Doc Du Comb, my hunting companion; Johnnie the cook; and Mac the horse wrangler.

"This looks like sheep country to me!" I observed as we all drank from the cold, clear creek.

'It is," Frank assured me. "We ought to see some sheep today, but we're likely to see only ewes and lambs. The big old rams are probably higher up."

*N*ot long after that, I saw my first sheep tracks in the sand of the creek bottom, then sheep trails and beds in the steep shale slides of the canyon walls. As we traveled, the sheep tracks grew more plentiful, and we began to see wolf tracks too. Then, as we rounded a bend in the canyon, Frank held up his hand.

"Want to see your first Stone sheep?" he asked quietly.

Right down in the bottom of the canyon, at the mouth of a side creek that flowed into the Nevis, were about a dozen ewes and lambs, my first Stone sheep. As you probably know, they are close cousins of the snow white Dall sheep of the Yukon and Alaska; also of the Fannin group of Yukon sheep, sometimes known as saddlebacks.

Except for its comparatively small size and its different coloration, the Dall (*Ovis dalli dalli*) is rather like the Rocky Mountain bighorn, and both the Stone and the Fannin are usually classified as subspecies of the Dall. The Stone is considerably larger, however, and its color pattern resembles that of the bighorns farther south – though the dark areas are darker and the whites are whiter, so the contrast is more marked. Also, whereas the bighorn has a white "doughnut" on its rump, the Stone (as seen from behind) seems to be wearing ankle-length underdrawers.

At least, that is the picture I had fixed in my mind, but I knew that this distinction doesn't always hold good. For while the pure-white Dall is at one extreme and the contrasty Stone at the other, with the Fannin somewhere in between, the color variations shade off almost imperceptibly from one form into the other.

*H*aving heard Stones called "black" sheep and "blue" sheep, I was surprised to find how light were the ones I saw now. Their heads and necks were a light gray that was almost white, and their bodies were a medium gray with white bellies and rumps.

"I didn't expect them to be that light," I told Frank.

"The ewes and young rams are," he said, "but some of the

old rams get pretty black."

In the side canyon behind that first small bunch was a much larger herd of 50 or more sheep. A little later we came around another bend to surprise still another little group. Very accommodatingly, they scrambled up a bluff and stood on a small ridge looking at me while I photographed them at a range of not more than 50 yards.

The show wasn't yet over. After traveling another mile and seeing a few ewes and young rams scattered along the rugged canyon wall, we spotted a bunch of 11 rams bedded down on a point about 500 feet above us. I doubt if any of those wilderness rams had ever seen a man, and I am sure none of them had been shot at.

Even if they didn't know what we were, we must have looked interesting. A couple of them got to their feet to see us better, but most of them simply lay there in the beds they had pawed out of the shale, chewing their cuds and eyeing us in mild speculation. They were only about 300 yards away and knocking one of them off would not have been too difficult.

One had horns that would probably have measured more than 37 inches in length; but I hadn't come all that way for just a so-so ram. One that stood up had a wide spread and perfect points, but he too was on the small side. Right there in the bunch were rams that ranged in color from the typical Stone with the medium-gray face and neck to the Fannin type with faces that from a distance appeared to be almost snow-white.

Later that day Doc Du Comb saw a wolf chasing two rams on a slide. He shot at the wolf and missed, but saved the sheep. We were in Stone sheep country at last!

Our first day of hunting on the Bessa River was, however, practically a complete blank. All the sheep mountains in that country are tough. They were very high, and the campsites, where water and horses feed are available, are low. The mountains are so steep and so brushy on the lower slopes that it is impossible to use a horse even for the preliminary phases of sheep hunting. All this I discovered that first day, and it held true through the balance of the trip.

Frank, Doc, Mac, and I set out to tackle a mountain a couple of miles from camp. First we climbed through thick jackpine where we couldn't see more than 25 yards. Then we came to a willow jungle. Above that was a tangled mass of what the Yukon natives call bug brush. It was noon before we reached the moss and lichens at the very top. It was beautiful and exciting country, but all the sign and beds were old, and the only sheep we saw that day were about four miles away, bedded just below the crest of a flat-topped mountain. Weeks later we saw the same mountain from the other side at Richards Creek, and what looked like the same bunch of sheep lying on the same slide!

Several days had passed before we hit rams again – and then we saw plenty. We were camped on the Prophet River. It had rained the night before, but in the morning it cleared, and after waiting a couple of hours for the brush to dry, the four of us took out up the mountain. In three hours we were on top and had our glasses on rams. That day we must have seen around 40 – big ones, little ones, very dark Stone-type ones, Fannins with white heads and necks. About half a dozen had really respectable heads that might have gone 38 inches. A beautiful Fannin that would have seemed more at home in the Pelly Mountains of the Yukon tempted me, and Doc cast greedy eyes at a good black Stone. From the time we hit the top of that mountain until we plunged over the side to fight our way back to camp through the willows and spruce, we were constantly within sight of rams.

Our next stop was at Lapp Creek, the camp from which L.S. Chadwick, accompanied by Roy Hargreaves and Frank Golata, killed the world-record Stone sheep. That was great sheep country when Chadwick was there in 1936, but not a sheep did we see. The wolves had cleaned them out.

On the Muskwa, where we camped next after taking the pack outfit over one of the toughest passes in the northern Canadian Rockies, it was the same story. We saw a few rams there, and also a few ewes and lambs. None of the rams we saw, however, were in the top trophy class. Two hung around across the canyon from camp about a mile away. We kept a 20X spotting scope set up to watch them. One was a typical dark Stone; the other a Fannin with a head and neck as pure white as that of any Dall.

Evidently, what had happened was that the weather was changing. We had had some snow. The big rams were pulling out of their summer range and were on their way to the lower country to meet the ewes and lambs, go through the late-November and December mating season, and spend the winter there. Our getting first-rate rams depended on finding some spot where a good many were resting up for a few days on their irregular migration route.

One of my days at the head of the Muskwa stands out as just about the most uncomfortable day I have ever spent in the mountains. The previous day it had rained and snowed, but that day we could see a faint glimmer of light in the overcast sky. We managed to kid ourselves into believing it would clear, so Doc and Frank went upstream from camp to look over some high glacier country while Mac and I set out to explore a big basin downstream.

We climbed through the thickest mass of alpine fir I have ever seen, up a slope that was almost straight up and down. About noon we were on the rim of the opposite side of the basin. We drew a complete blank – a few old sheep tracks, a few caribou tracks, but not a glimpse of the animals that made them.

Then it started to rain, snow, and sleet – the darndest mixture of cold, wet stuff you ever saw. We fought our way back to camp through shin-tangle and willow. Every branch was dripping frigid moisture and the growth was so thick that a good part of the time our feet literally didn't touch the ground. Somewhere in that jungle I lost the lens covers on my scope-sighted rifle, and when we finally got back to camp, even the inside of the scope was wet.

A few days later we were back on the Prophet again, still hoping to find a bunch of big rams availing themselves of stop-over privileges on the long, leisurely journey to the winter range. After a week of overcast sky and occasional rains and light snows, we awoke one morning to heavy frost and a cloudless sky. All at once I began to feel lucky. The weather was right, and the law of averages was in my favor. My luck couldn't be *all* bad!

The frost still lay thick and cold on the grass when Frank and I started up the long, steep shoulder of the big mountain where we planned to make our climb, get above timberline, and hunt. At first we went through heavy black spruce, then through an aspen forest where golden leaves rained down and the sun silvered the white trunks, then we were in the willows. Just before we came out over the hump, we climbed up over a series of slick, grassy slopes and rock slides.

Once on top the going was much easier. The country was a series of hills on top of a mountain – steep hills thick with grass, moss, and lichen, with here and there a patch of dwarf willow not more than two feet high. Behind these lush alpine meadows loomed great black cliffs streaked with snow. It looked like fine ram country – food in the meadows, refuge in the cliffs.

We were barely on top when we began to see fresh ram tracks and droppings. We sat down, took out our binoculars, and almost at once we saw sheep a couple of miles away. From that distance they were only little dots, but we set up the spotting scope on the tripod, got them in it.

They were rams – five of them, all bedded along a ridge. The sun was high now and a good deal of mirage was running. Because of this, the rams looked through the 20X scope like a photograph so greatly enlarged that the grain in the negative shows. We could see one big ram right at the top of the ridge on the skyline, another a little below him to the right, two others toward the bottom of the ridge, and another at the left. Their heads all looked massive and they evidently were old rams. For a long time we lay there watching them, but the mirage grew worse instead of better. The only way we could really size them up was to get closer.

The wind was blowing up the mountain, so it did not offer any problem. The stalk would be long, but not difficult because we could keep behind intervening ridges until we could get where we wanted to be. The only rub was that there was no cover near the rams and any shot would have to be a long one.

Something more than an hour later we lay on top of a ridge about 500 yards from the rams and perhaps 500 feet above them. All were big fellows, but the one that took my eye was a dark ram with a heavy, broomed head and a close curl. Carrying those massive horns around had evidently made him weary, because most of the time he lay there with his chin flat on the ground to rest his neck muscles. Through the spotting scope the rams looked so close that I could actually see the annual rings on their horns. Every one of the rams would be an excellent trophy worthy of inclusion in the record book. Not one of them, however, would be near the top of the list.

"How do you like the fellow with the heavy broomed head?" I asked Frank finally.

"He's a dandy ram," he said. "He has a big base and heavy horns, but his head won't measure out. Those broomed heads never do."

"Do you think he'll go 38 inches?" I asked.

"Just about," he said.

"I think I'll try to take him," I decided. "He's a fine old ram and an absolutely typical Stone. I have always liked those close curls with broomed ends, because that's the way good bighorns are."

"Suit yourself." Frank said. "You might get a bigger one and you might not."

"My second ram will have to go more than 40 inches, and I'd like for him to be a Fannin," I whispered. "But I won't be ashamed of this fellow one little bit."

We could do one of several things. I could shoot from where we were. The country was open, and the chances were that in spite of the distance, I could cut the ram down before he got out of sight. However, I never like to take a long shot if I can get out of it. We could sneak quietly and in plain sight toward the rams, depending on the fact that they had not been disturbed and that wild sheep seldom expect danger from above. *Or* we could simply sit tight and wait for a break. The sun was dropping now, and it was getting along toward suppertime.

For another half-hour the rams fiddled around. Now and then one of them would get up, take a few mouthfuls of the light-colored lichen which the natives call caribou moss, and lie down again. Occasionally, one would look right at us, but because we stayed frozen, none of them grew alarmed. It was a long way back to camp, at least five miles of very tough going, and something would have to happen soon. We waited.

I was about to stand up and walk toward the rams as far as I could get, and then risk a running shot, when the ram I had chosen decided he had napped enough. He stood up, stretched, playfully butted one of his companions, and then started walking slowly up the ridge toward me.

Now and then he stopped for a bite of lichen, but he always continued up the ridge. Perhaps he remembered some especially lush place to graze. I dug my heels into the ground, got my left arm into a tight sling with my left hand hard against the front swivel. The old ram was less than 400 yards away now. In a little while he was less than 300. I could have shot him easily from there, but it looked as though he'd come closer. He did.

When he was about 200 yards away, he stopped and began to feed in earnest. I kept the crosshairs of the 4X scope low behind his shoulder and watched him. Just why I didn't shoot sooner, I do not know. Maybe being that close to taking my first Stone ram had given me buck fever. At any rate, I must have sat there for several minutes watching the big ram through the scope, seeing those crosshairs sharp and black against him.

When my finger finally took up that last ounce of pull, the ram went down as if he had been struck with a giant hammer. The 130-grain Winchester .270 bullet had made a pulp of the old boy's heart.

The other rams threw up their heads, got one good look at us, and left for parts unknown.

We went down to measure and photograph the big Stone. His

161

head would look good in any company. The curl was 39 inches, the circumference at base 15¹/₂ inches. He was very old, for his horns had 13 annual rings and were so weathered that they looked as if they belonged to an animal long dead. Most of his teeth were gone and those that were left in bad condition. He was fat, but I doubt if he would have survived another winter.

Since he was the first Stone ram I had ever examined, I was greatly interested in him. He was a blocky, burly fellow. His head and scalp would weigh about 45 pounds, and field-dressed, he'd weigh about 225 pounds. His horns were of the close-curled big-horn type, and if they were mounted with a bighorn scalp, no one would ever suspect they didn't really match. Now the Stone sheep do not go south of the Peace River and the bighorns do not come north of it. Nevertheless, there must have been some contact between the two species at one time, because those Prophet River Stone sheep simply have too many bighorn characteristics!

With uneasy eyes on the sinking sun, Frank and I took the head, hams, and backstraps, and set out on the long trek back to camp loaded to the gunwales. Just as we were about to start down the long shoulder that led to camp, we stopped for a rest and Frank began to glass another mountain on the far side of a great canyon.

"Look over there, right on top of the ridge," he told me. "I see sheep, a whole bunch of them!"

We set up the spotting scope. The mirage was gone now, and even though the sheep were very far away, they were sharp against the sky with the rays of the setting sun focused on them like a spotlight in a theater. Those miniature sheep all had curling horns. Every one was a ram!

"It looks as though we've found ram heaven," Frank said, grinning.

FORTY YEARS OF HUNTING ADVENTURE
– A *Jack O'Connor* PORTFOLIO –

*J*ack and Eleanor shared a passion for hunting mule deer and whitetails in Mexico and the desert Southwest. They killed these mule deer on a 1931 hunt in Arizona's Kaibab Forest, which would serve as the setting for a number of Jack's magazine articles.

*J*ack aims his .22-250 Varminter at a distant prairie dog during a 1944 hunt at the Slade Ranch in Arizona. Looking on are Jerry (far left) and Brad. ≈∅≈ Jack, Eleanor and their four young children gathered on the lawn of their Tucson home for this 1940 portrait. From left are Jerry, Bradford, Caroline and Catherine.

*B*ig game and varmint hunts were usually family affairs for the O'Connors. Clockwise from top: Rancher Frank Seibold watches Jack secure a desert whitetail to his horse. ≈∅≈ Jerry, then 16, admires his first desert mule deer, taken in 1946 in the Huachuca Mountains of Arizona. ≈∅≈ Jack and a coyote (circa 1937) he killed with his .270. ≈∅≈ Jack and Doris Seibold with a Coues' buck taken in 1944.

*I*n 1935, when Jack took this Coues' whitetail, Mexico's Sonora region was a hunter's paradise, filled with deer and bighorn sheep, javelinas, coyotes, jackrabbits and desert quail. Jack was probably the first to write about hunting the little Sinaloa whitetail, or *cabrito*, which he described as a "diminutive, sub-tropical relative of the larger Arizona whitetail."

*C*lockwise from top: Jack was a superb rifleman, no matter the make or caliber. Time after time he dropped varmints and deer at distances over 250 yards, and he was amazingly skilled at hitting running game. ≈⌀≈ Oldest daughter Catherine O'Connor sports a custom Biesen Model 70 in 7x57 in this 1960 photo. ≈⌀≈ Eleanor with her Coues' buck on a 1935 hunt in the Cucurpi mountains of Sonora.

*C*lockwise from top: Jack killed this Stone ram, his next-to-last North American sheep, on a 1971 hunt in British Columbia. ≈∅≈ His best-ever ram was this Dall taken in 1950 on Pilot Mountain of the Yukon Territory. Next to Jack is Moose Johnson, one of his favorite sheep guides. ≈∅≈ Jack watched his son, Brad, kill this trophy bull moose in the Yukon Territory in 1975. It would be Jack's last hunt in the Canadian wilderness.

This beautiful, white-maned caribou was one of several Jack took during his horse-pack trip into Coffin Top Mountain on the Alberta-British Columbia border in 1943. Years later, in one of his *Outdoor Life* articles, Jack wrote that caribou "top everything else in beauty and strangeness," then added ". . . in spite of its looks, the finest bull caribou that ever trotted is a dumb-bell."

*J*n the mist and soaking rain of Admiralty Island, Jack took this Alaskan brown bear, his first of the species. His guide for the 1956 hunt was Ralph Young, who would host Jack and Eleanor on another bear hunt in the late '60s. ⟨⟩ In 1966 Jack kept many of his trophies and other memorabilia in a separate building just behind his home in Lewiston, Idaho.

'Connor shares his thoughts on "rough shooting" with John Amber (center), editor of *Gun Digest*, on their 1968 hunt in Scotland. In his story "My Highland Fling," he admitted to feeling a certain amount of pressure to shoot well, though he ended up as "high gun" on one drive. ≈∅≈ In 1955, surrounded by elephants and native beaters, Jack poses with his first tiger, which he killed with his .375 H&H.

*C*lockwise from top right: Jack set up a Wyoming antelope hunt in 1960 for Prince Abdorreza Pahlavi, brother of the Shah of Iran. ✑∅✑ The Prince had helped to guide Jack on this Persian ibex hunt the previous year. ✑∅✑ Jack killed this Trans-Caspian Urial on the same trip to Iran.

’Connor owned several hunting cockers and Brittany spaniels over the years, but Mike was his favorite. "Mike was the greatest bird-finder I have ever seen, a dog with a choke-bored nose, a tireless hunter," O'Connor wrote in his article, "Triple-Play Hunt." Here, Jack and Mike relax during a 1962 pheasant hunt close by their Idaho home.

'Connor enjoyed eight African safaris over a 25-year period, the longest for nearly two months. In this photograph from his 1969 hunt in Zambia, he uses his riflescope for a closeup view of elephants wading across the Zambezi River. ≈⊘≈ Eleanor watches as Jack examines the ivory on his first elephant, taken on the same trip. He killed the smallish bull with his .416 Rigby.

$\mathcal{C}$ lockwise, from top right: With an admiring Eleanor looking on, Jack wears a proud smile after taking this big-maned lion in Zambia in 1969. ✑⊘✑ He used a .416 Rigby to hammer this trophy Cape buffalo on the same safari. ✑⊘✑ A few days later Eleanor dropped this Zambian lion with her .30/06 Model 70 Winchester.

*T*he vast Kalahari Desert was the setting for this 1966 photograph of Jack and his Botswana trackers with a superb gemsbok. Guided by legendary professional hunter John Kingsley-Heath, Jack also "knocked off" (he loved using that phrase) a trophy lechwe and in the waning moments of his safari, a "Last Minute Kudu" (see page 209).

*C*lockwise from top right: Jack traveled to Tanganyika (now Tanzania) in 1959 to kill this magnificent kudu. ≈⌀≈ This beautiful 44-inch sable fell to Jack's 7x57 pre-'64 Model 70 in Southwest Africa (now Namibia) in 1972. It would be the O'Connors' last safari. ≈⌀≈ Jack and Eleanor relive their stalk of this handsome zebra, which she killed with her .30/06 while on their 1966 hunt in Botswana.

*J*ack O'Connor was in his early 70s, on a pheasant hunt in La Crosse, Washington, when he paused for this portrait taken by his son, Brad. Almost all of his hunts, even short afternoon sashays for quail, jackrabbits or pheasants not far from his home or office, sooner or later showed up in his 1,200 magazine articles, written over a period of 48 years.

PART THREE
Hunting in Africa & Asia

Jack O'Connor went on his first African safari in the summer of 1953. It was an extended affair that lasted over three months. Two years later he would experience his first *shikar*, a three-week hunt in India, followed by quests for red sheep and Persian ibex in Iran, where he was the guest of Prince Abdorreza Pahlavi. Over the ensuing two decades there would be seven more safaris, return trips to India and Iran, visits to Scotland and Scandinavia, and other foreign destinations. More often than not, Eleanor went along.

These grand adventures took place during the twilight of international hunting's Golden Age. It was a period that lasted just a bit more than a century, concluding with O'Connor's generation. This entire span produced splendid literature, and on a personal note, some of the most treasured items in my personal library are books written by such hunter/explorers as Sir Samuel White Baker and Frederick Courteney Selous and decades later by such literary giants as Robert Ruark and Ernest Hemingway.

Two distinguishing characteristics set O'Connor's international hunting forays apart. The first is the manner in which he provides detailed and insightful information on guns and ammunition. With the possible exception of renowned elephant hunter John "Pondoro" Taylor, no one has done it better. Arguably, Jack was first and foremost a gun writer, not a hunting writer, but he combined the two genres with a sure, deft touch. Second, he had an exceptional knack for setting a scene. He gave his readers a sense of time and place, taking them to far-away places that they would never visit but nonetheless could enjoy.

The selections here provide a solid cross-section of O'Connor's African and Asian experiences, his favorite big game animals and some of his finest hunts. I'm confident that these stories offer a solid sampling of what I consider one of O'Connor's real literary fortes – capturing the excitement of big game hunts in exotic locales.

BUFFALO MAKE ME NERVOUS

Most of the great 19th-century African hunters, men like Selous, Gordon-Cumming, and Cornwallis Harris, considered the Cape buffalo the most dangerous of the Big Five, so it was small wonder that the animal made O'Connor nervous. This lengthy story embraces a number of his hunting experiences with m'bogo and includes a few desperate moments with a wounded animal. August, 1963

*M*y first encounter with an African Cape buffalo endowed me with great respect for these big, wild cattle. Or to put it another way, my first buffalo scared the devil out of me. I know guys who just naturally bowl buffaloes over without giving the business a second thought. On my last trip to Africa, I went with two of them – Fred Huntington and Dr. Sib West. In both Mozambique and Angola, where we hunted, the big, mean black buffaloes were plentiful. Bag limits are generous, and if my memory serves me properly, these two characters knocked over four buffaloes between them.

I shot only one, and that is what I will tell you about in this story.

*B*ut first, let me explain why I am a trifle gun-shy so far as buffaloes are concerned. This goes back to 1953, when I was in Tanganyika on my first African safari. Don Ker, the famous white hunter, and I were cruising around one morning in his hunting car looking for lions. I still remember the day very vividly. It had been pretty crispy the night before, not frosty but cold and dewy, and that morning the air was fragrant with the odor of sun-cured grass as sweet as new-mown hay. Little Thomson's gazelles about the size of foxes were everywhere, skipping around in the tall yellow grass like sand fleas on a beach.

165

Herds of the larger Grant's gazelles stood under the flat-topped acacia trees and herds of dark wildebeests stared at us from a distance, tossed grotesque heads, switched tails and galloped off. Once we saw a young male lion with a half-grown mane walk calmly across an opening to bed down in a brushy donga and later we came across two sleek, golden lionesses and three cubs. They were lying on the gray granite rocks of a little boulder-strewn hill called a *kopje* (pronounced copy in Africa). Don and I watched them for a few minutes, hoping that an old male lion would show up, but apparently these ladies were divorcees or something.

So vividly is that day etched in my memory that I can still remember a lovely basin full of rich yellow grass, rimmed with dark thorn trees, and simply swarming with zebras.

*W*e continued through the valley, came over a low ridge, and drove through a grove of trees. A buffalo was the last thing in the world I was thinking of when I became aware that out of the corner of my eye, I could see what I took to be a buffalo standing under a tree. I turned my head, and sure enough, that's exactly what it was. This was the first buffalo I had ever laid eyes on, and it looked to me as if it was a bull and a good bull at that.

Trying to appear as calm and judicious as if I had spent half my life up to my neck in buffaloes, I turned to Don. "What about that bull buffalo over there under the tree? I said. "Is he any good?"

Don jerked his head around, stopped the car, and looked the bull over with his binoculars.

"Very good," he said. "You should take him."

He put the car in gear and drove about a quarter of a mile to a spot where the car was hidden. Then we prepared for the stalk.

"What rifle do you want, Bwana?" asked Thomas, Don's gunbearer of many years. Thomas, or Saidi as he was called by the Africans, had been a noncommissioned officer in an African regiment during the war.

"The .450," I told him, and he handed it to me.

The rifle was made for the .450 Watts cartridge, the wildcat predecessor of the .458 Winchester. It was the .375 Magnum case-necked out to .45 caliber, stuffed full of No. 4895 powder, and loaded with a British 480-grain soft-point bullet made for that great old elephant cartridge, the .450 No. 2 Nitro Express. The velocity I got was about 2,150 feet per second, just about identical to the later .458.

Don took his .476 Westley Richards double and set out. I

followed, and Thomas followed me. All the tales I had heard about people getting tossed and pounded by indignant buffaloes raced through my brain. I tried to appear as casual as if stalking 2,200 pounds of buffalo was something I did every day. Actually, if a chipmunk had squeaked at me I would have jumped right over a thorn tree.

When we neared the place where we had seen the bull, he was gone. But in a moment Don located him. He was lying down about 150 yards away, looking in another direction and philosophically chewing his cud.

I would have been content to shoot him from there as I would have appreciated the head start if he resented it and I had to run. I started to suggest as much to Don, but he shut me up and we began our sneak.

Presently, we were about 60 yards from the bull. He was still lying down, looking away and still working at his cud. As he lay there, his big, nearly hairless, black body was slightly quartering to my left. I figured that I could hold for a high lung shot and the bullet would have an excellent chance to penetrate through and break his sturdy neck.

Shooting from a kneeling position, I waited until the gold bead steadied down and then squeezed the trigger. The buffalo's head went down and his big body went limp.

"You killed him with one shot, Bwana!" Thomas said, pounding me on the back.

"Shoot him again," Don said.

This time I held for the heart to drive the bullet in low just back of the foreleg. When I shot the great black body rocked.

I then ejected the cartridge and stood up. I was reloading when, at the same instant, I heard a pounding of hooves and Don's surprised yell of warning. I looked up to see my "dead" buffalo coming at us with fire in his eyes and blood streaming from his nostrils. Don and I each threw a bullet into him. He staggered, turned, and fell.

An autopsy showed that I had correctly called my first shot, but when the soft-point bullet struck the massive spine, it had flattened out like a silver dollar. My second had gone through the bottom of the heart.

Since that time I have had profound respect for old *m'bogo,* the iron-plated, indestructible Cape buffalo. In fact, I have been so doggoned cautious that I began to wonder if I was afraid of the things.

*T*he next chance I got to take a crack at a buffalo was in French Equatorial Africa, where I hunted with Elgin Gates in 1958. One day, Elgin, Mickey Micheletti, our white hunter, and I sneaked right into the midst of a herd of probably 300 Chad buffaloes. These are smaller animals than the big Cape buffaloes of South and East Africa. We got to within 75 yards of three bulls. I rested a .375 in the crotch of a tree and put the crosswires of the scope right on the biggest bull's shoulder.

"What about it, Mickey?" I asked. "Is that a good trophy head?"

"No," Mickey said. "Not very."

"In that case, I'm not going to shoot it."

"I like to hear you say that," Mickey told me. "You are a real sportsman."

"Maybe I'm just chicken," I said.

"But I do not understand," Mickey said, puzzled. "You say you are the chicken, the barnyard fowl? I am puzzled."

"Skip it," I said.

*N*ext year I leveled down on *m'bogo* on the Kilombero River in southern Tanganyika. John Kingsley-Heath and I sneaked through half a mile of tall grass and got within 50 yards of a big herd of buffalo. They were standing in the open, just in front of some heavy brush. One of them was looking right at me. I sat down, poked the muzzle of the .375 out of the grass. The crosswires rested right at the sticking place.

"I have a 44¹/₂-inch head, John" I said. "Is that one any better?"

"I doubt if it is as good," he said.

"I won't shoot it then," I said. "Ask Kenebe to go back to the hunting car and get my movie camera. I'll take pictures." I shot some scenes through the grass, then stood up to spook the buffaloes to get some action. The pictures turned out very well.

"I admire you for not shooting that buffalo," John told me later. "So many sports want to fill their licenses with indifferent heads."

"Maybe I'm afraid of buffaloes," I said.

"In that case, why did you sit around 50 yards from them and take movies?" he asked.

"Darned if I know!"

*S*o in the spring of 1962, when I was getting ready to go on safari in Mozambique, my wife Eleanor came around to kibitz when I was packing the rifles.

"Good heavens," she said. "Four rifles! All I'm taking is my

7mm. What do you need three rifles for?"

"Well," I said, "This 7mm. Remington Magnum is a new rifle for a new cartridge and I want to write about it in *Outdoor Life*. The .375 is my lion medicine, and maybe I might pop a kudu or sable or something else with it."

"What's that other horrible looking thing for?" she demanded.

"That, Honey, is my .416 Rigby. I'm taking it along to shoot a buffalo. I've been wondering if I were afraid of buffaloes and this time I mean to find out."

"Afraid of buffaloes – those silly cows?" she asked.

"Listen," I said. "If you'd ever been charged by a dead buffalo, you'd whistle another tune."

So we went to Mozambique and started hunting on the Save River. We collected the mysterious and lovely antelope known as nyala with little trouble. We shot fine ringed waterbuck, good kudu, and various other antelope.

Every morning before sunup we crossed the Save River in a dugout canoe, shivering in our light down jackets. We would pick up the Japanese Nissan hunting car there, cruise until we found game, and then stalk. Sometimes we'd shoot. More often we would not.

The country on the south bank of the Save swarms with game. Impalas, the brick-red antelope that are about the size of a small whitetail deer, do not run as large in body and horn as their kinsmen farther north in Kenya and Tanganyika. They make up in numbers, however, what they lack in size. Every day we saw hundreds, if not thousands of them. There were also bush pigs, bushbucks, reedbucks, little gray antelope called oribis, and red ones called steinboks. Both of these are about the size of small foxes.

A couple of times we ran across herds of buffaloes. Once we located a bunch by a tremendous cloud of dust. Harry Manners, our white hunter, saw the dust first. "Buffaloes," he said. "Nothing else could stir up that much dust. Something has frightened them."

We drove toward the dust and made a circle downwind. Then we left the hunting car behind. Harry and I took .375s, my wife her little 7mm. Mauser. We sneaked up to within 50 yards or so of the herd. There must have been 200 of the big black creatures, but so far as we could tell, there wasn't a shootable bull among them. We backed off and returned to the hunting car.

On another occasion when we were hunting a plateau which Harry called Paolo's pantry, because a poacher there had once killed and dried tons of meat, we got right into the center of an enormous

169

herd. Again no shootable bulls. Paolo, incidentally, has reformed. He now works as a game warden for Safarilandia, the company that outfitted us. Instead of poaching game, he protects it. Nevertheless, it is considered wise to keep Paolo supplied with meat, so that he'll stay on the straight and narrow.

Harry had been leaving word around Sangan villages that his whiteman hunter was looking for a mossy-horned old he buffalo and that any villager who located one would not only get nearly a ton of meat, but would have his palm crossed with some escudos.

So there came a day when we stopped in at the village to see what the news was. The head man came out to receive us. He inquired about Harry's health, the health of his wife and his child, and the health of everyone back at camp. The women gathered around the hunting car, squatted in a circle. Europeans stand up to show respect, but in Mozambique the Sangan women sit down to show the same thing.

For a moment Harry talked to the Sangan, exchanging pleasantries. Then he turned to me. "The old boy has something to tell us," he said. "He's making a production out of it. Maybe they've seen a pride of lions or have a leopard located or something."

Then it came out. Grandly, the old man summoned one of his sons. This young man, he told us, this incomparable young hunter, had located a big buffalo. With the coming of the next sun, he would lead us to it.

So the next morning I left the .375 in the rack at camp and took the big .416 Rigby. It was particularly chilly that morning and I can still remember how the glassy water of the river steamed in the frigid air. I had given Joe a wool shirt, but even that didn't keep him warm.

We drove out from the village a few miles with the young hunter standing up in the back of the car to direct Harry. Except for an occasional dry watercourse, the country was as flat as a table and very dry. We twisted and turned through the brush and trees, and bounced over rough ground cut up by elephants during the rainy season.

Presently, the boy grew cautious. He told Harry to drive slowly. Then he said we should get out and go on foot. Every now and then our guide would stop, peer carefully around. Then we'd sneak ahead once more. When we went through thick brush, he'd stop, get down on hands and knees, and peer into the brush. We had just come out of a thick patch of brush when he stopped as if he had run into a wall and pointed. Across an *embugo* about 150 yards away, looking at us and partially concealed by brush, was a big, lone buffalo.

"There he is and he's a good one!" Harry whispered. "This lad is good. I think the blighter can smell buffalo."

Well, I said to myself, here we go again.

I crept around Harry and the guide and sat down. I could just see over the grass from that position. For a cannon, my old .416 is a very accurate rifle. It weighs 10^1/$_2$ pounds and I wouldn't have it weigh an ounce less. The action is beautifully smooth, and the trigger lets go like the breaking of a glass rod.

With my load of 105 grains of No. 4831 powder and the 400-grain Barnes heavy-jacketed bullet, the .416 kicks like the devil from a benchrest, but when fired at a bull buffalo, I can testify that it has no more recoil than a .22. When the heavy rifle settled down and the crosswires of the Weaver 2^1/$_2$X scope came to rest under the old bull's chin, I completed the squeeze. The bull collapsed.

"Good shot, by George!" Harry shouted. Then: "He's getting up!"

The bull staggered to his feet, turned and started to wobble off into the brush. I took a hasty crack at him, and Harry ran to the left and fired. An instant later Harry, the guide, and Joe all started bounding after the buffalo. Before they could go far, I heard the mournful death bellow of the buffalo, a sound as characteristic as the death cry of a stricken tiger.

A moment later we all stood beside the old bull. His head was just over 40 inches, good but not wildly exceptional. Like most good bulls, he was an old-timer that had been run out of the herd by stronger and friskier youngsters. My first bullet had gone low through the neck and had cut the big blood vessels over the heart.

"Well," my wife said when we were taking pictures, "do buffaloes still make you nervous?"

"You're darned right they do!" I said, and I meant it.

171

THIS DAY IN PARADISE

Robert Ruark likened his first African hunt to a sojourn in the Garden of Eden. Here "Bwana Four Eyes" gives an account of his first safari, taken in 1953. It covers some enjoyable mixed bag hunting, including reedbuck, the humble warthog and secretive bushbuck.
August, 1954

I first saw the Thing off to my right. It slithered through the tall grass by the wide placid river in Tanganyika, half phantom, half reality. When it moved I could see it; when it stopped it was invisible. It could have been a hyena, an antelope, a lion, even a human being on hands and knees.

Not far from the spot where this furtive creature moved through the grass was a great anthill, which a million generations of termites laboring for centuries in the darkness had built 30 feet high. I scrambled up it to look down and see what was slipping away from me through the grass.

When I got to the top and peered over, I could not for a moment see the creature at all. Then it moved off, and for an instant I could make it out quite plainly – a strange little antelope with the twisted horns of a miniature eland, a narrow pointed face, a slender body curiously marked with dots and stripes.

Then the creature vanished into a patch of reeds by the river and I did not see it again. I might have collected it – if I had carried a suitable rifle and shot very quickly. But in my hands that evening I had a 16-gauge shotgun I had carried out of camp in hope of knocking off a few francolins, those foot-racing, white-meated, exasperating partridges which are found in one form or another all over Africa.

One of the camp boys had gone with me to pick up the birds and to carry a .375, so I could defend myself if a lion tried to take a bite out of me.

173

He got as excited as I did over this furtive little creature I was so determined to get a look at, and once he tried to hand me the big Winchester so I could take a pop at it from my perch on the anthill. *"Mbwara – mbwara!"* he told me.

When the Thing faded off and we couldn't boot it out of the reeds, he shrugged his shoulders hopelessly, sighed, shook his head, and gave me a stream of Swahili in which the word *mbwara* was frequently mentioned. By his expression, I could see he felt that dealing with American dudes too dull of mind to learn even elementary Swahili and too addle-pated to make up their minds to shoot was enough to drive an honest man to the bottle. He also made it plain that I'd had my chance and if I didn't get a Thing, the fault was mine.

In the forest to the west, grass fires set by honey hunters were burning, and the smoky haze turned the swiftly dropping sun into a great red ball that swam in a sea of rose and gold. By the time we arrived in camp with a few hard-won francolins, the slender nut palms were black against the fading sunset. Across the Ugalla River a lion was roaring and out in the water before our tents a hippo splashed as he fed.

Syd Downey was sitting in front of the fire, a smile on his face, a sundowner in his hand, when the boy and I plodded up. "Ah," he said, "some birds. Good!"

"Syd," I told the white hunter, "I saw the darndest-looking little beast today. Horns a little like an eland, stripes like a kudu, not as big as a Grant's gazelle."

Syd turned to the boy, who began jabbering in Swahili. Again I caught the word *mbwara*. "What a pity!" Syd said. "You were very close to a bushbuck. The boy says he wanted you to shoot it with the .375, but you wouldn't. He is very unhappy about it. Not many Americans go home with a bushbuck."

"So that's a *mbwara!*" I said. "But honestly, Syd, I didn't get a good look at the darned thing until an instant before it did a fade-out."

"What a pity," Syd repeated gloomily, and he and the boy exchanged a what-we-poor-dude-wranglers-don't-have-to-put-up-with look.

Bushbucks, Syd told me, are also called harnessed antelope. They are relatives of the kudu and also of such fabulous beasts as bongos and sitatungas. They are widely distributed and fairly common, he said, but so shy and so nocturnal that few safari hunters ever take one out.

Of all the areas where Herb Klein, Red Earley, and I hunted in Tanganyika and Kenya in the summer of 1953, I believe the country along the beautiful Ugalla River was the most interesting. For half a mile on either side of the river the grass was as short and green and as close-cropped as that of a well-kept lawn. Great nut palms with slender trunks and feathery tops rose on every side. Because the area along the river was under water during the rainy season, no other trees grew on the flat except on the giant anthills. Some of these conical mounds were 30 or 40 feet high and each supported its own little forest of thick brush and gnarled old trees.

Back in the forest, the niombo trees were bare except for a few fluttering golden leaves. Gaunt red soil lay exposed between patches of blackened grass, and the whole country stank of stale fire and burned grass and smoldering ashes. There, ravenous tsetse flies as bold as burglars and as indestructible as little battleships leaped on the unwary.

But down by the river, away from the trees, there were no tsetses. Always a caressing little breeze blew – neither too hot nor too cold, too strong nor too weak. It kept away the insects, cooled the sweat on the feverish brow of the hunter, told him which way to stalk. Day and night this little breeze blew. When the sun was up it quickly dried the dude hunter's undershirt as it flapped from a bush in the sun. At night it stirred the dried fronds of the palm trees to put the weary dude to sleep with swishing delicate rhythm like that of a dreamy rumba orchestra. It was the sort of place where I had always imagined Adam and Eve setting up housekeeping.

There were dozens and scores and hundreds of animals along this magic plain by this silver river – not the common plains game like the little Thomson's gazelle, the homely kongoni, the fantastic wildebeest, the gaudy zebra, creatures that run in herds of hundreds. Instead, there were the aristocratic sable antelope with its curving scimitar horns, the big bulky roan, the dainty oribi, the slender and handsome reedbuck, and the rare and furtive bushbuck. At night the lions roared and herds of squealing elephants came crashing down to water.

Of the commoner African game along the Ugalla, there was the sleek topi with its pink coat and purple flanks, the homely warthog, and Lichtenstein's hartebeest or konzi. This last is about the size of the common Coke's hartebeest, or kongoni, a big, awkward, horse-faced antelope which we had seen by the thousands on the Simiyu and on the Grummetti, but the konzi has an entirely different angle

175

to his funny-looking horns.

The warthog is so incredibly ugly that in comparison he makes the next-ugliest animal you can think of look like Hedy Lamarr. Great warts sprout all over his long head. Irregular patches of bristles grow here and there on his scaly gray skin. He suffers from pimples and dandruff. He leers about stupidly from tiny myopic eyes, then whirls and slithers away as if he were on roller skates, his foot-long tufted tail straight in the air. His trot is so smooth and even that if he is in grass, he looks as if he weren't running at all but traveling on wheels. Like the rhino, the warthog is often accompanied by tickbirds. They squawk out warnings to him in exchange for the privilege of picking away the ticks with which he is infested and munching on the scales of dandruff.

I hadn't planned to take a warthog, but one day Syd and I saw a solitary boar with widespread, upturned tusks so good I simply couldn't turn it down. He won't make a beautiful trophy, but he'll make a spectacular one.

Most of the game animals on this beautiful floodplain were not greatly frightened by the hunting cars, as they seemed to consider them simply funny-looking and strange-smelling varieties of elephants or rhinos. We could always drive past, park the car, and come back to make the stalk without much difficulty. For instance, we all got reedbucks on the Ugalla. Red was first under the wire. Then one afternoon when Herb and I were hunting together, we got a couple of beauties, the two largest, I believe, that were seen on the trip, as between us we must have looked over dozens of males. In color, in conformation, in the shape of their pretty, delicate heads, they reminded me of the American whitetail. Like the whitetails, they liked brush and forest and came out early in the morning and late in the afternoon to feed.

But bushbucks were something else. Many times we saw their tiny pointed tracks, and sometimes we could tell we'd been so close that the noise of the automobile had spooked them. The curious-looking little creatures were as elusive as ghosts.

We saw and photographed hundreds of sable antelope, and some roans. Herb and Red tried to get too familiar with a lioness and her cubs with their cameras and had to flee like rabbits when she took after them.

Then late one afternoon, when Syd and I were cruising along in the hunting car, we saw a small antelope silhouetted against dry yellow grass clear across the yellow, placid Ugalla. Instantly Syd slammed on the brakes.

"There's our bushbuck!" he said.

But the little creature dived into some brush and never again came out. Apparently he'd heard the car and that was enough for him.

Then Syd hatched a scheme. Since bushbucks were so wary, the thing to do would be to hunt *across* the wide river – as the Southwestern hunter does who shoots his deer on the far side of the canyon. We knew where at least one good bushbuck lived, and where there was one, there should be others.

Mornings, as soon as we could see, and evenings, until darkness fell, we'd leave the car, then go quietly along the riverbank watching the far side. Often we saw other game – tiny oribis, dainty reedbucks, massive blue-gray roan antelope, which next to the eland is the largest of the African antelope.

Our quest ended one morning when I was about convinced that bushbucks were optical illusions. We had started out very early. The sun was not yet up, the dew was heavy on the grass, and the lions were still roaring. Couple of times as we hunted along the bank, we saw out in the river the flat curve of a hippo's back and his wide, flaring nostrils thrust above water like snorkels of submarines.

At the little native village we found most of the inhabitants at breakfast. One family had seined a quantity of what looked like young catfish. The smallest were about two inches long, the largest about six. They were piled on an iron grill with a fire under them. Now papa, mamma, and the kids were all squatted around the grill shoveling down the fish – heads, tails, and all.

All the natives along the Ugalla are hunters and fishermen. Because of the tsetse flies, they cannot raise livestock or even keep dogs, and we saw no attempts to farm. They seine fish, gather wild honey, and shoot game with muzzle-loaders. Around the village we saw scattered bits of bone and hide from roan and sable antelope, warthog, and oribi. Since the natives were bright-eyed and chipper, the diet must agree with them.

Tanganyika has for many hundreds of years been a land of much mixing of races, and one often sees natives who are exceedingly black but have Nordic features. The head man of the little village looked like a New York banker I know, and he had the same rich voice, the same hearty air. Another native looked like a well-known motion-picture actor.

"Any *mbwara* about?" Syd asked the banker.

Mbwara? . . . If a man wasn't careful as he walked through the grass he fell over them! Nothing the banker would like better than to show us a few, but when a man has a woman and a few *totos* to feed, he has to get out and scratch. He'd planned on fishing that day, but of course if the bwanas would polish off a roan so his young offspring wouldn't starve, he'd take the day off.

So off we went in the hunting car with the banker and the movie man. They directed us to a long point about two miles from the village. The river took a bend there and it was lined with nut palms that would be worth a couple of thousand dollars each if installed on an estate in southern California.

We hadn't walked over a quarter of a mile when the movie actor pointed.

"Bushbuck!" Syd said. "Across the river at the left of the small palm."

And so it was.

On the far bank, across the gleaming surface of the river, stood our bushbuck, sharply silhouetted against tall yellow grass. He was about 250 yards away.

I dropped into a solid sitting position, put the crosswires in the 4X scope right behind his shoulder, and sent a 130-grain Silvertip sailing out of the .270. The little buck went down as if flattened by a giant hammer.

Until that moment, the problem of how I was going to get my trophy after I shot it had not bothered my pretty head. I was appalled then to remember that the Ugalla is the home of crocodiles and hippos and that both of those strange beasts have been known to take bites out of those who invaded their domain. I was also shocked to think that the country is full of hyenas, vultures, and marabou storks, all of which simply dote on juicy bushbuck.

But Syd had an answer for that one, too.

While the banker remained with us to discuss international events and the strange doings of the stock market, Bito, Syd's driver and gunbearer, went with the movie actor on an errand to the village. The vultures found the bushbuck, but by shooting under their feet, I managed to to discourage them until Bito and the movie actor came back with a bark canoe perched atop the hunting car, and the two local boys paddled over and returned with my trophy.

He was an unworldly-looking little beast, chestnut in color, but curiously dotted and striped with white. Around his neck was a bare collar where no hair grew, something which I thought was a defect, but which Syd told me is characteristic.

*W*e had hardly started for the village before we saw a herd of sable antelope, in charge of a coal-black herd bull, slowly coming back from water.

"Here you are, Mac," said the banker in Swahili. "Here is some eating meat. Forget not your promise!"

"Alas, this cannot be," Syd told him. "Bwana Four Eyes is a stranger from a great country across the salt ocean. He has come to seek bones and bits of horn and hide which he will take back to his strange country and nail to the walls of his hut as fetishes. He has a paper for but one sable. If he should shoot another, the English in Tabora will seize his guns and his money, and throw him in jail."

The banker relaxed in sulky silence. Plainly, he thought he was double-crossed.

But luck came to our rescue. Bito thought he heard a shot. Syd stopped the car and turned off the motor so we could listen. We heard another – and another.

We drove in the direction of the shooting to find Herb Klein and Myles Turner bending over a big bull roan. Herb kept the head and scalp. I kept the bushbuck, which probably dressed out at not more than 90 pounds. The banker and the movie actor wound up with the roan, which must have weighed at least 500 pounds with head off and the insides out.

From now on, one of the fireside tales told in that little Ugalla village will no doubt be of the madmen from the far country who give away good, juicy meat and keep the horns and pieces of hide, who prefer little skinny bushbucks to big fat roans. So everyone may live happily every after!

ELEPHANTS ON THE ZAMBEZI

Jack, Eleanor, and Brad enjoy an exciting elephant hunt along the mighty Zambezi River, which concludes in dramatic fashion when Brad has to shoot a rogue female that repeatedly attacks the party. January, 1970

*A*s this story starts, my wife Eleanor; Ron Kidson, our professional hunter and part-owner of Zambia Safaris; and I were rolling down the road in Ron's Land Rover hunting car. It was late afternoon, and we didn't have a care in the world. I had not popped a cap that day, but Eleanor had made a nice offhand shot at a beautiful little bushbuck. We had seen a pride of lions, a very large bull kudu, and a great many elephants.

On our right, between the road and a range of rocky hills, was the dry African bush with low shrubs, thorn trees, and an occasional grotesque baobab, a strange and primitive African tree that looks as if it had been uprooted and put back into the earth upside down. On our left was a green floodplain of grass and swamp and towering trees, and beyond that the wide Zambezi, one of the great rivers of Africa and the world. Across the big blue river was the Rhodesian shore.

Eleanor sat in the front seat with Ron. I was in a back seat with a gunbearer. None of us was thinking of anything more serious than a bath, clean clothes, and a cold drink around a cheerful campfire as the swift African dusk came down and silhouetted the trees against a rosy sky.

Then ahead of us we heard a scream. No one had to tell me it was an angry elephant. It sounded exactly like the canned sound effects that one hears when elephants are shown on television.

As the sound registered on us, the head and trunk of an

elephant burst through the trees ahead and about 40 yards away. Instantly, Ron put the hunting car into reverse. At the same time he stuck his head around the windshield and started yelling at the elephant. I have never seen a car travel faster in reverse, and I doubt that I have ever heard worse language.

For about 50 yards the elephant was coming about as fast as the car was going, but presently the big creature slowed down and the car pulled away. When we were about 200 yards from where the elephant had jumped us, Ron stopped.

"Big bloody cow!" he said. Then he added, "Bad business!"

When the cow came for us, I handed the gunbearer the .338 I had in my hand and grabbed the .416 Rigby that was in the gun rack in a soft case. I almost tore off my fingernails getting it out. At the same time I could see that Eleanor was cramming cartridges loaded with 220-grain solids into the magazine of her .30-06.

I stood up, my head and shoulders and the big .416 clearing the hatch at the top of the car. The cow was about 50 yards away now. I could see her head and the top of her shoulders over some bushes. She stood there for a moment, then moved off to the right. I could make out three or four other cows.

Presently, Ron decided that the coast was clear, and he drove ahead. The cow was lying in wait for us. As we passed, she charged out of the bush right at us. I put the crosswires of the Rigby 2^{1}/2-power scope right between her eyes as she came, but she was behind us. Ron gunned the Land Rover and quickly outdistanced her.

A couple of nights before and at about the same place, our son Bradford and his professional hunter, Mike Cameron, had blundered into a herd of cows and calves and had been chased. Since there were elephants behind them and an angry cow coming for them in front, Mike had to turn off the road and outrun the cow by crashing out into the bush. Fortunately, he had good going.

When Brad and Mike told the rest of us about their experience, it had seemed rather remote. Things like that simply do not happen to decent people! Today, it no longer seemed remote.

"I don't like that at all!" Eleanor said. "That cow's dangerous. Someone's going to have to shoot her."

"I hope not," Ron said. "When anyone shoots a cow, there's

no end of red tape with the game department. It would be simpler to let the cow shoot the hunter."

*E*leanor, Bradford, and I were starting the third week of a 30-day safari in Zambia, a country in the southern third of Africa that was called Northern Rhodesia until it became a self-governing state a few years ago. It was Bradford's first safari, Eleanor's sixth, and my eighth. We had met Bradford in Rome and had then flown down to Lusaka, the capital of Zambia, by Alitalia, the Italian airline.

Our first camp was adjacent to the Kafue National Park and a day's drive from Lusaka. There, Bradford, who is outdoor editor of the *Seattle Times*, started his first safari with a bang by getting an enormous sable antelope, a buffalo, and assorted lesser trophies. Eleanor shot a lion, but I was still looking.

The Zambezi area, where we were hunting elephants, was clear across the southern part of Zambia from Sichifula, where we had begun our hunt, and not far from the great Kariba Dam, which has created what amounts to an inland sea by backing up the Zambezi.

The Zambezi country, which Ron Kidson and Keith Rowse, owners of Zambia Safaris, considered by far their best elephant country, was so far from our first camp that it took Bradford and Mike Cameron two hard days of driving to get there. Eleanor and I had it easier. We drove to Lusaka, spent the night there in a modern hotel, and then flew down to the camp by chartered plane.

There were many elephants on the Zambezi; some lions and leopards; lots of buffalo, bushbuck, kudu, and eland; and tens of thousands of guineafowl. Since elephants were among the 26 trophies that our $980 hunting licenses entitled us to shoot, we were giving some thought to collecting ivory.

Elephants are on the increase over much of Africa. There is little ivory hunting since it is worth only about two inflated dollars a pound now, whereas 60 and 70 years ago it was worth five very solid dollars a pound. Trophy hunters take some elephants, but far more are shot on "Control" to keep them out of native fields and to prevent their eating themselves out of house and home. I was told that the plan is to shoot 5,000 elephants in Kafue National Park, dry the meat, and process the hides into leather.

Where we hunted on the Zambezi, I could see that elephants

were a problem when they became plentiful. They are enormously destructive. They push over big trees to get at choice foliage. We saw hundreds of thorn trees girdled and thereby killed by elephants. The animals enjoy the taste of the bark.

We saw hundreds of elephant cows and calves, and we approached close to them when the wind was right. Once we saw with binoculars a herd of seven bulls on an island out in the middle of the Zambezi, but they were safe. They might as well have been on the moon.

A day or so later we were traveling along the road when I happened to see a bull elephant cross an opening in heavy trees and brush in the jungle close to the river. He disappeared before I could get Ron's attention, but we looked and found the seven bulls we had seen on the island.

An elephant is almost blind. But he hears pretty well, and his power of scent is among the best in nature. We sneaked up to within 30 or 40 yards of the herd. An elephant looks like a moving haystack at that distance. Expecting that we would knock one off, I looked toward Ron and raised an inquiring eyebrow. He shook his head. Afterward he told me that we had been between the elephants and the cover from which they had come. If they had stampeded, they would have come right toward us – and we had no large trees to get behind for protection.

We watched the elephants for several minutes. A big black one seemed to be the leader, and presently he walked to the bank of the Zambezi and plunged in. All the others followed. We ran to the bank and watched. Seeing those monstrous creatures almost completely submerged cross a channel of the river and then clamber ponderously up onto an island was one of the grandest sights I have ever seen. In itself, it was just about worth the trip to Africa.

Eleanor had herself keyed up to shoot an elephant, and when the herd swam across the river, she was let down.

"Do you think we'll get another chance?" she asked.

"Sure," Ron said. "If not tomorrow, the next day. They range on both sides of the river.

The next morning we quickly found the large black bull and three smaller ones near the river. They were about a mile away, across the grassy floodplain, moving slowly along, yanking a branch now and then, pushing an occasional tree.

We made up our task force. The gunbearer carried Eleanor's Winchester Model 70 .30/06, a light rifle that she had used on tigers in India and on mixed game in Botswana. Len Brownell, the stockmaker who is now a big wheel with the rifle division of Sturm, Ruger & Company, and I had planned the rifle in 1963 when Eleanor and I were hunting in the Yukon with him, Bill Ruger, and Robert Chatfield-Taylor. The ammunition was handloaded with 220-grain, full metal-jacketed (solid) bullets.

Ron was armed with a .458 and I carried a handsome, custom-built .416 Rigby on a Brevex Magnum Mauser action. The .416 is the ancestor of the .378 and the .460 Weatherby, and the case is the same as that of the Weatherby cartridges, except that it is not belted. The cartridge delivers about the same energy as the .458 by pushing a 410-grain bullet faster than the .458's 500-grain job. On this trip for buffalo and elephant, I used British factory ammunition with the steel-jacketed solid bullet.

At any rate, we had plenty of firepower to fall back on if things went wrong.

The little herd continued to poke along not far from the riverbank, and we were able to walk just a little faster than they were moving. When we were about 150 yards away, they stopped, apparently to think over whatever elephants think about.

Quickly we closed in on them. About 50 yards from the elephants were a couple of big sturdy trees, far too large for an elephant to push over.

"Couldn't be better," Ron whispered. "If those elephants should come this way, we can just step behind the trees and they'll rush by us."

Then he turned to Eleanor and said, "The one on the right. Remember – right between the eye and the ear hole."

I watched as Eleanor lifted her rifle. If she had any elephant fever, I could not detect it. Ron and I trained our heavy rifles on the bull in case anything went wrong.

Then Eleanor's .30/06 cracked. The bull collapsed in his tracks. It was an awe-inspiring sight.

"Eleanor brained him!" Ron shouted.

I turned and looked at the Storm and Strife. Her face wore a look of astonished unbelief.

"You didn't know your own strength, did you?" I said.

185

"Heavens!" she said.

Ron and I kept our rifles trained on the other bulls, but there was no need. Apparently the light report of the .30/06 and the instant death of the leader hadn't meant much to the smaller bulls. Ron yelled at them, and gradually they moved off. We had not realized it, but Eleanor's bull had been standing right on the bank of the Zambezi, and when it collapsed, its head had fallen into the river.

Not a bit of the meat from elephants shot by Ron's clients is wasted. The animals are cut up, the meat is dried into what we would call jerky, but what is known as biltong in Africa. Then it is turned over to the Zambia game department and distributed to the poor.

There is generally some action in elephant hunting – and the next day there was plenty. In the afternoon Eleanor, with her elephant behind her, decided to stay around camp and try to ambush a leopard. Ron and I went out to get an elephant.

We spotted two good bulls and began our stalk. The grass was head-high, and where we started the ground was dry. Presently, we were on damp ground, then mud. Before long we were walking in water that went over our shoe tops. Then it was above our knees and getting deeper. I told Ron that struggling through that morass was too much for me.

We floundered back through the swamp toward the car. Gloomily, Ron watched the two bulls moving away through the swamp in the distance.

"I wish Bradford would come along," Ron said. "We'd give those bulls a run for the money."

And the wish was the father of the event. No sooner had he said that than we heard the sound of an approaching car and Mike and Bradford hove into sight. Off went the task force, skirting the swamp at a trot in an effort to overtake the bulls. I sat there in the sun, trying to get dry.

About 20 minutes after they had left, I heard two quick shots and then another. I presumed they had overtaken the bulls and that Bradford had collected one. Not long after that, Bradford and one of the gunbearers came into sight.

"I suppose you got a bull?" I said.

"I'll say we didn't!" Bradford said bitterly. He was upset.

"What happened?" I asked.

"That damned old cow!" he said. "She jumped us, and we had to shoot her."

"Well," I said, "that was an experience."

"It was one I could sure have done without," he said. "It scared the hell out of me!"

He told me the story. They had been hurrying along on dry ground at the right side of the swamp. Some cows and calves were feeding out in the swamp not far away, but the hunters had their minds on the bulls.

Suddenly the men heard a scream and a crashing of brush and a big cow elephant came barreling out right at them not over 50 yards away. Bradford was carrying his .375, and Ron had a .416 Rigby that he had borrowed from Mike. One of the gunbearers had Mike's .458.

None of them wanted to shoot the cow. They all ran, but the lad with Mike's .458 had a head start and was endowed with very fair speed. Ron yelled at the cow and ran for the shelter of a big anthill. Mike, who himself has a good deal of talent for picking them up and laying them down, was going flat out after the gunbearer and yelling for him to stop. Bradford was just running.

When Ron got behind the anthill, he thought he had shaken off the cow, but an instant after he stopped, she shot around the anthill almost on top of him. He threw up the .416 and fired at her forehead. She was so close and the angle was so sharp that the heavy bullet missed the brain. However, it staggered the cow and she hesitated.

In the meantime Mike caught the gunbearer. He jerked the .458 from his hands and whirled around toward the cow just as Ron's shot staggered her. Mike let go a .458 solid that crashed into her brain, and she dropped just as Bradford fired. It had been a close one.

Ron was convinced she was the same mean cow that had been chasing the cars on the road. Since everything she had gone after had fled, she had been getting bolder and bolder, meaner and meaner. Whether she had been responsible or not I do not know, but along that road beside the Zambezi there is a big shiny ten-ton German truck wrapped around a tree. An elephant had chased the truck. The driver had lost control and cracked it up. Ten-thousand dollars of Zambian government money had become a pile of junk.

The next morning we went over to inspect the dead cow.

187

With us was the crew that was to cut it up for biltong.

"The wages of sin," Eleanor said, as she looked at the remains. "She deserved what she got." Since the day we were chased by the cow, my wife has had scant patience with ill-tempered lady elephants.

*E*leanor, Ron, and I continued to look around for an elephant. Because we had previously done a good deal of African hunting, we did not do much shooting. Bradford collected a good bull kudu and an eland.

My elephant, when I finally got it, was a piece of cake. We saw it standing all alone in tall grass under a tree. Eleanor elected to watch the stalk. She filled the magazine of her .30/06 with solids, just in case, and found a perch on a tall anthill.

Ron and I made a circle to keep the wind in our favor and moved slowly through the tall grass toward the lone bull. The eyesight of elephants may be very poor, but the bull must have seen a movement in the grass. At any rate, when we were about 50 yards away, the bull turned to face us. His enormous ears went out. His trunk came up. Eleanor, who was watching from her anthill with binoculars, said later that he seemed to be trying to focus on us.

Then slowly and ponderously – like a fat, tired old man – the bull started walking right toward us. I waited until he was about 15 yards away. Then I hoisted up the .416, put the intersection of the crosswires three or four inches below the line between his eyes, and squeezed the trigger. The bull went down as if the earth had been jerked from under him. The 410-grain steel-jacketed solid had gone through eight inches of solid bone and found the brain. I have since regretted that I had not been quick-witted enough to hand Eleanor my movie camera and tell her to take long-lens films of the stalk and shot.

*B*radford, who had been very lucky on everything else, had a tough time finding a shootable elephant. In fact, he did not get one on the Zambezi. He did not fire another shot at an elephant until we made our last stand of the safari on the Kafue River. There, he hunted a week from dawn until dark.

When he finally got his shot, he wanted to make extra sure. He knelt down within 20 yards of the bull to take a frontal brain shot, and held just below the line between the eyes. But his kneeling position made the angle wrong, and his bullet went in

188

above the brain. There was great trumpeting, crashing of brush, yelling, and rushing about, but Bradford and Mike Cameron got the bull down. Bradford had killed each of his buffalo bulls with one shot, but he was unlucky on elephants.

How much our ivory weighs I do not know. When we left, it had still not been pulled from the skulls. None of the tusks are fabulous 100-pounders, but all are good average ivory. The fact that hungry people are going to eat all that meat makes me feel better. Anyone who shoots an elephant leaves an awful lot on the ground.

TO CATCH AN
ELAND

Serendipity can sometimes mean
surprising success, which is the case
here as Jack ends up killing a huge
bull eland while hunting lions.
His description of the stalk
leading up to his telling shot with
a .375 Magnum is vintage stuff.
April, 1954

*B*ack when I was doing a lot of hunting in the Canadian Rockies and had shot a good many grizzlies, people sometimes asked me how to go about catching a grizzly. I'd tell them that the way I hunted the bears was to make up mind I was going to shoot a walloping big mountain sheep – and forget all about grizzlies. Then, as the days passed and I climbed around above timberline looking for the ram of rams, I sooner or later ran into a grizzly. The first silvertip I ever shot was up in the Alberta sheep country. Last one I took was likewise in sheep country – in a freezing, lonely basin in the Yukon's Pelly Mountains.

Now I'm beginning to believe that in Tanganyika the best way to get a good eland is to walk your legs off after a couple of big, fat he-lions – one with a yellow mane, the other with a black one. At least that's the way it worked out when I was in Africa.

*T*he eland is the largest antelope in the world, a big, heavy-looking tan-gray animal with some stripes across his back, heavy spiral horns, and a wad of brown hair on his forehead. Most African antelope have about as much fat on them as a racehorse or a good bird dog in midseason. The eland is an exception. He gets enormously fat, so he's greatly prized by the fat-hungry natives. He looks, more than anything else, like a Jersey bull with funny horns and a few bumps and lumps he shouldn't have.

A bull eland is a lot of antelope. He'll stand from 5 feet 9 inches to

191

6 feet at the shoulder. How much will one weigh? Darned if I know. Prof. Robert Ruark, the columnist and savant who did an East African safari some time before I did, says they'll run 2,000 pounds. I didn't weigh one and I don't believe Brother Ruark did either. I wound up shooting a very large bull, and he looked to me as if he would weigh a good deal less than an Alaska moose. Probably he'd dress out about like a run-of-the-mine Canadian bull moose – say about 1,200 pounds.

Once when I was stalking something or other by pussy-footing upwind, there on the African plains, I suddenly caught the overwhelming, familiar, and pleasant odor of a herd of dairy cows. It was so strong and so real that I'd have sworn there was a barn full of Jersey cows beyond the scrubby thorn trees, munching timothy hay and ready to give contented milk. What I smelled and then saw was a small herd of cow elands with their calves.

When they saw us they watched us for a moment and then the horrible truth dawned on them. They were off in great bounds. In spite of their weight, frightened elands can leap almost like those famous jumpers, the impalas. To see a bull eland weighing around 1,500 pounds merrily jump over an eight-foot bush – or another bull eland – is quite a sight.

An eland looks like beef, smells like beef, and tastes like beef. With all that delicious eating meat tied up in one bundle and going around on four legs, it is no wonder that the eland is a cautious animal. Lions are after him. Natives are after him. Wild dogs and hyenas like nothing better than to sink a tooth into a big fat eland.

In spite of all this, the eland is surviving and apparently increasing. He is found over a vast area of Africa – in forest and bush and plain – and he gets along and prospers because he is a sly, suspicious, and alert animal that moves off at the slightest noise, at the tiniest bit of tainted air. The typical view you'll get is of the south exposure of one going north.

I wanted, of course, to bring back a trophy head. The animal is not only the world's largest antelope, but he's typical of Africa. Getting one, I'd imagined, would be easy – something to be done at my leisure and when the mood was upon me. I was disillusioned early in the trip. The eland may look like a Jersey cow, but he doesn't act like one!

*D*on Ker and I were cruising around for lions one afternoon when we saw, standing right at the edge of some thin bush about half a mile away, four big bull elands. (The cows are tan, by the way, almost identical in color with a Jersey cow; but the bulls turn gray with age.) Don put on the brakes and lifted the Bausch & Lomb binoculars he wears around his neck almost as routinely as he wears his pants.

"Good bulls," he said. "One's a dandy!"

I still had the notion that I could pick up a trophy eland any time the spirit moved me, so I demurred. "I thought we were hunting lions," I protested grumpily. "I'd hate to spook a big one for a lousy bull eland."

Earlier that day we'd seen two lean and ornery-looking lady lions munching on what was left of a topi kill, also a young male with a fair-to-middling mane. I had lions on the brain and every time we came around a bush I expected to bump into the big-maned one of my dreams.

"That's not a lousy bull eland, chum," Don told me. "It is a very fine trophy eland. We of Ker & Downey take our trophies when and where we find them."

That was that, and we crawled out of the hunting car.

The four big bulls moved slowly away. Don, the two gunbearers, and I went after them. We'd keep brush between us and the little herd, but now and then we'd peek out. The bulls did not seem frightened. They strolled along, switching their tails to shoo off the flies, taking a bit of this or that, seemingly happy, content, and at peace with the world. Now and then they'd glance our way, but apparently they hadn't seen us.

Finally they discovered a plot of grass to their liking and began to graze. Rapidly we closed in until Don, muttering beneath his breath, stopped and pointed.

About 200 yards away, and high over a bush, was the head and neck of an enormous bull giraffe. Then another head popped up – and another. For a long minute the giraffes cased us thoroughly, and the more they saw of us the less they liked. They wheeled as if on signal, tucked their tails up alongside their fannies in that charming way giraffes have, and took off in their characteristic slow-motion gallop.

The giraffes saw us; the elands saw the giraffes – and that was the end of our stalk. Our last view of the elands was their big fat rumps disappearing at a gallop into the bush.

"Bloody butt-ins," said Don bitterly.

What I said was worse than that.

*I*n the days that followed, Don and I hunted lions long and hard. We were out as soon as we could see, and came back to camp only when the sun had set and the quick tropic darkness had descended on the veldt. I shot some Thomson's gazelles for our table, kongoni for meat for the boys. I also lucked into a very good buffalo bull. There were lionesses around – very handsome ones, too. Now and then we saw elands – usually cows, but sometimes bulls – and almost always they saw or heard or smelled us first and were rapidly disappearing. It began to dawn on me that one doesn't exactly go out and knock off trophy eland bulls with sticks.

The way to catch one, as I've said, is to hunt lions. Don and I, a driver, and two gunbearers were cruising one morning along the banks of the Simiyu River just before sunrise when we came upon two big-maned lions strolling along. They looked at us (or rather at the hunting car) mildly, and we looked at them hungrily.

Now, in Tanganyika and Kenya there is a game regulation forbidding shooting within 500 yards of a hunting car. There is also a rule that the hunter cannot bounce out of the car, let it move on 500 yards, and then open up. I can testify that Don Ker and Syd Downey observe the regulations – and to the letter – even though it means losing a good trophy. It would have been ridiculously easy for me to stick the muzzle of my .375 out of the car and knock over either or both of those lions. It would have been almost as easy for me to jump out of the car and pot them.

Don wanted me to get one of them as much as I did, but we drove on until we were out of sight and well over 500 yards from where we'd seen them. Then we jumped out of the car, dived into the almost-dry riverbed, and ran for our lions. I was fully convinced they had not been spooked, that they didn't know a hunting car from our aunt Cynthia, and that they would still be strolling along, whistling to themselves and with their big, fat, pendant bellies swinging.

But when we poked our heads up over the bank, there were no lions in sight.

We went back to where we'd last seen them and picked up the tracks. Apparently those big cats did know what hunting cars were, likewise what they meant, because the moment we got out of sight, they had run like rabbits.

After a council of war, we decided to track them. So off we went. The tracks were easy to follow when over open, dusty ground. But when they took us through high, heavy grass, they were very difficult. When we lost the spoor we'd circle, and sooner or later one of us would pick it up again.

The sun moved higher. It got hotter. We got farther and farther away from the water in the car and even from the stinking muddy waterholes in the parched Simiyu. The lions seemed to know where they were headed. They had long since stopped running and were walking.

*W*e had gone about five miles from the river, and it was nearing noon, when Don saw a little buck Thomson's gazelle staring fixedly into a brush patch, as interested and horrified as a youngster seeing his first burlesque show.

Don held up his hand for caution. "He sees the lions!" he whispered.

Leaving our boys behind, we sneaked into the brush, eyes straining in the gloom to spot those lions before they saw us. But we had given them the jitters and they were on the lookout. We were sneaking upwind, so they must have seen us or heard us. Possibly the Tommy ran and gave us away. At any rate, my first awareness of the lions was a glimpse of them running at right angles through the thicket about 50 yards away. I could see the silhouette of their big manes and bulky bodies through the bush.

I raised my .375 and was following one of them, the crosshairs on his shoulder, when Don stopped me. "Don't shoot!" he cried. "We don't want a wounded lion."

So I didn't shoot.

Don and I took out after them, hoping to get a shot in the clear. I saw them again when they were about to go into thick bush 300 yards away. The opportunity was poorer than the first.

Defeated, we headed back to the car, which was beside the Simiyu, a good five miles away. All at once I was tired, hungry, thirsty, footsore, and almost ill with disappointment. I surrendered my .375 to my gunbearer and slogged along under the hot sun, feeling 95 years old.

It is one thing to walk five miles after starting fresh in the cool of the morning and thinking you're about to come to grips with a couple of he-lions at any moment. It is another to walk five miles in the heat of the day, thirsty and tired, after a couple of lions have made a chump out of you and have weighted your feet with disappointment.

The equatorial sun got hotter and hotter, and I got thirstier and thirstier. It suddenly occurred to me that I had it in for he-lions, particularly those two fat slobs we'd seen. They looked so dog-goned brave, but they ran like rabbits . . .

We were almost continually in sight of pretty little Thomson's gazelles, and now and then we'd see a small herd of kongonis staring at us for a moment before they took off in a clumsy, spavined gallop. Once we spotted a couple of hyenas sneaking away from the bare bones of a lion kill.

But I was more interested in getting the load off my feet and finding a drink. As I grew thirstier, my sights went lower and lower. At first I dreamt of a cold and beaded glass of beer in some air-conditioned bar. Then I began to dream of an ordinary drugstore soda. Soon I was ready to settle for a glass of cold water – then simply for a glass of water. Before long I was dreaming voluptuously of the waterhole on the Simiyu with the dead hyena in it. Now, if a man just went to the other end of the pool, held his nose, and didn't look at the hyena . . .

Suddenly Don stopped. His binoculars came up to his eyes. "See the bull eland?" he whispered.

I indeed saw an eland standing in the thin shade of a thorn tree a good half-mile away. I looked at him with my 9X glasses, but couldn't discern much about his head through the mirage dancing off the hot, bright plain.

"Terrific head," Don said. "Feel fit enough to try for him? It will be a difficult stalk, but maybe we can make it, and he's worth no end of trouble."

For a moment the rolling mirage let up and I got a good look at the bull's head. I could tell the horns were long and massive, better than those of the bull the giraffes had beaten me out of. Then my internal chemistry began to work. Suddenly I wasn't tired. Nor was I thirsty. In fact, I felt swell.

So off we went to stalk one of the wariest of all African antelope across an almost barren plain. We bent over so that the eland would not get the hated upright human silhouette. We walked on our knuckles with an apelike shuffle and moved only when the bull was looking elsewhere. When he looked toward us, we stopped. Flies chewed on us. The sun beat down. Safari ants stung us, but when that bull was looking our way, we moved not so much as a muscle.

Minute after minute passed. We progressed at the rate of about 100 yards per half-hour. Gradually the bull grew larger and larger, and the horns looked better and better.

From Sonora to the Alaska boundary, I have stalked many a fine mountain ram. I have also stalked elk, antelope, and deer, but usually in mountainous or cut-up country where I could get out of the animal's sight and sneak up behind a ridge or other cover. Here, we were slipping from bush to bush, trying to keep the eland from seeing us moving, as well as camouflaging our ugly human forms with twigs and shadow.

When we were about 350 yards from the bull, we paused for minutes behind a red anthill. "I think I could knock him from here," I whispered to Don.

"No," he said. "Let's make sure."

Crawling on our hands and knees, we sneaked about 100 yards closer and stopped in the shade of a thorn tree. For the last 50 yards I'd been afraid to look up, since the only cover we had was an occasional sickly shrub and some thin grass.

"Think you can hit him from here?" Don whispered.

"Of course."

"It's a pretty long shot, but I am afraid he'll run if we get closer."

I took the .375 Magnum from my gunbearer's hand and wiped the lenses of the scope, which had gotten dusty. Poor Don almost died of heart failure when he saw me dig out the white handkerchief.

Then I slowly rose to my feet, put my left hand against the trunk of the thorn tree, and rested the forend of the rifle over it. The wary bull had spotted me and seen the movement. He was watching me and I was about to let him have it.

Then I got a break. The eland was suspicious, but not frightened. He decided to come closer for a better look before he disturbed his midday rest by running. So he trotted about 50 yards our way and stood quartering toward me. Through the bright field of the $2^3/_4$X scope, he looked sharp and big and beautiful. I had the intersection of the crosshairs behind his shoulder for a high lung shot. Gradually I increased the pressure on the trigger. The big gun roared. The bull gave a great jump and took off, running at right angles to me.

"He's hit!" Don shouted.

"In the lungs!" said Thomas, our headman and Don's gunbearer.

I bolted another cartridge into the chamber, swung the crosshairs along with the running eland, and touched off my second shot. He went down as if a house had fallen on him and was dead when we got to him. The first shot had gone exactly where the crosshairs had rested. The second was a bit farther back and higher.

"Hell of a head!" Don said as we approached.

And it was. An East African eland with 27-inch-long horns, measured "along the straight," as they say in those parts, is a very fine specimen. Mine went $29^3/_4$ inches and was very heavy and massive.

Most of the African white hunters are Englishmen and for food they prefer small antelope, such as the Tommy, that taste like mutton. They leave the big sorts for the camp boys. But while our three were scrambling for the choice bits, particularly for the masses of suet, and while Don wasn't looking, I sneaked in with my little pocketknife and cut out a backstrap as long as your arm and as big around as your thigh.

That night, before we went to bed, Herb Klein and Red Earley, my safari partners, and I broiled fillets over the coals and ate them like cookies. In case anyone asks you what bull eland tastes like, tell them it has the exact flavor of charcoal-broiled steaks cut from corn-fed prime beef and that cost from three to six bucks at good restaurants, where they don't even throw in the horns.

197

GRAND SLAM IN CATS

There's no African equivalent of the Scottish Macnab (a salmon, grouse, and stag taken in a single day), but on this safari in Tanganyika, O'Connor kills what he describes as a "Grand Slam" in cats – lion, leopard, serval cat, and cheetah. May, 1954

Whenever I think of Africa, I remember our hunting camp in the great cat country along the Simiyu River in Tanganyika – and one of my most vivid memories is the way it looked at dawn. The night was still very dark when our personal boys woke us up. One moment I'd be lost to the world. The next I'd be conscious that tall, grave Suleiman had set my hot tea on the ground beside my cot and was taking down the mosquito netting.

I am a quick starter; morning is the best part of my day. As quickly as I could I'd bounce out of bed, gulp my hot tea, then dress, wash up, and go outside. But Herb Klein, who starts late and finishes strong, would lie in his bed, groaning in horror at the spectacle of anyone who could greet the dawn with cries of joy.

Dawn comes quickly in equatorial Africa. One moment the sky is remote and black and the stars glitter with white incandescence. The next, the eastern horizon begins to show pink and the stars fade to pale silver. As I write this, I can still see the interlaced branches of the thin-leafed thorn trees behind our Simiyu camp black against the rosy glow, as intricate and lovely as the pattern of a black-lace dress over a pink slip.

Quickly the eastern sky would change from pastel pink, to deep rose, to violent red. Then the red would rapidly fade. The stars would disappear, and the country around – the distant trees, the low round hills, the fragrant grassy plains – would emerge in the cold flat light of the early day like a photographic print in the developing bath.

At almost every dawn, as the day was born and the sweet chill wind blew across the plains, we'd hear the morning song of the great cats. Downstream, a pride of lions would usually be winding up the night's hunting, and we'd hear them roaring. *Harumph . . . harrumph, HARUMPH . . . wump, wump, wump.* A leopard lived upstream less than half a mile away and often, between the roars of the lions, we'd hear its coughing grunts.

Our party was one of the last to hunt the Simiyu country; not long after we pulled out it was made part of the Serengeti National Park. But what a hunting country it was when we were there!

Don Ker, the white hunter who was to steer me around during the Simiyu portion of our trip, told me this was the greatest cat country in East Africa, and after our first afternoon's tour of it, I was in full agreement.

Don and I were hardly a mile out of camp when, across a donga, we saw the cruel, sculptured perfection of a lioness' head watching us from the yellow, rustling grass. Then we saw another and another. It was a great pride of lions – 18 in all. Farther on we saw two more lionesses, lovely with sleek golden hides and taut, lean, coiled-spring beauty.

As we drove around in the hunting car I marveled at the game we saw – eland, waterbucks, impala, giraffes, little Thomson's gazelles by the thousand. Once, Don stopped the hunting car and picked up his binoculars. Lying under a tree were two cheetahs, those round-headed, round-eared, long-legged cats that are the fastest animals on earth – animals that can, for a short distance, speed along at the rate of over 70 miles an hour, animals that with their short, swift rush can overtake the fastest antelope.

This was indeed cat country!

But I didn't know half of it. I was dying to get back to camp and tell Herb Klein and Red Earley about the wonders I'd seen. Those two Texans would be deeply envious. But when we drove up, we found Red with a triumphant leer on his face. On his first afternoon in the cat country he had gone out and killed himself a very handsome lion with good blond mane. As he and Herb were cruising around with Myles Turner, their white hunter, they had spied this handsome male lying in the tall grass under a tree and making goo-goo eyes at a girl friend nearby.

While Herb remained perched about 600 yards away on an anthill, where he could watch the whole business with binoculars,

Red and Myles crept through the grass on hands and knees for half a mile to get within 75 yards of the two great cats. When they reached the thorn tree from which they planned to shoot, Red was winded, as a substantially built and well-fed man of middle years has every right to be. So he and Myles lay there in the warm sun, out of sight in the high, rank grass until Red had his wind back. Then Red got slowly up, rested his Winchester Model 70 in .300 Magnum in the crotch of a thorn tree, and put a 180-grain bullet right through the burly golden neck of that beautiful lion.

That night after dinner all of us, white hunters and dudes, sat around the campfire. Its warmth was welcome, because it gets chilly in those East African highlands as soon as the sun goes down. The stars glittered white and cold, and the Southern Cross came out. It is before a fire that hunters like to dream and plan and boast. On other nights and before other campfires – in the Yukon, on the Middle Fork of the Salmon River in Idaho, in Texas – Herb and I had planned this very trip. Now our dream was a reality.

By the flicker of the firelight we could see, golden against the black night sky, the exotic-looking, flat-topped thorn trees. And we could also see one of the safari waiters, clad in a green fez and green vest over a long, white, night-shirtlike garment, straightening up the table.

As the darkness deepened, a prowling hyena began to keen and gibber on the other side of the Simiyu, not over 100 yards away. Incredibly bold, these hyenas. They come around camp to see what they can find in the way of garbage and scraps. They'll eat anything, from the tender hindquarter of a Thomson's gazelle to a pair of hunting boots or a rifle sling. Almost every night they'd walk through our camp, and once I woke up to see one staring at me from the open door of the tent.

Now our pride of lions downstream began to roar. Next the leopard upstream joined the chorus. I shivered a little as I thought of the death that must walk this African night . . . of the waterbuck pulled down by the lions, of the trusting little Tommy murdered by the leopard and carried up into a tree . . . of the young topi and impala that would be caught and killed by the great obscene jaws of the hulking hyenas.

"Listen to it," Herb said to no one in particular. "Lions downstream, a leopard upstream. Jack and Don saw cheetahs this afternoon. Red shot a lion. How many kinds of cats are there around here anyway, Myles?"

"Big three, of course," Myles said. "Then the serval cat. Little chap. Slender. Plain black spots. Lives on birds, the smallest bucks, that sort of thing."

"You know what I'd like to do here from this camp?" Herb asked.

"What?" said Red.

"I'd like to get all four of the cats – lion, leopard, cheetah, and serval."

"Might as well wish for a polar bear too, just as long as you're at it," said Red.

"Want to put up a little dough that says I don't?" Herb snapped.

"Fifty bucks!"

"It's a deal."

Herb and Red were always making bets – on who'd get the largest buck, on which safari car would have a flat tire first, or (one in Paris) whether the first redhead to pass the sidewalk café where we were sitting would be going north or south.

Now I told myself that Herb had made himself a hopeless bet, one he was bound to lose. It wasn't much of a trick to get a lion – just any lion – there in the Simiyu country, but getting an old he-lion with a big mane was no cinch. Big-maned lions are not common and those that are in circulation move mostly at night, bushing up during the day.

Getting a leopard is even tougher because leopards are more difficult to bait than lions, and even more nocturnal. I had already seen a couple of cheetahs, but perhaps they'd be the only ones we'd spot on the entire trip – they are even scarcer than leopards. Serval cats? They were so rare that no one I knew who had hunted in Africa had ever seen one. For once, I thought, this Klein character has got himself out on a limb!

The very next morning I had occasion to think of Herb and his wild bet. Don, Red, and I were cruising around on the other side of the Simiyu when we saw vultures drop on swishing wings out of the blue sky, to perch in a big thorn tree. Don drove over to investigate and we found that a couple of cheetahs had killed a young impala. Too bad Herb wasn't there. Red and I could have knocked them off as they loped away, but the best way to see rare game is *not* to have a permit to shoot that particular species.

I was getting worried. I had come to Africa primarily to get a big trophy lion. I was concentrating on lions to the extent that I hadn't even taken out a leopard or cheetah license. As the days went by, I saw female lions, cubs, and young males; but the big-maned lions eluded me. The more I hunted the more hopeless the quest seemed. Herb had shot some good buffaloes and antelope, but he was as catless as I. Nevertheless his confidence remained.

"Keep your pants on, amigo!" he told me one night when I was feeling blue. "My hunches are almost always right. I feel it in my bones that you're going to shoot the damnedest lion that ever drank from the Simiyu. It may sound silly, but I still think I'll get all those funny cats."

He was right; next day his luck took a turn for the better. He and Myles Turner, peppery, sandy-haired white hunter, were cruising in their hunting car when they saw a big black-and-orange leopard lying beneath a thorn tree reflectively chewing on a little Thomson's gazelle it had just caught. As it caught sight of the car, it abandoned its kill and took refuge in a patch of high grass.

"We'll get that leopard!" Myles muttered, as he stepped on the gas and took the hunting car to a spot half a mile away, where he could park it out of sight.

Then he and Herb came cautiously back. That staunch friend of the African hunter, an anthill about five feet high, loomed up about 75 yards from where they'd last seen the cat. Cautiously they approached it, creeping through the grass on all fours. Finally they made it without giving the cat their wind or a betraying sound.

Herb lay behind the anthill for a moment until his breathing became normal, then cautiously poked his head over it. For a moment he saw nothing and thought the leopard was gone. But the Tommy still lay beneath the thorn tree and Herb had hopes. Presently the round, spotted head of the leopard showed cautiously over the grass. The cat was still torn between hunger and fear of the automobile, and was taking no chances before he resumed his meal.

Slowly Herb brought the crosshairs in his scope to bear on the leopard's head until he could see them sharp and black against an ear. When the .30 Weatherby roared, the cat's head disappeared, and Myles, who had seen hair fly, gave a yell of triumph. The 220-grain Remington Core-Lokt had taken that leopard just behind the ear and luckily did practically no damage to the scalp.

*I*t is an old safari custom that when one of the paying guests knocks off a major trophy (lion, leopard, buffalo, rhino, elephant, or cheetah), the boys carry him from the hunting car to his tent, whooping and hollering and chanting improvised verses in his praise, such as "Brave bwana Fatso shot a lion. Now he will be happy and give us silver shillings!"

When the hunting car came honking in triumph up to camp that day with the leopard, the safari boys grabbed Herb and carried him around camp. He did not know it, but he was in for a lot of free rides during the next few days. When the Klein luck starts rolling, it really rolls!

That afternoon Herb and Myles went out to shoot a lion bait. They had found a rocky little hill with a good deal of lion spoor around it, so they shot a kongoni, and hung it in a thorn tree nearby.

Next morning the hunters went out just after sunrise and crept up over the little hill, in order to look down and see if there was a lion on the bait. But when they peered over, they saw nothing. The kongoni was untouched. Both Herb and Myles were bitterly disappointed, but suddenly they became aware of a noise in thick brush in the rocks below them, a noise that sounded suspiciously like some large animal having a meal – *crunch, crunch, chomp, chomp, growl, growl.* Cautiously they crept forward and peered into the brush below. The noise continued. Finally they made out the shadowy form of a big male lion. He was eating what they afterward found was a warthog.

To shoot or not to shoot? They didn't want to try to plug the big cat through the brush, for fear the bullet would be deflected. The thing to do was rout him out and knock him off in the open.

They crept silently back over the little hill and told their gunbearers to pound on the bait tree and throw stones into the brush to make the lion move. They thought he would run directly away from the noise and the gunbearers, so they stationed themselves behind a bush on the opposite side of the hill.

But instead of coming toward them, the lion took off at right angles across an open plain for another hill, and before they knew it he was a couple of hundred yards away and really scratching gravel.

Herb's first shot hit him in the flank and spun him around.

"Got him!" Myles yelled.

But the lion recovered and was off once more.

The next shot struck the big cat in the foot, slowed him, but didn't stop him.

Herb was pretty concerned by this time. Here he had a wounded lion on his hands and through his mind flashed all the stories he had read about indignant cats escaping into the brush and then knocking down and chewing up those who went after them.

Running as fast as he could, he took out after the lion, trying at the same time to reload his almost-dry magazine. The gunbearers say he fell on his face twice. He has no memory of that, but he did come in with skinned knees and with hide off his left palm and elbow.

He quickly found, though, that even a wounded lion can run faster than a desk-bound executive who gets his exercise by pacing the floor while he thinks heavy thoughts. He was short of wind, and the lion was getting closer and closer to shelter. It was now or never. He stopped, got into a kneeling position, and tried to calm his tortured breathing. By now the lion had turned broadside to the hunter and was but a few yards from cover.

Herb swung along with the running beast, got the crosshairs well ahead of it, muttered a brief incantation to the gods, and touched one off. The big 270-grain .375 bullet landed on the cat with a solid plunk. The lion went down. Then it got up and crawled feebly into the brush. Herb stood up, but his wind was short and his legs were so shaky he almost fell down a third time.

When he and Myles approached the bush, they could see the big yellow cat lying back among some rocks. He was still growling, but the bullet had smacked him in the lungs and he was through. He was a fine, big blond lion, with a heavy mane. Between pegs he measured nine feet four inches from the tip of his nose to the last joint of his tail – and that is a lot of lion.

*W*ith his leopard and his lion behind him, Herb had passed Red and me with a slash of speed. Red was hunting leopard and not seeing any. His luck was particularly annoying because mornings and evenings we could hear the leopard a few hundred yards up the Simiyu coughing and grunting, and one morning we woke to find that the beast had walked within a few yards of our tents.

Now that Red had his lion, he saw several of the kind of big-maned males that I was looking for, and because he didn't have a cheetah license, he saw more of those small-headed, long-legged cats.

For my part, I couldn't find the big trophy lion I wanted, but I did see the leopards Red was after. One morning I saw a glorious big male leopard, shining in the glory of deep-gold hide and rosette spots, working on an old bait that Herb and Myles had left. By this time it was pretty high and if there is anything a leopard loves it is well-cured meat. Another time just at sunup Don and I watched a beautiful leopard gallop across an open plain. This was *cat* country!

Red and I, both envious of Herb's luck, thought it had deserted him when he came in one evening to report he had seen a cheetah and had missed it. He and Myles had been after buffalo when they spotted a cheetah out in the open, where it could not be stalked. He had tried a shot with the 300-grain bullet in his .375 Weatherby Magnum, but misjudged the range and missed.

But here in the Simiyu country his luck was rolling. The day after he got his lion, he and Myles were cruising around and spotted a big male cheetah that had just dined – too well and very unwisely, since he had eaten a whole Thomson's gazelle and then taken a big drink of water. His enormous, swollen belly weighed as much as he did, and he simply could not travel fast.

The cat was lying on an anthill getting the sun and digesting his kill. Myles and Herb ditched the car and began the stalk. Cover was thin and the cat saw them. He took off. To get a vantage point, they ran to the anthill where he'd been lying. In a moment they spotted him about 500 yards away, moving slowly through thin grass. Herb took a crack at the cat, but the bullet hit just below him and once more he ran.

As they watched, the cheetah disappeared into a brush patch more than half a mile away.

"Come on!" Myles yelled. "He's full of meat and won't go fast."

So off they went. Herb, who used to be a fast end on the University of Wisconsin varsity, bitterly regretted his desk-bound years. On this African trip, his fate seemed to consist of running as fast as he could over the veldt after big cats.

With chest heaving, he made it to the brush where the cheetah had disappeared. He and Myles moved warily up one side of the thicket, watching the other. Presently, as Herb pussyfooted through the brush getting his wind back, he saw the cat in a little opening about 150 yards away, looking back over his shoulder at Myles. The gorged cat could hardly travel. Herb simply dropped to one knee, put the crosshairs behind the cheetah's shoulder and let him have it. For the third time in a few days, the camp boys gave him a free ride.

That very afternoon Don Ker and a couple of the boys went out to put up bait, while Herb, Red and I went out with Myles to get camp meat and photograph some game. I remember knocking off a Tommy and I think Red shot an impala. We were driving back to camp when Myles suddenly put on the brake and hissed, "Serval cat!"

I had almost forgotten Herb's wild-eyed bet, but it suddenly dawned on me that now he had a chance to do something which, so far as I know, has never been done by another American on safari – collecting on one trip all four of the major African cats.

This *was* a piece of luck. Here was the rarest, the most nocturnal, and the shyest of the larger cats right out in the short grass of the open plain in *daylight*. And Herb had a special license for serval!

About 100 yards from the car was a tree- and brush-filled donga; it was the only possible approach to the serval. The two hunters got into the donga without being detected by the cat. Red and I had a ringside seat as we watched with binoculars from the hunting car. We could see the cat lying in the grass, and we could also see Myles and Herb sneaking along the donga.

Then the action slackened. We could no longer see the hunters, and the serval cat lay down in the grass. He too was out of sight.

"Klein'll never get him now," Red said. "He can't see him!"

"That guy's riding a streak of luck and I wouldn't give you five cents for that cat's life," I told him. "I don't know how he'll get him, but he will."

I had put down my binoculars when suddenly Red snorted: "Guess where that jughead is now. He's climbed a tree. He's got his rifle with him. By golly, he's going to shoot!"

Then I heard the sharp crack of the little Remington .222, followed by the thud of a striking bullet.

"What did I tell you?" I said.

As we drove back to camp, Herb rubbed it in a little.

"What you two buzzards need is a little luck," he told us smugly. "Here we are up to our necks in cats, but Red's still looking for a leopard and Jack still hasn't shot his mangy old he-lion. You guys are smart and you're handsome. Trouble is you aren't lucky!"

The next morning when I got out early to breakfast, I suddenly felt clammy, greasy hands on my face and neck. It was Herb at work. He had covered his hands with grease from his lion and then wiped it on me to bring me luck. When unsuspecting Red came out, he too was given the treatment – with grease from Herb's leopard.

Funny part is that it worked.

Within an hour I shot a big lion that measured nine feet seven inches between pegs, and Red caught up at last with the leopard that lived a quarter of a mile up the Simiyu. It was a lady leopard, a spinster, and Red nailed her through the neck when she came out to investigate a bait.

Maybe Herb did succeed in passing on some of his fabulous luck, but maybe the fact that we were hunting in the world's greatest cat country also had something to do with it.

LAST MINUTE KUDU

The kudu was one of O'Connor's favorite African game animals (lions were also at the top of his list), and on this safari in Bechuanaland he kills a superb bull with his favorite caliber of rifle, the .270.
June, 1968

*W*e saw our first Bechuanaland bull kudu early one morning when we headed out in the hunting car to look over some red lechwe and to try to find a lion. The kudu broke out of the brush on one timbered "island" and ran 200 yards or so across an open valley to another patch of timber. He was a handsome creature with his spiral horns, his gray body with its white stripes, and his slender legs.

When the bull shot out of the brush, my wife Eleanor and I both clutched our rifles as though we were about to leap from the car and open up. But John Kingsley-Heath, our white hunter, didn't even slow the vehicle down.

"You wouldn't want him," he said. "He's only about 50 inches. Shootable, but not for old African hands."

The kudu disappeared in the brush, but his curiosity was too much for him. He came back and climbed to the top of an anthill about ten feet high. As we drew opposite the hill, he stood there facing us like an equine statue on a pedestal – his nostrils flaring, his chest heaving from his run.

I yelled to John to stop the hunting car. Then I grabbed for my movie camera, switched to the long lens, and shot about 15 feet of film.

"Isn't he beautiful!" Eleanor said, just as the bull decided he had seen enough and jumped down from the anthill. "After he posed like that, I wouldn't have shot him if he had gone sixty inches."

"If you ever turned down a sixty-inch kudu, I'd quit hunting," John said. "When I thought Bwana M'zee (the Old Man: me) had missed that sixty-incher down on the Great Ruaha in fifty-nine, I contemplated suicide."

"Don't be silly," Eleanor said.

Everything was moving that bright clear morning along the Okavango Swamp. Warthogs – their white tusks glistening in the sun, their tails up like automobile radio aerials – trotted as smoothly over the short green grass as if they were on roller skates. Once, we saw a herd of eight cow and calf kudu galloping off on their little feet. The kudu's curious "sore-footed" gait is reminiscent of that of a vain woman wearing shoes that are too small.

Now and then we saw a pair of reedbucks, antelope about the size and appearance of whitetail deer and having sharp, round horns 12 to 16 inches long. The strange water antelope called red lechwe were everywhere, in herds of a half-dozen to 100 or more. They were feeding on the shore or standing in the swamp's shallow water.

The Okavango Swamp covers hundreds of square miles in what was Bechuanaland when we hunted there, but has since become the independent nation of Botswana. This great swamp is a watery world of fish and of the raucous fish eagles that devour them; of crocodiles; of the mysterious situtunga, a shaggy little water antelope with twisted horns like those of his relative, the bushbuck; of islands covered with brush and grass and tall trees, where leopards and black-maned lions find happy hunting and where herds of big black buffalo doze and graze.

We were traveling on a sand spit that thrust far out into the swamp. Generally it was above water, and on it were "islands" so high that water never covered them and trees grew upon them. Out in the swamp itself, we could see other islands dark with trees. In some places the water was but a few inches deep; in others it was a dozen feet deep.

We had hit the Okavango at a bad time, John told us. There had been a drought lasting several years in Bechuanaland. Thousands of cattle owned by the natives had died. The water level had fallen so much that a hunting car could be driven around among islands that were high and dry, and you could hunt just about everywhere.

But then heavy rains had come, both in Bechuanaland and in Angola to the north. The water level had risen. The game-filled islands had been cut off, and the game that had concentrated on the outskirts of the Okavango for water had scattered to the vast brush country surrounding the swamps.

*W*e had left Richard and Sarah Jane Harris, our companions for this safari, at our main camp near the end of the sand spit about 40 miles away.

A lorry lumbered behind us as we rolled along in the bush vehicle. Presently, John stopped and showed the boys in the lorry where to pitch camp.

John's plan was to see if we could get a couple of red lechwe trophies and use the carcasses as lion bait. There were a good many greater kudu in the area, some buffalo and lions, and some leopards and cheetahs. But the shooting of cheetahs is forbidden, and the area's leopards are rarely seen – they come to baits even less often than the lions.

Some magnificent male lions have come out of Bechuanaland and also from Angola. I knocked off my finest lion trophy in Angola in 1962.

Collecting a couple of sizable red lechwe, we figured, should not be difficult. Apparently that part of the Okavango is red lechwe heaven. We were never out of sight of dozens if not hundreds of these animals, which were scattered along the shores of the swamp, nibbling the tender grass. They stood in herds in the shallows, staring at us.

Every now and then a bunch of lechwe would panic. They'd gallop through the shallow water, throwing spray 15 feet high with a sound like the roar of the surf.

Just as the mountain sheep survives because he can travel faster over rough ground than the soft-footed animals that chase him, so does the lechwe survive in shallow-water areas. There he can run faster than the lions, the leopards, and the hyenas that chase him.

Nevertheless, the Okavango's predators must live well. They can lie in wait on the wooded hummocks and rush the lechwe that venture out to feed on the tender grass along shore. In our travels we must have seen the remains of 40 or 50 freshly killed lechwe.

While riding along, we paused now and then to glass promising herds of lechwe. Many of the animals looked good to me, as I had seen lechwe previously in Angola, where they were not nearly so plentiful and their heads did not run so large.

Presently, John laid his binoculars down and turned to Eleanor.

"Mama Kali," he said, "I see a nice one for you. See the big animal in that far bunch? He's got a very fine head. We can snake

211

through the island there and get a pretty good shot."

(Our Swahili-speaking gunbearers and skinners – and John, too – call Eleanor Mama Kali, meaning the deadly or dangerous woman, because she never misses.)

While I sat on an anthill and watched, Eleanor and John disappeared into the brush on the island. But something spooked the herd of lechwe. I saw them go plowing away through the water. Then I heard Eleanor's .30/06 go off. The big male sagged at the hindquarters, but kept on with the rest of the herd.

"Gut shot," John said gloomily when he and Eleanor rejoined me. "They started to run before Mama Kali was ready. She could only shoot once, because other lechwe got in the way."

We drove around to the other side of the lake and finally located the wounded ram. He was standing, humped up and with his head down, at what appeared to be 350 to 425 yards away.

I took a good rest over a termite hill, held so that I could see light between the bottom of the horizontal crosswire and the top of the ram's back, and squeezed one off. The lechwe dropped at the shot, and a moment later the sound of the striking bullet came floating back.

John took off with the two gunbearers, carrying his .470 double as insurance against crocodiles. It took them several minutes to find the lechwe, and John had to shoot it again. The ram was hiding in four feet of water with only its nostrils showing.

Either the ram had been farther way than I had thought or I had yanked the trigger, because the bullet had hit low and a bit farther back than I had intended. The lechwe was a good one – 28¼ inches along the curve of the horn. The best we had gotten in Angola was about 26 inches.

The red lechwe belongs to the kob family along with the true kob, the waterbucks, and the pukus. The meat of all members of this family is coarse, strong, and tough, and few humans can stomach it. But apparently it tastes pretty good to predators, so we found a good spot and hung the carcass where lions had been hunting and feeding.

When we got back to camp that night, the sun was setting in a rosy, glowing sky, and the waters of the Okavango were like polished silver.

The fly camp was all set up – a green bugproof sleeping tent for my wife and me, a cot draped with mosquito netting for John, and a table on which sat a bottle, a jug of ice, and some charged water. There were chairs by a cheerful fire, and on another fire 50 yards away the cook was roasting a hindquarter of reedbuck I had shot a couple of days before. Basted with white wine, butter and pepper sauce, the roast smelled very nice while we sat around the fire sipping sundowners.

During the night we heard lions roaring, and the next morning, after a fast breakfast, we went out to check our bait. The carcass had been pulled down and devoured. Nothing remained of the tough old lechwe but some of the stomach contents, the hooves, some bits of bone, and a few scraps of hide.

"The lions should be close by," John whispered.

We set out – Eleanor with her .30/06, me with a .375, and John with his .470 double. The mound on which we had put the bait was about 200 yards long and 50 to 75 yards wide. Covered with brush, trees, and waist-high grass, it wasn't the best place in the world to have a fight with a lion – and Bechuanaland lions have a reputation for ferocity unparalleled in all of Africa.

We inched forward into the gentle morning breeze. I was certain I could smell lion. Then I saw brush move perhaps 40 yards away, and in an opening I could see the sleek yellow head and the cold yellow eyes of a lioness. She seemed to have eyes only for me. She watched me for about ten seconds and then walked slowly to our right.

Again we moved on. Before going 20 yards we heard brush rustle and saw a lion with a yellow mane staring at us within shotgun range – skeet No. 1, at that.

"Take him," John whispered to Eleanor. She had shot two tigers, but never a lion. I had killed four lions, so she was to have first shot.

The lion gave a deep, rumbling growl, and I put the crosswires of the Weaver K3 right on his shoulder.

"Shoot!" John whispered again.

"He's not very good," Eleanor whispered back.

A moment later we saw the lioness again. She was still moving slowly off. Again we went forward. Presently, in a little opening, we saw the male standing beside another yellow-maned lion and watching us.

John and I each picked a lion and covered it. Then the lioness came out of the brush and joined the two males.

"Are you going to shoot?" I whispered.

"No!" she said.

For a moment I was tempted to squeeze the trigger of my .375. The crosswires looked very sweet on the lion's shoulder. In that moment I thought of many things – the fact that I had previously shot four lions, one of which was about as good a lion as you can get, and the fact that we'd be in a tough spot if a couple of them came for us at once. I must admit, too, that I wanted to hold off for a better trophy.

Which of these thoughts swayed me, I cannot say. At any rate I didn't let the shot off. We heard a lion growl farther away as the big cats moved off.

All of us had been pretty tense while playing ring-around-the-rosy with the lions. Now that they were gone, we heaved a collective sigh. I had never been in a pickle with lions, but John had been badly mauled and almost killed by one some years before. Eleanor had once cut down an enraged tiger that was about to gobble up an Indian beater, and both of our gunbearers had seen plenty of fast action with lions and leopards.

We all had a great deal of respect for the big cats.

"I was disappointed that you didn't shoot, Mama Kali," John said as we walked back to the car. "Someone ought to knock off a lion for the good of the safari."

"If I ever shoot one," Eleanor said, "it's going to have a better mane than either of those. I just don't see any point in shooting a so-so lion."

Then John turned to me and said, "When you leveled down on that fellow, I expected to hear that .375 go off. Didn't you want him?"

"I'm holding out for a better one," I said.

Thinking that we might get more lions to come to bait, we hung another lechwe that Eleanor shot. We were returning to camp for lunch when one of the gunbearers whispered *"Tendalla!"* and pointed to a brushy island. With my binoculars I could see a bull kudu staring at us from the other side of some brush.

"Ordinary," said John, and we drove on.

The funniest incident of the whole safari occurred late that day, as we headed back toward camp. It was almost dark, and a pair of warthogs had turned in for the night in their den in a ten-foot-high termite hill. Apparently they were dozing off when one of them looked out and saw our hunting car bearing down on them. Uttering loud *"Oink-oinks,"* both of the animals shot out of their hole, missing the car by inches.

We must have been in a warthog city, because an instant later seven or eight other warthogs raced out of their holes within a radius of 75 yards and, giving vent to noisy *"Oink-oinks,"* fled desperately into the dusk. I suppose they thought they were being attacked by a pride of lions.

Kiebe and Edward, the gunbearers, howled with laughter.

John wiped sweat from his brow.

"It gave me a bit of a start," he said. "For an instant I thought we were being charged by a herd of rhinos!"

Since the lions had been roaring the night before, we decided to get up just before first light and drive in the direction of the roars. To me, this seemed a good idea – almost a sure thing.

I awoke about midnight to the tune of roaring not very far away, and for the rest of the night I slept fitfully, spending most of my time listening. There seemed to be two prides of the big cats. I remembered how in 1959, on our first trip with John in Tanganyika, we had hunted toward a roaring pride at dawn and I had knocked off a galloping lion with a shot I'll never forget.

But my lion luck, something in which I had great confidence, had apparently run out with my fourth and best lion. As the night wore on, the roars got farther and farther away, and I was certain that at least one of the prides had left the sand spit and crossed to an island.

And so it proved. We were out before first light, and though we saw no lions, we did hear some impressive roaring far out in the swamp. As far as we could tell, all the lions had left the spit.

But we did see a magnificent cheetah. He was lying atop a termite hill, his coat glowing golden in the first rays of the sun, watching us with hooded yellow eyes.

We checked our baits, but none had been touched. If we got lions on this trip, it would have to be somewhere else, as the cats had left the sand spit and we could not follow them through the swamp out to the islands.

Luck is an odd thing. If a hunter's luck is good, he can be heavy footed, a poor climber, a lousy shot – and yet he can get game. If his luck is bad, he's had it.

Up to now my lion and kudu luck had always been so good that I felt I was specially blessed. On my past hunts I had seen at least 200 lions and far more than my share of bull kudu. My wife also felt that she was specially favored – particularly with cats. She had encountered dozens of lions, leopards, and cheetahs in Africa, and far more tigers in India than anyone had any right to expect. She had also bumped into many big kudu bulls.

But on this trip a jinx was riding on our shoulders. Heavy rains filled the Okavango and made hunting tough. Along the way, our gun cases had been broken open and most of our ammunition stolen. We had a narrow escape with a wounded Cape buffalo. And as I write this, our fine gemsbok and lechwe trophies are long overdue in New

York and are presumably lost.

It seemed that we had turned our kudu luck over to Richard Harris, our hunting companion. Early in the trip he knocked off a very good kudu, and he could hardly go out of camp without stumbling onto coveys of big bulls. He and Frank Miller, his white hunter, saw so many bulls that they called the area "kudu alley."

But our kudu luck was out. Frank and Richard would come into camp and say that they had just seen five big bulls peacefully browsing a mile or so away. We would rush out there and the kudu would be gone. Out of our last camp in the Kalahari Desert, Frank and Richard saw one big kudu bull five or six different times in the same place. They never went there without running into him. John, Eleanor, and I haunted the locality. We found the bull's fresh tracks, but never laid eyes on him.

Our lion luck was just as bad – and Richard Harris shared it. The country around our camp on the Kalahari swarmed with zebras and wildebeest, and two or three prides of lions were preying on them. We heard the lions roaring at night, and in the morning circling vultures would lead us to the kills. On three or four occasions Richard and Frank encountered female and young male lions, but never did they see an old lion.

But though our luck was bad, I enjoyed the hunt – the frosty nights of southern Africa's winter, the warm sunny days, the sundowners around the fire before dinner.

Eleanor and I collected good gemsbok, springbok, and our quota of zebras. Both Eleanor and Richard shot roan antelope, and Richard got an eland.

Finally, only two days remained before we would have to drive to an airstrip to meet our chartered plane that was to fly out from Johannesburg to pick us up.

We spent those two days hunting near a series of great salt pans about 35 miles from camp. The pans, an interesting feature of the Kalahari Desert, are depressions covered with a silvery chemical that is brought to the surface by underground water. At a distance the pans look like lakes or ponds. The alkali flats of the American Southwest are much the same thing. Some of the pans extend for miles in intricate and irregular patterns. Their surface is as smooth as pavement, and an automobile can speed across them as if on a superhighway.

The country we covered the first day was sandy and as flat as a pool table, and on it grew sparse grass and scattered thorn trees. It looked much like the desert country of southern Arizona.

Now and then we came upon a barbed-wire fence built at great expense by the veterinary department of Bechuanaland to keep the game away from water, so that it would die of thirst. The scientific mind is often inscrutable to a peasant like me.

The small, skinny cattle of Bechuanaland are sold in Rhodesia for an average of $12 a head. A native who wants to shoot and skin a zebra can sell the hide in Maun or Francistown for $100 (zebra hides are highly regarded in both the United States and Europe by interior decorators, who use them for rugs and for upholestry).

I was told by a Bechuanaland official that the building of one drift fence caused the death of 25,000 game animals, mostly zebras. It may be entirely logical to destroy a $100 zebra, which is perfectly adapted to the desert country, in order to raise a $12 cow, which is not. But I am too dumb to understand such logic.

I noted with pleasure that in many places the thirsty animals had broken down the fences, which had not been repaired.

*W*e had one more day to hunt. But since John had to go to the airstrip to meet another party the next day and since I could very well spend most of that day packing, today was really my last. I had just about forgotten there was such a thing as kudu.

I pricked up my ears.

"Kiebe says he sees the tips of a kudu's horns in the brush," John said softly. "Why don't you go over and collect him."

The veteran gunbearer and I sneaked through brush for about 74 yards. Then I could make out the rear end of one kudu, its tail busily switching flies. I could also see the horns of an adult bull.

I walked 15 or 20 feet to my right until I could see the top of the adult bull's back. I shot offhand with the .270 and saw the kudu fall. Two other kudu ran out – a young adult with two spirals on each horn and youngster with no more than a foot of horn just beginning to make the first turn.

We photographed the kudu, skinned out the head, and left for camp with the meat and trophy. The kudu was by no means my best, but I'd never hunted longer or passed up more bulls before I shot one.

It was late and dark when we got back to camp. Frank Miller and the Harrises were around the fire belting their sundowners, and the cooks were keeping the dinner hot. All of us were a little sad, because we had only one more night out on the veldt of southern Africa.

217

he plan the next morning was for Frank, Richard and Sarah Jane Harris, and Eleanor to go over to an area where the grandfather of all Bechuanaland kudu hung out, to see if Eleanor could bushwhack him.

The kudu hunt was to be a simple and easy one. Eleanor was philosophical. If the bull turned up and was larger than any she had shot, she would do her best to pot him. If he didn't turn up, she would not go into a decline.

The kudu hunters drove off, and I spent the morning getting ready to leave. About 12:30 the head boy came and told me that lunch was ready. I asked him to hold off until the others came back. But they didn't return, and I finally ate alone at 2 o'clock.

I wondered what had happened. I decided that Eleanor must have wounded a kudu and that the members of the party were trailing it.

I went back to my tent, tried reading a book, and fell asleep.

I was awakened when Eleanor came in just before sundown. Her face was dirty and scratched. Her safari jacket was torn, the knees were out of her pants, her hair was disheveled, and her hat was askew.

"What in the world have you been doing?" I demanded.

"Hunting lions," she said.

"It looks as if one of them caught you!"

"We never went to the kudu place," she told me. "We weren't far from it when we saw this wonderful, big black-maned lion. He ran when he saw the safari car. Richard and I piled out, but before we could shoot, this darned lion was in thick brush.

"I remembered how Joe Shaw got killed by a lion in thick brush in Angola and how John got mauled in Tanganyika, but I knew we were leaving tomorrow. If I got et by a lion, at least everyone could say I got et by a good lion.

"Well, anyway, that brush patch must have been lousy with lions, and the only way we could move was to follow the runways the lions had made. That's why the knees are out of my pants. I had to crawl a lot.

"Most of the time I could smell lions. A dozen times I heard the lions growl only a few feet away, and three times I saw a lion moving off through the brush. I didn't shoot because I couldn't tell what lion it was. Once a lion growled a long time and didn't move. I wondered if it was going to come at us. But we were all set."

Eleanor had been sitting on her bed. She leaned over and started to unlace her boots.

"Ask the boys to fix me a bath," she said. "I'm absolutely filthy. And see if you can get Number One boy to promote me a long, cold drink.

"You know," she continued, "I wish you had been along. Then we could have surrounded them."

Finally, she sighed and said, "A real fun day!"

*W*e flew back to Johannesburg the next day and then boarded a plane for Rome by way of Leopoldville in the troubled Congo.

I have never had a more interesting flight. It was a clear, beautiful day. We crossed Bechuanaland and from 20,000 feet we could see the country we had been hunting – the Kalahari dotted with salt pans, the silvery Okavango. We stopped over in Leopoldville, where the Congo River looked to be five miles wide, and then continued on over the great Congo rain forest, which eventually thinned out into the brush country fringing the southern Sahara.

For three hours the big Alitalia DC-8 jet sped over the sand dunes and rocky hills of the seemingly endless desert. It looked as if nothing could live there, but I knew there were Barbary sheep on the rocky *jebels* and addax browsing in the *wadis*. Dusk was coming on when we saw a sprinkling of lights that marked cities of the Mediterranean coast of Africa. Not long after that we were seated in a sidewalk cafe on the famous Via Veneto in Rome. Eleanor had gotten her hair done in Johannesburg. Her scratches had healed, and she wore a light dress now in the pleasant September air of this ancient city. She didn't look the least bit like a lady lion hunter.

"Well, I said, lifting a glass of Cinzano and soda, "here's farewell to Africa."

"Don't say that," she said. "You break my heart!"

SABLE IN THE MAGIC FOREST

Hunting in Tanganyika's sable country with renowned PH John Kingsley-Heath, both Jack and Eleanor take excellent trophies. Jack takes three shots and Eleanor chides him a bit, conveniently forgetting she missed on her first chance. November, 1962

I must admit that my wife takes a dim view of mounted big-game heads. She calls them my stuffed animals, and she regards the collecting of such things as a sign of retarded development if not indeed of complete mental collapse.

But gradually through the years I have worn her down, and she has learned to live with the fact that, in some respects, I am highly irrational. She has always reacted to mounted heads in much the same way as she has toward my compulsive acquisition of firearms.

When we married, I was dead broke, just out of graduate school, and had but one gun, a Winchester Model 54 in .270. When, after I had drawn a few salary checks, I brought home a shotgun, she was bitter because it was not a vacuum cleaner. From that time on there was a rhubarb in the O'Connor mansion every time I sneaked in a new gun. That was until I had six. She became a good big-game shot, but all guns looked alike to her. If I gave her a .375 to go deer hunting with and told her it was her .257, she wouldn't notice any difference except that the rifle kicked more than usual. After I had acquired my sixth firearm, I was aware that either her spirit was broken or she couldn't count over five.

And so it was with big-game heads. Once, when she found a taxidermist's bill, I thought she was going to leave me, but now when the expressman brings a crate, she simply sighs, puts on her I-married-a-maniac look, and goes out to play golf.

All of this wind in the willows in the way of an introduction is

221

simply to let you know how astounded I was when, just before we took off for an African safari, she paused one day in front of my big sable antelope head, looked at it reflectively, and said: "That is a beautiful animal!"

I was thinking of Africa then and of my English white-hunter friends.

"Quite!" I said in my best, clipped British accent.

"Will I get to hunt them?" she said.

"Raw-ther!" I said. "You jolly well will. Chap who is to be our white hunter on the second leg of our safari says we'll nip over to an extraordinary bit of sable ground and have a delightful shoot. Quite!"

"You really fracture me when you get humorous, Douglas Fairbanks, Jr.," she sneered. "That phony English accent would curdle milk. If I read tomorrow that Westminster Abbey has fallen down, I'll know it's because every dead Englishman in it turned over in his grave."

"Really?" I said.

"What I was about to tell you," she went on, "when you put on your impersonation of Col. Randolph Edward Tudor Stokes-Brown, M.C., D.S.O., of the Fourth Inskinning Rifles, is that I think sable antelope are terrific and I'd like to hunt them. Most of the poor creatures from Africa that you got stuffed, look as if they had been created by Dr. Seuss, but the sable is beautiful. If I get one, I'd like to get it mounted. At least it would be something that I could brag about for a change."

"Honey," I said, "it's as good as mounted."

So it came to pass that one day early in November, 1959, my wife and I were sitting in the front seat of a Land Rover hunting car with our white hunter, John Kingsley-Heath, driving through mud and pouring rain and looking back every few minutes to see if the lumbering truck that held our tents, supplies, and safari crew was still with us.

It had been raining hard most of the day down there in southern Tanganyika, and when we turned off onto the muddy track that led into the sable forest, it was touch and go whether we'd make it.

The weather wasn't going according to plan at all. Up north, where we had been hunting leopards in the high country, the rains had already started, but down here in the south, the short rains were not scheduled to begin until about November 21. But here we were in the first week of November, riding through the rain. The curtains on our Land Rover were down, and up on top of the safari car, the boys were clothed in their raincoats and looking as unhappy as drowned rats.

Our last hunting camp on Great Ruaha River had been very hot and everything had been bone dry. I had shot a tremendous greater kudu there, a monster bull with a 60-inch head. We had rested a day, shot some guinea fowl, and worked over the rolling stock. Then we had pulled out through the dust and heat after what had been a wonderfully lucky and successful safari, and headed for our last camp and our last trophy, the sable antelope, the only one my wife wanted badly.

We had two days of long, hard driving. We went through Iringa, where, when we had flown down from the north to a landing strip on the Kilombero River, we had stopped to gas up the plane. We camped about 60 miles short of the pretty town of Mbeya, where the next day we bought some American and British magazines and a few supplies. As we climbed a high hill to get out of town toward the sable camp, the rain started pouring down.

"Frightful luck," John said through clenched teeth as the rain drummed on the roof of the car and the windshield wipers chattered merrily. "The rain will scatter the sable and that's where we're headed. There is a spring that is the only permanent water in many miles, and the sable come in and are never too far away. Now, with water everywhere, they'll scatter all through the forest. Only good thing I can say is the tsetse flies won't bother us when it's raining."

Of all Africa's wonderful antelope, the sable is one of the very handsomest and one of the best trophies. He gets his name because, though he begins life as a tan calf and turns brown as a young adult, he comes black as an adult bull. In the northern part of the sable range the cows are brown, but I have been told that in some areas farther south the old cows are almost as black as the bulls.

The underparts of the sable are brilliant white. The lower jaw is white and there is a long white strip along the inside of each eye. The tail is long and tufted, and, like many other African antelope, the sable is higher at the front quarters than at the rear.

With the long, sharp horns of both sexes, the sable is a well-armed and courageous animal. Marauding lions have been killed by sable and so have hunters who have approached wounded animals carelessly. A good bull sable looks to me as if he would weigh about 500 pounds. He is smaller than his relative, the similarly marked roan antelope, but he has far longer and handsomer horns.

Africa's finest sable are found in Portuguese West Africa, a colony which is also called Angola. The record giant sable from

223

Angola had 64¼-inch horns. The season is now closed there, but some years ago my fellow native Arizonan and world-wide big game hunter, George Parker, killed one under special permit. It had horns over 60 inches long.

As you go north, the sable get smaller. The average trophy head in Tanganyika runs about 38 inches and anything over 40 is considered very good. In 1953, Herb Klein and I hunted sable farther north on the Ugalla River. We saw hundreds. Herb hunted hard and looked over a lot of sable, but the best he could find, if I remember correctly, was about 41 inches. I was very lucky and got one that measured 44¼ inches. At the time, it was the largest bull a client of Syd Downey, my white hunter, had ever shot and was in the first five in the Tanganyika records. Later, three or four larger than the old record of 46 inches were shot.

The sable is a forest animal, generally preferring rolling country and fairly open forest interspersed with *embugos,* or open meadows. Usually, sable travel in small herds up to 20, but like old bighorn rams, the largest bulls are often found alone or with a male companion or two.

The fact that the sable generally lives in more open country and is less spooky than the brush-dwelling greater kudu makes him easier to get, but he is still a much more difficult trophy than most of the common plains antelope. He bears the reputation of being a tough animal to bring down, but like the other African antelope, I found him easy to kill if I placed my shot right. My 1953 bull was killed stone dead in his tracks with one shot from a .300 Weatherby.

*I*t was with mixed feelings that we plowed through mud in the mist of that dripping forest east of Lake Rukwa late that afternoon. Once we drove by four big black buffalo bulls sleek with the rain as they grazed in a gleaming *embugo.* A couple of times the truck got stuck and we had to pull with the Land Rover and the boys had to push to get it out. Presently, the sun went down and darkness began to creep up in the canyons.

Suddenly, from our left, a bull sable, his mane waving, galloped across the road. His coal-black hide was glossy from the rain and his magnificent horns were long and beautifully curved.

"Good bull. Maybe 41 or 42 inches. Under the circumstances, we might consider him," John said. "We might get a better one and we might not. Anyone interested?"

"Eleanor gets first pick on this jaunt," I said.

"All right, Eleanor," John said, "let's go."

Eleanor reached back to the gunbearers in the back seat and one of them put her little 7 x 57 in her hand. In a moment she and John, creeping along like burglars, were sneaking from tree to tree toward the spot where the sable had disappeared.

But it wasn't meant to be. The bull had stopped in a patch of brush in a canyon to watch his back track. He saw the hunters before they saw him and went off at a gallop. Eleanor's hasty shot smacked into a tree.

As we pushed off again, the little woman was wet, thoroughly chilled, and full of gloom.

"I really booted that chance," she said. "Maybe I would have hit him if he had been standing. I'll bet I never see another bull like that."

"Chin up, my dear," I said smugly. "Faint heart never won big sable and that sort of thing."

"Shut up!" she said.

We turned off the main track onto a dim trail that headed south. The ground grew softer and softer, and once we had to hitch the Land Rover onto the truck to yank it out of a mud hole. Finally, we wound up in the dark and in the rain, cold, tired, and miserable, by a collection of grass huts which had been built some years before by a government survey party.

In a few minutes, our efficient safari boys had a fire going, and while the tents went up, we sat in camp chairs with drinks in our hands. Eventually, we ate a hot dinner in the dining tent, then fell asleep to the sound of the drumming rain.

Next morning we were out early in the wet, shining forest. Now and then we glimpsed gray oribis, small gray antelope with sharp little horns, fleeing as if the devil were after them. A couple of times we saw small herds of tan Lichtenstein's hartebeests standing at the far end of *embugos,* but they wheeled and galloped off. The tsetse flies were out and now and then one chewed on Eleanor in spite of the fact that she was covered with bug repellent.

Twice we ran into the long and pointed tracks of sable. Leaving the hunting car, we followed them a couple miles without their getting any fresher. The sable were traveling.

About noon, when we were almost back to camp, we saw our first sable of the day, a small herd standing in the timber, switching their tails to keep off the flies. There were two bulls, a couple of cows, and two calves. But one quick look with the glasses showed that the bulls were still quite brown and that their horns did not have the sweeping curve of mature sable.

"Won't go over 35," John said disdainfully.

That afternoon we hunted long and hard but saw no sable. We did, however, see a magnificent bull eland. We had stopped the car to watch a little herd of hartebeests when the eland walked out of the timber and right down the track toward us, switching his tail and looking now to the left, now to the right.

The eland is one of the spookiest of all the African antelope as well as the largest. Eleanor and I were not interested in him as both of us had taken fine eland previously. We wondered when he would get over his fit of absent-mindedness and see the hunting car.

Preoccupied, he continued to walk toward us, sleek, handsome, and as large as a Jersey bull. He didn't notice the hunting car until he was about 50 yards away. If I have ever seen an animal do a double take, it was that eland. For a moment he halted in frozen surprise. Then he made a great jump, wheeled, and tore for the timber.

Time was growing short, and when it rained again during the night, all of us began to worry about the roads to Tabora, where we planned to catch a plane for Nairobi. Until that dry run on the first day, I had planned to look over a good many sable and see if I couldn't beat my 44 1/4-inch trophy.

The rain had made it wonderfully cool up there in the green and shining forest. The next morning dawned chill and gray, but before long it warmed up. The sun shone intermittently and the tsetse flies were really out. I don't enjoy tsetses, particularly since their bite feels as if one had been stuck with a small, red iron. Otherwise, they don't do me much harm. But my wife is allergic to the bites. Once, when we were hunting leopards, we ran through a narrow but bad tsetse belt. She hadn't put on her bug dope, and by the time we got back to camp, her ankles were red, feverish, and twice their normal size. So that day she was really prepared. She was so covered with bug repellent that she smelled like an oil refinery. She had tied up the bottoms of her slacks so that the tsetses couldn't climb up her legs. She wore gloves and a mosquito net.

Again we saw a good deal of fresh sable sign, but no sable. We extended our range and drove several miles west. Then the gunbearers, John, and I climbed a rocky hill to glass the *embugos* and the openings in the forest below.

Dainty little klipspringers peered at us from the rocks. Off in the distance, circling vultures told us that the night before a lion had killed. At the edge of a long and narrow *embugo*, a herd of buffaloes lazed.

Then John stiffened. Presently he turned to me and handed me his glasses. "Here, old boy, have a look. I've picked up a herd of sable." They were about a mile away, right on the edge of heavy forest, and for a moment I had difficulty seeing them. At that distance, we could not make out horns, but three of the sable looked big and black.

Since the hunting car was in the opposite direction, we sent one of the gunbearers to tell Eleanor and Dave, our second white hunter, that we were off on a sable hunt on foot and to head in the direction we had taken.

When we finally reached the area, we saw the sable across an *embugo* about 250 yards away. There were about 15 of them, including three very respectable bulls, any of which would go around 40 or a bit above.

We sneaked forward until we finally ran out of cover. Then I put my left hand around the trunk of a small tree and rested the .375 against it.

"Which is the best, John?" I asked.

"The one right in the middle behind a cow."

I had my eye on the same sable, so I waited. For a long time the animals stayed there, moving little. Then they began slowly to feed to the left. That perverse bull stayed behind the cow, but then she moved away. For a second or so I had a broadside shot at the bull, but the wind sprang up just then and shook the little tree so hard I couldn't keep the intersection of the crosswires on the sable's shoulder. Then the whole herd turned and started to wander into the woods. It was now or never.

I touched off the shot as the bull quartered away from me, but the tsetses were chewing on me and the tree was wobbling. John called a hit along the ribs, but the bull bucked and the whole herd ran. We had to track for a half-hour before we caught up and put the bull down.

My first shot had raked along the ribs, just touching a lobe of one lung.

*W*e had hardly got the bull down when we heard the rumble of the hunting car, and Dave and Eleanor drove up. Eleanor stood by while we measured the horns – 41½ inches.

"I thought *I* was going to get the first shot at a sable," she said bitterly. "Now I'll bet you've chased all the sable out of the country. Three shots! Even back where we were it sounded like the battle of Tarawa!"

"Honey," I said lamely, "the hunting car was in one direction and the sable were in the other. We thought we'd save time –"

"Yes, I know," she said, "big-hearted of you!"

The atmosphere in the hunting car was a bit chilly as we drove back to camp with the sable head. Eleanor had on her mosquito net and I couldn't see the expression on her face. It must have been the I-married-a-selfish-creep look. She does that one extraordinarily well.

But we hadn't gone more than a mile when one of the sharp gunbearers clutched my shoulder and pointed.

"Pala pala," he whispered.

We looked where he was pointing and saw about 400 yards away through a long passage in the trees a herd of sable moving slowly away. John jammed the glasses to his eyes.

"Damned good bull with them," he said. "Fine sweeping curve. Eleanor, grab your rifle and pile out. This is your show."

I hadn't seen mamma move so fast since she stepped on a hoptoad in her bare feet one summer evening long ago. As she followed John, bent double and wearing gloves, scarf, and mosquito netting, she looked formidable enough to haunt a large house.

I grabbed a camera and followed. They circled to keep the wind right as the sable moved slowly and erratically. Presently they climbed up on an anthill. I saw John take another look with his binoculars. Then Eleanor's 7mm. came up. She steadied it and then shot. I heard the thump of a solid hit and heard John shout, "Shoot again!" Then I heard Eleanor yell, "He's down."

The beautiful bull lay about 200 yards away, shot twice through the lungs with the 145-grain Speer bullet in front of 46 grains of No. 4320.

He was a very old bull and his horns had a pronounced and beautiful curve, but the long sharp points that add length to a sable head had been worn off blunt. It went just under 41 inches.

"He doesn't have quite as long a head as yours," Eleanor said, "but it's prettier and anyway, I didn't have to chase him, fire volleys at him, and scare all the game out of the forest."

"He is indeed a handsome bull and I congratulate you," I said.

She seemed thoughtful as we rode back to camp in the Land Rover.

Then she turned to me. "Do you think I'd be silly if I had my sable mounted?" she asked. "I mean not just on a shield, but really stuffed like your big one."

"I'd think you were just getting smart."

"You know," she went on, "it wouldn't cost much to make the trophy room longer. Then we could put up my sable and some of my other things."

It started to rain again about the time we hit camp, and John decided we'd be wise to pack up and drive back to the main road before the muddy track into the sable forest got any worse.

Late that afternoon we made camp by the road. It was raining a little and my heart was heavy with the realization that my third African safari was over. It had been wildly successful as well as highly selective.

My wife, who had told me that aside from sable she was mostly going along for the ride to see the natives and the game, had got a very respectable bag – eland, sable, mountain reedbuck, zebra, puku, waterbuck, and impala. In reality, she had shot more stuff than I had. My key trophies had been my first leopard, a very good one, a record-class puku, a fine $31^{1}/_{2}$-inch eland, one of the very best taken in East Africa in several years, a good lion, a good sable, and the wonderful 60-inch greater kudu I had shot on the Ugalla. Aside from the few trophies, we had taken some animals for camp meat and leopard bait. All in all, we shot fewer than 25 animals, but there is little reason for anyone on his third safari to be anything but selective.

Eleanor had had the time of her life. She enjoyed camp life, the hunting, the natives, and the charming Britishers we had met. As an old hand at shoestring hunting trips and a veteran Dutch-oven cook, she was delighted to have someone else sweat over the campfire for a change.

It took us three days to plow through the mud to Tabora. There, we spent the night in a beautiful hunting lodge that had been built for the last kaiser of Germany when Tanganyika was German East Africa. No tsetses chewed on us, no mosquitoes hummed, and no lions roared.

John and Dave had to put the hunting car and the truck on a flat car and go by train out of the rainy area. My wife and I flew back to Nairobi, and a few days later we parted in Rome. She was to go back to Idaho by way of London, the polar bear route, and Seattle, and I was headed for Iran to hunt wild sheep and ibex.

"Well, it's all over," I said as I bade her goodbye at the Rome airport. "You've seen a lot of Africa. You've been on safari and have done some shooting. Did you have fun?"

"I've loved every minute of it," she told me. "I'd start back to Africa tomorrow if you asked me. I have my safari clothes and my rifle. All you need to do is raise a few thousand bucks."

A WEEK IN NOAH'S ARK

This story, one of several growing out of Jack's first African safari, echoes the magic and mystique in its title and text. He takes a record-book impala, shoots a couple of zebras, and derives particular joy in killing a bull dik-dik "weighing all of nine pounds."
June, 1954

There are a thousand Africas. To some, Africa means high, cold mountains, damp and chilly, where dark jungle frames lush, light-green grassy meadows, where the mysterious bongo, Africa's rarest antelope, has its shadowy being, where the mountain zebra barks, and where the great black buffalo crashes through the bamboo forest. Africa also means the harsh and terrible deserts of the upper Sudan and the coast of the Red Sea, where the shaggy ibex with his back-swept knotted horns lives on fantastic mountains as bare and black and dead as the face of the moon.

And there is the bush country of the great sable antelope, a land of shoulder-high grass and nyombo trees, a land where elephants prowl and lions roar, and where the voracious tsetse fly makes life miserable for man and beast.

There are a thousand Africas, but the Africa most of us think of is the open plains country where herds of game feed on short grass, where there are scattered patches of brush and a few thorn and euphorbia trees, an Africa where zebras run in hundreds, wildebeests in thousands, where impalas leap fantastically into the air as though built of rubber and filled with hydrogen, where tiny dik-diks skitter from one bush to another, and where Thomson's gazelles bounce around in herds of hundreds like so many sand fleas on a beach. This Africa we think of must also have herds of giraffes, its truculent buffaloes, its hyenas, its waterbucks, its topi, its baboons, its elands. Lions must roar around camp at night and monkeys have to chatter in trees.

231

This – sort of a contemporary Noah's Ark – is the Africa that Herb Klein, Red Early, and I encountered in Tanganyika in 1953 when we hunted for a week on the Grummetti River, which empties into Speke Gulf, Lake Victoria. If I didn't have still photos and movies to prove it, I wouldn't dare to tell about it, much less write about it. One of the big surprises of my African trip was how many giraffes there were – and how many ostriches. Surely we saw thousands of each, and both were plentiful on the Grummetti. And the amount of game we saw was fantastic.

The North American hunter, who is used to thinking of deer as being plentiful if he sees twenty in a day's hunt, finds it hard to comprehend encountering thousands of head of game, of having six or seven species in sight at one time. There is nothing like it in any part of North America. The only thing one can compare to it is a heavily stocked cattle range.

This, of course, is the Africa of the movies, the Africa of the plains game. All Africa isn't like this. Many a man has hunted the big, gray, spiral-horned greater kudu for a month – and returned without one. He may go for a week or more without firing a shot, and see so little game that he has to eat corned beef and buy domestic goats for his boys. The man after a trophy sable may find it almost as tough. But the Grummetti country lives up to all advance notices. This is Africa! This is *it!*

During the rains the great Grummetti River overflows its banks and for three or four miles on each side the ground is soaked. When the dry season comes, when the grass on the high plains shrivels up, when the smaller streams become rock and sand, there is always water in the Grummetti, always lush and succulent green grass. Then the game moves in and the leopards and lions follow. Down in the river bottom the big burly waterbucks bush up each day but come out to feed as the shadows lengthen. Herds of great black buffaloes graze along the banks, wallow in their mudholes among the reeds. Handsome little reedbucks, which look much like our smaller sorts of whitetail deer, live close to the river in the tall grass and reeds. Now and then a rhino moves ponderously through the country, and flocks of francolin – African partridges – and guinea fowl scurry off in front of the hunting car.

Up on the green and level plains, game is so numerous that it almost ceases to be game. Wildebeests, looking strangely like a cross between buffalo, horse, and antelope, were so numerous when my two Texas friends and I were there that I could never bring myself to shoot one. The topi, a beautiful antelope with short cowlike horns but a pinkish coat, yellow stockings, and purple patches on his flanks, is there by the thousands. My license called for four topi. I shot one for meat for the boys on the Simiyu River, and one for lion bait, and that was all. Hundreds of zebra were there for the taking.

The finest game animal on the Grummetti is, I believe, the impala, a cleanly built, lithe little antelope with beautiful lyre-shaped horns. He is about the size of an American pronghorn or a smallish whitetailed deer, and Americans who've seen him in movies have marveled at his ability to make fantastic leaps. One bound will put him 10 feet into the air and 30 feet across country. It's routine to see one jump over another impala's back and clear it by six feet.

I got my impala on the Grummetti, the only impala I shot in all of Africa. I had seen a good many specimens on the Simiyu when we were hunting lions, but partly because we didn't want to make unnecessary noise and partly because we'd seen no rams that came up to Don Ker's high notions of what a trophy impala should be, I had not shot one.

Then one morning when the white hunters and I were cruising around looking for whatever we might devour, he suddenly stopped the car and lifted his binoculars to his eyes. "That big impala ram over in the herd at the edge of the bush is a dandy," he said. "It will be a long time before you see another as good."

In a moment my own glass was on the ram. Even I could tell I was seeing an exceptional trophy, as the horns appeared to be several inches longer than those of any of the many impalas I had seen.

Don drove the car on a half-mile or so, then we got out, and with Thomas, the gunbearer, we doubled back toward the marked ram, hiding behind anthills, skulking behind bushes. But stalking thirty animals is a lot tougher than stalking one. Presently a ewe had her eye on us, then another ewe – and the whole herd was in flight.

Not knowing impalas, I was ready to throw in the sponge. Don wasn't. "Let's watch them," he said. "They aren't very frightened. The ram doesn't know what the ewes saw. They'll calm down."

After running half a mile, the herd stopped on the open plain about 300 yards from a patch of brush and thorn trees. They figured that whatever was after them wasn't going to sneak up through the tall grass and bite them.

Don, Thomas and I made a long detour to get the patch of brush and trees between us and the herd. Then we closed gradually. In the last stages I used a five-foot anthill for cover. There was no mistaking the big ram; he was standing facing me, somewhere between 250 and

233

300 yards away. I thrust the light .300 magnum around the anthill and rested it on my hand. Through the 4X scope the ram loomed big and bright, and the crosshairs were steady against his chest. As the rifle recoiled the ram gave his last great leap into the air, then fell in an inert heap.

He was a beauty, with horns that taped 30¹/₂ inches around the curve. This is one of the largest impalas, according to Zimmerman, the Nairobi taxidermist, to be brought out in years. What the current world-record impala is I don't know; the latest edition of *Rowland Ward's Records of Big Game* gives 33 inches as tops.

Herb got a fine impala in this wonderful Grummetti country, but lost one that may have been even better than mine. He, Don Ker, and I were out one day when we saw the big ram with a herd of ewes. Herb and Don made the sneak while I waited in the car, chewing my fingernails. Presently I heard a shot. Herb had fired his .257 Weatherby Magnum just as the ram turned. The bullet broke the shoulder and practically took the leg off, but did not get into the body cavity. We trailed the impala until it was so dark we could no longer see. Twice we jumped him, but he was watching his back track and always got out before Herb could shoot.

Next morning we took up the trail again. But soon we came to the end. During the night hyenas had found and killed the wounded impala, and all they left of him was a patch of blood, a few hairs, and the contents of his stomach. They even carried away those beautiful record-book horns, and we never did find them.

*B*ecause game is plentiful, there are many predators on the Grummetti. There are the jackals, lithe little coyote-like animals that always hunt in pairs. And there are cheetahs, serval cats, wild dogs, bat-eared foxes, and hyenas. Hyenas, which are genuine predators as well as scavengers, are there by the hundreds, insolent, big, stinking. To me the hyena is the most repulsive animal in nature, a creature which looks as though he'd been buried and later dug up. Most African animals are fated to go down the maw of the hyena. Even the lion, as he grows old and stiff and weak, is pulled down and devoured by hyenas. The hyena devours the young of all species, the crippled, the old, the sick, and the weak.

One day Herb and Red surprised a leopard that had just hung a tommy in a tree – a Thomson's gazelle, that is – to keep it away from hyenas. *Chui*, as he's called in Swahili, shot into a patch of brush to get away from the snorting monster of a motorcar, and took refuge in a warthog hole. Ah, the lads thought, we'll run him out of his hole and get movies of him. They were taking readings on their light meters and unlimbering their cameras when the leopard tired of it all. He uttered a couple of coughing grunts, bounced out of his hole, and came full tilt at the car. Red grabbed his .300 Magnum, Herb almost fell out of the car in astonishment, and Myles Turner saved the day by putting the hunting car into gear and making a quick get-away. Otherwise the boys from Texas would have had the indignant leopard right in their laps.

Red collected his buffalo on the Grummetti. Herb and I had previously shot ours on the Simiyu, where we were hunting lions. We'd found old bulls that had been driven out of the herd. Mine was a loner, Herb's had only a single companion, also mean and battle-scarred. The more buffaloes there are, the greater the chance the hunter takes. Red and Myles, completely undaunted, went right into the middle of a herd in heavy bush to find and shoot a herd bull.

Except for Red's buffalo, all our Grummetti River trophies were what in East Africa is known as "little stuff." A zebra may weigh around 800 pounds, but compared to the *big* game – lions, rhino, buffalo, elephant, and leopard, the dangerous animals, the ones that shoot back – he's still small. A waterbuck is a big, shaggy, heavy-footed antelope almost as large as an American bull elk, but he too is small game. There were literally hundreds of giraffes on the Grummetti and a giraffe is enormous and incredibly tall. I suppose he's small game too, but none of us shot a giraffe; few Americans do. And the same is true of ostriches.

We shot some zebras on the Grummetti, as the zebra is as typically Africa as the lion, and all three of us wanted zebra rugs for our trophy rooms. There were zebras by the thousands – in herds of a dozen, fifty, hundreds. There isn't much to getting a zebra on the Grummetti. We'd see a herd at a distance. We'd part from the hunting car, make a stalk from behind a screen of brush. Then we'd pick out a stallion and the gunner would sneak quietly out from behind the clump, sit down, and shoot. Failing a one-shot kill, he is probably in for a long chase, because a zebra can carry around a lot of poorly placed lead.

The green grass of the Grummetti was kept as short as that of a lawn by the grazing game. In some areas there were great open vistas of this lovely greensward, but in others the parklike sweep was broken by small clumps of dense brush about 50 feet across. Each clump was a tangle of little trees, tall grass, brush, thorns, and each ended as sharp and abrupt as a hedge.

Only the smallest creatures could penetrate these dense clumps,

235

yet it seemed that in each one a pair of the incredible dik-diks lived. Their cousins the elands – world's largest antelope, weighing almost as much as a Jersey bull – had survived by growing huge. But the little dik-dik chose the other way. To be safe he became so tiny that he could dart through spaces where no jackal or hyena would think of going, and where even the little bat-eared fox could not force his way. The eland will weigh 1,500 pounds or more; the dik-dik, seven or eight.

When we were after lions on the Simiyu, I had occasionally seen a dik-dik skitter through the tall grass, and I would not have been any more astonished if I had seen a basilisk. A dik-dik was on my must list as being one of the most interesting of all African animals. So badly did I want a specimen that many times on the Simiyu I had groaned in frustration when Don Ker had advised against shooting one for fear that I might spook some unseen lion.

"I wouldn't shoot that," he told me again and again. "When we get to the Grummetti we'll see them by the dozen."

And he was right.

One morning with my record impala in the bag, and a couple of zebras for rugs, we set out to collect a ferocious dik-dik. When we'd been hunting something else, the tiny antelope had stood around their lairs staring at us, but this day the word had evidently been passed that we were out for blood. Every dik-dik that saw us took off as if we'd been preying on their kind for years.

Presently, though, we spied a bull dik-dik – weighing all of nine pounds, or almost as much as an antelope jackrabbit – standing just beyond a thin screen of brush by his fortress. He was gazing at a mixed herd of zebras and topi, which in turn was gazing at us. Carefully Don focused his binoculars on the dik-dik.

"Take him," he whispered. "His horns are tremendous!"

I could hardly shoot for laughing. The thought of a funny little dik-dik having a tremendous head killed me.

When we compared its measurements later with those in *Records of Big Game,* my astonished respect for Don Ker's knowledge of trophies, which was already high, went even higher. If memory serves me right, my great big ferocious bull dik-dik was within a quarter of an inch of the East Africa record, a monster to make all the other dik-dik hunters green with envy!

Don Ker had to return to Nairobi to go out with another safari. Syd Downey, another of Africa's topnotch white hunters, came to replace him. Syd and I took pictures, did some varmint shooting. The weather was sunny and perfect – cool enough for good sleeping at night, chill of early mornings, warm at midday. Monkeys chattered in the trees around the camp. Sometimes when I'd wake up in the quiet, starlit night, I'd hear lions roar on the other side of the river, a sound so wild, so thrilling that I hope it can forever be heard on the African veldt.

It was a wonderful life, this living in a natural zoological park with more game than Noah's Ark ever housed, game that ranged from the tiny dik-dik to the great eland and the monster rhino. But it couldn't go on forever.

One night Myles gave us the news. "Well, chaps, the soft life is over. Tomorrow we move south to work, sweat, grief, and tsetse flies!"

THE TIGRESS OF ELEPHANTVILLE

Jack had already killed a big tigress and Eleanor pooh-poohed it as being a simple process. Her first tiger doesn't come quite as easy, but once taken, it gives her heroic stature among the natives.
January, 1966

When I shot a big tigress the first day we hunted in India in the spring of 1965, my wife Eleanor decided there was nothing to tiger hunting. "It's like taking candy from a baby," she said. "You just tie out a water buffalo calf. A tiger comes along and kills the calf. He eats three-fourths of it, drinks, goes off, and goes to sleep. Then the hunter climbs a tree. A flock of village characters in white, dusty diapers wake the tiger up and run him past the tree. The sneaky hunter pops the tiger. Tiger dies. Everybody shakes everybody else's hand, poses for pictures with the tiger and looks heroic. They all whoop and holler. Big deal!"

I wish I could say she got her first tiger as easily as she thought she was going to, but she didn't.

In the national forests of India, the hunter leases the hunting rights to a certain area, called a "block," for a specified period of time. The forest department sets a limit on the number of animals he can take in each block. Our outfitter, Tigerland Shikars of Jabalpur, had reserved two blocks for us, one of which was called Ghatpiparia. I had killed my tigress within its boundaries, and most of the time while we were hunting we lived in a rest house near a village after which the block was named. The other block was likewise named after a village – Hatibad, which means in Hindi, the place of elephant, or Elephantville.

When you are at Hatibad, you are really in the boondocks. We saw no elephants there, but it is famous tiger country. On several

239

occasions tigers have killed bullocks hitched to carts, and two or three years ago a tiger killed a villager who was driving a bullock cart and who belted the tiger with an ax when the big cat jumped one of his bullocks. The tigers live almost exclusively on cattle, and since the villagers always stay with their cattle during the day and drive them into corrals in the village at night, the tigers have to knock the cattle off in the daylight with the herders whooping and yelling. The villagers of Hatibad never travel alone in bullock carts. Two or three men go together, since the more men there are, the more noise they can make. The shrieks and howls of human beings disgust and unhinge tigers, and if the villagers can see the tigers in time to get their vocal chords operating, they save their bullocks.

Two or three days after I had shot my tigress (see "First Day Tiger," *Outdoor Life,* November, 1965), we drove over to take a look at Hatibad. It was a small village of mud houses huddled on a little rise. A lone palm grew in front of it and blue hills covered with teak jungle rose a mile beyond. A well had been dug about 100 yards from the village, and there were women around it, gossiping and drawing water.

*W*e parked under an enormous tree about 200 yards from Hatibad, and in a few minutes people began to gather. One was the forest guard. He had a khaki jacket and a bicycle, and he smelled a tip. Another was the law. He wore a blue jacket and sported an imposing pair of moustaches that made him look like a pre-World War I Hungarian cavalry officer down on his luck. He too smelled a tip.

I don't suppose the villagers of Hatibad see an automobile twice a year or a "European" once in ten. To them, Eleanor and I were Europeans. They had heard vaguely of the United States, but precisely where it was and what Americans looked like, they did not know. I was that old European *sahib* and Eleanor was called the European *memsahib*. After she had shot a tiger she was variously known as "the brave little European woman," or "that savage little European woman." I liked that last name best. Occasionally she was referred to as "the Old *Sahib's* Young Wife." She liked that best.

Everyone told us we had really come to *the* place, that a tiger was in the bag – or several tigers, if necessary. A hunting party in a village means that sooner or later a lot of rupees are passed out, a glimpse into the lives of strange and outlandish people, excitement, something to talk about for months and even years.

The villagers showed us where several tiger kills had been made recently, but almost all evidence of them had long since been carried away by ants, hyenas, and vultures. We found pug marks of a good-size tigress and of a large tiger, but none was fresh.

We returned to our rest house at Ghatpiparia. We would hold Hatibad in reserve. There were tigers there and they were like money in the bank.

*N*ot long after our return, a tiger killed one of the water buffalo calves we'd set out as bait in a nullah in the Ghatpiparia block. We drove the jeep as far as we dared, then made the hot and dusty hike to our machans. The "stops" climbed into trees along the route they wanted the tiger to take. If the tiger started to sneak out of the beat, they were supposed to tap on the trees with sticks to keep him coming. Prince Abdul Quayum, our gentleman shikari, and Tinsa, who was in charge of the Ghatpiparia beaters and whom we called the old *shikari,* placed the men who were to drive. They were to move in a long line making all the noise they could.

Far in the distance the whooping and hollering started. A sambar doe and her leggy fawn came galloping by. Then we saw a young male chital (the spotted axis deer) with spike horns, then some jungle fowl and monkeys. Last of all were the peafowl, some of them magnificent cocks with glittering plumage and long tails.

"No tiger in the beat," said Muthu Swamy, our Tamil jeep driver, who was up in the machan with me.

Quayum and Eleanor, who were in the other machan about 100 yards away, presently came marching over.

"The tiger wasn't in the beat," Quayum called to me. "It has moved. The beaters tell me they heard a sambar belling and the monkeys giving their alarm call over in the big nullah next to the hills. We'll beat there."

The new machans were two or three miles away. Quayum and the old *shikari* instructed stops and beaters, and the rest of us took off for two other machans Quayum had ordered erected before we arrived for the shoot.

My machan was nearly 40 feet above the ground, and it overlooked one fork of a big nullah, or ravine. It was a logical route for a driven tiger, but it had one disadvantage. For about 50 feet directly by the machan, the area was quite open. I knew a tiger would cross that bare space with great reluctance. If he crossed it at all, it would be on a dead run. Eleanor's machan on the other fork was lower – not over 15 feet above the ground and well within range of a tiger's leap. But the nullah there was much brushier and afforded good concealment.

I heard the whooping and hollering of the drive, and quickly there came the usual parade of jungle folk – a sambar doe and fawn, the jungle fowl, the peacocks. The beaters drew nearer.

The monkeys high in the tree opposite mine began giving their harsh, grating alarm call. "They see the tiger," Muthu Swamy whispered. He had never seen a live tiger and was on his first tiger hunt, but maybe he'd been reading up on the sport. I frowned and raised a finger to my lips.

The monkeys were going crazy now, and I knew the tiger was near.

It was a still, very hot day without a breath of air. Suddenly, I was aware that I could smell the tiger. He was directly below me, in the nullah right on the edge of the opening, and his scent was rising. I gripped my .375 and waited. Then there was a deep, rumbling growl – silence.

The monkeys went wild for a moment, then they stopped yakking. They were looking over toward Eleanor's machan. I knew the tiger had decided not to cross the open area and had doubled back to try his luck in the next fork.

Now the beaters were swarming by my tree. Something was going to have to happen. I heard a shot, followed by a heavy, roaring growl and an outburst of shouting. But there was no sound of the second and finishing shot every tiger hunter puts in.

Somehow, Muthu Swamy and I managed to get down from our machan without breaking our necks. He lugged my camera case and I my .375 as we ran to the other machan.

Eleanor and Quayum were at the foot of the tree, plainly angry. Before them stood one of the beaters with a shotgun in his hand. As I watched, Quayum reached out and took it away from him.

"What goes on here?" I asked.

"All my life I have wanted to shoot a tiger, and there he came, sneaking along," Eleanor said. "I saw him go behind a bush and I could just barely see some of his hide. I had my rifle aimed right where he was going to come out and he had to cross an open place about a yard wide. He stuck his head out and looked around. A moment later I could have got a shot at his shoulder. Then this stupid dolt here blazed away at him with a shotgun from about 60 yards. I was so startled, I darned near fell out of the machan, and the tiger let out a growl, did a double flip-flop, and beat it."

"That's a tough break," I said.

She turned to Quayum. "Tell that beater for me that if he ever does anything like that again, I'll cut his heart out and make him eat it."

Quayum translated. The color drained out of the beater's face. A moment before he had been half defiant, but Eleanor's threat shook him up. He turned to sneak away, and Tinsa, the old *shikari,* gave him a resounding kick in the rear. We never saw him again.

*A*fter this catastrophe, we decided to go over and take a whirl at the Hatibad tigers. We loaded a bullock cart with tents, equipment, and utensils and sent it on its lumbering way to Hatibad. We hired two villagers to carry our beds over their heads – 25 miles for their asking price of two rupees, less than 50 cents.

When we got to the village at sundown, the tents were up, the beds were made, and a little warming fire was burning in the front of the tent Eleanor and I were to use. A small table had been set up, and on it was a bottle of Indian whisky, a bottle of soda, and a thermos jug full of ice cubes. Two calves had been tied, and Tinsa said there was fresh tiger sign about. As we nibbled on our sundowners, we heard the cursing of a bunch of monkeys and the belling of sambar.

"*Shere,*" whispered Tinsa.

"Tiger," said Quayum. "One has gone to water in the pool in the nullah about a quarter of a mile away."

The villagers had told us there were two tigers not far away. One was a tigress that lived in the nullah close by and who made a regular practice of killing cattle in broad daylight. The other was a big male whose tracks they regularly saw about four miles away. Calves had been tied to tempt each.

When we hit the hay that night I felt lucky. Somehow I felt the presence of tigers. Then off in the distance a tiger began to roar, *Ooom, ooom, O-O-O-MMM.*

"Hear that, Eleanor?' I asked. "It's a tiger roaring."

"I'll be darned," said Eleanor. "I wondered what it was. I'm glad I have heard one, but I think roaring lions are more fun. Anyway, I hope the tiger doesn't decide to find out what's inside this tent."

"I feel lucky," I told her. "You're going to get a tiger in a day or two."

*W*hen I awakened at dawn, Ran Kahn, our Moslem cook, had a fire going in his mud stove and Babu Lal, the table boy, had built another fire in front of our tent and had set the table for breakfast.

243

We finished our toast, soft-boiled eggs, and coffee, and I was in the midst of a shave when Tinsa and the bait boys showed up leading one calf.

"Well," said Prince Abdul Quayum, "the big male tiger has killed, but he has left the beat. Tinsa thinks he plans to come back, so we'll have to sit up." Sitting up, incidentally, means waiting all night in the machan, hoping the tiger will come back to feed on his kill.

We went up the road three or four miles, left the jeep, and walked to the tiger kill. Tracks of a big male tiger were all about. He had killed the calf, dragged it into a thicket, and eaten about three fourths of it. Then the tiger had left the thicket, walked down the road for a couple of miles, and turned off toward some hills.

"He may come back tonight. He may come back tomorrow night. He may never come back," Quayum said. "At any rate, we'll have to sit up, as we have no idea where he has gone for his nap."

So Tinsa, the bait boys, and some villagers built and tied a machan in a tree about 35 yards from the spot where the calf had been killed. Then they dragged what was left of the calf back to the tree to which it had originally been tied. They fastened it to the tree with stout rope and covered it with branches to keep the vultures off.

About 4 p.m., Quayum, Eleanor, and Babu Lal left for the machan. They were warmly dressed, had chairs to sit in, and blankets to wrap themselves in. Babu Lal had a powerful spotlight hitched to an automobile battery. If the tiger came to the bait, he would get it in the spotlight and Eleanor would blast it.

In my limited tiger-hunting experience, the tigers have come back to the kill early or not at all. That night I lay in the tent reading and keeping an ear cocked for the sound of a shot. At 11 o'clock, I turned out the light and went to sleep, convinced that the tiger was not going to return to feed on his kill.

When I woke up, the cook was standing by my side with my morning tea. He indicated that Muthu Swamy had already left for the machan with the jeep.

Not long afterward the jeep came back. All the machan-sitters looked a bit worse for wear.

I had told Eleanor that sitting up all night for a tiger and hearing the jungle go to sleep and then awake was an experience she should not miss. She agreed, but added that she'd just as soon not do it again.

She had been cold and cramped and miserable. Babu Lal went to sleep every half an hour or so and shivered so hard from the cold that Quayum had to wake him up. His shivering almost shook the machan down. The machan wasn't very strong, and it tilted so that Eleanor had to brace herself to keep from sliding out of her chair.

*A*fter breakfast, Eleanor went into our tent to catch up on her sleep. Quayum, Muthu Swamy, and I went out in the jeep to see if we could run across some horned game for meat, since we had devoured a nilgai, or blue bull, we had knocked off early in the hunt and we were now living on canned meat. All we saw, however, was a little herd of five *chinkara* (which the British used to call "ravine deer") running off about 400 yards away across a field. A *chinkara* is a little fellow about the size of an East African Thomson's gazelle.

We got back to camp about lunch time. Eleanor had finished her nap and had put on fresh clothes. We used the last of our ice to make what we called a Ken River Special – charged water, gin, fresh limes, and sugar. We ate. Eleanor decided to take another nap. Quayum went to his tent for a snooze. I sat in the shade and read a book.

All the Hatibadians with nothing else to do had been hanging around our camp since shortly after dawn. Now, most of them had gone back to the village for their naps. One of the only ones left was an old man whose job seemed to be babysitting. Wherever he went he carried with him a little girl about two years old. She was convinced that I ate little girls, and every time I looked directly at her she hid her face and howled. When she thought I was not looking, she peeked at me shyly.

Suddenly, a lad about 16 came charging into camp, jabbering madly. Tinsa picked himself up from under a tree where he had been sleeping and went over to him. Quayum came out of his tent to talk to the boy. Then I heard wooden cowbells, and more herd boys came barreling out of the jungle, driving the village cattle.

"What goes on?" I asked Quayum.

"We're in luck," Quayum said. "The tigress has killed a cow. She drove the boys away by roaring and threatening to charge. She is on the cow now. We can use the machans I had built before you came. We'll have a beat as soon as we can collect enough villagers."

I never saw beaters collect so quickly. The Hatibadians bore no love for the tigress, since she had been living right in their back yard for a couple of years. She was very bold. She thought

245

nothing of charging into a herd of cattle, killing one, and then threatening the herders.

When enough beaters had gathered around our tents, Quayum and Tinsa gave them a lecture on the proper way to beat. Tinsa would take charge. Quayum, Eleanor, and I would go ahead and get into the machans.

I told Quayum to put Eleanor in the most likely machan and I'd take the other. Muthu Swamy and I shinnied up into ours. Presently, I could see Eleanor and Quayum about 80 yards away in a machan across the treetops. It was by a hillside on the other side of a wide nullah. I could see the stops in trees on both sides.

Then in the distance I heard the beat start with the usual yelling, shouting, and jabbering. Tense, I waited with the .375 trained on the most likely spot, a cartridge in the chamber, the safety off.

The beat grew nearer. I heard an outburst of jabbering.

"The tiger is in the beat," Muthu Swamy whispered. "Someone has seen it."

A stop in a tree to my left began to tap. Then one began to tap on the right in the direction of Eleanor's machan. About a dozen peafowl went streaming by Eleanor's machan. Some monkeys in a tree up on the hill above her were going crazy.

Then I heard the sharp crack of Eleanor's .30/06. There was no growl, no roar. A moment later I heard another shot from the .30/06, and I was sure she had connected. Then the beaters began to shout.

"Memsahib has killed the tiger," said Muthu Swamy. "The tiger is dead." He took off his shoes and climbed down, but I was afraid I'd break my neck. In a few minutes he came back with the bait tiers and the rope ladder.

I found Eleanor standing beside a very handsome and very dead tigress and shaking hands with about 40 enthusiastic and happy Hatibadians.

There had been nothing to it, she told me. The tigress had come strolling out from behind a bush and had stopped broadside not more than 30 yards away to look back at the beaters. Eleanor had put the intersection of the cross-wires right on the cat's left shoulder and had squeezed one off. The 180-grain Remington soft-point Core-Lokt bullet killed it so dead, it didn't have time to growl. Quayum had told her she must always put a second shot into a tiger, so she shot again.

We took photos, then put the tigress across the hood of the jeep and drove in triumph back to camp. On the way, an old man stopped us. When he was told that it was *memsahib* who had shot the tigress, he bowed and wept and put his head on her feet. This tigress, he said, had almost ruined him as she had killed seven of his cows and a prize bull that had cost him 500 rupees.

Soon every man, woman, and child from Hatibad and other nearby villages was on hand. When we drank our sundowners in celebration, we were completely surrounded. The men stared at Eleanor with wonder and respect. The children wanted to touch her. The next day all the matrons of Hatibad put on their best saris and came to call on her. They prostrated themselves before her and put their hands on her ankles.

"What are they saying?" I asked Quayum.

"This one here," Quayum said, pointing, "just told the others that when an Indian woman hears a tiger, she runs to her house and closes the door, but when this fierce little European woman hears a tiger, she gives a cry of joy, seizes her *benduck* (gun) and rushes into the jungle! . . . This one here has just said your wife was very brave, and this one said she was very beautiful and very brave, but for a woman very savage."

"That's it exactly," I said. "Tell the good woman she doesn't know half of it."

THE WORLD'S MOST BEAUTIFUL DEER

*Jack never lacked for an opinion,
always stated in unequivocal terms.
The chital sat at the top of his list of
deer when it came to beauty, "a fawn
with horns on him." This was
his first Indian shikar.
December, 1955*

It was a fresh, dewy morning and our temperamental jeep was roaring down a dusty, twisting road through the Indian jungle. Suddenly to my left, framed by feathery green trees and standing knee-deep in tawny grass, was a herd of deer. And such deer you never saw in your life. There were seven of them and every single one was a buck with lofty antlers. But the payoff was that all these handsome bucks were wearing the white-spotted, red-brown coat of a fawn.

I had a .270 in my hand and my hunting companion, Lee Sproul, had a .30/06. We were all set for just such an occasion, but our jeep driver was bent on getting back to the forest rest house where we had hung our hats. He went roaring on, looking neither to the left nor to the right. Screams and yells in English were just noise to him.

By the time we got the jeep stopped, with the aid of A.D. Mukerji, our outfitter, that herd of wonderful deer had been spooked. Lee and I piled out, but we caught only a glimpse of their shining antlers and their sleek, spotted hides as they streaked away through the tall grass and trees.

The deer Lee and I saw that day was the chital, or spotted axis deer, probably the most common deer of the Indian jungle and, for my money, the world's most beautiful.

Members of the deer family have a way of being good to look upon. Even the great pendulous-nosed bull moose, although not pretty in any conventional sense, has the beauty and impressiveness of mass and grandeur. A big buck mule deer or sleek whitetail is a sight to

249

gladden the heart, and a large bull elk is a thing of noble beauty. But the chital or axis deer is the most beautiful of all.

Imagine a deer about the size of an average whitetail, one that would weigh on the hoof somewhere between 150 and 200 pounds. Then picture this buck in the universal garb of fawns – a red-brown coat spotted with white. Now put on his head a set of elk-like antlers, and you have the chital.

He comes by his elk antlers honestly, since, along with most Asiatic deer, he is a distant relative of the North American elk, or wapiti.

The chital is found over the whole of India and in Ceylon. And he's extraordinarily plentiful. He has to be. Tigers eat him. Leopards eat him. Wild dogs and wolves eat him. So do natives and sportsmen.

A common way of hunting chital in India is to cruise along a road at night in a car equipped with a spotlight. If you are an Indian, you're probably armed with a shotgun of some sort and the shotgun is loaded with buckshot. Every time you see a herd of chital you blast away. Of course, you wound many more than you get, but there are plenty of chital. Being an Indian, you do not mind.

The most trigger-happy character I have ever run into was an Indian forest guard. He owned a cheap Spanish shotgun, and he had a supply of shells loaded with buckshot. Every time he saw a bunch of chital he poured shot into it. I never saw him bring down a single one, but two or three times Lee and I could see he had wounded one, and so we finished it off with our rifles. How many deer that character wounds in a month I have no idea, but it must be plenty. He wears that shotgun like a pair of pants and apparently the Indian government furnishes him plenty of buckshot shells.

This kind of night hunting is illegal in the United States, and rightly so, but it's an old Indian institution – even though frowned upon by the government and prohibited in forest lands.

I must admit that there is much charm in hunting the Indian jungle at night with a spotlight. When dusk settles down, the jungle grows suddenly quiet. One moment a thousand doves of half a dozen different kinds are talking their sweet soft language, making a low background of sound for the shrill cries of the peafowl, the crowing of pheasants and jungle fowl. Then as darkness comes, the birds grow silent. Presently, the belling of a sambar, a big, coarse-bodied elk-like deer, or the sharp warning call of the barking deer, warns the other forest inhabitants that a tiger or a leopard is on the move.

During the day the chital lie down in thick brush and high grass and are seldom seen. But as the sun drops low and the jungle cools, they move out into the grass-scented glades to feed. All during the night they're afoot and the beam of a spotlight shows their eyes gleaming like diamonds back in the trees.

One of the oddest night hunts for chital that Lee Sproul and I made in India was by handcar along a stretch of railroad through lovely semi-open jungle near Kashipur. We were first taken by automobile to a town about 40 miles from Kashipur. Then at dark Lee, a chap named Joe Hardy, and I set out for Kashipur in a handcar. Our "motor" consisted of four men. Two would push the car for a mile by running barefoot on the rails behind it, then the other two would take over. The fact that it's cheaper to hire four men to push an inspection car than it is to buy a little gasoline engine tells a lot about wage scales in India.

That night a half-moon lit the open jungle with a misty glow as the little handcar clicked along. We could hear the whisper of the pushers' bare feet on the rails, the distant barking of village dogs. Once, from far away, came the thrilling *ooom – oom – ooom* call of a wandering tiger.

Now and then our car would click through a darkened village where humpbacked work oxen lay resting on the ground, softly revealed by the moonlight. Startled dogs would yap at us briefly, and once a woman, as if having a nightmare, yelled shrilly from a hut.

But of the long ride along those clicking rails, I remember mostly the glittering eyes of the chital. We must have seen 300. Time and time again the car would slow, and Joe, who was manning the spotlight taken from the jeep, would play the beam over a herd of those lovely deer. Of does and fawns we saw many. Of youngish bucks we saw a few. But big trophy bucks – not a single one.

It was surprising how well we could see to shoot by spotlight with the medium crosshairs in the 4X scopes Lee and I had on our rifles. Up to 50 or 60 yards I could plainly see the intersection of the crosshairs against the neck or shoulder of a chital. At somewhat longer ranges, I could usually see enough of the crosshairs, against light-colored grass or foliage, to tell where they came together. But it was just a night of sighting at chital and passing them up. None were big enough to pull the trigger on.

My first chital stag came on a night shoot in a patch of jungle down out of the national forest. We were tearing along in the jeep when about 60 yards to the left of the road we saw a constellation of blazing eyes. As the jeep slowed and stopped, the spotlight reached out and put its long bright finger on a very respectable chital stag. Since it was my turn to shoot, I swung the .270 around until the crosshairs came to rest on the stag's neck. The 150-

grain soft-point bullet hit squarely and he never moved.

In India, where many of the animals live in tropical and subtropical forests, the seasons are mixed up. I was surprised to find that this, my first chital stag, was in velvet, but that he was beginning to rub his antlers clean. I was told that my stag was actually behind schedule – that most of them had already cleaned their antlers. The chital, then, is just six months ahead of (or behind) our American whitetails, as he is about as far along in his annual cycle in mid-April as the whitetail is in mid-October.

I was also told that a chital doe has twin fawns and breeds twice a year. I can hardly believe the latter, as there simply wouldn't be time, unless the gestation period is very different from the seven-month period of American deer.

In ages past, the ancestors of North American deer – and probably all deer – must have worn spotted coats as adults, because biologists say that the young show ancestral characteristics. The chital is one of the few species that has simply refused to grow up.

But he isn't the only deer in India – not by a long way. One of the most interesting we saw was the hog deer, a little gray fellow that probably won't dress out at more than 40 or 45 pounds on the average. The hog deer, like the chital, belongs to the same big family as the North American elk, but our elk is the largest of the family and he's one of the smallest.

He lives in high grass and survives because he can sneak off without being seen. A scared hog deer can come about as near to crawling as any animal I've ever seen. He puts his head down, bends his knees so that he'll stand about half his usual height, and sneaks off. Most of the time we saw our hog deer from the backs of elephants, but even from that vantage point, they're none too easy to make out.

Another very interesting Indian deer is the *barasingha*, or swamp deer, an animal which is decreasing because the grassy swamplands where he lives are being drained and put into farms. Another relative of our elk, the *barasingha* looked to be somewhat bigger than our largest mule deer. Lee and I saw several magnificent stags in the first area where we were hunting tigers. Once I started to shoot a superb fellow that trotted off about 200 yards away. But our outfitter was always afraid we'd spook a tiger, so we came home without *barasinghas*.

When we were trying to find a cooperative tiger in the foothills of the Himalayas, we saw a good many sambar – shaggy, also elk-like, and even larger than the *barasingha*, but never did we see a big bull.

Another sort was the furtive little barking deer. His kind kept us informed as to where the tigers were, but we never had a chance to shoot one.

*T*he days of our Indian hunt slipped by. Lee got a tiger reasonably early in the game. We shot a few peacocks for the pot, sometimes knocked over a dove or wild pigeon. Now and then we bought a sheep from a native. But mostly we lived on the handsome chital.

Lee and I got fair enough chital heads while hunting camp meat, but nothing outstanding. We still wanted big ones and hunted hard for them, patrolling the roads early in the morning and late in the evening in jeeps, rocking along on hunting elephants through the dewy forest at dawn, still-hunting at dusk while the jungle fowl crowed and the big peacocks flapped away into the trees dragging tails that looked 20 feet long.

Finally, when our time was running out, I got my chance at a handsome trophy chital. We were taking a turn in the jeep at dawn one morning, and it was Lee's turn to have first shot, as I had nailed a small stag for the pot a couple of days before. We were rolling along when we saw a little herd of chital does and fawns and slowed a bit to see if by any chance there was a stag around.

Apparently there wasn't. Mukerji spoke to the driver. He stepped on the gas and the jeep started to pop and sputter and pick up speed. Right then the best chital stag we had seen during the whole trip broke out of a little clump of trees about 100 yards away and began galloping to the right.

Mukerji yelled, the driver slammed on the brakes, and Lee piled out, switching off the safety of his .30/06.

For want of anything better to do, I also piled out. Lee ran around the rear of the car to have a clear shot. I went around the front. The stag galloped on. About the time I expected Lee to shoot, I saw the stag swerve to the right. Then I heard Lee shout, "Better take him if you can. He's behind trees from me."

When my .270 came up, I could see the stag quartering to my right through the Leupold 4X scope. With the intersection of the crosshairs about two feet ahead of the stag's nose, slightly below, and moving along as fast as the stag was moving, I touched one off. The stag piled up. The 150-grain bullet had gone in behind the shoulder and come out.

The others jeeped over to pick the stag up, but I paced the distance off. The big chital had fallen just 220 steps from where I had fired – a long shot for the Indian jungle.

That was the best shot I made in India, and luckily it was on the largest chital stag we saw. I'm going to get that beautiful head mounted, and when I do, those who come into my trophy room will say, "Golly, look at that fawn with horns on him!"

WORM IN THE TOOTH

An attention-catching title, intriguing Iranian folklore, and sheep hunting with a difference form the ingredients of a compelling yarn. Jack takes home a fine red sheep from this grand expedition.
March, 1956

Lee Sproul and I were supposed to hunt Persian red sheep on the little mountain the next morning, but neither of our two Luhr guides was feeling well. Both had gone out to scout that day and had come back to say that they'd seen two bunches of rams, but also to report that they felt like the very devil.

The trouble? Each had an abscessed tooth. As it stood, they told us, they could show us some rams if they only had the strength, but those teeth had their heads jumping and their legs filled with lead.

Our hunting companion, Prince Abdorreza Pahlavi, brother of the Shah of Iran, has something of a reputation as healer among the villagers and tribesmen of this Iranian back country. Wherever he goes he takes a hardwood box full of medicine and implements. He's equipped to remove a splinter from a finger, combat a major infection, or set a broken leg. And the guides plainly expected him to dive into his magic box and pull out a major miracle for them.

"Oh dear!" groaned the prince. "I'm no dentist. I can give them some aspirin, but that is about all."

"Your highness," said Lee, "would you ask these men to open their mouths and point to their aching teeth? Maybe I can think of something."

And so the three of us inspected the two guides' molars. Each had one that was a dilly, fearfully decayed and badly abscessed.

"I'm no dentist either," I said, "but I know enough about teeth to know they're beyond treatment. Isn't there somebody in the village

255

who pulls teeth?"

The prince translated for me and I could see the guides recoil in horror at my suggestion.

"The old guide says *never!*" the prince told me. "He says that once a man here in the village pulled a tooth for him and that the pain made him die a thousand deaths. This tooth my kill him, he says, but at least he'll die but once."

Lee dug around in his kit, got out some cotton, and stuffed it in the molar cavities. The prince contributed some aspirin and I some pills a physician friend of mine had given me before I left home. I also dosed them with some antibiotic pills I had.

As he took all these remedies, the old guide shook his head.

"These European medicines are all very well, no doubt," he said, "but back in the mountains grows a certain rare plant. Each plant produces but one lovely blossom, and in each blossom when it is exactly mature and is shedding, its exquisite fragrance for many yards around lives a small green worm. If I could but catch one of these worms, I'd put it in my bad tooth. The pain would stop like magic and the tooth would be good as new."

Our two Luhr guides were handsome men, hawk-nosed, sharp-eyed, with the broad shoulders and powerful legs of good fullbacks. The old one wore a big sweeping mustache that gave him the look of an amiable bandit – a man who wouldn't cut a throat unless he considered it absolutely necessary. The young guide looked to be about 35 as against the old one's 50. Tough characters, these Luhrs. They can climb like ibex, ride like madmen, and carry loads that would break down a donkey. They have been famous warriors for thousands of years.

*L*ittle Mountain, on which we were to hunt, rose tall and gray and barren across the green valley from where we were camped. It was Little Mountain only in relation to Big Mountain, which soared above our camp, its flanks white with snow, its head swimming in clouds.

Our camp was beside an ancient Persian watchtower built to warn the villagers against raids by the wild and predatory Luhrs, the ancestors of our two guides. It was about 6,000 feet above sea level. The peaks in the great Big Mountain range rose to over 13,000 feet behind us, whereas those of the little mountain only went up to 10,000.

Centuries of overgrazing and cutting had destroyed the once-heavy forests on Big Mountain and almost all the grass was gone. But now in the springtime it was green with weeds clear to snowline. Little Mountain, though, was the cold, dead gray of barren limestone. The eroded slopes and rocky escarpments looked as sterile as the face of the moon.

But it did look like sheep country. Down in Sonora, Mexico, where I first started hunting mountain sheep many years ago, I had often found sheep on ranges that were lower, but which look no less barren than these.

The next morning our two guides said they were still in pain, but that they'd slept a little during the night and felt equal to a mild bit of climbing. We dosed them up with more pain-killers and antibiotics and set out to hunt.

Lee, the prince, and I rode little Arabian horses, but our helpers swung out ahead with long, distance-eating paces. We each had a gunbearer and horse-holder. Another Luhr went along to carry water, still another to lug nested silver dishes that contained our lunch, and yet another with a burden of movie cameras. A couple of spare Luhrs came to carry the trophies, if any, down the mountain.

Across the green irrigated valley we went. We forded the river, crossed the Teheran railway tracks, and headed up a long valley that led into the heart of the range.

As our horses labored up the steep mountain trail, I saw sheep sign now and then – tracks that could have been made by miniature Rocky Mountain bighorns. The sight made my heart race because I've always loved to hunt wild sheep, and if I shot a ram today it would be the sixth kind of wild sheep I had collected.

The sheep we were after this time are commonly known as the Persian mouflon or the Persian red sheep. Their scientific handle is *Ovis orientalis erskinei*. They are larger than the tiny Sardinian mouflon, which are native to the Island of Sardinia in the Mediterranean Sea. But the Persian mouflon is a good deal smaller than any of the American wild sheep I've hunted – even smaller than some dwarf Stone sheep my son Bradford and I found on a barren little range up in the northwest corner of British Columbia back in 1951.

My friend Herb Klein, who had hunted in Iran with Prince Abdorreza a year or so before, told me that the little red sheep were the smartest, wariest sheep he'd ever seen. I was to find that he was right.

North American sheep for the most part live in wilderness areas where they see few men and have little fear of humans. I remember

257

dressing out a bighorn ram I'd selected from a herd of seven. While I worked, the six others stood 75 yards away and stared at me as if I were the most curious creature they'd ever seen.

But once a wild ram learns that human beings are not to be trusted, he's one of the spookiest animals that breathes. Down in Sonora, where the desert bighorns have been shot at for many generations, the rams are the wildest I've ever seen in North America. In Iran, the little red sheep have been dodging spears and arrows since the dawn of historical times. And now they're eluding people with scope-sighted rifles. If it has two legs, the red sheep want no part of it!

In mountains where there are many canyons, ridges and peaks, it's not difficult to stalk close to wild sheep. The hunter who watches the wind and stays out of sight can usually get a pretty good shot. But this particular range in southwestern Iran didn't lend itself to an easy approach. In spite of its Little Mountain name, it's built on an enormous scale, with wide canyons and great hulking ridges.

Mostly the side canyons were few and shallow, and distances from one ridge to another averaged 1,000 yards or more. Although Little Mountain looked like the barren Sonora ranges, it had the tremendous proportions of the limestone mountains at the head of Muskwa and Prophet Rivers in British Columbia.

*W*hen we left our horses behind, we were probably somewhere between 1,500 and 2,000 feet up the side of the mountain and the crest was still 2,500 feet above us. Like most climbing when a man hunts sheep, this was not dangerous, as it so often is with goat hunting, but it *was* work – lifting one foot up, finding a place where it wouldn't slip, then hoisting up the body, lifting the other foot. And so on and so on and so on . . . .

We worked around a long open slope, climbing gradually higher and higher. To our right we could see the black streak that was the railroad, the silver sheen of the river, the green checkerboard of fields. The white dots far across the valley were our tents, pitched by the tumbled adobe huts of the ancient Persian village. Across the valley, lofty, austere, and snowcapped, rose the serrated peaks of Big Mountain. It made me feel little just to look at it.

At each side canyon that broke off the ridge under which we were climbing, we'd cautiously poke our heads over the sheltering rocks and glass the country below us. It was April. The ewes were lambing and ranging apart from the rams.

Once we got within 200 yards of a ewe with a lamb that couldn't have been more than a few hours old. It was wobbling around on ridiculously long legs and coming back now and then to nurse from its patient mother.

A little later the old guide poked his head over, focused his binoculars, and broke into a wide grin. He indicated a spot far below and I put my own glasses on it. I could see a whole swarm of ewes and lambs. The ewes were lying around content and motherly; the lambs were sleeping, nursing, skipping, playing – all the usual lamb antics.

"I don't like the looks of things very much," Prince Abdorreza told me a few moments later, as we plowed on toward the crest of the range. "We are seeing nothing but ewes and lambs. We've had some pretty warm days here, and the old rams may have crossed the valley to Big Mountain. It's a lot higher and cooler. Let's hope for the best, though."

A little later we climbed up a cliff that wasn't very high but just about vertical for 150 feet. Above that was a ridge that ended at the highest peak in the range. As I picked my way up, it occurred to me a 100-foot fall would kill me just as dead as one of 1,000 feet. We were at almost 10,000 feet, and the air was getting very thin. I labored along, wheezing like a leaky pipe organ.

At the top, the prince was waiting to lend me a hand. "We may have a bit of luck now," he told me. "The old guide thinks that if there are any rams in the range, they'll be in a basin we can glass from the top here."

*A*nd so it was. At the very crest the two guides peeked over, then turned and motioned to Prince Abdorreza. He took one look and turned to me with a jubilant smile. Then he held up his right hand with all five fingers extended – five rams.

I inched up to a place where I could look down in the great basin and focused my binoculars. Presently I saw the rams, lying there looking out over the country below them as wild sheep do all over the world.

"Well," said the prince, "there they are. You and the old guide better take off. I'll be in the cheering section."

Motioning with his hand for me to be quiet and careful, the old Luhr took my rifle and led the way. We dropped off around a peak, scrambled down a cliff, made a wide circle, and came out behind a rock with the rams some 350 yards away and about 700 feet below us.

I looked them over carefully with my binoculars. Now I could see six instead of five there in the rocks. I picked out what seemed the largest head. In spite of the range, I was in a good position to shoot,

259

for I could cushion my rifle on a rock rest. If I missed, I'd have plenty of time to fire other shots.

I held out my hand for my rifle, but nothing doing. The old guide refused to surrender it. He spoke to me severely in Persian, apparently telling me that the range was too long and we'd get a better shot.

So we backed off our lofty perch, dropped into a canyon, and approached the sheep from a lower level. And the last stages of our stalk must have been something to watch. We had to crawl along a sloping bench of solid rock for about 100 yards. The guide crept along on knees and one elbow, holding my rifle with the hand of the arm he was crawling with. He used the other hand to press down on the top of my head. If I got my nose more than six inches in the air, he'd grind it into the limestone once more.

I wanted to tell him that I was in no position to shoot and for the love of Mike to give me my rifle so I could sneak ahead and pot myself a red sheep. But I couldn't speak Persian and he couldn't speak English. Consequently, we continued to wiggle along that sloping limestone shelf like two drunken crabs.

Presently, the Luhr paused and raised his head. Things seemed to look all right to him, for he handed me my rifle. I peeked down into the basin, and the first thing that caught my eye was a ram about 250 yards away looking right at me. At the same time he was getting to his feet.

*T*alk about spooky sheep! These Persian red sheep make the wild-eyed and suspicious Sonora rams seem confiding. Most of the rams I have stalked will pause for a moment when something moves. They want to make out what it is. These Persian sheep jumped the instant they saw me. Before I could get into a sitting position, they were bounding over the rocks like golf balls – and instead of six rams, I now saw more than a dozen.

I did some quick looking through my 4X scope to see which was the largest ram. The one I picked was headed for the ridge, leaping from rock to rock, moving faster than I have ever before seen a wild sheep move. My first shot was two feet behind him, my second apparently right over his back. On the third shot he rolled, and I thought I had him. I was allowed another and turned to pick him out.

Then the prince, who had come up from behind, yelled, and I saw that my wounded ram had got to his feet and was about to go over the ridge into the big basin beyond. I'd hit him too far back. I had time for one more hasty shot and then he was gone. I thought I'd lost him or was in for a long, long chase, but I didn't know my host.

"I'll catch him for you!" the prince shouted, and he took off like scared ram himself, traveling at a dead run and leaping from rock to rock down the canyon and up the other side. A moment after he disappeared I heard a shot. Then I saw his tiny figure against the sky, signaling for me to come and get my ram.

Carefully and painfully I picked my way over the rough country the prince had galloped over. It must have taken me half an hour to cover the country that incredible mountaineer had traversed in a couple of minutes.

I had an assist on my ram, but I was proud of my first Asiatic sheep nevertheless. He was a lean, sleek, handsome fellow with horns entirely different from those of North American sheep. We couldn't weigh him, but he looked to be about the size of an American pronghorn antelope – about 100 pounds hog dressed.

His horns measured 27 inches around the curls. According to the record book, this is a very good sheep, but Prince Abdorreza has a dozen trophy heads much bigger than that – the first seven or eight in the world records.

*B*y that time it was midafternoon, blindingly bright and very hot up there in the thin, high air. The prince and I finished what water we had and ate some stewed chicken from one of the silver dishes with our fingers. Then we headed down for the spring to which our horses had been taken.

The two lads who came along to carry the trophies decided to drink at the spring, so – carrying head, scalp, and meat between them – they *ran* down that mountain, leaping from rock to rock.

When the prince and I reached the spring, the old guide was happy and beaming, sprawled out on the grass and at peace with the world.

"How's the tooth?" the prince asked.

"The tooth? Oh yes, the one that gave me pain. It's all right now." He tapped his jaw. No longer was it swelled.

"Ah," said the prince. "The medicine worked. Those antibiotics have killed the infection."

Said the Luhr, "I found the beautiful flower and in this flower was a worm. I put the worm in the tooth and now it is as good as new."

I SHOOT A CLIFF HANGER

O'Connor had a knack for titles, and in this one the "cliff hanger" conveys something of a double meaning. His ibex hunt in Iran costs him a broken rib, some anxious moments with his guns, and plenty of sweat equity. Along the way we get some lessons in ancient history that tell us how deeply and widely O'Connor read.
February, 1956

I t was lonely up here in this rock blind on barren point, and it was also improbable. The rich little carpet that kept my rear end off the sharp stones was a genuine Persian rug. The ruddy-faced, sandy-haired guy with blue eyes in the blind with me looked like Joe Doaks, the American pal you bowl with every Wednesday night, but he was a Persian, or Iranian, if you wish. The vast empty country that stretched out below was part of the ancient and fabled land of Persia – a land once ranged and ruled by such mighty warriors as Cyrus, Alexander the Great, and Genghis Kahn.

And to make the story even more improbable, the tall handsome hunter in the other blind up the ridge from me was a real flesh-and-blood prince – Prince Abdorreza Pahlavi, brother of the Shah of Iran. He's a crack shot, superb mountain climber, and probably the boldest and most skillful ibex hunter going.

Because my Rhode Island friend Lee Sproul and I were a couple of softies, we were, that first day of our hunt in Iran, being treated to an ibex drive. Our host, who had arranged things for Lee, the prince, and me was a genial retired colonel of the Iranian army who looked enough like General Franco, the Spanish dictator, to be his twin brother. Early that morning he had sent a horde of husky villagers out to work along the rugged comb of a mountain range that soared above the level valley and the rolling foothills. When we reached our blinds, they were only about a mile away and were moving ibex before them. All we had to do after we had scrambled 1,500 feet to our rocky hiding place was to wait and shoot.

This was regal hunting. The night before, we had left Teheran by royal train emblazoned with the coat of arms of the ruling Pahlavi family. We dined voluptuously in the lounge of a private car, slept to the clicking of the rails and the song of the Iranian wind. Then, after a typical Persian breakfast of preserves, cheese, toast, and coffee, we were whisked to the colonel's romantic castle, in a green and lovely garden surrounded by a high adobe wall.

When the colonel did things, he did them right. We were taken as far toward the ibex mountain as we could go in a passenger car. Then we were transferred to jeeps. When the country got too rough and steep for those little rock hoppers, we were put aboard magnificent Arabian horses. But any horse will quickly break his neck in real ibex country, so presently we had to pile off and climb the rest of the way afoot. Soon the three "guns" – Lee, Prince Abdorreza, and I – were crouched in our blinds, peeking through cracks between the stones, waiting for a glimpse of this most surefooted of the world's mountain dwellers, the ibex.

*I*f you're not up on your natural history, the ibex is a true goat of the Capra group. His is the long-horned branch of the family, whereas the white Rocky Mountain goat of North America is a member of the short-horned branch. The short-horned group, including the serows and gorals of Asia, is vaguely related to the antelopes. There are ibex and ibex-like animals in rugged mountains from Pakistan to Spain and from China to Arabia and northeastern Africa.

The Persian ibex is called the *pasang*, which means rock-footed, in his native land. If I were naming him, I'd call him the glue-footed or the suction-cup-footed. He's the greatest rock expert in the world. Nothing I ever saw can compare as a mountaineer to the shaggy, evil-smelling *pasang* of the Persians.

Lee Sproul and I took some movies of ibex. They show them walking straight down what appears to be a perpendicular cliff. They also show them trotting merrily along the sides of seemingly vertical walls. The darned things *must* have glue on their feet.

I'm jittery and restless by nature. Waiting on a stand for deer or sitting immobile in a duck blind sets me to chewing my fingernails. So I was prepared to be bored stiff until the ibex showed up.

I don't think my sandy-haired *shikari* and I had been in the blind more than ten minutes, however, when he whispered something and pointed. Peering through a crack between two rocks, I focused my binoculars on the spot he indicated. For a moment I could make out nothing but heaps of barren brown rocks, great soaring cliffs, treacherous slides. Then something moved and the glass resolved it into a shaggy nanny ibex. Cautiously, she picked her way over the stones. Sometimes she'd leap boldly from rock to rock, but when things got tough, she'd travel carefully. Now and then she'd pause to look and listen. Then another nanny with two kids appeared. The kids were little larger than house cats and had probably been born only a few days before. Nevertheless, they skittered over the rocks like experts.

Then two youngish billies trotted around a point. I had seen many pictures of ibex, as well as the magnificent heads that Prince Abdorreza had hanging in the beautiful trophy room of the palace, so I knew that these two billies wore mediocre horns. I let them travel.

They, like the nannies and kids, ran the gantlet of the blinds unmolested. Then two billies with longer horns popped up. They were older and smarter and had waited until the last moment, for I could see the drivers like black ants on the skyline just behind them.

Right now was a pretty good time to become an ibex hunter, I decided, so as the two billies trotted closer, I swung ahead with the little 7mm. Mauser I was using that day. The ibex I selected was about 250 yards away, but traveling slowly. I led it five or six feet and squeezed the trigger. The billy gave a jump and disappeared behind a rock. I thought I'd missed. Then Lee touched off the .270 he was using. I saw the other ibex collapse.

When I toiled up there after the shooting was over, I learned I hadn't missed the billy after all. The prince had found a blood trail while looking at Lee's billy and had followed it up to find the other ibex as dead as dead could be about 75 yards up the mountain.

Lee and I were using borrowed rifles that day because of a snafu. The 7 mm. I was shooting is the one the lovely Princess Perisima, Abdorreza's wife, is, as I write this, using in Africa. Lee had borrowed a .270 from my brother-in-law, John Barry, who is an executive of an American engineering company and lives in Teheran.

We had to borrow rifles because ours were confiscated. When Lee and I flew from Karachi in Pakistan, to Teheran, I innocently assumed our troubles with customs were over. That anyone would seize our rifles and ammunition en route was too fantastic to consider.

But that's exactly what happened. Our American-piloted DC-4 landed at a remote village called Zhidan just inside the border of Iran, and before long the pilot came to tell me that Lee and I were in trouble. The customs inspector, he told us, refused to pass our rifles, and we couldn't apply for a permit to possess rifles at any point nearer than Teheran, about 600 miles away. Without a permit, we couldn't transport the rifles farther by plane, the adamant customs official told us.

In my usual foresighted way, I didn't have with me so much as a letter from the prince, but I told the customs officer that we were to be guests of the Shah's brother, and that if he didn't let our rifles go, I'd call the United States marines. The pilot backed me up. He swore that Lee and I were big shots of such importance that if we were inconvenienced in the slightest, governments would fall, heads would roll, and there would be bloodshed and rioting over half the world.

Plainly, the customs officer thought that Lee and I were fantastic liars and that the pilot was simply backing us up because we were fellow Americans. No permits, no rifles, he said. So presently we winged away despondently, leaving our rifles and ammunition behind in Zahidan.

But that wasn't the end of the story. While Lee and I went on with borrowed rifles, the Iranian chief of staff set out to right our wrong. He flew a bomber bristling with machine guns the 600 miles from Teheran to Zahidan, picked up the rifles, and flew them back to the capital. There, another plane flew them 250 miles to the village station where we had left the royal train. Then, the local chief of police rushed them by automobile 60 miles to our host's castle. I still beam each time I visualize that bomber bristling with guns and high brass buzzing down on the customs official.

I have already said that our first host, the Iranian colonel, looked like General Franco, the Spanish dictator. Throughout the hunt I was struck by the similarities between Iran and Spain. I have been in Spain and I have traveled among people of Spanish blood in Latin America. The average Iranian could be set down in Madrid or Barcelona and look just like his neighbor. One sees precisely the same faces in Iran that he sees in Spain, the same Spanish faces that look out at him from the paintings of Goya, Velazquez, and El Greco. Both countries once possessed great empires, and both countries are largely high plateaus from which big mountain ranges rise.

To complete the parallel, both countries have been gutted by centuries of overgrazing and deforestation. Mountain ranges once covered with forests so dense that whole armies hid in them back in the days of Cyrus the Great and Xerxes, now have not a tree. Mountain slopes where grass once grew bell-deep to a horse now support only weeds. Hordes of sheep and goats have ravaged the grass; charcoal burners have mopped up the trees.

As we flew over the country around Zahidan, where our rifles were seized, we could see the end products of erosion. The topsoil was gone from the mountains, and even the sand and pebbles had been washed off the hills and had covered the fertile land of the valleys. The country was bleak as the face of the moon. Land that great armies once fought over now supported only a handful of camels and domestic goats.

But this deforestation has made Iran the greatest sheep and goat country in the world. When the mountains were heavily forested they harbored the maral, the Persian red deer which is related to our elk. There were also roe deer, and there were tigers. Now the forest game has disappeared, and the bare ranges have become the home of the lithe Persian red sheep and the shaggy ibex. Maral, roe deer, and tiger are now found only in the Caspian provinces where the much heavier rainfall keeps cover growing.

Our first drive that day netted us the two billies, and when we got down to our horses, we found that our host had shot a small sheep that had somehow got mixed up in the goat drive.

That afternoon our beaters drove for the Persian gazelle, an animal about halfway in size between the African Tommy and the Grant's gazelle. The herd came by Prince Abdorreza about 300 yards away. He picked out the largest buck, swung ahead of it with his .300 H&H Magnum, and neatly knocked it over. He's the best game shot I've ever seen. He can do with open iron sights what most people wish they could do with a scope.

The world over, goats are better adapted to the roughest country than wild sheep. If a ram is let alone, he'll feed and bed down in smooth, lush, hillside pastures. Usually he chooses his grazing ground close to cliffs, so that he can escape his enemies, but if he's not bothered he'll move out to round-topped grassy hills over which a horse can gallop. I've seen both Stone and Dall sheep in such country, and in northern Iran the urial, another species of wild sheep, are found in country a jeep can be driven over.

But that wild goat, the ibex – now there is a mountaineer! He's perfectly at home on cliffs where any other living animal would stand trembling. One day I was climbing painfully and dangerously up a knife-sharp ridge, headed for the top of a great barren range. To my left, across a narrow canyon, was an almost straight-up-and-down cliff. Suddenly, something made me look to my left, and there was an ibex billy. He'd probably been bedded in some cleft in the rocks, and now he felt he ought to get out of there. His feet found narrow projections, little ledges, cracks; but from where I was, not over 100 yards away, it looked as if he were walking on air.

I wish now I hadn't shot, but I did. As the .270 cracked, he collapsed and plummeted straight down. It seemed minutes before I heard the body thud on rocks 1,500 feet below. Later that afternoon a couple of the native helpers got to it and carried it out. It looked as if it had been run over by a fleet of trucks.

I was hunting ibex in the colonel's country when I had the accident which handicapped me throughout the rest of my Iranian trip. Lee was ailing that day, so Prince Abdorreza and I climbed to about 10,000 feet for ibex. We got three billies and a young ram. When we came down, our host had mules waiting for us, and we rode on toward more level country. As I got off my mule, my left foot caught in a narrow stirrup and my right foot slipped off a stone. I crashed into a sharp rock as I fell, and from then on I was in constant pain. As I climbed around at from 9,000 to 12,000 feet, every deep breath I took was like getting stabbed with a knife.

Later in Teheran, when we were reoutfitting before going to the Caspian provinces, I went to see an American physician. I had a broken rib and a couple of cracked ones.

"Rib's broken all right," the doctor said, as he wiggled it back and forth. "Do you spit blood? No? Well, it'll be painful, but all you can do is to sit it out."

So I sat it out. I remember one night after the prince and I had been up to almost 13,000 feet. We couldn't get our horses over a snow field and had done most of it on foot. When we reached the crest, a great canyon fell away beneath our feet. Around us was an endless panorama of brown rocks, snow, and cliff after frightening cliff. At the very bottom of the canyon, perhaps a mile below the ridge on which we stood, was a brown and agitated little stream fed by the melting snows.

Here and there, as much at home on these terrible ledges as eagles in the air, were ibex, little brown animals in a brown wilderness of stone. Some were bedded, a few were on foot and feeding; but all were out of reach. The prince showed me a point where, a year before, he and a native guide had walked in from below to take a fine trophy billy.

"You must be part ibex yourself," I told him when he pointed out the incredible route.

Against Prince Abdorreza's advice, Lee and I had chosen a bad time for our ibex hunt. The Luhr tribesmen were moving their flocks of domestic sheep and goats through the mountains, and all the game had been spooked and driven to the roughest country. However, we had wanted to hunt tiger in India in late April and early May and we had taken our chances. If I ever go back to Iran, it will be either in the fall or earlier in the spring.

Yet an off-season hunt did produce one of the finest Persian ibex ever shot – and a recklessly courageous mountaineering feat.

The prince, Lee, and I had spent a long day hunting ibex without having any luck. Very early, we had seen a small bunch of fine red sheep rams, but they scented us and took off. The ibex we'd seen in the cliffs had either been in places where they couldn't be approached or had moved on before we could reach them.

The three of us had spent the midday hours – when no game is moving – lying on our backs with our heads under the same bush to keep the searing high-altitude sun off our faces. About 3 o'clock we started hunting again. At a great distance we found with glasses the rams that had eluded us that morning, but it would have taken a day's travel to reach them. We also discovered an ibex now and then with the glasses, but either the animals couldn't be reached or their heads were not worth taking.

We were thinking of going back to our horses and heading toward camp, which was seven or eight miles away, when one of the guides spotted a beautiful billy in the rocks far below us. The goat had fed on some dry grass and weeds on a ledge a few inches wide and 1,000 feet above the river for a few minutes. Then he decided to move up. We watched his fantastic climb with the glasses. He came within 400 yards of us, and I'm sure that any of us could have killed him. But if we had, he'd have fallen a mile.

We were just about to call it a day when one of our two Luhr helpers, who had gone around a point for a look, came back excited. He had, he told the prince, located the biggest ibex billy he'd ever laid eyes on.

We all scrambled over to where we could glass him. He was at least 1,500 feet below and on a ledge about four inches wide. But no denying it – this was an ibex among thousands.

"Will you go after him?" the prince asked me, "I think he's one of the very finest trophies I have ever seen."

I looked at the declining sun. I felt my aching ribs.

"Your Highness," I said. "I am a family man. I have a beautiful wife and two charming daughters to support. Besides, the very thought of those cliffs scares the dickens out of me!"

"Do you mind if I try, then?" the prince asked.

"Of course not! Lee and I will be your cheering section."

*B*ecause time was running short, the prince and his two Luhr guides started off on a run. They decided to make the descent around a point out of the big billy's sight. The prince had his .300 Magnum strapped across his back by the sling, and he wore gloves to keep the sharp rocks from tearing his hands.

Down and down they went, like flies on a wall. They'd work along a ledge, find where one below widened out, then drop to it. Just watching them made Lee and me shudder.

As they descended, the sun went down and the deep canyon began to fade into darkness. Finally we heard a shot. Then another, and another – five in all. When the prince finally got within range of the great billy and on the same level, it was so dark he couldn't see his open sights. He had to aim by looking along the barrel as he would point a shotgun. Yet he got the billy.

By the time they got the head skinned out, it was so dark they were afraid to start back up the cliffs, so they perched on a ledge until the moon rose. Then, by the yellow misty light, they crept and clutched their way back up the cliffs.

At camp after midnight, the steel tape revealed that this big billy was not only the largest the prince had ever shot, but ranks among the five largest Persian ibex on record. Horn length was 48⅝ inches.

And that's the way a great trophy should be taken: A daring stalk, good shooting, and all in a wild and rugged setting. The ibex may look a lot like somebody's back-yard billy goat, but he's one of the world's greatest trophies and one of the most dangerous to hunt. He won't chew you up like a lion or a tiger or gore you like an elephant or a rhino. Nor will he toss you like a buffalo. But anyone who follows him into his native cliffs takes the chance of breaking every bone in his body.

PART FOUR
Miscellany

or most sportsmen, Jack O'Connor's name evokes thoughts of Coues' deer, sheep hunting, shikar and safari, flat-shooting rifles and, of course, challenging quests for big game. All of these are accurate perceptions, but there was a great deal more to the man as a writer and as a hunter. He loved fine shotguns and wrote extensively on them. During some of his jaunts to Asia and Africa, he made stopovers in Europe to visit the premises of great gunmakers on the continent and in England, and from reverence for his grandfather's Parker as a boy to acquisition of lovingly crafted smoothbores late in life, shotguns always loomed large in his life. Nor should it be forgotten that roughly half of one of his best-selling books, *Complete Book of Rifles and Shotguns*, dealt with them.

O'Connor not only wrote about shotguns; he used them. Some of his most coveted experiences as a hunter came when following a joyous Brittany, usually accompanied by a family member, hunting birds. He delighted in all sorts of varmint hunting and relished easygoing days spent plinking with rimfires. Few things gave him more simple pleasure than a day of chasing Gambel's quail. He introduced his children to the outdoors through small game hunting, and I've always been intrigued by the manner in which Eleanor's wingshooting (even when on big game hunts) enters into his stories. Similarly, Eleanor loved to fish and from time to time Jack makes mention of that fact.

The selections that follow reflect these diverse, too often forgotten interests, each a reminder of O'Connor's wide-ranging abilities – he knew a lot about many kinds of hunting and many types of guns. There's bird hunting at home and abroad, a mixed bag hunt for jackrabbits and coyotes, and even a trout fishing piece. His article on the .270 is but one of dozens he wrote about the caliber, which he admired so much and used so widely. It is the only selection in the book that originally appeared as a column as opposed to a major article, but no representative look at O'Connor's work would be complete without such a piece.

FIGHTING TROUT A MILE DOWN

*This might well be the only fishing
story O'Connor ever wrote. It comes
from a trip, probably made in 1932, to
the remote, trout-filled reaches of
Bright Angel Creek in the Grand
Canyon. December, 1935*

Trout a mile down? Impossible, you say. Anglers don't go down
for trout; they go up, up into the high mountains where the
altitude makes the water cold and the fish pugnacious.

This observation may be true, as a rule. This yarn, however, isn't
concerned with the rule, but with the exception. That exception is the
bright-hued depths of the Grand Canyon. Here, a mile below the
timbered Arizona plateau, are trout as big, as colorful, and as scrappy
as any that ever darted through crystal waters on a mountain slope.

A mile may not sound like a great distance. Horizontally, it isn't.
But vertically it's something to view with awe. In the case of the
Grand Canyon, this plumb-lined mile takes you from the cool, tree-
dotted brim down to desert. The terrifying descent of the narrow trails
takes you through a dozen strata of rock formations, a trip which,
geologically, carries you back to the beginning of earthly time. This
descent may fascinate you with its beauty and color; it may make you
a bit dizzy as you glimpse the silver thread of river far below. But
you'll take it, if you want to find the sort of fishing you've never had
except in your dreams.

You must get to the very bottom of this tremendous gorge, down
to the river, rushing ice-cold through a desert that sizzles with heat as
high as 120 degrees in the shade. You need not be amazed at this
paradox; Arizona is a land of paradoxes.

In Tucson, for example, you can swim in outdoor pools in sight of
snow-capped mountains. You can suffer frostbite in the morning and
ten miles away, prickly heat in the afternoon. I'll admit, though, that
the Grand Canyon trout are a little more paradoxical than most
oddities Arizona offers. A cold-water stream, flowing through cactus,

273

prickly pear, desert willow, mesquite, and other hot-country vegetation, is strange enough. The fact that such a desert stream should teem with large trout is almost incredible. In most of the Southwest, a trout stream below 7,000 feet is almost unheard of, yet Bright Angel Creek is only 2,500 feet above sea level – 4,500 feet below the south rim of the canyon and more than a mile below the north rim.

Both the cold water and the trout are easily explained. The source of Bright Angel Creek is the high, cold Kaibab Plateau on the north rim. It rises in places to more than 9,000 feet and snow often lies on it more than 25 feet deep throughout the winter. There are no streams on the Kaibab. The water drains down great sink-holes in the limestone, finally gushing out thousands of feet below in a series of cold brawling springs.

Roaring Spring, which is one of these, is the source of Bright Angel Creek, home of the biggest, gamest trout in Arizona. It bolts out of the rocks with a roar that is audible on the north rim thousands of feet above. Its water is so cold it is almost impossible to drink it. Thence for ten miles it rushes through Bright Angel Canyon so fast it never has a chance to warm up. The fall of the stream is approximately 200 feet to the mile and in many places it is from 20 to 30 feet wide.

In spite of the incongruous desert vegetation, Bright Angel Creek is one of the finest trout streams imaginable – white riffles, boiling rapids, deep, green pools where the big fellows lurk. A little below Phantom Ranch, the creek flows into the Colorado, father of Western rivers and digger of canyons. Its clear, cold waters are lost in the swirling, muddy current of the treacherous larger stream.

Fine trout stream though it is, Bright Angel Creek is relatively unknown and not overfished. Few of the thousands of sportsmen who visit the Canyon annually have even heard of its battling rainbows and Loch Levens. If they had, they would stay to try their luck rather than travel on after inspecting the gorge from the rim.

These mile-down trout are not for weaklings and the timorous. To get at them, the angler must drop down precipitous trails into ever-thickening heat. From the beginning of the Kaibab trail on the south rim, the journey takes two and a half hours on muleback. On foot it takes an hour longer. The trip from the north rim is shorter, but steeper. Mules and guides are obtainable on either rim, and board and room at Phantom Ranch near the mouth of the creek are astonishingly cheap, considering that every morsel of food eaten must be packed by mule into the canyon.

Many hardy souls walk both ways. I have hiked in and out on both trails. In the summer of 1934, my wife and father-in-law hiked from the north rim to Bright Angel Creek, fished all day, and hiked out. I'll guarantee, however, that they'll never do it again in one day. It is almost too much for human endurance.

*U*ntil a few years ago, Bright Angel Creek was an ideal trout stream with no trout. The warm, muddy waters of the Colorado formed an insurmountable barrier to cold-water fish. Then, in 1928, the National Park Service made its first planting of rainbows and Loch Levens. Rangers built a hatchery at Roaring Spring and, by 1931 when the stream was opened, the fishing was the best in Arizona. Food in the cold, swift water is plentiful, and the fish grow rapidly. The fishing has held up beautifully. Almost every day someone takes a trout longer than 20 inches, 18-inchers are common, and few under 10 inches find their way into creels.

If you plan a trip to the Canyon, remember that, no matter how cool it is up above, it will be warm on the creek. Leave your waders at home and dress lightly. And don't try to go in and out on the same day!

I took one trip into the Grand Canyon on which I was not the hero. Instead, I was only a stooge, a captor of grasshoppers, and a taker of pictures. I had, stupidly, left my rod at Flagstaff. After all, it mattered little. My wife is a far more ardent and skillful fisherman than I, and the other member of the party, Tom Bellwood, is a genuine *maestro*. His deftness with the fly rod is almost sinful.

*W*ith a guide to keep us from jumping our mules off the cliffs, we left the rim at 1:30 on a late August afternoon and wound swiftly down into the vivid depths of the canyon. By 5:30 we had obtained two cabins at Phantom Ranch, were cooled off after a swim in the pool there, and were at the stream. Even in late afternoon the temperature was around 100 degrees, but the water could not have been much over 50.

The costume my wife evolved was one of the strangest get-ups a trout fisherman ever wore, and I have no doubt but that some of the fish died of astonishment on beholding it. However, it was suitable for the work in hand. Because it was hot, she wore a sun suit. Then, because the brush along the streambank scratched her, she put on the guide's chaps. Tennis shoes and a felt hat completed the bizarre ensemble.

275

Because it was nearing the dinner hour, the fishermen of the party decided to try their luck near the ranch. They rigged up their tackle, both putting on Gray Hackles, found promising looking pools a hundred yards apart, and cast.

Their reward was – catfish!

By dinner time, they had pulled out a half-dozen 10- and 12-inch channel cats apiece, but nary a trout. To say they were mystified would be putting it mildly. I had never heard of fly-fishing for cats. Perhaps the catfish hadn't either and didn't know they were being unconventional. The way they went after the flies was amazing. We afterwards learned that the cats invaded the stream from the Colorado and were found as high as Phantom Creek, which enters Bright Angel, a couple of miles above the mouth.

My wife is thoroughly practical when it comes to trout. Although she is descended on the paternal side from a dyed-in-the-wool fly-fisherman who thinks anyone who'd take a trout on live bait is a menace to the integrity of American institutions, she always aims to give the critters what they want. She'd rather fish with flies, but if the trout crave worms, worms she gives them. If they like grasshoppers, that's what they get. If they'd take no other bait but the front page of the *London Times*, she'd use that.

So the next morning, after a rather late start, I found myself capturing grasshoppers. At first she tried flies – Gray Hackles, Black Gnats, Sliver Doctors, White Moths, Coachmen. None of them worked well. By 9 o'clock she had a couple of small ones, and I was catching grasshoppers.

I'll never forget one big devil, a potbellied Lock Leven which turned out to be 15 inches long. He was feeding in a riffle behind a stone and, as fast as my wife let the 'hoppers drift by him, he'd gently detach them from the hook. He almost killed me. I caught him black grasshoppers, yellow grasshoppers, and big, green grasshoppers which flew like ducks. Presently, he lost his caution and, instead of toying with the bait, he struck hard. From the trail above I watched the battle. He took for deep water and I could see the line cutting the smooth surface of the pool. But my wife worked him into shallow water and landed him.

Shortly after that battle, our guide joined us with our mules and we worked up the creek, alternately fishing and riding. By noon we were at Ribbon Creek, which flows into Bright Angel about five miles upstream from the ranch. We ate behind Ribbon Falls where the little creek tumbles a hundred feet over a cliff into a deep pool in which some big rainbows lurk.

Bright-Angel Canyon is an astonishing place. The creek, in the millions of years that it has been running, has cut out a narrow canyon from solid schist and granite, the oldest exposed rocks in the United States. In some places, the walls go up almost straight for a thousand feet; in others they slant enough to be climbed by a hardy mountaineer.

The sun strikes the bottom of the canyon only in the middle of the day, and for that reason, fishing is fair at times when it would be futile even to try elsewhere. Occasionally we caught glimpses of the north rim a mile above us, dark with its thick growth of fir and spruce. Through the mouth of the side canyon we could see the buildings on the south rim.

Our guide, Ed Cummings, an old fellow townsman of mine, has guided at the canyon for 15 years and is a mine of information on its geology, history, and wildlife. While Tom Bellwood and my wife fished, Ed and I talked. He told me of mysterious Indian cliff ruins hidden in lonely side canyons, difficult of access and never explored. He spun yarns on enormous old mountain rams, driven from the high walls of the canyon by deep snows and made tame by hunger; of wise, big bucks which live in the depths the year around and clean the velvet off their horns on sandstone instead of venturing up on the mesa where they might be shot; of wild burros as wary as hawks. And he told me strange stories of happenings in the canyon country – of a locoed pack mule which jumped from the Kaibab trail and fell 1,500 feet to the rocks below; of the happy honeymooners who started to go through the canyon in a boat and so far as Ed knew, were never heard from again.

*D*arkness comes swiftly in that narrow canyon. By the time we finished our talk and went to take the mules to the fishermen, dusk was coming fast. We came on Tom first. He had a heavy creel and a face wreathed in smiles. He had the limit of ten trout and every one was a dandy. A few minutes later we heard a shrill scream above the roar of the water and saw my wife, grappling with a big boy in the shallows. She had worked him up to the bank, but just as she was about to grab him, he had flopped free of the hook. She pounced like a cat and got him.

All of the fish that afternoon had been taken by the fly route, Tom and my wife told us as we rode back to the ranch. They were biting on both Gray Hackles and White Moths, and the darker it got, the more they favored the Moths. During the last of the season, flies undoubtedly work better than live bait, and our experience that morning was only the exception which, they say, proves the rule.

The next morning was to be the last. We were up early and at it. Curiously enough – you never can tell about trout – the later it got, the better the fishing became. Both my wife and Tom tried out their flies until they finally hit upon Coachmen. What happened from then on seemed more like a wish than actuality. There was a big fellow in every pool and every one of them seemed to have been waiting wistfully for a Coachman. Smaller ones wanted them, too, but the big lads usually beat them to it. Fish under ten inches went unceremoniously back into the water, and, by 10 o'clock, both anglers had their limits – ten big fish.

Back at Phantom Ranch, we chilled the fish in the electric refrigerator, wrapped them in paper and then in canvas, and started across the suspension bridge over the Colorado on our mules. In an hour we had climbed out of the 1,400-foot deep inner gorge and were bidding good-by to Bright Angel Creek. In another hour we could smell the cool, pine-ladened fragrance of the upper plateau and, three and a half hours after leaving the ranch, we topped out and were thanking Ed for one of the best hunting and fishing trips of a lifetime. A mile below we could still see the creek, scene of the finest trout fishing in the West.

*I*f you'd like to try it yourself, here are a few tips. If you must walk, by all means take a pack mule for your food and bedding. Unless you are as hard as nails, getting yourself in and out of the canyon is about all you will be able to do. Wear shorts and an old pair of shoes, preferably with hobnails in them. Too many clothes will spoil your trip, for you will find that it's everlastingly hot down below in trout season. However, don't forget to take a sweater along. You may run into a shower the last couple of thousand feet of your climb out and, in this higher altitude, it can be surprisingly cold.

Dry flies are about as effective as lures and are more sporting because it will take you longer to catch your limit. Have plenty of flies, as it is easy to lose them on the brush, and have them tied on rather large hooks, nothing smaller than No. 8, if you don't wish to be plagued by the little fellows.

By far the best fishing is in the lower end of the stream between Phantom Creek and Ribbon Falls. Below this magic stretch, there are too many channel cats, many of them fresh from the Roaring Springs Hatchery.

The stream is steadily but not heavily fished, and the fact that the Park Service plants about 45,000 fingerlings annually would seem to foretell fine sport for many years to come. The difficulty of getting to the stream protects it from automobile fishermen and the tin-can tourist.

There is talk now of installing a tramway to haul passengers from the south rim to Phantom Ranch. If that is done, the trip will only take a few minutes instead of hours, but about three-quarters of the fun will be gone. Old Bright Angel will then be just another stream where there used to be good fishing, like thousands of others in the country.

I hope I never live to see that day!

GAMBLING FOR GAMBEL'S

Time and again in O'Connor's work one comes across mention of the decorative little bundles of feathered dynamite that we call Gambel's quail. They provided fine fare for campfire meals, afforded challenging sport, and were plentiful in the desert Southwest during Jack's heyday. In this story we see O'Connor's conservationist side when he reminds readers that "clean farming" and quail are like oil and water – they don't mix.
December, 1946

Perhaps it's simply luck. Perhaps it's some sort of obscure instinct which guides a hunter. Or possibly it is as the Indians believe – if you live right and observe the proper rituals, the spirits of the woods and prairies will take you by the hand and lead you to good hunting. I know that for my part, some of the best sport I have ever encountered has come to me through no conscious process on my part. It has been as if I were guided by some unknown hand.

The quail of the little *milpas*, which is what the Mexicans call their farm fields, are a case in point. I discovered them by accident. I discovered them because I needed them, because I had to have them if I were to get in much bird shooting. It was as if some beneficient spirit had conjured them up for me out of my need.

Now the Gambel's quail of the Southwest is almost entirely a desert bird and not, like the Eastern bobwhite, a dweller on farms and fields. The Gambel's does not get on well in the modern world, and for the most part he has disappeared from the big irrigated valleys of the Southwest. Clean farming, the habit of burning off the grass each winter, and predator domestic cats which all Americans seem to love (as well as the ever-present and just as predatory small boy with his

281

BB gun and his .22), all serve quickly to exterminate him around most farms. The birds have survived in hordes in the deserts, but civilization nearly always spells their doom.

So I had no right to find those coveys where I did. They were simply born of my need.

There is excellent bird hunting around Tucson, Arizona, but most of it is from 20 to 40 miles away and out of reach of the man who holds a job and must confine his longer jaunts to weekends. I wanted a spot where I could shoot a few birds after my day's chores were over – and I found it – easily, quickly, almost as if I had known about it all the time and had just remembered.

*I*t was a few years ago, and I had just moved to Tucson from the high, cold Coconino Plateau in northern Arizona, where no quail live and where wild turkeys are the only native nonmigratory game bird. Turkeys, of course, afforded considerable excitement and exercise, but not much shooting, since in those days the bag limit was two. So I was desperately anxious to polish up my quail technique.

Gloomily I went to my job the morning of opening day while more fortunate human beings headed for the desert and the merry Gambel's quail. At 3:30 p.m., when I could slip away, I gathered up the wife and a couple of guns and went out aimlessly, wistful but planless.

We passed the suburban homes of wealthy Easterners and of not so wealthy natives, tourist hotels, beer joints, and filling stations. Surely there were no quail around here.

About three miles from home I saw a little-used road turning off into a patch of cholla and greasewood toward Rillito Creek. Still aimless, I took it.

"Where are we going?" my wife asked politely.

"I don't know," I told her.

After a quarter of a mile, a barbed-wire fence stopped us. I got out to open a gate, and there, fresh and sharp in the soft dust, were quail tracks – unmistakably quail tracks, the sign of a good-sized covey.

So we took our guns and moved cautiously into the mesquite thicket on the other side of the fence. More tracks crisscrossing the soft earth, feathers, dust baths. In the distance I heard the sweet, flutey call of a cock Gambel's quail.

So we mooched along, straining our ears, guns ready. Presently we came to a little irrigation ditch bordered by a high, thick pomegranate hedge full of red and orange fruit.

Then, *B-b-b-b-b-*, the unmistakable sound of a flushing quail.

There he was, a beautiful cock, towering up out of the pomegranates. I shot and saw him collapse – and heard a yell with distinctly Mexican overtones.

Astonished, I pushed through the hedge and saw something the presence of which I hadn't expected – an adobe house. And standing in front of it, beside a washtub, was the angriest Mexican woman I have ever seen. She gripped a soapy quail in one hand and waved it furiously as she sputtered at me.

Mexicans, I am convinced, are the fastest-talking people on this globe, and when angry, they talk at least nine times as fast as when they are calm.

She told me what she thought of *gringos* in general, of hunters as a race, and of me in particular. She also remarked about the morals of people who went about shooting quail so that they fell into washtubs and frightened good Christian women half out of their wits. She even brought my grandmother, my great-grandmother, and my great-great-grandmother into the discussion.

My wife, fortunately, didn't understand much Spanish, or perhaps I should never have regained face with her. We both stood there and took it.

Then a tall, solemn Mexican appeared, hoe in hand. He listened impassively, now and then stroking his handlebar mustache. But after a few minutes of it, he caught my eye and slowly winked. I grinned, and he grinned.

La madama turned then, saw her spouse, and landed on him. Would he stand there like a big rat, she demanded, and simper when a gringo had just shot her with an *escopeta* (gun)? Ah, if she had only married a man instead of a spineless *huodido* that could be trodden upon like a worm! Out of breath, she paused then, as he shrugged. She was resigned to her fate, helpless with indignation.

*I*t was my turn now. I assured her, in my best Spanish, that if I had known so lovely and gracious a lady was working on the other side of that beautiful hedge, I should never have shot, that I was the most humble and remorseful of men, with a head that must remain forever bowed in contriteness and shame.

She favored me with a smile then, the first rift in the clouds, and my wife completed the peace treaty by making friends with a shy four-year-old girl who came peeking out of the adobe hut.

So we met Juan and Mercedes, and we also met the quail – the *"muchos codornices"* which Juan told me about. "Don't shoot the cow or the children," he said to me, "and you are welcome."

A little exploring gave us the explanation of why the quail were there. Although we were hunting only a few miles from the center of Arizona's second largest city, we were for all practical purposes in Sonora, Mexico. A dozen Mexican families lived along the creek there, farming little *milpas* of corn and beans and chile, raising scrubby chickens, tending gnarled little orchards, and now and then butchering one of the steers that fed in the mesquite pasture. They were poor, hard-working people and, like their relatives in Sonora, almost never hunted. If they did pot something now and then with a rusty old single-barrelled shotgun, it was a cottontail or jackrabbit, never a quail or a dove, since they didn't have the skill to hit the birds on the wing and felt it a waste of money to shoot them.

Mexicans of their class stew up everything with chile, garlic, and onions anyway, so they think jackrabbit meat is just as good as quail, and one shell gets far more of it. The only time I felt Juan's downright disapproval was one day when he showed me a closely huddled covey that I could have practically exterminated with one shot. I refused to shoot, and he showed plainly that he thought I should have my head examined.

Those *milpas* were really lovely, a fit setting for hunting the smartest, gamest bird in the Southwest. The big feathery cottonwoods along the ditches were just turning then, flaunting great masses of clear, bright yellow against the transparent blue of the southern Arizona sky. Scarlet strings of chile hung against the light-brown adobe houses, and the fields were checkerboards of green and gold.

When we left the adobe of Juan and Mercedes that first day, we hadn't gone more than 50 yards when we flushed a covey out of an ancient cottonwood overgrown with grapevines. I had heard about such things before – or, rather I had read about them in stories of hunting bobwhites and ruffed grouse – but never before had I seen Gambel's quail eating grapes. But I was warned and when, 50 yards or so farther on, another covey burst out of a brush pile, we both went into action and got three.

Writers are fond of generalizing about the habits of game, and I have done some plain and fancy generalizing myself. I honestly thought I knew about as much about the habits of Gambel's pretty quail as anyone. Yet that day I had to discard practically everything I had learned from tramping over the deserts for nearly 30 years. Those birds were Gambel's quail in form, in color, in calls; but in action, they were like bobwhites. Hunting them was bobwhite hunting in a Mexican environment.

One field had been planted to wheat, and it must have contained six or seven coveys of from 10 to 20 birds each. Juan had harvested it with a hand scythe and the stubble was a good six inches high, high enough to conceal the feeding birds and also to make them fairly hard to find when we grassed them, unless we kept our eyes open. Those birds did not run when they heard us coming as Gambel's so often do. Instead, they hid and burst out from beneath our feet when we were almost ready to step on them. Sometimes they flew over into an adjoining field, but usually they fanned out, scattered, and hid again in the same wheat stubble.

Ordinarily, the quail of the deserts flush at from 20 to 30 yards; sometimes, when they are wild and the ground is quite bare, from 35 to 40. These birds exploded at our shoe tops. Bobwhite hunting? Nothing else! And for the first time in my career, I longed passionately for two things almost no Southwestern hunter ever buys – a really good bird dog and an open-bored gun.

Used to longer flushes, I ruined the first three birds I took out of the stubble patch. I shot too fast and even with the modified barrel I reduced them to masses of pulpy feathers. After that I waited them out and took them at ordinary range – or what is ordinary range in the Southwest. A good bird dog would have been in his element then, as the birds lay well.

I followed one covey into a thick patch of mesquite, and there I got what I imagine grouse shooting is like. They had scattered and at least half of them lit in trees. I'd hear the whir of wings and see them driving through the foliage. I won't tell my score. I'm no grouse shooter. I'd like to be, but I have never had the opportunity. So those who have hunted grouse know about what an open-country shot armed with a close-bored 20 gauge with 30-inch barrels would be likely to do under such circumstances.

I could hear the little woman's gun popping in the stubble still, and when I joined her, I found her picking up the bird which completed her limit. I still lacked two, but we had enough. So we headed back toward Juan's by the way of a brushy draw to pick up some cottontails for our host.

We rolled three and missed as many more by shooting over them with our straight-stocked guns. I completed my bag of quail with a pair of shots I still remember voluptuously, although the misses I had made in that pesky mesquite thicket seem somehow to have escaped me. We were strolling along, expecting nothing, when two birds exploded from the top an of old peach tree on the edge of a field. I made as neat a double on them as I have ever made, shooting the moment they were silhouetted against the sky. I found them both on the far side of the tree, so dead they hadn't moved – and that, for a Gambel's quail, is very, very dead indeed.

As if we hadn't already had enough sport, we ran into a fine flight of doves. We had seen a good many that day, scattered and feeding in the stubble, but we had ignored them for the quail. Now we took our stands beside some high cottonwoods and shot while the doves came streaking over, headed for their roosts in the bottom of Rillito Creek a quarter of a mile away. We found ourselves shooting cleanly, swinging smoothly, and in a few minutes we had ten doves.

The sun was about to set, so we knocked off, delivered our thanks and our rabbits to Juan and Mercedes, and headed for the car.

Would our kind hosts have either doves or quail? No, not they! But on the other hand, they were very fond of weenies. We said we'd bring them some next time. And we did.

*T*wo or three afternoons a week for the rest of the season we shot on Juan's place, delivering our tribute of hotdogs and returning with bags of sporty birds, large, fat, and delicately flavored from eating all sorts of food ordinarily unknown to desert-dwelling Gambel's – grapes, dried apricots, wheat, and milo – even maybe a spot of chile now and then.

Never did those little *milpas* fail us. Without intending to, Juan had arranged an ideal set-up for birds. He had never heard of clean farming, so his ditches and field corners were high with brush and weeds. He didn't prune his fruit, so his trees did just as well for roosts as the horny paloverdes of the desert. He raised crops to eat instead of to sell, and as a consequence the birds had plenty of food, whereas most Americans in the Southwest now raise either truck or cotton.

I wish this story could end on a happy note, but our first season there was our last. A wealthy Easterner with a yen to be a Southwestern country gentleman saw Juan's place and was so charmed by its rustic simplicity that he bought Juan out, and Juan and Mercedes went back to Sonora.

It's a model American farm now. The fence corners are clean, so are the ditches, and the fruit trees have been pruned and sprayed. The fences now bear "No Hunting, No Trespassing" signs, but there is no need for them. The quail are no longer there.

MY HIGHLAND FLING

Jack regularly made stopovers in Europe in connection with his safaris, and in this case he gets a fine taste of the traditions associated with driven bird hunting in Scotland. In this rather long story he captures the essence of proper Scottish sport, touches on British "bests," and retains his distinctly American identity by shooting a Winchester Model 21. He even manages to come out as high gun. August, 1960

Toughest shooting in the world, old boy," Tommy Morgan, the little Welshman, told me. "Better get a good night's sleep and take an extra dose of vitamins. Tomorrow you'll need it. Most of the American chaps who come over here to shoot grouse can't hit a bloody thing for a week."

"Don't let him worry you," said Eric Roberts, one of my hosts. "You shouldn't find grouse too difficult."

I must admit I was a bit worried. All my life I'd been reading of Scottish grouse shoots. I had read how the grouse come in like bullets, and many an American in describing his experiences had said he shot a dozen shells on the first day without getting a feather.

As a lone American shooting with a bunch of Britishers, I was in a good position to be embarrassed by a poor performance.

"Look, Tommy," I said. "Don't get the idea that I have my sign up as a crack shot with a shotgun. I've seen worse shots than I am, but I've also seen many who were much better. In fact, if you went out to any American skeet club and threw a rock into the crowd, you'd probably hit a better scattergun marksman that I am. Don't expect too much of me."

As we talked we were in Eric Roberts' suite in the Railway Hotel at Aberdeen, Scotland, nibbling on the distilled elixir manufactured by the firm in which Eric and Sandy Gordon, my other host, were directors. It was September, but fall weather had already settled over the Highlands above the east coast city of Aberdeen. Outside it was raw and chill, with mist rolling in from the North Sea. In the hotel room, my Scottish friends warded off the chill with a coal fire in the open grate and with an occasional nip of Scotch.

Two days before my wife and I had landed at Prestwick, the airport for Glasgow. But since the grouse shoot was strictly stag, my wife was off to tour the island of Great Britain. At the end of the shoot I would meet her in London. We were headed for Africa, where I was to make my third safari and my wife her first. Eric Roberts had asked me to stop here and do a spot of grouse shooting with him. I was eager to take a whirl at it. I'd never shot a Scottish grouse and had never seen a Scot on his native heath. For that matter, I had never seen any part of Great Britain except London. Since I had a grandmother named McConnell and a lot of Scotch blood in me, I thought I'd like to see what an uncorrupted Highlander looked like.

We spent a couple of days driving across Scotland from west to east, and among other things we saw Loch Ness, where the famous sea monster is reputed to make his home. It was the monster's day off; he wasn't there to greet us. We also stopped at the Grant distillery on the Fiddich River, a tributary of the Spey in the region where all the world's fine Scotch whiskey is made from malted barley dried in peat smoke. The water of the little river combines with the peat and with the Scottish know-how to give this wonderful booze its characteristic smoky taste.

As I was to find out, the thrifty Scots discovered generations ago that it was cheaper to wear thick wool clothing and to stoke their internal fires with an occasional slug of Scotch than it was to heat a house. Most of their homes are still heated with fireplaces. There's little timber for fireplace wood, however, and coal and even peat are expensive. An American reckless enough to get more than five feet away from the feeble fires in the country homes of Scotland will soon have frost on his ears.

But apparently the mist and the cold, the herring, the oatmeal porridge, oatcakes, and Scotch whiskey all agree with the Scots. I have never seen a finer looking lot of people – big brawny men, lovely girls with flower-petal complexions. Around Aberdeen, anyway, the great majority of the people are fair, and I have never seen so many redheads in my life.

While Eric, Sandy, and I were crossing Scotland, I pumped them about grouse shooting. In the British Isles, they told me, there's nothing that corresponds to the casual public shooting in the United States. It's considered that the owner of the land is also the owner of the game on it, and likewise the owner of the banks of a stream is the owner of the fishing rights.

Anyone who shoots in Scotland must either own the land, lease the shooting rights, or be invited by someone who has shooting rights, as I was.

Businessmen who like to shoot grouse, but who own no land, form syndicates. They lease the shooting rights from landowners and hire gamekeepers to trap and shoot vermin, keep off poachers, burn the heather at the proper time so conditions will be right for the grouse, and raise and put down pheasants if any of the country is suitable for such birds. The keeper also hires beaters and manages the drives for grouse.

Each member of the syndicate pays his share of the costs of shooting. All of the birds taken are put into a common pool and sold. There's no bag limit. If a member wants to keep some of his birds, he pays the market price for them and the money goes back into the syndicate's common fund. The host on a grouse shoot may invite a guest to help himself to birds out of the bag, but the fact that a man has killed grouse gives him no right to it. From first to last, those who own the land or the shooting rights own the game.

All game is widely sold in Britain – rabbits, grouse, pheasants, Hungarian partridge, red and roe deer. When I went on to London, my wife and I wandered into Fortnum & Mason, the world-famous food store where the clerks wear striped pants and cutaways. Displayed beside such foods as rum cakes, truffles, and quail eggs were my old friends the Scottish grouse, looking somewhat bedraggled and selling for one pound sterling ($2.80) each. Knowing a little about the cost of a Scottish grouse shoot, I did some mental arithmetic and decided that the thrifty way to get grouse is to buy them at the market. I'd bet that every grouse shot in

289

Scotland costs someone at least $15. However, it's sport the Britisher is after, not meat.

Incidentally, the insides are never taken out of gamebirds in Great Britain until they're dressed for cooking, and the British look with horror on the American custom of removing the internal works of the birds the moment they are brought to bag. They also deplore the American habit of refrigerating their birds until such time as they're cooked. Such treatment, they say, doesn't allow the flavor to develop or the meat to get tender. One day I casually told Sandy Gordon that I froze pheasants and quail and kept them in the freezer until I wanted to eat one. A look of pain and amazement spread over his face. "Shocking," he said.

The British may have something with their tenderizing treatment. I ate some roast grouse while I was in Britain; they were both tender and delicious.

A grouse shoot in Scotland is a social occasion of no mean proportions, and the next day the syndicate members and guests gathered for the shoot in a little valley surrounded by rolling, heather-covered hills. Most of the "guns" (those who were to shoot) wore tweed jackets and matching knickerbockers of the plus-four variety that were fashionable in the U.S. back in the 1920s. Some wore the picturesque kilts. They also wore neckties and tweed or felt shooting hats. Their shoes ("boots," to them) were stout jobs with hobnails and six- or eight-inch tops. I wore an old tweed jacket, a red wool shirt, a pair of khaki cotton pants, which I'd later wear to hunt lion and kudu in Africa, and a pair of silicone-tanned waterproof boots with eight-inch tops. More of the red shirt later. I was a bit out of uniform, but I'm sure my host forgave me. If I ever shoot grouse in Scotland again, I'll wear plus-fours or kilts and whatever the Scots wear under them. I found my cotton pants miserably wet and cold.

Every "gun" was armed with a beautiful British shotgun of famous make – by Holland, Purdey, Boss, Westley Richards, Tolley. All had two triggers, straight-grip stocks of fine European walnut, the small forends which many American refer to as "splinters," and 28- and 30-inch barrels. These British game guns are chambered for $2^{1}/_{2}$-inch shells and their grouse load is $1^{1}/_{16}$ ounces of British No. 6 shot. That's about the same as our 20-gauge Magnum load, but I can testify that it will knock grouse for a loop out to 40 yards. Light recoil makes it very pleasant to shoot.

All of these fine guns were carefully taken out of leather cases lined with felt. Some of the hunters had matched pairs of guns, as before the war it was the custom for each "gun" to have a loader to take his empty weapon and hand him a loaded one. Many of the guns were 40 and 50 years old, but their owners thought nonetheless of them because of it. There's a brisk market for second-hand guns in Scotland and England, and an ancient fowling piece by a famous maker will sell for several times its 1910 cost. Prowling through sporting-goods stores, I saw a few American guns, and the prices asked for them were staggering.

My own gun was a 12-gauge Winchester Model 21 with 26-inch barrels bored modified and improved-modified. If I hadn't been so conscious of the excess baggage rates on airplanes, I'd have taken along my extra set of barrels bored skeet No. 1 and 2. They would have been better for grouse. Since I planned to use the same gun on tough and wild francolin and guineafowl in Africa, I decided to make the more closely choked barrels do for both Scotland and Africa. My Scottish hosts examined my double with great interest. They liked the selective single trigger, but disapproved of the pistol grip and the beavertail forend at first. Before the shoot was over, however, they had come to like these radical innovations.

Each shooter here had a leather cartridge pouch, which he carried over one shoulder, a flask of highland dew, and a shooting stick – a contraption which is sort of a cane with a folding leather seat, a very handy gimmick, by the way.

*E*ach of us was given a card listing the "butts" we were to occupy during the various drives. After each drive, the guns move to another line of butts and change numbers. That way, each gun has a crack at good shooting, because as a rule the butts in the center of the line see more birds.

I must admit that I awaited the results of the first drive with some trepidation. Could I hit these feathered rockets I'd heard so much about? Presently I'd see.

Sometimes the butts are simply flimsy brush blinds just thick enough to break up the gunner's outline, but sometimes they are built of sod or of moss-covered stones. The same butts and drives have been used to fool countless generations of grouse. Our hunt was in the middle of September and the grouse season had been on for six weeks. The birds were fast, strong of wing, and not so easy to fool as the young and unsophisticated birds taken when the season opened on what the Scots call the Glorious 12th of August.

S o I sat there on my shooting stick behind a brush blind, puffing from the climb up the hill and sweating slightly from grouse fever. Superficially, the grouse country of Scotland looks much like the rolling caribou barrens of the Yukon. The heather is about as high as the dwarf birch or "bug brush" of the Yukon, and the rolling round-topped hills with their patches of timber in the draws look much the same. Far in the distance we could see our line of beaters, each waving a white flag and each accompanied by a bounding springer spaniel.

Presently, I saw a covey of grouse sweep low over the contours of the ground and head toward the left end of the line of guns. A fearful popping of guns broke out and couple of grouse dropped.

A moment later someone down the line shouted "Mark!" and I could see a covey headed right at me. I was so interested in seeing what the birds looked like that I waited too long before shooting. Then I stopped my swing and missed clean with my first barrel. I whirled around and shot fast with my second. The bird wobbled down, hit on the edge of the pattern. He was a cripple, which the Scots call a "walker," but later one of the springers picked him up.

Right then and there I decided that these grouse weren't impossible. Some came low, some high, some swerved when they saw the guns. However, they didn't twist and dive like mourning doves. They were speedy, but not as fast as some of our ducks.

Another bunch came over. I picked out a bird that was quartering to my right, about like the No. 2 low-house bird in skeet, and knocked it cold. I missed with my second barrel, and the only alibi I could think of was that I had too small a shot pattern. I switched my single trigger then to fire the improved-modified barrel first.

My next shot was a high, wandering single and I took him about 40 yards out and possibly 75 feet up, killing cleanly. On the next go-round, according to what I scribbled in my notebook at lunch, I got a right and left. My Scottish friends were beginning to believe an American gun could nail grouse after all.

Presently the shooting was over for that drive. The drivers came up to the line of guns. With the aid of their springer spaniels, they picked up all the birds. Each gun is supposed to remember how many birds he's grassed and about where they fell – no easy task when one gun may knock down six or eight birds on one drive. The little springers were slow but very thorough, and I'm certain they found every bird I knocked down during the entire shoot.

On the second drive the line of guns crouched behind a cut

bank by a road. The shooting was fast and furious, and there I made my best shot of the day. I was watching a bird that had been lightly hit flutter down behind the line of guns when suddenly I saw a single coming right at my blind and almost on top of me. It was exactly like a No. 8 high-house target at skeet, and I cracked that bird about 20 feet from the muzzle and just ahead of me. On another occasion on that stand, I killed two birds in front so fast that I didn't see the first bird fall. I knew I'd scored a double after the second bird fell, because I could see a puff of feathers hanging in the air where the first bird had been.

After three drives we knocked off for lunch. The ladies of the country squires on whose lands we'd been shooting had all manner of food laid out on a long table. Most of the guns and the beaters had an aperitif in the form of anywhere from a half-tumbler to a whole tumbler full of whiskey. Then after lunch, my hearty companions had another one for the sake of their digestions. They tossed these heroic portions off without batting an eye, and if it affected their walking or their shooting, I failed to see it.

When the day's bag was toted up late that afternoon, I found to my surprise that I was high gun. I had shot slightly more than one-fourth of the birds taken by eight guns. I think I got the breaks, and the way the draw on the butts turned out, I was usually in a pretty good position. I made several "right and lefts," or doubles, as we call them in this country. I found the way to do this is to take one bird well in front as the covey comes in and then to take the other overhead but a bit in front.

On several occasions I killed my first bird, missed my second. Part of the reason for second-barrel misses was that the second bird would be so close that the small pattern of my modified barrel handicapped me somewhat. Some of the guns used by my companions were bored full choke in the right barrel, cylinder in the left. I think that's about right for Scottish grouse. Barrels bored skeet No. 1 and No. 2 (approximately modified and cylinder) would also do very well, and an American shooting grouse in Scotland should do his best shooting with a gun so bored.

The second morning of the shoot in Scotland it was raining, raw and miserable. The birds were coming in low and most of the shots were about like the No. 1 and 2 low-house targets at skeet, with an occasional No. 8 high-house shot thrown in. I was hot as a pistol that morning and on one drive I killed six birds with seven shots.

293

However, I wasn't high man that second day, or anything like it. My shirt was partly responsible for my lower score. After lunch the sun came out. I was quite hot in the butts and I peeled off the neutral-color tweed jacket and shot in my scarlet wool shirt. Never let anyone tell you that Scottish grouse are color blind. Every time I stood up to try to take a bird out at 40 or 45 yards, the whole covey would swerve and leave me in the lurch. All up and down the line of guns the lads were shaking their heads at my wild costume. Another reason I wasn't high gun was that a guest who had joined the party the second day was one of the finest shots I've seen.

To give me a complete picture of their upland gunning, my host took me on what they call a "rough shoot." A long line of guns preceded by a gang of busy and enthusiastic springer spaniels walks through the fields, popping at everything that gets up. We took pheasants, Hungarian partridges, and big hares about the size of our largest jackrabbits. Turnip fields are favorite cover for both the Huns and pheasants, and one is apt to jump a hare anywhere. But compared with the excitement of driven game, rough shooting struck me as being a bit dull.

I'd like to try a British driven pheasant shoot sometime. The guns stand behind a line of trees and the pheasants are driven over them. It must be tough shooting.

In its way, shooting driven grouse is an exceedingly interesting sport, a type of hunting completely unlike anything we have in this country. I wouldn't call it the most difficult shooting in the world. For me, pass shooting mourning doves is harder.

But grouse offer plenty of action, and one of the best things about it is getting to know the Scottish gunners. They're keen sportsmen and good shots. They expend a lot of time, money, and energy maintaining their shooting on that tight little island.

They tell me that in the old days of more grouse and bigger drives, many a practiced Scot was able to take two birds in front, exchange guns with his loader, and take two behind. That's something I'd like to see.

VARMINTS MOVE AT DAWN

Today, plinking for varmints is enjoying something of a resurgence, as hunters find that hunting predators, jackrabbits, crows, and the like offers a fine way to extend their times afield, sharpen their marksmanship and, in the case of critters like coyotes, to face real shooting challenges. O'Connor relished this type of hunting. This article appeared with the byline of Joe Ryan, one of O'Connor's many pseudonyms. March, 1942

"Boy, I've found them!" Don shouted over the telephone, "It took plenty of looking, but when I found . . ."

"Found what?"

"Jackrabbits – by the dozens, by the hundreds, by the thou –"

"Hey, wait a minute!" I said, "Don't make the story too big. You're going to have to show them to me, you know!"

"And I saw a couple of coyotes too," he went on. "Sure, I'll show them to you. Doing anything in the morning?"

"Nothing that can't wait for a jackrabbit convention."

My trigger finger had been itching for a really good varmint hunt for some time. Like any desert animal, jackrabbits are to some extent migratory. They have to keep up with the feed that shoots up after spotty rains. For more than two months I had been unable to locate really good shooting, and my favorite stretch of jack-and-coyote country had gotten gradually worse, drier, dustier, more barren. Where it was once common to see a hundred jacks in an afternoon, now a dozen made a big day in the Arizona desert.

But Don evidently had them located once more, so the next morning we drove through the deserted streets of the city and headed north into the desert while it was still dark. By the time we struck this new jackrabbit country, gray dawn had come and it was almost light enough to shoot.

Seen at midday and at dawn, the same section of the Southwestern desert affords an amazing contrast. In the middle hours the sun is high and hot and glaring, and the land looks desolate, uninhabited. A few cattle droop in the sparse shade of a mesquite or ironwood, and the jackrabbits dozing behind the brush are torpid as lizards, slow to move and hard to see. Nesting doves and whitewings mourn with melancholy voices in the heat and glare, and the quail are invisible. One who did not know the country would swear it was as lifeless as the face of the moon.

But at dawn the creatures of the desert are out in all their amazing variety. Now, just as Don and I turned into this new section he had discovered, my eye caught a movement in a patch of cactus, and when we stopped we saw it was a big desert mule deer, a buck with enormous blood-swollen horns in full velvet. It was ridiculous to see an animal so large try to hide in a piece of cover so small, yet if I had not noticed movement, we probably would have passed him by. When he knew he was discovered, he trotted off, stopping a couple of times to watch us, and finally disappeared over a ridge.

A pair of Gambel's quail with long, dark topknots led a big covey of little ones across the road in front of us, and in the distance we could see a badger waddling home from his night's hunting.

"Yesterday when I was out here I saw two coyotes run into that draw over there," Don told me, as we watched the badger disappear. Then his voice quickened with excitement: "Hey! There they are now!"

Ahead of us the land rose gradually, and on the hump, silhouetted against the dull red of the sunrise, were two coyotes trotting slowly in single file. When we jumped out of the car, Don with his .30/06 and I with my .270, they stopped and stood watching us.

"I'll take the one on the right," I whispered.

Our two rifles cracked as one, but it was instantly evident that we had judged the range badly, as both bullets kicked up spurts of dust beneath their feet. Those coyotes went into high, and for a few seconds they were in sight along the skyline. My second bullet struck right at one's tail and made him switch on his supercharger, and Don's kicked up dust right beneath his belly.

I am a great hand to figure things out *after* it is too late to do anything about it, and it struck me that the cause of our missing those coyotes so far was an optical one. They were on the skyline just in front of the coming sun, and they looked large – just as a rising sun or a rising moon looks larger than it does when it is well up. We thought they were about 250 yards away, whereas in reality they were probably a quarter mile from where the car was parked.

*R*ight then we turned that jackrabbit hunt into a coyote hunt. We split and made a wide circle of a mile or so, hoping to intercept the coyotes in their flight or to kick them out where they were hidden. Don had been right when he said there were plenty of rabbits in that country. During the walk I must have seen fifty – lithe, swift, wary black-tails, and big, stupid antelope jacks that ran in bunches of from two to five, with their conspicuous white rump patches flashing in the first low rays of the sun. We were after bigger game just then. But no luck. When we met at the car, Don said he had seen the coyotes disappear over the horizon 600 or 700 yards away, but he didn't even try to shoot at them.

I soon saw why the area was alive with jacks. It was drained by a great wash, where an underground stream ran just below the sands. On the uplands everything was dry – grass, weeds, shrubs. There was food but no moisture, and even desert game needs some water. But along the wash, the grass and weeds were green, succulent. Quail were thick there, present literally by the hundreds. Cottontails scurried into the brush. Jackrabbits came to nibble the green stuff to wash down and soften up their dry feed, and the coyotes followed them.

We got action the moment we struck the wash – a couple of large black-tails sitting in the sand, silhouetted perfectly, digesting their breakfasts and thinking matters over. Our shots were followed by the hollow plop that comes from the impact of high-speed bullets, and those two jacks were flattened as by sledgehammers.

Over at the next side draw we jumped a bunch of five antelope jacks. We got two on the sit and two on the run. The last one stopped under a bush almost 300 yards away and froze. Don drew the shot, held so he could just see the animal's head peeking over the flat post of his scope, and squeezed. I watched

297

that jack fly apart as if a bomb had exploded inside him.

Seldom have I had such shooting as we found in the next half hour. We took everything that came. We hit and we missed. Almost always the black-tails took to the low brush and weeds on the far side of the great wash, where we could just see their ears and their backs as they tore along. Then we had to work hard to keep from over-shooting. The antelopes, though, struck for the open flat and depended on their speed. We could empty our rifles at them, correcting our leads by the spurts of dust.

If anyone thinks that *any* bullet travels so fast that running game does not have to be led, shooting at a few speedy antelope jackrabbits will soon disillusion him. Even a .220 Swift, shot stationary at a running jack, will put the bullet yards behind at 200. The .270 I was using that day drove a 120-grain bullet at a velocity of 3,250 feet a second and I was swinging ahead of the rabbits, yet at that, most of my misses came from underleading.

In shooting running jacks, elevation isn't hard to maintain. As nearly as I can estimate, I have to swing past them about six inches at 50 yards, 18 inches at 100, and at least three feet at 200. This is all figured for a jack running at right angles. Change the angle and it's something else again! Even a good shot will miss a lot of those babies, but connecting with one in the middle of a jump is compensation for a flock of misses.

We were now feeling like pretty fair hands with a rifle. The sun had been up an hour or so when Don made a long shot at a jack in the grass which we could not determine as a hit or a miss. We decided to go over and investigate. Nothing was in sight just then and our guard was completely down.

But suddenly Don shouted, "Look out for that wildcat!"

Twenty feet away, a big bay lynx was coming at me, fleeing from Don. I gave a startled yell and jumped about five feet. The cat swerved, brushing by my leg, and fled. I had my rifle over my shoulder by the sling, but I unslipped it, threw off the safety – and shot right under that confounded lynx as it jumped over a bush. Don's .30/06 crashed with like result. The cat darted into a side draw, and that was that.

We paused, made appropriate remarks. Both of us were bitterly disappointed and humiliated at having missed a mark the size of a bobcat at about 50 feet. But so goes it.

Chastened, we went back to the car. In the next half hour or so we picked up a couple of jacks apiece and Don made an astonishing shot at a Cooper's hawk a good 250 yards away. However, any success now was as dust and ashes. It isn't often that a varmint hunter gets a whack at a bobcat, wicked killer of quail and young deer, as the animals are even more nocturnal than coyotes. Letting that one get away made us feel like a pair of lugs.

*G*radually we worked back into the country where the coyotes had disappeared that morning, hoping against hope that we would see them again in spite of the fact that the sun was getting high and hot now, and it was time for them to brush up.

As it happened, the two had bedded in the brush near the bottom of a very narrow little draw and we almost stepped on them. In fact, they let us walk past them, and then I happened to see them sneaking off just behind us.

"Coyotes!" I yelled.

I got off a shot just as they disappeared into the brush. Even as I pulled the trigger I knew that I had missed, but somehow the hunch came – as it often does in hunting – that my luck was going to be good.

The arroyo into which the animals had disappeared was narrow but brushy, and my hunch was that they were so leery that they would dash out of it. Don disappeared at a dead run right at their heels, but I went through the arroyo, up the other side, and watched.

Presently, in the thin brush of a side draw about 200 yards away, I saw a movement. I couldn't tell just what it was, but I felt sure it was one of the coyotes. I knew, too, that I was in the ideal situation for the hunter; I had located the game before it had located me. Even better, that coyote was running from Don – and wouldn't expect me.

I sat down, threw off the safety, and waited. Again I saw the brown flash of a coyote's back going up the draw through the brush. When it got to the head where the brush played out, I'd have a clear shot.

When it came, the shot was all I could have hoped for That coyote came out of the brush, stopped dead still, and looked back over its shoulder toward Don. My flat-topped post came to rest against that shoulder and I squeezed off the trigger. For an instant the recoil blotted out the field, and when I looked all I could see was a brushy tail that waved gently against the horizon three times – and then was still. Just why coyotes that are hit with a high-velocity bullet wave their tails three times is something I don't know, but almost always they do.

I walked over to where the perp lay. He was stone dead, and the bullet had struck exactly where the top of the post had rested.

I had forgotten Don and the other coyote in the excitement of my own good luck, but a moment later I heard his rifle crack. He, too, had had a plan. He had followed fast on the heels of the coyote that had stuck to the bottom of the arroyo, and had run him out at the head. The coyote was loping along about 250 yards from Don and about 400 from me. At his first shot, a spurt of dust flew up right at the animal's heels. At the second, I could see that Don had hit a hind leg low. The coyote stopped for an instant and then moved off toward the protection of a grove of mesquites. But he was going more slowly. I got him in the field of the scope, was swinging with him and starting my squeeze, when he collapsed. A moment later the thump of a bullet came floating back, and I heard a whoop: "I got him!"

We met by Don's coyote, compared notes, congratulated each other, and felt like able fellows once more after the fiasco on the bobcat. On our way back to the car, we found why the coyotes had been loath to leave the vicinity. They had caught a cow in labor – on the evening before, evidently – and had killed her newborn calf. The little thing lay torn and half-devoured in the arroyo. With worlds of rabbits, their natural food, available, the coyotes hadn't been able to resist a chance for some veal. It had been their undoing.

Just as we reached the car, a big lazy antelope jack loped away from us – a perfect, easy running shot. I lifted my rifle, followed him with the post.

"Hey!" Don said. "Let's leave that one for bait!"

"Right!" I said.

The jack galloped on and on, across the big open stretch, into a shallow arroyo, out again, and over the horizon.

TRIPLE PLAY HUNT

We meet one of a series of Brittany spaniels owned by O'Connor in this story, and while he wasn't the "dog of a lifetime," Pete provides some fine mixed-bag bird hunting. Pheasants, sharptails, and Hungarian partridge offered Jack and Eleanor a world of fun in their later years. October, 1973

*W*e found a motel in Great Falls, Montana, stowed our luggage and guns in our room, and while Eleanor fixed her face, I took Pete, my Brittany spaniel, for a walk. Pete was pretty discouraged by then. That October morning he had joyfully entered the portable aluminum kennel in the back of the station wagon and had snuggled down on his bed of straw. The dog had assumed that we were headed out into the Idaho countryside or across the line to Washington for a bird hunt. But instead of a ride of a half-hour or an hour, he had been in the car all day.

The first time we had stopped at a filling station so that Pete could stretch his legs and have a drink, he leaped out joyfully – and ready to hunt. As the day went on and we had more pointless leg-stretchings, Pete grew more and more puzzled. That night he was plainly depressed. He sniffed the unfamiliar odors in the chill Montana air and then looked around halfheartedly. It was all I could do to get him to finish his supper.

Pete is a better old man's dog than Mike was. He is more tractable. He stays closer, minds better, and is a much better retriever. Mike generally retrieved well, because he had a strong sense of ownership, and he believed firmly that any bird that went down belonged to the two of us. If there was competition from another hunter or dog, Mike never failed to get there first and bring the birds to me.

But if we were hunting alone, he always ran over to the fallen bird. If it was wounded and ran, he chased it, caught it, and held it until I came up. But if the bird was dead, Mike always looked around to see if I had seen where the bird was. If he thought I had, he was off. He was interested only in live birds. Dead ones bored the hell out of him.

But Pete has always enjoyed retrieving, and he has saved my aged and creaking legs from a lot of wear and tear. I remember a day we were hunting along a road that clung precariously to the side of a very steep mountainside overlooking the Snake River. Chukar partridge were plentiful, but the hill was so nearly straight up and down that about the only way it could be hunted was for me to stroll along the road, while Pete ranged back and forth in front of me.

That day I was using a Winchester Model 21 chambered for the three-inch 20-gauge Magnum shell; with No. 6s it threw 1 1/4 ounces of shot. Some of the birds I hit must have fallen 500 to 1,000 feet away from me. But to tough little Pete, finding the birds and scrambling back uphill with them was a jolly romp.

That night in Great Falls, after I got Pete bedded down in the warm, thick layer of straw in his kennel, I joined Eleanor in our room. She was waiting impatiently for me.

"You look terrible," she said. "Your hair needs combing, your tie has a big spot of grease on it, and your shirttail's out. Hurry and make yourself fairly decent. I am starving!"

The next morning I fed Pete, gave him some water, and walked him while Eleanor got ready to travel. Pete is an enthusiastic character. When he is being taken for a walk, his diminutive tail usually wags madly and enthusiastically. But that morning it was glued between his legs. He slumped along, his leash slack, and he was too depressed even to smell the posts we passed. Pete had no idea of what we were up to, but whatever it was, he didn't trust it.

I left the motor running to warm up the car while we ate

breakfast, and when we returned the heat had melted the frost off the windshield – but it was still a quarter of an inch deep on the roof. The day was cold but clear. As we headed north toward the Canadian border, I turned toward Eleanor.

"Well," I said, "I don't think there's anything to worry about. Not a bit of snow."

"What's that white stuff over there – alkali?" she asked sourly.

I looked. A bit ahead and a little to the right was a patch of snow on the north side of a bush. The patch was no larger than a catcher's mitt – but it was snow. A quarter of a mile farther on we saw another and larger patch, then another. The snow patches thickened as we went north. Presently they ran together, and by the time we had crossed the Canadian boundary, the snow was six or eight inches deep on the level.

Some days before, our host Alva Bair had called from Alberta to say it was snowing like mad and that we had better wait until the weather cleared. Later he called to say the snow had stopped and that the forecast was for clear weather. Alva added that the snow should be off the ground by the time we got there. Alas, it was not.

Bair and Lawrence Helmwrath met us in a little village a few miles north of the Canadian line, where we ate lunch and bought our hunting licenses. As we followed Alva to his farm over muddy roads, endless wheatfields in every direction were covered with snow. Once in the distance I saw a couple of cock pheasants, and twice we saw flocks of ducks on the horizon.

Alva's pretty wife Nellie welcomed us and showed us to our quarters – Alva's basement trophy room. Like many modern farmhouses, the Bairs' place is as mechanized as a battleship. All manner of mounted heads stared down on us – sheep, bears, antelope, and even a lion, since Alva has hunted in Africa as well as extensively in his native Canada.

Alva told us that we had time for a short hunt before dark, so we changed clothes and put our guns together. Eleanor was using a Model 21 Winchester skeet gun that we had added to our arsenal back in 1940, when it retailed for $115. I was using a little Spanish Arizaga double side-by-side with nicely engraved sidelocks and an American single trigger made by Miller.

As we drove off, Alva told us that there were plenty of birds – pheasants, Hungarian partridge, and sharp-tailed grouse – but that the snow might make the hunting unpleasant for a couple of days. We saw our first birds about two miles from the farm – a

303

covey of Huns black against the snow about 100 yards ahead. Alva proposed that we stop and walk them up.

We let Pete out. He circled around. He came to life, and his tail started to wag when he smelled the aroma of gamebirds. A moment later he was pointing the Huns from a distance of 35 yards, as experience had taught him that he couldn't crowd Huns or they would take off.

When the covey buzzed up, I nailed a bird with my first barrel, missed with my second. Eleanor missed with her first shot, knocked one down with her second. The snow in the ditch beside the road was about two feet deep, but Pete plunged through it, found both birds, and brought them back.

A little farther on was a row of trees and brush perhaps 300 yards long and 30 feet wide. Alva and Eleanor went down one side and I down the other. Pete ranged in between. He was enthusiastic and birdy, and his little tail was revolving at about 3,000 r.p.m.

We hadn't gone 50 feet when Pete's bell stopped tinkling. I moved up opposite the spot where I had last heard the bell. Then I heard the flutter of wings and Alva's shout: "Sharptail!"

A large gray-and-white bird came by high and about 30 yards away. It was the first sharptail I had ever seen. I was so interested in looking at it that I didn't get my head down on the comb of the stock, and I shot high. Before I could slap the trigger a second time, Eleanor's 16 cracked and the sharptail went down.

A minute or two later I redeemed myself – after a fashion. Pete's bell stopped again. I moved ahead a few feet. I could see the dog, rigid with his nose pointed at some thick stuff about six feet in front of him. I made a snowball and threw it at the spot. Out came a magnificent rooster pheasant thrashing his wings and cackling like a mad thing. The little Spanish 20 gauge cracked, and the old cock bird landed in the snow with a thump. By dark we were back at the farm with three or four pheasants, a half-dozen Huns, and about that many sharptails.

*I*t was clear and very cold the next morning. Our first hunt was on Lawrence Helmwrath's place. The spot was a patch of brush, weeds, cattails, and high grass surrounding a little pond. Lawrence said there were nearly always pheasants there. He suggested we come in toward the pond from different directions.

We had hardly started when two ducks took off. I cracked one down and Alva got the other. The duck I had shot fell in the pond. Pete jumped in and retrieved it in great shape – his first water retrieve I can remember.

After Pete had brought the duck (a greenwing teal) to me, he circled around in front of Eleanor. She shouted that he was on point. I told her to walk in, and a moment later I heard the cackle of a cock pheasant and the thrashing of wings. I caught a glimpse of him as he broke into the clear on the other side of a shrub. Then Eleanor's 16 gauge cracked, and the bird folded.

It warmed up that day, and the snow was settling, but it was still several inches deep in the fields and about two feet deep in the roadside ditches. The birds were mostly along the grass and weeds of the fencerows. We'd see them ahead, let Pete out of the car, and walk them up. The sharptails almost always flew toward the snowy fields, and Pete never failed to bring them back when we dropped them.

We found the birds easy to hit (although I missed some), and once they were hit, they didn't carry much lead, certainly much less than a pheasant. Once on the ground, the sharptails lay there. Every day that we hunted we all got limits of sharptails, but we didn't always fill out on pheasants and Huns.

Sometimes I shoot a shotgun better than I do at other times. The first three days on that Alberta hunt, I missed some pretty juicy shots. I remember one in particular.

We were coming down a curving hill toward a brushy creekbottom when we saw a handsome cock pheasant and a couple of hens strolling along the edge of the road. We drove past, out of sight, then we sneaked back, guns in hand, with Pete cruising just ahead of us. The cock didn't like the looks of the dog. He cackled and took off, offering me a perfect crossing shot at about 30 yards. I shot, but I must have slowed or stopped my swing, as I didn't get a feather. An instant later Eleanor shot, and the bird plunged down and out of sight across a ridge. Pete was right after him.

We followed and found Pete on point beside a little gully. I took a color photograph as Alva and Eleanor walked in. A moment after I took the picture, the pheasant came out dragging a broken wing. Pete grabbed him.

The muddy ground along the road was tracked up by pheasants, so we decided to hunt through the brush along the creek to see what we could find. I remember one cock that flushed just ahead of Pete's nose and 25 or 30 yards from me. He rocketed almost straight up, cackling like a devil. I caught him with the center of the pattern from the modified barrel of my little 20. Feathers flew in every direction, and he dropped like a stone.

I shouted to Pete to fetch the bird. I could hear him moving around in the thick brush. I heard him whine. Presently, he came out without the bird. I sent him back again, but the result was the same. Then I tried it myself. The brush was so thick I couldn't crawl through it. I am sure the bird was stone dead, and I imagine he fell into some brush so high that Pete could not reach him.

I heard Alva shoot on the hill above me and saw a cock pheasant tumble, and an instant later another one came sailing by. It dropped when I shot. Pete brought him in, and a moment later he put up another rooster that I nailed just as he cleared the low trees. We got six fine cocks out of that brushy creekbed, and we ate lunch there in the sunshine.

The snow had been going, and that night it "Chinooked," and we awoke to find a warm wind blowing from the west and the snow gone. We hunted some stubblefields the next morning and picked up our limits of Huns and sharptails.

That afternoon we had a lovely pheasant shoot. We hunted a belt of very thick brush and trees that bordered a little creek meandering across a lush, grassy pasture. Pete, his bell tinkling, plowed through the heavy brush, and when the beautiful cocks came flailing and cackling out we nailed them.

*E*very day we saw more sharptails than anything else. The snow had pushed them into the fields from the grassy plains where they hatch their young. It can get bitterly cold there in southern Alberta, and the snow can lie deep. Snow and cold, Alva and Lawrence told me, bother the other gamebirds more than they do the sharptails, which are native to the area and are perfectly adapted to it. The speedy little Hungarian partridge comes from a similar climate in Europe and does well in Alberta's alternating grasslands and wheatfields. Pheasants need more cover than do either of the two other species, and they are never found far from woody cover. Alberta is a great bird country, because the bulldozer has not taken out all the brush along the streams and because the crops have not been doused with poisonous sprays – something that has happened in many areas of the United States.

On the last day of our hunt, we teamed up with Lee Straight, a rod-and-gun editor for the *Vancouver Sun* in British Columbia along with his brother and a friend. They had a couple of German shorthairs with them.

I did pretty well that day. Once, I cracked a big rooster with each barrel of the little Spanish 20 gauge. I also made two doubles on sharptails – no great feat, as they are big, dumb birds that get off the ground slowly.

But it was Eleanor who really wound up in a blaze of glory. On one turn through a stubblefield she made a double on Hungarian partridge. Then she made a double on sharptails. She still had only one pheasant. We were all headed home when 50 or 75 yards ahead Alva saw the head of a cock pheasant sticking out of some weeds along a fencerow.

Everyone watched as Eleanor stuffed a couple of shells into her 16 gauge. She walked slowly up the fencerow. At about 30 yards, the cock had seen enough and took off. She had just started to swing when a second cock came pounding out. She dropped both of them. Pete brought them in. Everybody cheered.

PHEASANTS, I LOVE YOU!

In this story, under the pseudonym of Bill Ryan, Jack shares his passion for hunting ringnecks – for watching his irrepressible Brittany spaniels bounce about, for the challenge of gunning the wily old cock-birds, and for enjoying the camaraderie of friends and family. July 1950

My pal, Al Sprague, and I were high on a hill in eastern Washington one morning when we saw a cock pheasant that had been put up in the valley below slant down into a weed patch about 200 yards away. It looked as if we had him. The patch wasn't very large. We would approach on one side. On the other side was a fence that bounded an open stubble field. So we walked back and forth through the weeds. We covered every square inch of the patch. No pheasant!

Finally we concluded that somehow he had sneaked away, so we decided to cross the fence into the stubble and hunt a weedy hillside we could see beyond. It looked simpler to crawl under the fence than to try to get over, so we broke our double-guns, laid them down, and began to wiggle on our bellies below the bottom wire.

Pow! There was a splutter of wings and the beautiful cock came bursting out, literally in front of our noses.

I wish I could relate that we bounced nimbly to our feet, seized our trusty fowling pieces, and gathered the big bird in. We didn't. Al almost tore off his coat trying to get back out from under the bottom wire. And I practically chinned myself on the same wire. By the time we had our guns in hand, the bird was gone.

Smart, those pheasants!

I often hunt down a rough road along the bank of a big river. In the side canyons are California valley quail. There are also a good number of pheasants. When the season was on for both quail and pheasants, I would see plenty of quail, an occasional hen pheasant, never a cock. The quail season lasted two weeks longer than

309

the pheasant season. The day after pheasants ceased to be legal game, I drove down the road toward a favorite quail spot. This time gaudy cock pheasants swaggered across the road, sat in trees eating berries, gaped at me from fields. How did they know the season was over? Sounds as if they read the papers.

Actually if I caught a big rooster doing just that, I wouldn't be greatly surprised. A pheasant is smarter than my dog, Sam. Sam is smarter that *I* am, and *I* can read.

The pheasant is the most intelligent bird I have ever run into – smarter than a quail, than any grouse, than an old, woods-wise wild turkey.

I shot my first pheasant in the fall of 1948 – and the occasion is one that I am sure I'll never forget. A pal and I had just waded across the very cold Boise River in south Idaho in order to get to a weedy island that was supposed to be crowded with cock pheasants. My friend's dog came to a point right on the river bank and a big, gaudy, glorious cock came bursting out, cackling like crazy. It was an easy quartering shot and in spite of my buck fever, I dropped him right in the river.

The dog went in after it, carried it to the other side, and then lay down and masticated on the bird reflectively like an old-time rube comic in vaudeville chewing on a straw. While I pleaded, threatened, and wept, the dog lay there on the sand of the bank thinking about this and that, watching the cool, bright sky, now and then remembering the pheasant she had between her two paws and taking another bite at it as if to keep her molars in condition. Finally she let the pheasant lie there and swam back to join us.

"Susie isn't very well trained yet," her owner told me.

"You're telling me!" I said. "I'm going to hop right in that water and get my bird!"

"Oh, don't do that! We'll be coming back this way in an hour and your pheasant will still be there. It'll keep!"

With distinct foreboding, I gave in, hoping against hope that my bird would be all right when we returned. Sad to say, the magpies got at it, pecked all the flesh off one side of the breast, and strewed gorgeous feathers all over the sand.

So I killed the first cock pheasant I ever shot at. I also killed the second. I might also add that I must have missed the next ten.

The thing the boys didn't brief me on was that a cock pheasant, when he has had time to get his steam up, can really make knots. Before I ever shot at a pheasant, I had hunted Gambel's quail for more years than I like to remember. I had shot my share of other species of quail, of ducks, doves, and whatnot. I was considered a fair hand at any of them, and then for a couple of days I had a heck of a time hitting pheasants.

How come? Everything I had heard about the birds convinced me that pheasants were not fast flyers and that they were easy to hit. The pheasant is a heavy bird. For his size, his wings are small and he has a high wing load. It takes him some time to get going. When he does, though, he can scat.

It happened that after I had nailed my first two birds, I got a long string of shots at cocks that had been spooked by someone else and were going past at from 35 to 45 yards with the throttle open. I didn't connect, decided I was overleading, led less and missed as before. Finally, I tried swinging about twice as far ahead and took some feathers off a cock's tail. From then on I hit the birds pretty well.

Before I shot pheasants I had done a good deal of reading about them and I had gathered that as gamebirds, they weren't so hot. They would do, many writers said, where the more sporting native birds would not thrive; but at the best, they could only serve to give the less-sophisticated lads something to pop at so they wouldn't go about riddling signboards and assassinating the farmers' chickens. Pheasants often did not lie well to a dog, they said. They ran or crept away and drove a pointing bird dog nuts. Instead of staying in the wheat stubble where the going is easy and it's a joy to watch the dogs work, the cocks take to the brush in the bottoms, to canyons, to steep hillsides covered with high weeds and made dangerous by rocks and boulders. In other words, the pheasant is a mean and un-co-operative bird.

To me that's a cockeyed criticism. One might as well have it in for the whitetail buck because he will lie close in the brush and let a hunter walk past him. Or one might as well denounce the bighorn ram because he hangs out high on the peaks where a man must climb his heart out to get a shot at him.

I believe I was lucky in that I did my first pheasant hunting where the birds were difficult to get and where only cocks could be taken. Friends who hunted in South Dakota in the days of great pheasant numbers, when either cocks or hens could be taken, have told me how a group of drivers working a cornfield would send literally clouds of pheasants out the end of a field. They would start hunting at noon and have their limits in half an hour or less.

311

Once a friend of mine who had been in South Dakota wrote me a long letter giving me his opinion on pheasant hunting. When I answered him, I told him I had never shot or eaten a pheasant. By return mail he wrote me that when he received my letter, his heart bled for me, so he picked up a gun, walked out into one of his fields, and killed three cocks in ten minutes. He was sending them to me to devour.

Pheasant hunting like that would surely be an experience, but as a steady diet, it would be too easy. The harder the hunter has to work for something, the more he values it.

A few days before I wrote this, I was working over a covey of California valley quail in a willow jungle along a riverbank, when I put up four cock pheasants. Another time I was shooting California mountain quail high on the side of a rugged mountain. Below me I could hear a pal popping away and apparently having a great sport. I thought he was into another covey of the beautiful mountain quail, but when I got down there, he had been shooting valley quail.

Once I led a friend into a canyon where not long before I had seen two big coveys of valley quail – and we had some fine Hungarian partridge shooting. In one hunting day in Washington, I got two cock pheasants, three mallard ducks, three Hungarian partridges and three bobwhites.

So here they all are! Just about every kind of upland gamebird found in the United States can be shot in the radius of a few miles and sometimes, indeed, within the radius of a mile or even less. Actually, in a pasture in eastern Washington, I saw in the air at one time a covey of Huns, a covey of quail, and about a dozen pheasants.

And what do the boys hunt? What bird bears 90 percent of the hunting pressure?

The pheasant!

The average hunter will take a pop at a covey of Huns if it rises within range, but he will not follow one up. Many will not bother to shoot at quail, because to do so might disturb nearby pheasants. The latest season in eastern Washington lasted 30 days on pheasants and Huns and was extended two weeks on all varieties of quail. As long as pheasants were legal game, the hunters were out in droves. When only quail were open, anyone who wanted to hunt them had the country practically to himself.

I love to hunt quail. I like to hunt them in the brush, in the stubble, in the open grasslands. In fact, I like to hunt them anywhere and of whatever species. I have shot every variety of quail found in the United States and a couple of varieties found only in Mexico. Until about a year ago my idea of heaven was someplace where I could pick up a gun and get into a covey of quail any time I felt like it.

Now I have revised my notion of the quail; just give me some pheasants to shoot at!

To me, the difference between quail hunting and pheasant hunting is about the same as between quail hunting and *buck* hunting. Getting into a scattered covey of quail and knocking them off as they get up is a lot of *little* thrills. Hunting deer all day, seeing does and fawns, then having a big burly buck come busting out on the other side of the canyon . . . well, that's a *big* thrill. To me, that big thrill more than overbalances all the little thrills.

The big concentrated kick when a fine cock gets out in range is just one of the ways that pheasant hunting is like big-game hunting on the Washington-Idaho border country. When the cocks have been shot at a couple of days, they leave the brushy stream bottoms, the stubble fields, all the easy places, and head for the steep draws, the rough hillsides. I have hunted pheasants in country as rough as that used by mountain sheep and I have been just as tired hunting pheasants as I have been when hunting sheep. The wily cock affords the same sort of problem as the shrewd old whitetail buck. Solving it gives the same sort of satisfaction.

Toward the end of last season, I had hunted two hours in country where previously I had seen many cocks. So far I had not raised one. Below me were beautiful brushy draws and grassy hillsides where I had hunted, but which this day had produced no pheasants. The birds *had* to be around somewhere. They *couldn't* have flown back to China.

About half a mile away in a bare plowed field, I noticed a rocky knoll that had not been plowed and which was covered with grass and weeds. I also noticed there were no tracks of hunters leading across the plowed field to the knoll. The spot was an unlikely one. It was small. The cover was not dense. No doubt 50 other pheasant hunters had cast a speculative eye on it and said to heck with it.

The more I looked at it, the stronger my hunch grew. I called my dog, admonished him to stay close, and started plodding over the plowed field toward those rocks and weeds.

About 15 feet from the edge, I stopped, switched off the safety of my 12-gauge double, and sent the dog in. There must have been 20 big roosters in there and I dropped two of the gorgeous birds out on the bare brown earth.

I have run into smart pheasants and I have run into dumb pheasants, but the smart ones outnumber the dumb ones. Once a pal and I were hunting along the edge of a stubble field when we saw a cock fly into a narrow weedy strip of cover along a small ditch. On either side was open stubble. It looked easy to get him out. I'd walk down the cover from one end, he from the other. The bird would have to get out. But when we met, we had seen no pheasant.

Then I checked the stubble on one side. I saw what looked like a dark stick thrust up from the golden stubble. It also looked like the tail feather of a cock pheasant, but that could not be. No cock would be so dumb as to hide there in that sparse stubble with his fanny up in the air.

I decided to investigate. The closer I came, the more it looked like a cock's tail and the less it looked like a stick. Twenty feet or so away, not only could I see the tail plainly, but I could see most of the pheasant. His hind end was up and his head was buried in the stubble.

I got set, said *boo* to get him going, and took him when he was out about 25 yards.

That pheasant didn't leave any more descendants. In that country the dumb birds that sit tight in the stubble for the dogs, that hang out in the cornfields and fly right into the waiting guns at the far end, get eliminated. The fathers of the new generation are the ones that hit for rocky hillsides, that flush wide and wild, or that sit so tight that they are almost impossible to get up. Old-time hunters say they are getting wilder every year, and well they might, because they are begotten by the smartest, wildest, shrewdest fathers.

In my two seasons of pheasant hunting, the score is largely in favor of the pheasants, so much so that it sounds like Notre Dame vs. Goose Creek Normal. But when I *do* outthink a pheasant, figure out what he's going to do before he does it, I feel like a scrub halfback who has run over a couple of all-American tackles and straight-armed an all-American end to make a touchdown.

In a country of hills and rocks and canyons, of wheatfields perched on mountaintops, of mountainsides where a goat would break his leg, pheasants can really work you over.

But the meaner they are, the more I love them. I have walked through a covey of scattered bobwhites, while singles exploded at every few steps. I have held my fire because I was reasonably sure that if I did so, I'd get up a cock pheasant within 100 yards. And when a hunter does that, greater love hath no man!

The .270 Can Do Big Things

Just the other day, a long-time friend mentioned that he was still shooting a Remington .270 he bought decades ago as a result of reading Jack O'Connor's countless pieces on the rifle. "It has never let me down," my hunting buddy wrote. Jack would have heartily approved of those words, and for my friend, like many of our generation, O'Connor's name and the .270 were virtually synonymous. Given that consideration, it seems only fitting to complete this anthology with one of his "Arms & Ammunition" columns on the rifle. December, 1943

Assuming that a cartridge can make its way on merit alone, that cartridge is the .270 W.C.F. In its early years it sat in the corner, dressed in sackcloth and covered with ashes, while few riflemen suspected that underneath it had a figger like Miss America, a disposition like an angel, and that it could bake pies like Mother used to make. The .30/06, its papa, had all the prestige of government adoption behind it, as well as the boosts of the gun writers. Further, in those early days, the rifleman could buy all the government ammunition he wanted at prices ranging from around one cent for 1918 wartime stuff to about three cents for later M-1 cartridges with nonfouling gilding-metal jackets. No wonder the .270 had a tough time getting started!

Gun writers of the 1920s and early '30s did the cartridge no

315

good by saying that it would do nothing the .30/06 would not do, that its velocities were not so high as claimed, that it was not so accurate as the .30/06, and that it was a great little hand to change its center of impact.

Time has proved all those statements baloney of the purest ray serene. The typewriter pounder who even now is so often quoted as saying the .270 would do nothing the .30/06 would not do, never in all his life shot a head of game with a .270. Unless he kept a yogi or a swami chained in the backyard so he could consult him when in doubt, I'll be darned if I know how he got that information.

As for the statement that .270 velocities are not so high as claimed, Winchester .270 rifles loaded with 130-grain Winchester ammunition were tested some years ago. The results of average instrumental velocities for ten-shot strings taken at 150 feet came out as follows: 3,126, 3,125, 3,115, 3,038, 3,028, 3,109, 3,029, 3,038, 3,017, 3,034. The average for these 100 shots, checked by several different chronographs and fired from several different rifles, comes out 3,075 *incremental* – that is, actual velocity over the given range. Add the arbitrary figure of 70 feet to it, and you get a muzzle velocity of 3,145 foot seconds.

*A*s far as accuracy goes, it has long since been discovered by those who have actually fired good scope-equipped .270 rifles from benchrests that the average factory .270 will outshoot the average factory .30/06 with factory ammunition. In comparative tests of the best handloaded ammunition in the two calibers, the .270 will also turn the trick. The average .270 will, in my experience, outshoot the average .220 Swift and shoot right along with a .257.

What about changing center of impact? Well, in 1938 I sighted in a tailor-made .270 on a Mauser action with the 130-grain Winchester factory ammunition. In the spring of 1943, when I took the rifle to Bill Sukalle for a new barrel, I still hadn't touched either windage or elevation. It was checked repeatedly at the target, and I shot hundreds of rounds at small marks like hawks, crows, jackrabbits, and coyotes.

I might add here that as far as big game went, up to about 250 yards it made no difference what sort of fodder I put into that rifle. It would keep any 130-, 150-, or 100-grain factory load well within a 6-inch bull at 200 yards, and with the best factory or handloads, it would shoot minute-of-angle groups all day long if I did my part.

Is that an exceptional .270? For a time I thought so. I began to suspect it wasn't when a friend of mine was targeting in a stock Model 70 Winchester with a Weaver 330 scope. His first five-shot group measured slightly more than an inch across. So did his second.

When my .270 Mauser began to develop a case of throat erosion, I walked into a sporting-goods store and wrote a check for the first Model 70 .270 the clerk pulled out. I had Al Linden stock it and M.L. Stith fit it with a 330 Weaver. It shoots just like the first one.

Jake Schoeller, former member of the Dewar Cup team, fine shot and an accuracy nut, has a standard .270 with a Zeiss scope. With his handloads, it is good for minute-of-angle groups. Al Ronstadt, now of Washington, D.C., wanted a .270 with a medium-heavy barrel and had one put on a Model 70 standard stock and action. I saw him shoot a 10-shot group well under one inch with the powerful combination of 53 grains of No. 4350 and the 160-grain Barnes Bullet.

This is not to say that there is no such thing as an inaccurate .270, or one which changes point of impact. Any rifle with a crooked or poorly bedded barrel, or with a fore-end so cut that it can warp hard against the barrel, will give poor accuracy and change its center of impact. However, the relation between case capacity and bullet diameter in the .270 evidently makes for clean burning of powder and for good accuracy, just as it does in the .257 and the .22 Varminter. The .270 has that somewhat mysterious quality known as "balance."

The .270's reputation was made, however, not on the target range, but out in the hunting fields, particularly in the West and in Canada and Alaska, where ranges are long. Hunters using the .270 discovered that with it, they could hit game at longer ranges than with anything else, and that when they hit, they got a higher percentage of one-shot kills.

The explanation is simple. The trajectory of the .270 with the 130-grain bullet at a muzzle velocity of 3,140 foot seconds, or the 100-grain bullet at 3,540, is very flat; for all practical purposes it corresponds to that of the Swift over 300 yards and is flatter beyond. Consequently, the hunter is less likely to undershoot at long range. Sighted to hit the point of aim at 200 yards with a scope, the 130-grain bullet drops only 5 inches at 300 yards, not enough to miss even a small deer with a hold in the center of the chest. (That drop from line of scope sight works out only 4.5 inches for me, by the way, and it also did for the late Capt. E.C. Crossman.)

If the hunter wants to turn his scope-sighted .270 into a real long-range rifle, let him sight in for 300 yards. In that case the bullet rises 1½ inches at 50 yards, 3 inches at 100, 4 inches at 150, 4 inches at 200 and 3 inches at 250. It's at point of aim at 300, 4 inches low at 350, 10 inches low at 400, and 18 inches low at 500.

317

All of which means that, so sighted, a .270 has a point-blank range of over 350 yards on even a small deer, a bighorn, or an antelope, and that by holding high on the backbone, the hunter would not have to bother his pretty head unduly about trajectory even at 500 yards, which under most conditions is too far to shoot.

With a higher-mounted scope, the trajectory is apparently even flatter, and under most conditions of plains and mountain hunting, the rifleman needs only to put the top of the post or the intersection of the crosshairs on what he wants to hit.

The other part of the ease of hitting with the .270 lies in the fact that the bullet gets there fast and cuts down on necessary lead. The 130-grain Peters and Winchester sharp-pointed bullets arrive at 300 yards still zipping along at 2,440 foot seconds, and the 100-grain gets there with a retained velocity of 2,600, or *faster than the fastest factory load for the .220 Swift*. The Swift gets the 46-grain open-point bullet to 300 yards with a velocity of 2,130, and it gets the 48-grain soft-point Spitzer there with 2,570.

For the sake of comparison, the 150-grain Western open-point .30/06 bullet, which leaves the muzzle at 2,980, gets to 300 yards with a retained velocity of 2,070 and the best-shaped 150-grain .30/06 bullet, the Remington 150-grain bronze point, retains 2,260. For the sake of another comparison, the 180-grain Western open-point bullet for the .300 H&H Magnum is traveling at only 2,080 at the 300-yard mark, or only 50 foot seconds faster than the 180-grain Remington bronze point .30/06 bullet with its initial velocity much lower than that of the Magnum.

All these little figgers preach a couple of powerful lessons – that for long ranges, bullet shape and sectional density are very important, and that the hunter ought to keep his eye glued to velocity figures out where the game is and not at the muzzle.

This high retained velocity also explains the spectacular killing power which everyone who has used the .270 has noticed at from 250 to 400 yards. Long ago I made up my mind that in order to be reasonably happy, I had to live where I could do a lot of hunting. I have used three .270 rifles since 1925. In that period I have also done some hunting with three .30/06 rifles, a 7mm., a .358, a .257, a .30/30, a .35 Remington, and a .30/40. The only cartridge with as good a record as the .270 is the 7mm., but it happens that the longest shot I ever made with it was 200 yards.

As nearly as I can remember, I have shot at and hit 39 head of big game with .270s. The longest shot (an antelope) was around 500 yards; the shortest (a whitetail), about 50 feet. The average was about 300 yards. One deer was hit and lost, but it was no more than scratched. Three took more than one shot; and 35 were killed with one shot. Most of those 35 didn't move out of their tracks. In 18 years I believe I have also shot about 100 coyotes with a .270, several of them being killed at 400 yards or more. Of all of them, only one wasn't killed instantly, and he, strangely enough, was less than 75 yards away.

Once upon a time, the owner could get any bullet he wanted for the .270 just so long as it weighed 130 grains. In late years, however, the picture has been greatly complicated. All major concerns load a 150-grain soft point with muzzle velocity of 2,770 foot seconds. Peters loads a 130-grain bullet similar in shape and construction to the original Winchester pointed expanding, and Remington loads the round-nosed, but very strong 130-grain Core-Lokt.

Both Winchester and Western load a 100-grain bullet at the very high muzzle velocity of 3,540; Winchester in a protected point similar to their 130-grain, and Western in a Spitzer soft point. Both Western and Winchester load the .270 with the 130-grain Silvertip. Western also loads a 130-grain hollow-point boattail, and of course, Winchester still loads the 130-grain "pointed soft point" or "pointed expanding" bullet originally designed for the cartridge.

Further to complicate the picture, bullets weighing 100, 120, 140, and 160 grains were available from Fred Barnes before the war, and bullets weighing 95, 100, 130, and 150 grains were manufactured by the Western Tool & Copper Works. In normal times, the only fly in the ointment is that there isn't any such critter as a cheap .270 bullet, as there have always been cheap .25 and .30 caliber bullets. The cheapest sold for about two cents, the most expensive for about three, whereas good .25 and .30 caliber jacketed bullets could be bought for around one cent. Handloads for the .270 have always cost somewhat more than for many other calibers.

The best all-around .270 game bullet has always seemed to me to be the 130-grain pointed expanding bullet designed for the cartridge and made by Winchester. Along with the 180-grain Remington bronze-point .30/06 bullet, it is almost a perfect ballistic job, combining a sharp, wind-bucking point with good sectional density. The base is very thick and heavy, the jacket becomes slightly thinner toward the point (which in reality is a sharp soft point of lead covered with a thick jacket of copper to keep it from battering in the magazine).

I have never seen one of those bullets fail to expand well, even at

319

long range, and I have never seen one that failed to penetrate deeply. I have found it practically perfect for medium-size big game, weighing from 100 to 350 pounds on the hoof; and hunters in Alaska and Canada say its penetration is adequate for moose and grizzlies.

Why so little has been said about the virtues of that bullet is a question I cannot answer. Some years after it had been on the market, a German firm brought out a line of bullets which was practically identical, and the gun writers almost broke blood vessels shouting its praises. The only explanation I could give was that some Nazi designer had taken the trouble to section a 130-grain Winchester .270 bullet, whereas some of the gun writers hadn't.

For anything from a big mule deer on down, the 130-grain Winchester Spitzer or the similar Peters job looks like the best medicine. In spite of the fact that men like Russell Annabel of Alaska and Jim Osman of Canada have used it on elk and moose and have found it satisfactory, I'll make a guess that the controlled expansion bullets like the Winchester-Western Silvertip and the Remington Core-Lokt would be a good deal better.

I base that on some hunting of broomtail horses, which are about the size of elk. Two .270 rifles were used by government hunters who had to exterminate the beasts on forest lands. The boys started out with the 130-grain Winchester bullet, and got pretty sloppy kills. They then shifted to the Remington Core-Lokt, and got deeper penetration and far more one-shot kills.

The same thing can be said of the Winchester-Western Silvertip – a bit too much penetration and not enough expansion for light game. For me, the Silvertip worked excellently on the one antelope and the few deer I have shot with it. Most deer and antelope hunters, however, have wanted less penetration, more expansion. In wooded country where shots have to be taken through brush, I'd prefer either to the pointed expanding.

A correspondent in Michigan made extensive tests, shooting the Remington Core-Lokt through all sorts of cover, and wrote that because of the round nose and thick jacket, it drives on through twigs and even small limbs with a minimum of deflection. The Silvertip, the Core-Lokt, and the Western boattail all retain less velocity than the original pointed expanding bullet does, for they get to 300 yards with a retained velocity of 2,260, as against the pointed expanding's 2,440.

I have always felt that the 150-grain soft point was a fine hunk of cheese for which there was little excuse. It has neither the flat trajectory and the shock power of the sharp-point 130-grain bullets, nor the penetration of Silvertip and Core-Lokt. It reduces the .270 to the power of a 7mm., which is a fine cartridge, but definitely not a .270.

For the handloader who likes to experiment and who is never satisfied with things as they are, the custom-made bullets offer definite possibilities. The 120-grain Barnes spitzer bullet is lightly constructed and, when driven at about 3,200, the most deadly small deer, coyote, and antelope bullet I have ever seen. Whitetail deer, hit anywhere solidly with that bullet, are almost always stone dead before they topple over. I have seen about 15 deer and antelope killed with that bullet, and I have never seen one move three feet after being hit. However, it would go to pieces too quickly to be absolutely dead sure at all angles on large mule deer.

The 140-grain bullet seems a shade too light to burn No. 4350, that great heavyweight powder, and No. 4064 will give it only 3,000 foot seconds. I'd stick to the 130. The heavy custom-made bullets in combination with No. 4350 are something else again, and anyone wanting to use the .270 on the heaviest game should look them over. Fred Barnes made a fine 160-grain semi-Spitzer of great sectional density, a small soft point, and a thick, heavy jacket of pure copper. It can be given about 2,800 with 52 grains of No. 4350, and 2,850 with 54 grains. With my Model 70 sighted in for 300 yards with the Winchester 130-grain factory load, the 160-grain bullet in front of 52 grains of No. 4350 is exactly on at 200; a fact which comes in very handy for the sheep hunter who wants to take along a few cartridges loaded with the heavier bullets in case he runs into a grizzly. The 150-grain Western Tool & Copper Works bullet is a formidable baby, which 54 grains of No. 4350 will drive along at 2,950 foot seconds. Wow!

It was the 100-grain bullets, with their very flat trajectory, their astounding accuracy, their freedom from ricochet, and their ability to buck wind, that made the varmint and coyote hunters sit up and get interested. As we have seen, these bullets retain more velocity at 300 yards than any factory load for the .220 Swift. Because of the small time lag, they are much less wind-sensitive than the standard hot-shot .22 bullets, and they can be depended on to make longer sure hits on chucks, crows, hawks, and what not.

Many a varmint shooter who has spent plenty of moola dallying after those painted hussies, the super-duper .22s, has discovered that the little old .270, who has been sitting in the corner all the time masquerading as a big-game rifle and nothing else, has exactly what he has been looking for. If he can manage it, he gets a ten-pound .270 with a medium-heavy barrel, slaps a 10X scope on it, use those 100-grain bullets at 3,540 foot seconds – and discovers he has the doggonedest long-range varmint rifle in the country.

*I*t is my notion that it will be some time before a better cartridge than the .270 makes its bow. The cartridge even now has only slightly less recoil than the .30/06, and a heavier bullet at a higher velocity means more recoil, perhaps so much that the average hunter will not do his best work in the field with it. Actually, the .270 was a 1940 cartridge, which happened to be introduced in 1925, a long way ahead of its time. It took the riflemen of this country many years to catch up with it.

On the other hand, the .270 is by no means always the rifle for the one-gun man. Lots of other calibers will serve just as well or better for the once-a-year deer hunter in the wooded East. The .270 has always been and probably always will be an expensive proposition to handload because of the odd-size bullets. Furthermore, just about one chuck hunter in 100 has enough skill to take advantage of the extra range the .270 gives him.

Working pressures are a good deal higher in the .270 than in the .30/06, and barrel life is shorter. If a man does much rapid fire, or shoots many ten-shot groups, both of which heat the barrel up, he will see a good deal of erosion in 1,000 shots, and he may find his accuracy falling off in less than 2,000 shots. Barrel life is, I believe, about 30 percent longer than that of the Swift and 30 percent shorter than that of the .30/06. My figures may be on the gloomy side, because I do a lot of experimenting, which is tough on barrels.

Because of the cheaper bullets, longer barrel life, and lighter recoil, I'd rather do most of my varmint shooting with a .250/3000 or a .257. For hunting the largest game, I'd get a lot more comfort out of the fact that the .30/06 tosses a 220-grain bullet, but until something better comes along, I'll stick to the .270 as a Sunday gun on anything from coyotes on up to mule deer, if the shooting has to be done at long range.

BIBLIOGRAPHY

*J*ack O'Connor left an extensive and remarkably varied literary legacy. It includes hundreds if not thousands of articles in outdoor magazines, a solid shelf of original books, major contributions to many other volumes, selections in numerous anthologies, and posthumously published collections belonging to essentially the same genre as this work. What I have compiled, while based on considerable research, is by no means complete. Indeed, a truly comprehensive O'Connor bibliography would be a massive undertaking of the sort which earns hard-working graduate students advanced degrees in library science.

No attempt has been made to provide listings of his magazine articles – there are far too many for inclusion – but mention of the major magazines for which he served as a regular contributor should serve as a guidepost for anyone who might want to delve deeply into his writings.

O'Connor wrote his first piece for *Outdoor Life* in the mid-1930s, and for almost four full decades he was a regular contributor. Interestingly, one of his earliest contributions dealt with trout fishing. To my knowledge, "Fighting Trout a Mile Down" was his only published effort dealing with angling. In late 1939 he became a *Outdoor Life* columnist under the title, "Getting the Range." This was changed to "Arms and Ammunition" in the June, 1941 issue, a title that remained until November, 1952. At that point O'Connor's column was listed in the table of contents simply as "Shooting."

His last "Shooting" piece, "Hail and Farewell," appeared in July, 1972. Over this period O'Connor not only wrote hundreds of columns, he contributed scores of features as well, and those of my generation will always remember him as an *Outdoor Life* man.

After his retirement from *Outdoor Life*, O'Connor was persuaded to join the staff of a newly established publication, *Petersen's Hunting,* as executive editor. He worked in that capacity until his death in January, 1978. His first article for *Petersen's,* "Buck Fever," was published in the February, 1974 issue, and his last, "The Art of Tracking, Tracks and Sign," appeared in the July, 1978 issue. Over this time-span he had a piece in the magazine every month, a total of 54 articles.

Before he became a staffer for *Outdoor Life,* O'Connor wrote for

Field & Stream, Sports Afield, Esquire and *True,* among others. In *The Last Book,* he comments that once he took the position at *Outdoor Life,* he did not have time to contribute to *Esquire*, which at that time was edited by noted fly fisherman and sportsman Arnold Gingrich. Presumably, that was true for his other freelancing efforts, although he did write some pieces for *Gun Digest.* O'Connor was a paid staffer at *Outdoor Life* and perhaps his contract prohibited contributions to rival magazines.

He did, however, use a number of pen names early in his career, including Bill Ryan, Carlos Ryan, II, Joe Ryan, Barry Williams, L. E. Chamberlin, Jr., Jim Hack, and Henry E. Peters. Quite possibly there were others, and assiduous research might well reveal other O'Connor writings. Interestingly, his use of various pseudonyms is not widely known, witness the absence of any such mention in Ken Callahan's fine reference volume, *A Dictionary of Sporting Pen Names* (1995).

As we add this volume to the O'Connor shelf, it is appropriate to take a retrospective look at what already exists. His major books form an impressive list. Furthermore, many of them were expanded, revised or updated, so forming a complete holding of all the myriad printings and versions would be quite an undertaking.

So appealing and widely distributed (through the Outdoor Life Book Club as well as regular trade channels) were his works that I feel fairly comfortable in stating that he is the most popular of all American sporting scribes, at least in terms of total books sold. Certainly, anyone who regularly browses the lists of out-of-print dealers is aware of his enduring popularity and the ready availability of his most popular titles. By the same token, some of his earlier works, including his novels, the one book he did for Eugene Connett's famed Derrydale Press, and *The Last Book*, are highly collectible.

O'Connor's first book was *Conquest* (New York: Harper & Brothers, 1930), a novel which is quite rare in the original edition. Subsequent works, in chronological order by date of their first appearance, include:

Boomtown (New York: Alfred A. Knopf, 1938);

Game in the Desert (New York: The Derrydale Press, 1939), later reprinted with some minor changes, first as *Hunting in the Southwest* [(New York: Alfred A. Knopf, 1945) and later in both limited and trade editions as *Game in the Desert Revisited,* with the original title but a new Foreword by O'Connor (Clinton, NJ: The Amwell Press,

1977, in a limited, numbered, and signed edition of 1,000 copies and subsequently in a 1984 trade edition)];

Hunting in the Rockies (New York: Alfred A. Knopf, 1947 and a reprint by Safari Press in 1988);

Sporting Guns: How to Choose and How to Use Them (New York: Franklin Watts, 1947);

The Rifle Book (New York: Alfred A. Knopf, 1949);

Hunting with a Binocular (Rochester, NY: Bausch & Lomb, 1949 – a 24-page promotional pamphlet);

The Big Game Rifle (New York: Alfred A. Knopf, 1952);

Sportsman's Arms and Ammunition Manual (New York: Outdoor Life Books, 1952);

Jack O'Connor's Gun Book (Popular Science Company, 1953);

Outdoor Life Shooting Book (New York: Outdoor Life Books, 1957 – a small 80-page paperback, later offered in revised and expanded form as *The Hunter's Shooting Guide*);

Complete Book of Rifles and Shotguns (New York: Harper & Row/Outdoor Life Books, 1961);

The Big Game Animals of North America (New York: E. P. Dutton, 1961);

Jack O'Connor's Big Game Hunts (New York: E. P. Dutton/Outdoor Life Books, 1963);

The Shotgun Book (New York: Alfred A. Knopf, 1965);

The Art of Hunting Big Game (New York: Outdoor Life Books, 1967 – second printing in 1971 and a slightly revised edition in 1977);

Horse and Buggy West: A Boyhood on the Last Frontier (New York: Alfred A. Knopf, 1969 – autobiographical);

The Hunting Rifle (New York: Winchester Press, 1970);

Rifle and Shotgun Shooting Basics (New York: Outdoor Life Books, no date but circa 1970);

7-Lesson Rifle Shooting Course (New York: Outdoor Life Books, no date but circa 1970 – an excerpt from *Complete Book of Rifles and Shotguns*);

Sheep and Sheep Hunting (New York: Winchester Press, 1974);

The Hunter's Shooting Guide (New York: Outdoor Life Books, 1978).

    Posthumously published works include *The Last Book: Confessions of a Gun Editor* (Clinton, NJ: Amwell Press, 1984 – in a limited, numbered and signed edition of 1,000 and a trade edition);

Hunting on Three Continents with Jack O'Connor (Long Beach, CA: Safari Press, 1987 – issued in a deluxe edition of 500 copies signed by Brad O'Connor and a trade edition).

$\mathcal{A}$s has already been noted, there have been previous compilations somewhat similar in nature to this work. Two of these were published during his lifetime. *Jack O'Connor's Big Game Hunts* contains 26 stories, all of which had previously appeared in *Outdoor Life*. They range widely in subject matter and geographical location, from caribou to oryx, sheep to sable. *The Best of Jack O'Connor* appeared shortly before the author's death. It contains selections from three of his books (*Conquest, Boom Town,* and *Horse and Buggy West*), two selections from *Gun Digest*, and 28 from *Outdoor Life*.

Hunting on Three Continents with Jack O'Connor focuses on writings from the latter portion of his career, when he wrote regularly for *Petersen's Hunting*. The book contains 30 of the 54 pieces he contributed to the magazine along with a two-page Introduction from another noted hunter and sporting scribe, John H. Batten. Finally, *Jack O'Connor: Catalogue of Letters* (Agoura, CA: Trophy Room Books, 2002) includes portions of 287 letters written to John Jobson, his good friend and confidante, between 1960 and 1977. It includes "A Special Tribute" by Jim Rikhoff and a "Cataloguer's Introduction" by the publisher, Ellen Enzler Herring. Many of the excerpts are quite brief and really serve as teasers designed to sell the letters (the publisher, a noted bookseller, offered all of them individually, and the price is given with each letter).

While I have not made a concerted effort to trace them, O'Connor's name appears in many anthologies as a contributor. They include:

Treasury of African Hunting, Peter Barrett, editor (New York: Winchester Press, 1970);

The Bear Book, Jack Samson, editor (Clinton, NJ: Amwell Press, 1979); *Arizona Wildlife Trophies* by Eldon Buckner, (Mesa, AZ: Arizona Wildlife Federation, 1995);

Hunting Dangerous Game, Vin Sparano, editor (Lakeland, FL: Larsen's Outdoor Publishing, 1992);

The Greatest Hunting Stories Ever Told, Vin Sparano, editor (New York: Beaufort Books, Inc., 1983);

Classic Hunting Tales, Vin Sparano, editor (New York: Beaufort Books, 1986);

Complete Book of Shooting (New York: Harper & Row/Outdoor Life Books, 1965 – written with Roy Dunlap, Alex Kerr and Jeff Cooper);

Gun Talk, Dave Moreton, editor (New York: Winchester Press, 1973);

2000 Ideas for Sportsmen (New York: Grosset & Dunlap, 1948 –

O'Connor wrote lengthy sections on "All About Rifles" and "All About Shotguns");
Sportsman's Encyclopedia (New York, 1947);
Outdoor Life's Gallery of North American Game (New York: Outdoor Life, 1946);
Mexican Game Trails: Americans Afield in Old Mexico, 1866-1940, Neil Carmody and David Brown, editors (Norman, OK: University of Oklahoma Press, 1991);
The Hunter's Encyclopedia, Raymond Camp, editor (Harrisburg, PA: Stackpole and Heck, 1948);
The New Hunter's Encyclopedia (Harrisburg, PA: Stackpole Books, 1966);
Arizona in Literature by Mary G. Boyer (Glendale, CA: Arthur H. Clark Co., 1935);
Last Casts and Stolen Hunts, Jim Casada and Chuck Wechsler, editors (Camden, SC: Live Oak Press/Countrysport Press, 1993).

For detailed information on O'Connor's life, the logical beginning point is his own books, several of which are autobiographical in nature. This is particularly true of *The Last Book*, an interesting and at times scathing look at the outdoor industry, magazine editors, writers and writing, and related subjects. Those who want to understand the man and his roots should also read *Horse and Buggy West* and his two early novels, *Boom Town* and *Conquest*.

O'Connor was a tireless correspondent who did his dead-level best to answer each and every letter directed to him (his son Brad, indicates that at times in the 1950s, Jack answered as many as 3,000 fan letters a month with the help of a secretary and some standardized responses).

Some of O'Connor's exchanges with friends have been published. These include: "The [John] Jobson-O'Connor Letters" (*Sports Afield,* Nov., 1981, pp. 64 ff. and Dec., 1981, pp. 80ff) and "The Jack O'Connor Letters' (*Outdoor Life,* Feb., 1989, pp. 66ff. and Mar., 1989, pp. 80ff. – correspondence on hunting issues with Robert Chatfield-Taylor).

There is also a biography, Robert Anderson's *Jack O'Connor: The Legendary Life of America's Greatest Gunwriter* (Long Beach, CA: Safari Press, 2002). Published in a boxed, limited edition of 1,000 copies and a trade edition, the book includes three chapters by Eldon Buckner. The book is, in my opinion, a disappointment in many ways. The portions written by Buckner, including a capsule coverage of O'Connor's career, a look at the guns he liked and used, and a

327

chronology of his life, are first-rate. Similarly, a bibliographical essay by Henry van der Broecke (it only covers books written or coauthored by O'Connor) is thorough and helpful. The heart of the biography (the portion written by Anderson), on the other hand, is uneven, with important aspects of O'Connor's career receiving little or no attention and reflecting incomplete background research. No fan of O'Connor should overlook the book, but it is by no means definitive.

There are also numerous biographical sketches, word portraits and articles relating to O'Connor's life or dealing with specific aspects of his career. Those produced by family members are especially noteworthy. They include: Brad O'Connor's "The O'Connor Legacy" (*Sporting Classics*, May/June, 1999, pp. 54-62) and "A Final Farewell" (in *The Last Book,* pp. 239-43). Caroline O'Connor McCullam's "A Daughter's Remembrances' (*Sporting Classics*, May/June, 1999, p. 63) appears in this book along with Brad O'Connor's article for *Sporting Classics*.

Also deserving of scrutiny are "Trophy for O'Connor" (*Outdoor Life,* Feb., 1958, p. 127); "Jack O'Connor Remembered" (*Outdoor Life*, July, 1989, pp. 38-41), and the obituary notice in the *New York Times* (Jan. 24, 1978).

I have written several pieces on him, including "Jack O'Connor: America's Greatest Gun Writer" (*Shooter's Bible*, 1990, pp. 60-67); "Jack O'Connor: A Sporting Bibliophile's Delight" (*AB Bookman's Weekly,* June 5, 1989); one of my Books columns in *Sporting Classics* (July/Aug., 1999, pp. 138, 141); "O'Connor as a Mule Deer Hunter" (*Mule Deer Magazine*, Spring, 2003, pp. 36-39); and "Remembering Jack O'Connor" (Jan., 2002 issue of *Outdoor Life,* pp. 35-37, a biographical overview and introduction to a special section celebrating the centenary of O'Connor's birth and reprinting excerpts from eight stories).

Art Popham, Jr., who studied under O'Connor and later became a noted outdoor writer in his own right, wrote "Elk with Eleanor" (*Outdoor Life,* Sept., 1968, pp. 56-57, 98-99). It is a fond reminiscence of hunting with Jack and Eleanor during the author's college days. Another piece of similar nature by Eldon Buckner is "Coues Deer O'Connor's Way" (*Petersen's Deer Hunting – 1990*, pp. 118-21).

There are entries on O'Connor in a number of major reference works. Perhaps the most useful can be found in *Contemporary Authors*, but also of note are *Who's Who in America* (there are listings in the 38th, 39th and 40th editions), James Vinson (Editor);

Twentieth-Century Western Writers, and *Texas Writers of Today.*

Among many articles on O'Connor or reviews of his books that deserve special note are those in *Booklist* (May 15, 1947); *Books* (Oct. 5, 1930, p. 7 and Feb., 6, 1938, p. 8); *Library Journal* (Jan. 1, 1948 and Mar. 15, 1969); *New York Times* (Feb. 6, 1938, p. 23) and *Saturday Review of Literature* (Feb. 19, 1938).

All bibliographical endeavors never really come to an end. The information I have compiled constitutes a meaningful start toward a comprehensive bibliography, but no more. In that regard, the editor would welcome any input on omissions or recommended additions, especially for material which appeared under pseudonyms or in out-of-the-way places.